An Introduction to Korean Culture

Edited by John H. Koo & Andrew C. Nahm

AN
INTRODUCTION TO
KOREAN
CULTURE

Edited by John H. Koo & Andrew C. Nahm

 Hollym

Carlsbad, CA and Seoul

An Introduction to Korean Culture

Copyright © 1997
Edited by John H. Koo & Andrew C. Nahm

First published in 1997
Ninth printing, 2020
by Hollym International Corp., Carlsbad, CA, USA
Phone 760 814 9880
http://www.hollym.com   **e-Mail** contact@hollym.com

⎡J Hollym

Published simultaneously in Korea
by Hollym Corp., Publishers, Seoul, Korea
Phone +82 2 734 5087   **Fax** +82 2 730 5149
http://www.hollym.co.kr   **e-Mail** hollym@hollym.co.kr

ISBN: 978-1-56591-284-7
Library of Congress Control Number: 97-74941

Printed in Korea

Table of Contents

List of Contributors 9
Preface 11
Pronunciation of Korean 13

1. The Land, Climate, and People
1. Location, Size and Population 17
2. Topography and Physical Features 20
3. The Economic Geography of North and South Korea 30
4. The People 34

2. History
1. Background 41
2. Premodern Korea:
   Through the Prehistoric Ages to the Dawn of Statehood 42
3. From the Three Kingdoms to a Unified State 46
4. Korea after Reunification 53
5. Modern Korea:
   Twilight of the Kingdom Choson 72
6. Japanese Colonial Rule and the National Liberation Movement 79
7. Liberation and Partition 86
8. The Korean War and After 91

3. Language
1. Introduction 101
2. Korean Writing 102
3. Dialects 104
4. Honorifics 105
5. Onomatopoetic Words 108
6. Dual System of Native and Sino-Korean Words 110
7. Some Grammatical Features 111

4. Folk Beliefs and Shamanism
1. Introduction 121
2. Shamanism 126
3. Variations of Shamanism 131

5. Confucianism

1. Introduction ··· 137
2. Historical Setting ·· 139
3. Confucian Ideology ·· 141
4. Monuments ·· 143
5. Education ·· 145
6. Ceremonies ··· 147
7. Confucianism in the Modern World ··· 149

6. Buddhism

1. Introduction ··· 155
2. The Teachings of the Buddha ·· 156
3. The Korean Adoption of State-centered Buddhism ···················· 159
4. Buddhism and Korean Culture ·· 162
5. Modern Buddhism Confronts the Christian Challenge ················ 164
6. The Monastic Core of Korean Buddhism ·································· 168
7. The Buddhist Faithful ·· 171

7. Christianity

1. Introduction ··· 179
2. The First Christians ·· 181
3. The Arrival of Protestantism ··· 183
4. Christianity, Nationalism, and Modernization ···························· 185
5. Growth and Division after Liberation ·· 189
6. Korean Characteristic of Korean Christianity ···························· 194

8. Korean Culture and Worldview

1. Introduction ··· 203
2. Shamanistic Worldview ·· 205
3. Buddhistic Worldview ·· 207
4. Confucian Worldview ··· 210
5. Christian Worldview ··· 213
6. Symbiosis of Divergent Worldviews in Korea ··························· 216

9. Political Tradition and Contemporary Politics and Government

1. Traditional Political Culture ·· 221
2. Contemporary Politics and Government ····································· 230
3. Conclusions ·· 241

10. Politics in South Korea since 1993
1. Introduction ·· 247
2. Civilian Government ·· 248
3. Anti-Corruption Reforms ·· 250
4. Democratization ·· 252
5. Relations with North Korea ····································· 255

11. Traditional Culture and Society
1. Introduction ·· 261
2. Confucianism and Patrilineal Ideology, Institutions and Practices ········· 263
3. Filial Piety and the Separation of the Sexes ···················· 265
4. Patrilineal Corollaries: Marriage, Inheritance, Adoption, and Widowhood · 268
5. Patrilineal Groups and Institutions ······························ 272
6. Confucianization as a Political and Ideological Process ················ 276
7. Confucianism and Social Stratification ··························· 277
8. Confucianization as a Cultural and Social Process ················· 280
9. Confucianism and Cultural Resistance ···························· 282
10. Conclusion ·· 285

12. Education
1. Introduction ·· 289
2. Education in Traditional Korea ·································· 292
3. Christian Mission Education in Korea ··························· 298
4. Education under Japanese Colonialism ··························· 300
5. Current Education in North Korea ······························· 302
6. Current Education in South Korea ······························· 305

13. Painting ·· 311

14. Traditional Music and Dance
1. Introduction ·· 325
2. Origins and Historical Background of Traditional Korean Music and Dance 327
3. The Classification of Traditional Korean Music ··················· 331
4. Particularities of Traditional Korean Music ····················· 337
5. Folk Music ··· 339
6. The Dances of Traditional Korea ································· 346

15. Stone Pagodas and Buddha Images
1. Introduction ·· 359
2. Stone Pagodas ·· 360

3. Stone Buddha Images ·· 365

16. Architecture and House Furniture
1. Introduction ·· 377
2. Characteristics of Floor Plans in Traditional Houses ··················· 378
3. Upper-Class Homes ··· 380

17. Traditional Ceramics ·· **385**

18. Papermaking and Printing
1. Introduction ·· 401
2. Movable Metal Type ·· 402
3. Innovations Under King Sejong ·· 404
4. Wood Block Printing ··· 406
5. Papermaking ··· 408
6. Bookmaking ··· 411

19. Oral Literature
1. Introduction ·· 415
2. Narratives ··· 416
3. Songs ·· 421
4. Sayings ··· 423

20. Modern Poetry and Literature
1. Introduction ·· 429
2. History and Memorabilia of the Three Kingdoms ····················· 431
3. Young Man Ch'ŏyong and Sea View Temple ························· 434
4. Sixteenth Century Korean Verse Literature ························· 440
5. Sixteenth Century Korean Verse: A Sampler ······················· 442
6. Seventeenth and Eighteenth Century Prose ························· 448
7. Modern Korean Literature ·· 452
8. Modern Korean Literature to 1945 ·································· 455
9. Post-Division, Post-War Korean Literature ························· 459

Appendix: Holidays and Festivals ····························· **465**

Index ··· **471**

List of Contributors (in alphabetical order)

Nancy Abelman, University of Illinois, Urbana-Champaign
Donald L. Baker, University of British Columbia
In-hak Choi, Inha University
Byung-ok Chun, Korean Traditional Design Institute
Alan C. Heyman, Researcher in Korea
Han-kyo Kim, University of Cincinnati
Kumja Paik Kim, Asian Art Museum of San Francisco
Robert H. C. Kim, Western Washington University
John H. Koo, Arizona State University
Junghee Lee, Portland State University
Kwang-kyu Lee, Seoul National University
Won-sul Lee, Former President of Han Nam University
David R. MaCann, Harvard University
Andrew C. Nahm, Western Michigan University
John Kie-chang Oh, Catholic University of America
Mark Peterson, Brigham Young University
Marilyn M. Rhie, Smith College
Clark Sorensen, University of Washington

Preface

With a history of more than 4,200 years, the culture of the Korean people is one of the oldest in the world. Because of the geographic proximity
of the Korean Peninsula to China, and the relationship that developed
between Korea and China long before the beginning of the Christian era,
the cultural development of the Korean people has been influenced by
Chinese cultural patterns in many ways, creating numerous similarities
between the cultures of these two countries. Consequently, many people
have the mistaken notion that the Korean culture is a mere reflection of
the Chinese.

The impact of China up to the eve of modern times was considerable, as was that of the West after the opening of Korea toward the end
of the nineteenth century. Some visitors from abroad who are casually
acquainted with Chinese culture may first be struck by the similarities
between the two cultures, but more careful observers will detect the subtle, yet distinctive, differences between Korea and Chinese patterns. All
will become aware of the fact that old and new cultures combine to constitute, in remarkable harmony, the Korean culture of today. Moreover,
one soon realizes that in the midst of Korea's multifaceted processes of
modernization and Westernization there is a resurgence and revival of certain cultural aspects which had been fading away.

A considerable number of English-language books on Korea have
been published in recent years, reducing the dire shortage of source materials on the history and culture of the Korean people and showing the

efforts they have made in the recent past to bring about economic development, modernize their society, and improve their way of life. Nevertheless, most of these books are for specialists or for those who have substantial knowledge about Korea. Consequently, the need remains for comprehensive, introductory reading materials on Korean culture for the general reader. Although English-language periodical journals on Korean culture, published by such organizations as the Korea Foundation, the Korean National Commission on UNESCO, and the Korean Cultural Service (in Los angeles) are valuable sources, they are unfortunately not readily available to most of those who could best profit by them.

This book is intended to meet the needs of the general reader. Major aspects of traditional, as well as modern, Korean culture are discussed by reputable scholars specializing in particular fields, and each chapter is prepared specifically to introduce a particular aspect of culture. A brief survey of Korean history and other cultural information are provided to enable the reader to fully appreciate the roots of Korean culture and the ways in which it has grown and transformed through out the ages. For those who wish to continue their quest for greater knowledge, a selected bibliography is provided at the end of each chapter.

Since chapters and portions of some chapters have been written by different authors, the contents of the book may overlap and duplicate certain information. There will also be different views on, and interpretations of, particular aspects of Korean culture, while other views may have been omitted. Such is the common nature of all books of this kind. Be that as it may, our aim is to present a book that will be enjoyable and interesting to general readers and help them to gain a broader knowledge of and appreciation for Korean culture. We hope that, in some way, this goal has been met.

Editors of this book wish to express their appreciation for the financial assistance given by the Korea Research Foundation for the undertaking of this project. They also wish to thank those who enthusiastically agreed to participate in the project by contributing valuable expertise and articles.

Finally, I would like to thank Mr. Boye De Mente, Mr. James Foley, Ms. Susan Michel and Sue-jung Kang (Hollym Publishers) for their editorial contributions and proofreading. Special thanks are also due Mr. Lee F. Sharra and Mr. Ryan Clarke for their computer technical assistance in editing the manuscript.

John J. Koo

Pronunciation of Korean

With the exception of certain personal and place names, along with names of firms and institutions, all Korean words are Romanized in accordance with the McCune-Reischauer System, which was modified by the Minister of Education of the Republic of Korea. Generally, the basic vowels, **a**, **e**, **i**, **o**, and **u**, are pronounced as in English.

a as in father	**e** as in end
i as in India	**o** as in Ohio
u as in rule	

The vowels o and u with the mark over them (ŏ and ŭ)are pronounced as follows:

ŏ as in ton	**ŭ** as in foot

Some compound vowels are pronounced as a single vowel:

ae as the **a** in apple	**oe** as the ö in German
ui as the **u** [ü] in the French word *lune* 'moon'	

Otherwise, all vowels must be pronounced separately (without gliding):

ch as *j*, **k** as *g*, **p** as *b*, **t** as *d*

When these consonants are aspirated which is shown by adding an apostrophe(') behind the letter, they are pronounced as in the English works:

ch'   like the **ch** of **ch**ance
k'   like the **k** of **k**ing
p'   like the **p** of **p**eace
t'   like the **t** of **t**oy

In certain cases, an apostrophe is also used to separate the pronunciation of two consonant sounds as in the cases of *Tan'gun* and *han'gŭl*, etc. Serveral compound consonants are pronounced as single consonants:

ss like the **s** of **S**am   **tt** like the **d** of **d**am

Those Korean words not Romanized in accordance with the McCune-Reischauer System, not widely used or well-known, are kept in their original form They include personal names such as Syngman Rhee, names of places such as Seoul and Pyongyang, industrial firm names such as Hyundai and Daewoo, and educational institutions such as Ewha Womans University and Yonsei University. In contrast, all Chinese words are Romanized in accordance with the Pinyin System.

1

The Land, Climate, and People
by Clark Sorensen

1

Location, Size and Population

Korea occupies, in addition to a small part of the adjacent Asian mainland, the central of three large peninsulas (Kamchatka, Korean, Malaysian) that protrude south from the eastern edge of the Asian continent. A mountainous country of some 220,847 square kilometers, Korea extends north to south some 1,000 kilometers, from 43 degrees north latitude along the arc of the Tumen River in North Hamgyŏng Province to 33 degrees north latitude on the southern coast of Cheju Island, Korea's latitude is similar to that of the most populated parts of Japan, of Spain, or of the American state of Virginia.

Sheltered from the Pacific Ocean by the main islands of Japan, Korea is surrounded on three sides by smaller seas that both separate and connect it to China and Japan. To the east is the deep, cold Sea of Japan(the East Sea) on which are located the important North Korean ports of Najin, Ch'ŏngjin, Hamhŭng, and Wŏnsan, as well as Russia's two most important naval and commercial ports on the Pacific, Vladivostok and Nakhodka. Ch'ŏngjin and Najin, having good rail connections to the interior, can serve as outlets for northern Manchuria as well as Korea. In recent years, North Korea has been setting up a free trade zone in the area around Najin and its neighboring harbor of Sŏnbong, in cooperation with the United Nations Development Program. In contrast to North Korea and Russia, South Korea and Japan have few important ports on the Sea of Japan. South Korea's east coast is separated from the most populated parts of the country by the rugged T'aebaek Mountains and has few good harbors. The Japanese port of Niigata is on the Sea of Japan, but most of Japan's important seaports are on the east (Pacific Ocean) side of Japan.

To the west is the shallow, warm Yellow Sea upon which both North and South Korea have important ports Namp'o and Haeju in the north, and Inch'ŏn, Kunsan, and Mokp'o in the south. Unlike the east coast, the west coast of Korea has great tidal variations: 5 meters at Namp'o, 7 at Haeju, and 9 at Inch'ŏn, where low tide exposes extensive tidal flats going out thousands of meters. Because of these tides, the dock areas of both Namp'o and Inch'ŏn are protected by dikes and locks to maintain water at a constant level. China's Shandong Peninsula is within 180 kilometers across the Yellow Sea from Cape Changsan in North Korea's Hwanghae Province, and it has long been an important destination of seaborne trade between the two countries. The Yellow Sea also extends north past the Chinese port of Dalian, gateway to Manchuria, and connects with the Gulf of Bohai upon which is located Tianjin, the main port for Beijing. Ferries run from Inch'ŏn to Tianjin and the Shandong Peninsula.

The southeast corner of the Korean Peninsula faces the Korea Strait that separates Korea from Japan. Here is located South Korea's most important port, Pusan. By ferry from Pusan to the Japanese port of Fukuoka across the strait is some 200 kilometers, but the Japanese Island of Tsushima, located in the middle of the strait, is just visible from the Korean mainland on a good day.

The southwest corner of the peninsula faces the East China Sea served by the port of Yŏsu. Cheju Island, a large volcanic cone some 80 kilometers south of the Korean mainland in the East China Sea, is the southernmost part of Korea.

Since 1948, Korea has been divided into two competing states, one socialist, the other capitalist. In the north, the socialist *Democratic People's Republic of Korea* (DPRK), or North Korea, occupies 122,100 square kilometers. To the south the capitalist *Republic of Korea* (ROK), or South Korea, occupies slightly less than 100,000 square kilometers of the peninsula. In terms of land area, North Korea occupies about 55 percent of Korea and South Korea 45 percent. In terms of population, on the other hand, South Korea, with almost 44 million residents, has about 65 percent of the population, while North Korea, with slightly more than 22 million residents, has about 35 percent.

South Korea is one of the most densely populated countries in the world with an overall density of 440 people per square kilometer. North Korea, on the other hand, has a population density of only 181 people per square kilometer. South Korea's population density is higher than Japan (329), China (121), or India (266), and is surpassed in Asia only by Bangladesh (778) and Taiwan (572). Although by the end of the colonial period in 1945 some three quarters of a million Japanese and around 75,000 Chinese lived in Korea (primarily in the large cities), virtually all of the Japanese and a good number of the Chinese left after liberation. Except for some 30,000 overseas Chinese concentrated in Seoul and Inch'ŏn, the population of both parts of Korea is entirely ethnic Korean.

North Korea shares a 1,025 kilometer border with China along the Yalu and Tumen Rivers. In the extreme northeast, North Korea also shares a border with Russia along the last 25 kilometers of the Tumen River which empties into the Sea of Japan. A rail line between Vladivostok and Najin runs across this common border. Because of the North Korea-Russian border, China does not have direct access to the Sea of Japan from Manchuria. There has been some talk of dredging the shallow Tumen River to allow shipping to sail directly up the river to an inland Chinese river port, but the economic and technical feasibility of this project has not yet been determined.

South Korea's only land border is with North Korea. The original border, the 38th parallel that cuts across the Korean peninsula some 40 kilometers north of Seoul, was an arbitrary boundary agreed upon by the Soviet Union and the United States for the purposes of disarming Japanese troops in 1945, and was not intended to be permanent. The development of the Cold War and the creation of two separate states on the Korean peninsula in 1948 led to a civil war from 1950 to 1953 between the North and the South that eventually involved troops from the United States and twelve other members of the United Nations on the side of the south, and China (with the support of the Soviet Union) on the side of the north. The present boundary between North and South Korea follows the armistice line agreed upon by the United States, North Korea, and China on July 27, 1953. It runs considerably north of the 38th parallel in the mountainous east, but south of the 38th parallel along the Imjin River in the west just north of Seoul. This boundary is heavily fortified and is bordered by a four kilometer demilitarized zone (DMZ) on either side. A neutral compound where the two sides can meet, if necessary, is maintained on the DMZ near the village of Panmunjŏm.

2

Topography and Physical Features

Koreans celebrate their nation as extending from Mt. Paektu to Mt. Halla. Mt. Paektu, at 2,755 meters the tallest mountain of Korea, is an extinct volcano on the North Korea-Manchuria border whose crater is filled by Lake Chŏnji from which flows the headwaters of Manchuria's Sungari River. Mt. Halla, whose cone rises symmetrically from the sea to 1,950 meters to form Cheju Island, is the tallest peak in South Korea. Mt. Paektu last erupted in 1702 A.D., and Mt. Halla in 1007 A.D. These volcanoes are not actually typical of the Korean Peninsula, which is geologically stable and not subject to the violent volcanic eruptions and frequent earthquakes of Japan and the Philippines.

The mountainous nature of Korea means that only 20 percent of the land can be cultivated. Although Korea's mountains outside the far north are not particularly high, the slopes are steep, and they determine much of the geography of the peninsula. Mountains frame the river valleys, densely populated with people; they separate the provinces; and they shape the transportation routes that tie the different regions together.

T'aebaek System

The main system of mountains that forms the backbone of the Korean Peninsula is the T'aebaek Mountain System which runs south from Mt. Paektu along the boundary of North Korea's Kanggye and Yanggang Provinces, curves around Yŏngdŭng Bay, and then runs along the east side of the peninsula as far as the Taegu-P'ohang Valley in South Korea. The northern portion of this mountain system, known as the Nangnim Range, runs south from Mt. Paektu on the Chinese border to just north of the city of Wŏnsan, and has peaks more than 2,000 meters high. The southern portion of the system, known as the T'aebaek Range, runs from the famous and scenic 1,500 meter peaks of the Diamond (Kŭmgang) Mountains south of Wŏnsan to the Taegu-P'ohang Valley in South Korea. These two ranges, connected by a number of minor ranges with peaks seldom reaching more than 1,000 meters high, have a general northeast-southwest orientation. These lower ranges allow the east coast port of Wonsan to enjoy good communications with Seoul, along the Chugaryŏng Valley (pass at 600 meters), and with P'yŏngyang along the more serpentine Ahobirŏng Valley.

Hamgyŏng Range

East of, and almost perpendicular to, the Nangnim Range is the high Hamgyŏng Range that parallels the Sea of Japan coast and separates North Korea's inland Yanggang Province from the coastal provinces of North and South Hamgyŏng. Along with Mt. Paektu, the Nangnim and Hamgyŏng Ranges together form a triangle that encloses the rugged Kaema Upland (Yanggang Province) around the upper reaches of the Tumen River. To the east of the Nangnim Range, the Hamgyŏng Range continues as the Myohyang Mountains that separate the provinces of Kanggye, and North and South P'yŏngan. This is a somewhat lower range than the Hamgyŏng, but it has spectacular scenery second only to that of the Diamond Mountains.

Sobaek Range

Farther south beginning at T'aebaek Mountain in the T'aebaek Range, the Sobaek Range that separates South Korea's Yŏngnam region from the rest of Korea, branches off in a southwesterly direction terminating in 1,915 meter Mt. Chiri in the southwest corner of the peninsula.

The general tilt of the Korean peninsula is from east to west. The T'aebaek Range hugs the east coast of Korea providing for only a narrow coastal littoral along the East Coast. The crest of the T'aebaek Range, while only 20 kilometers from the Sea of Japan, is more than 100 kilometers from the Yellow Sea. The eastern escarpment is thus steep with short, swift rivers, but the western side is more gentle with longer, larger rivers the Taedong, Imjin, Han, and Kŭm. The Naktong River which originates in the Sobaek Mountains is the only major river that flows south. It empties into the Korea Strait near Kimhae. Thus, with the exception of the Hamhŭng plain, all the large plains—P'yŏngyang-Chaeryŏng plain, Kyŏnggi lowlands, North Chŏlla plain—and the population concentrations are on the western side of the Main Korean Range, or south of the Sobaek Range. Even the largest of these plains, however, does not compare in size with the Kantō Plain of Japan nor with the huge North China plain. On the whole, Korea has a small-scale landscape that traditionally was dotted with small villages of several dozen houses and occasional towns, rather than the big cities and large villages of China with several thousand households.

Table 1 : Korea's Rivers

A. Rivers that empty into the Yellow Sea

	length	navigable length
Yallu (Amnok)	813 km	
Taedong	431	243
Han	482	298
Imjin	254	121
Kŭm	402	120

B. Rivers that empty into the Korea Strait

	length	navigable length
Naktong	526 km	340 km

C. Rivers that empty into the Sea of Japan

	length	navigable length
Tumen (Tuman)	516	

Climate

Korea's climate is characterized by alterations of the continental influence of the large land mass of Asia and Siberia, and by the maritime influences of the seas surrounding the Korean Peninsula. In the winter, continental influences predominate leading to a cold, dry season. During the summer, maritime influences predominate bringing warm, moist air from the southern seas. Most areas get between 100 and 200 centimeters of annual precipitation concentrated during the growing season, so that Korea supports a lush native vegetation of great variety, as well as good agriculture. The climate of the peninsular parts of Korea, where maritime influence is strongest, is warm-temperate. The coldest month has an average temperature near freezing, while the hottest month (usually August) has a temperature above 25 degrees Centigrade. This is similar to comparable latitudes on the East Coast of the United States. North of a line linking Anju with Sŏngjin, and in highland regions, continental influences predominate and the climate is cold-temperate. More than three months have a mean daily temperature below freezing, though the hottest month (usually July) still has a mean daily temperature above 25 degrees.

The southernmost parts of the Korean peninsula receive rainfall throughout the year, but most of the Korean peninsula exhibits striking seasonality in precipitation. Only small amounts of rain or snow fall from October through March, while the rains that begin in the spring gradually increase to a peak in July or August, then taper off in September. This cycle is caused by global wind patterns ultimately attributable to the large size of the Asian continent, to the height of the Himalayan Mountains, to the spin of the earth on its axis, and to the uneven heating of the earths surface.

During the winter, extreme cooling of the Asian continent causes a large mass of dense, cold air to settle over northeastern Siberia. This dense mass of air, known as the Siberian High, drains toward lower pressure areas, such as the West Pacific, sweeping over Korea and North China on its way. The winter winds from Siberia have not been able to pick up moisture, so they are dry as well as cold, and little precipitation falls during the winter. The opposite happens in the summer. The summer sun heats up the Asian continent—particularly north India and Mongolia. The hot air rises, creating a low pressure zone, the Mongolian Low, that draws in warm, moist air from the oceans. This moist air, the Northeast Asian Monsoon, brings the steady, heavy rains to Korea (and North China) in July that are known in Korean as the *changma*. As the summer progresses, the heat and the low pressure zone move farther and farther north drawing the summer monsoon, and the rains it brings, farther and farther north, reaching the most northern portions of Korea in August.

As the oceans in the western Pacific warm up in late summer, typhoons become more and more likely. Hurricanes in the Pacific Ocean are called typhoons. Korea, being fairly far north and protected from the Pacific Ocean by islands, is not as subject to typhoons as the Philippines, Taiwan, the South China Coast, or even Japan, but typhoons that form in late July or early September sometimes hit the southern part of Korea. By the time they reach as far as Korea, they often have lost some of their strength. The most danger tends to be from floods and landslides caused by intense rain rather than wind damage. If the typhoon hits in September, however, it may knock down the rice crops that are almost ready for harvest, and this has a devastating effect on the agricultural areas hit by the typhoon.

Agriculture

Until the post-war industrialization of the peninsula, most Koreans subsisted by peasant agriculture. Each household endeavored to produce most of what it needed on land it either owned or rented. Farms were exceedingly small, averaging half a hectare (1.2 acres).

Koreans divide their land into two categories: riceland, or *non*, and rainfall field, or *pat*. Riceland consists of fields suitable for the cultivation of rice that have been leveled, diked, and provided with a source of irrigation. These are the most valuable lands. Rainfall fields are used for unirrigated grain and bean crops, vegetables, and orchards.

Although some people kept horses for riding purposes, most plowed with oxen who were fed on straw, kaoliang, grass cut on the hills, and weeds growing alongside paths and irrigation ditches. Deliberately cultivated pasture was rare, and dairy farming unknown. Farmers with little or no land sometimes moved into the hills and practiced fire-field (*hwajŏn*) farming, a type of farming in which they would burn over the natural vegetation on steep slopes, plant field crops for a couple of years, and then abandon the fields to let them rejuvenate with natural vegetation.

Which crops were grown depended upon household needs and environmental conditions such as length of the growing season, availability of irrigation water, and amount of rainfall. Wherever possible, people leveled and terraced fields to make them suitable for rice growing. Two fifths of the total cultivated acreage of Korea was riceland (not all of which had a secure source of irrigation) with the rest being rainfall field. Each household tried to farm a little of each type of land so that they would have a variety of food to eat. Ideally they would grow enough regular rice to feed their family, and enough glutinous rice to make rice cake (*ttŏk*) and brew rice beer (*makkŏlli*). The rest they would sell for cash. On part of their rainfall fields they would grow vegetables for home use—cabbage, hot peppers, radishes, garlic, lettuce, zucchini, and squash. On another part they would grow field crops such as barley, millet, kaoliang, beans of all types (soy, red, mung), and wheat; and if they still had some field left over, they might plant mulberry trees whose leaves are used to feed silkworms. Peasants often planted a fruit tree or two near their house—persimmons in the south, and cherries, jujubes, apples, pears, peaches, or chestnuts in other areas. Specialized fruit orchards were not common because transporting fruit to market was difficult. In addition to food crops, people grew hemp, ramie (a kind of fine grass that was woven into cloth), and cotton to make clothes, and such specialized crops as tobacco and sesame (which was pressed into a cooking oil). In coastal areas people commonly planted sweet potatoes, while in the mountains they often planted buckwheat and white potatoes.

The diet consisted of steamed grain, seasonal vegetables, and usually a soup. Rice was the preferred grain, but it was so expensive that poorer families often sold their rice for cash and purchased cheaper grains such as barley, millet, or kaoliang that were grown at home or imported from Manchuria. A large proportion of the rice crop was exported to Japan, where it was well-appreciated since Korean rice is the same as that grown by the Japanese. Peasants often ran out of rice toward the end of winter and subsisted on barley. They called the time of food shortages, barley pass (*pori kogae*), in the early spring, when agricultural work is intense but crops are not yet ready to be harvested. Fresh fruit and vegetables followed the seasons. Housewives put great effort into making *kimchi*, a mixture of cabbage, radishes, red pepper, and garlic preserved in brine. It was important in providing vitamins during the winter when no fresh vegetables were available. People often added roast chestnuts and sweet potatoes to their diet at that time of year. Wheat and buckwheat were not made into bread, but rather into noodles which could be substituted for steamed grain. Beans could be steamed like grain, but many were eaten as sprouts. Soybeans could also be mashed and mixed with wheat to make a fermented soup stock known as *toenjang*. Sometimes soybeans were also made into a beancake known as *tubu*. Koreans like meat (beef, pork, chicken, goat, even dog) eggs, and fish, but until recently only the wealthy ate meat very regularly. Seaweed, however, was a good source of protein for coastal people. People ate the brown kind known as *miyŏk* in a soup flavored with sesame, while the green kinds known as *kim* were dried, pressed into thin sheets, and wrapped around balls of rice.

The growing season varies in different parts of Korea. On the south coast, or on Cheju Island, the growing season lasts almost eleven months, but in the north it may last only seven months. Five different agricultural regions can be distinguished: (1) the subtropical south, (2) temperate south, (3) central, (4) north, (5) Kaema upland. The subtropical south is confined to Cheju Island, a very narrow strip along the south coast warm enough so that crops can be grown almost all year round. Both riceland and rain-fall field are double cropped, and certain tropical crops that do not grow elsewhere in Korea (such as taro and Mandarin oranges) can be cultivated.

The temperate south includes the rest of North and South Chŏlla, and North and South Kyŏngsang Provinces. Here half or more of the land was riceland on which rice was grown from spring to fall, and a catch crop of barley was planted in the winter. Because riceland is so productive and requires a lot of labor, farms in this part of Korea were small averaging about a third of a hectare (less than an acre). Bamboo grows in this part of Korea, and some villages in south Cholla province specialized in producing bamboo implements in the off season.

Central Korea, consisting of Kyŏnggi and the Ch'ungch'ŏng Provinces, was similar to the temperate south in which riceland predominated. The growing season was too short to grow winter barley on riceland because the barley harvest came too late for the rice to be planted on time. Winter barley could be grown on rainfall fields, however. In the northern zone—Hwanghae, North and South P'yŏngan, and North and South Hamgyŏng Provinces—less abundant water and a shorter growing season made rice cultivation more difficult. In these provinces fewer than a quarter of the fields were riceland, and such rainfall field grain crops as wheat, millet, kaoliang, soybeans, and maize were widely grown. Because rainfall fields are less productive than rice fields, farms on the average were 2/3 of a hectare twice as large as in the temperate south. The Kaema—upland North Korea's Chagang Province was unique. Here farmers cultivated little rice and concentrated on oats, millet, buckwheat, beans, and potatoes on farms of a hectare or more. Firefield farming was especially common here.

Before World War II, farm tenancy was a serious problem. Over the years of Japanese rule, many Korean farmers had lost their land so that by 1931 more than half of all the agricultural land was cultivated by tenants who were the majority of the farmers and paid rents to landowners amounting to about half of their crop. In the north, less than half the land was tenanted, but in the rich rice-growing areas of the south, almost three quarters of the riceland, and more than half the rainfall field, was owned by landlords who did not cultivate their land. Some of the largest landlords were Japanese, but the great majority were Korean. The largest landlords tended to live in the cities and left their lands in the care of agents. The tenants most commonly were sharecroppers who paid half their harvest to their landlords, or paid a rent in kind determined by the landlord on the basis of the crop. Because rents were so high, most tenants barely lived at the subsistence level and had little incentive to improve their agricultural practices.

Not only did the tenancy system discourage agricultural innovation, but it aggravated rural poverty and created resentment and political unrest, so that upon liberation from Japanese rule in 1945, the question of land reform was one of burning importance. Land reform was carried out in North Korea in the spring of 1946 when lands were expropriated from landlords without compensation and distributed among tenants. A large number of the former landlords fled to South Korea at this time. Buying and selling of land in North Korea was prohibited. The lands distributed to tenants were collectivized after the Korean War. Since 1958 agriculture in North Korea has been carried out on cooperative farms (*hyŏptong nongjang*) that are coterminous with administrative villages. Many people moved to the cities to work in factories during the period of collectivization so that today only about a quarter of the North Korean GNP is provided by agriculture. The present-day collective farms are run by managers answerable to local and county farm committees. North Korean agricultural policy has concentrated on attaining food self-sufficiency by encouraging large-scale grain farming using scientific methods. Tractor stations are maintained in rural administrative centers to encourage mechanization. This system has led to productivity improvements, but not to the hoped for extent. Reports of food shortages have periodically emerged from North Korea. As North Korea is almost entirely in the northern agricultural zone where rice is less commonly grown, even today almost 60 percent of the grains grown are rainfield grains such as wheat, barley, maize, and kaoliang.

South Korea also embarked on land reform after 1945, but in a more gradual manner. The ten percent of the agricultural land in the south that had been owned by, Japanese was seized and managed by the American Military Government's New Korea Company until sold to tenants for three times the annual harvest in 1947. The Republic of Korea's land reform law, with similar provisions, was passed in 1949 and was implemented between 1950 and 1955. According to its provisions, tenanted land was to be sold to tenants, and farm size was limited to three hectares. About 25 percent of the land of South Korea changed hands in this manner. There were many irregularities, however, and another 25 percent was privately sold from landlords to tenants during the 1945-1955 period. Even so, by 1955 tenancy rates in South Korea had been reduced from almost 70 percent to less than five percent. Although successful in reducing the tenancy rate, the South Korean land reform was less successful in the short run in improving agriculture and rural living standards. Many of the new farms were too small to be viable, so many who received land soon sold it for subsistence. Those who were able to succeed at farming rarely had capital for improvements or the technical knowledge to improve their agriculture. South Korean agriculture has gradually improved since then, however, due to a combination of rural-urban migration, changed market conditions, and government support.

The industrialization and urbanization that began in the 1960s in South Korea drained unemployed and surplus population out of the countryside and created urban demand for agricultural products. At the same time, the government instituted price supports for the basic crops and implemented a comprehensive agricultural extension program run through the Agricultural Guidance Office and the Office of Rural Development. The Agricultural Cooperative was merged with the Agricultural Bank in the early sixties to form the National Agricultural Cooperative Federation, a comprehensive organization with branches in each rural township that could disseminate seed, fertilizer, tools, and credit to farmers while providing a cooperative means of marketing their crops. These measures have led to a profound change in South Korea's agriculture. The number of farmers has fallen drastically to less than 15 percent of the population, while farm size has tripled to an average of 1.2 hectares (about 3 acres).

Most farmers now plow with small tractors, use chemical fertilizers, control weeds and pests with insecticides, and may even transplant rice mechanically. Rice productivity has shot up, while field crops such as wheat, barley, millet, rye, and sorghum have been declined to less than 15 percent of the grains grown. Grains such as wheat can be purchased cheaply on international markets, so they have been replaced by higher value fruit, vegetable, medicinal, and industrial crops. Cheju Island, for example, now specializes in citrus, while some farmers on the south coast grow cut flowers for the Japanese market. Animal husbandry has become much more important. Cattle are no longer used as draft animals, but hundreds of thousands are raised for slaughter, as are even larger numbers of pigs, chickens, and ducks. Dairy farming has emerged around the major cities.

The living standard of South Korean farmers has improved greatly over the years, but improvement of the standard of living in rural areas has lagged the cities. This has been a major cause of rural to urban migration. Farm price supports are a significant government expense. Farmer indebtedness has emerged as a problem when farmers borrow to expand their scale of production or to cultivate a new sideline only to find that prices have crashed. South Korean farmers are especially fearful of a crash in agricultural prices if domestic markets are freely opened to international imports.

3

The Economic Geography of North and South Korea

North Korea has built its economy by using its abundance of natural resources. The mountainous terrain provides many opportunities for developing hydroelectric resources. Coal (anthracite) is found in North and South Pyŏngan Provinces and South Hamgyŏng Province. Iron ore, gold, silver, copper, lead, and zinc are also found. The Tanchŏn and Kŏmdŏk mines in South Hamgyŏng Province are said to contain the world's largest deposit of magnetite. South Korea also has good hydroelectric power sources, but its mineral sources (though they include cement and coal) are inferior to those found in the north. This lack is made up in part by superior agricultural potential in the south.

Both North and South Korea have become highly industrialized and urbanized since 1945, but the pattern of urbanization in each is different. In 1990, South Korea was almost 75 percent urban, and was dominated by a few very large cities—Seoul, the capital, with almost 11 million residents, and five other cities with more than a million residents each. Sixty-three percent of the population lived in cities larger than 100,000 in 1985. North Korea was 60 percent urban in 1987, but the capital, P'yŏngyang with 2.4 million, was the only city of more than a million, and 61 percent of the urban population lived in cities smaller than 100,000.

Table 2 : Largest Cities in North Korea (1987)

Cities	Population
Pyŏngyang	2,355,000
Hamhŭng	701,000
Chŏngjin	520,000
Sinŭiju	289,000
Tanchŏn	284,000

Table 3 : Largest Cities in South Korea (1991)

Cities	Population
Seoul	10,918,000
Pusan	3,877,000
Taegu	2,286,000
Inchŏn	1,728,000
Kwangju	1,234,000

The North Korean economy is based on the ideology of *Juche* (self-reliance) and is centrally planned. The North Korean leadership endeavors to create an economy that can provide for as many of its own needs with domestic production as possible, by importing only what is absolutely necessary and by exporting only after domestic needs have been met. Trade amounts to less than 20 percent of the GNP, with Russia, China, and Japan being the major trading partners. Domestically mined coal provides some 90 percent of North Korea's energy, with hydroelectric power contributing the rest. The nuclear plants at Yŏngbyŏn are still considered experimental, so big nuclear power generation capacity is not expected for North Korea until the late nineties. Since petroleum has to be imported from either Russia, China, or the Middle East, North Korea has avoided heavy dependence on this as a source of energy.

Heavy and chemical industries have been given great emphasis with major concentrations near P'yŏngyang, Hamhŭng, and Ch'ŏngjin. Iron and steel and the machine-building industries are all important, with the steel mill at Kimch'aek being the largest. Light manufactures have been given more emphasis in recent years than in the past. Many consumer goods are produced locally rather than in the large industrial cities.

North Korea has a well-developed railway network. In 1980 they had more than 5,000 kilometers of track, 63 percent of which had been electrified. Some 90 percent of North Korea's freight and passengers are carried by rail. Since trains can be powered by domestically produced electricity or domestically mined coal, heavy dependence on rail transport facilitates energy self-reliance. Highway transport that requires the use of imported petroleum is less developed, but more than 350 kilometers of superhighway connect P'yŏngyang with Namp'o and Wŏnsan.

Table 4 : North Korean Ports by Tonnage

Cities	Tonnage
Namp'o*	about 1,500,000
Ch'ŏngjin*	
Hamhŭng	

* Foreign ships may land

The South Korean economy is capitalist but with significant government planning and ownership of infrastructure such as rail, power, and steel. Since the sixties, international trade has fostered rapid growth in GNP and per capita income. Per capita GNP has passed $10,000 vaulting South Korea into the lower ranks of the world's high income countries. Trade amounts to about 75 percent of the GNP. South Korea imports machinery, intermediate manufactured goods, petroleum, and other raw materials and exports finished manufactured products, from consumer products like microwave ovens to steel, ships, and automobiles. Textiles, clothing, and footwear, important industries of the past, have begun to decline and move offshore to China and Indonesia as Korean labor has become more expensive, but they are still important to the economy. Similar to North Korea, South Korea has well-developed hydroelectric power resources and modest coal deposits, but all domestic sources together supply only about a third of the country's power needs. Almost half its energy is supplied by petroleum imported from Saudi Arabia, Kuwait, Malaysia, and Indonesia. Almost 15 percent of its energy (half of the electricity generated) is supplied by nuclear power.

A large portion of South Korea's industry is located near Seoul, particularly in the Kuro and Pup'yŏng districts between Seoul and Inch'ŏn. Other concentrations of industry are in Taegu (textiles and automobile parts), and the southeast coast including P'ohang (iron and steel), Ulsan (chemicals, automobiles, shipbuilding), Pusan (shoes and shipbuilding), and Masan (machine tools, textiles). The Yŏsu peninsula on the southwest coast has a large concentration of chemical refining plants. The concentration of industry in Seoul and the southeast has recently become a source of political tension. Efforts are now being made to spread industry more evenly around Korea.

South Korea has a well-developed railway network with almost 6,500 kilometers of track in 1990. Only 3 percent of that track is electrified. The country has concentrated much more than North Korea on developing highway transport. South Korea has more than 40,000 kilometers of paved highway and more than 1,500 kilometers of superhighway connecting all parts of the country. South Korea's railways, while they haul in tonnage about as much as North Korean railways, haul a much smaller proportion of South Korea's total freight and passengers. Railways and the subways in Seoul and Pusan together carry about 10 percent of the passenger traffic, with the rest going either by bus (both high-speed highway and rural), or increasingly by private automobile. In 1989, 28 percent of the freight went by rail, 60 percent by highway, and 11 percent by ship. In recent years, as private car ownership has skyrocketed, South Korea's highways have begun to suffer from the clogged traffic typical of developed countries.

Table 5 : South Korean Ports by Tonnage and Cargo

	Most important cargo	Tonnage
P'ohang	iron ore, coal, steel	35,416,000
Kwangyang	oil	34,679,000
Pusan*	general cargo	31,301,000
Inch'ŏn*	general cargo	22,877,000
Ulsan	automobiles	14,338,000
Tonghae	general cargo	10,038,000

* Foreign ships may land

4

The People

The discovery of Paleolithic artifacts proves Korea was inhabited as long ago as 500,000 years. However, any inhabitants of the Korean peninsula that far back in history would have been premodern (Homo erectus or neanderthalensis) and are not likely to be directly ancestral to today's Koreans. Today's Koreans are descended from numerous waves of migrants from Northeast Siberia, Mongolia, Manchuria, and North China who began drifting into Korea from around 5000 B.C. These migrants undoubtedly belonged to a variety of tribes and cultures who came to Korea at different times and gradually merged, intermarried, and developed a common society on the Korean peninsula. Koreans today consider themselves a homogeneous race and culture, but the merging of originally distinct tribes into a single common society was not completed until after Shilla united the Korean peninsula in 668.

Based on linguistic and archaeological evidence, the basic stock of the Korean people seem to have migrated from northeastern Siberia into Manchuria and then down into the Korean peninsula. Some continued across the Korea Strait into Japan, which has continued to receive Korean migrants, though the number has been relatively small since the Shilla unification. The original northeast Siberia stock received significant admixtures of blood from China—particularly during the 400 years, from 100 B.C. to 300 A.D., that Chinese commanderies existed in north Korea. Significant migration of ethnic Chinese and northeast Asian tribes from

China and Manchuria continued through Koryŏ times when significant numbers of ethnic Koreans also migrated to China's Shandong Peninsula for trade purposes. Because of these ancient migrations to and from Korea, and because of the mingling with neighboring people, Koreans physically closely resemble northern and eastern Chinese to their west, and Japanese of the Inland Sea area to their east.

Koreans are a medium-sized people. Studies done during the thirties found the men to average 163 cm (5'4") and the women 148 (4'10"). This was several inches shorter than Chinese from Hebei near Beijing, about the same as Chinese in the eastern provinces of Jiangsu and Shandong, and one to two inches taller than the Japanese or southern Chinese. Both men and women tended to be somewhat taller in the north than the south. Improved nutrition since World War II has led people to grow taller than in the past in both Korea and Japan. Studies in the late fifties in South Korea showed most men ranging between 161 and 171 cm (5'3" and 5'7") and women between 152 and 162 cm (4'10" and 5'3"). The stature of South Koreans today is now probably an inch or so taller than the earlier studies found, because nutrition has improved since that time.

Multivariate studies of Korean skull measurements show them to be quite similar to those of Manchus, Mongols, and northern Chinese. Koreans tend to have a relatively large head—tall and broad in front, but narrow front to back. Like Mongols and Manchus, Koreans tend to have prominent cheekbones with a relatively straight nose. These protruding cheekbones give the face a somewhat flat aspect. It is thought that high cheekbones might function to protect the eyes from wind and glare. Most Koreans have an oval face. Almost all Koreans (like the Chinese and Japanese) have straight black, or chestnut, hair (which tends to be darker on males than females). A small number of males (less than one percent) have slightly wavy hair. Most Koreans have chestnut colored eyes, though the darkness varies somewhat from person to person and tends to be somewhat lighter in females than in males. Skin color for Koreans, as for Japanese and northern Chinese, is quite light, comparable to southern Europeans. The slight yellowish tint of East Asians' skin comes from a subcutaneous layer of fat that protects people's faces from cold rather than from skin color per se. Many Koreans' cheeks turn bright red when they are exposed to cold, when they exercise, or when they drink alcohol. About 80 percent of Koreans have an epicanthic eye fold, but up to 20 percent are completely without this feature.

Studies of the ABO blood groups show Koreans to be typical for northeast Asia: 28% O, 32% A, 30% B, and 10% AB. As in all of East

Asia, Rh negative blood is extremely rare. The distribution of blood types in Korea is notable primarily for the low frequency of O type blood, the type that is most common worldwide. High frequencies of A type blood are characteristic of Europe, but B type blood is relatively uncommon there. On the other hand, B type blood is extremely common in Northern India and Mongolia, but A type blood is relatively uncommon. Korea, Japan, and Manchuria are characterized by relatively high frequencies of both A and B type blood, hence low frequencies of O type. It has been hypothesized that frequencies of blood types might be a consequence of each type's superior resistance to different endemic diseases, as well as heredity, but no comprehensive explanation for the world-wide distribution of blood types has been forthcoming. In Korea the frequencies of A and B tend to vary from north to south with B type blood slightly more common in the north, and A type blood more common in the south. This shows the transitional character of Korea, in that A type blood is more common in Japan (closest to the south) while B type is more common in China and Mongolia (closest to the north). Like many peoples for whom dairy farming is not traditional, adult Koreans often lack the enzyme lactase that aids in the digestion of fresh milk. These adults, if they consume fresh milk, are likely to get stomach cramps or diarrhea.

Although in the aggregate Koreans have a distinctive physical profile, one should not underestimate the diversity of the Korean people. There is a good deal of overlap in the features of Koreans, Japanese, and north Chinese. Although one might be able to statistically distinguish a large group of Koreans from a large group of northern Chinese or Japanese on physical features alone (that is, even if they wore the same clothing and had the same hair style), it is difficult to do this on an individual level since the features of most northern and eastern Chinese, Japanese, or Koreans fall within the normal range of variation for all of these countries. All of the physical features found in Korea are also found in Japan and China, but at different frequencies. Ethnic Koreans who have grown up in China or Japan and have learned to speak the local language and dress and act according to local norms, have easily blended into the local population. Ethnic Chinese and Japanese could do the same in Korea, though this has rarely actually happened for cultural and economic reasons that have nothing to do with physical or racial appearance.

Suggested Further Reading

Bartz, Patricia. 1972. *South Korea*. Oxford: Clarendon Press.

Bunge, Frederica. 1981. *North Korea: A Country Study.* Washington, D.C.: U.S. Government Printing Office.

Eberstadt, Nicholas and Judith Banister. 1992. *The Population of North Korea*. Berkeley: Institute of East Asian Studies, University of California. Korea Research Monograph No. 17.

Lautensach, Ott. 1988. *Korea, A geography Based on the Author's Travels and Literature*. Berlin and New York: Springer Verlag.

Sorensen, Clark. 1988. *Over the Mountains Are Mountains: Korean Pesant Households and their Adaptations to Rapid Industrialization*. Seattle: University of Washington Press.

2

History
by Andrew C. Nahm

1

Background

Culture in present-day Korea is a sum total of various elements which developed through several historical periods. Although not all Korean historians agree regarding the periodization of Korean history, general consensus is that Korean culture as we know it now developed during the three historical periods—the ancient, the middle, and the modern following a longer, prehistoric period.

Each historical period left its particular marks on the cultural development of the Koreans, always sowing new seeds for further changes in subsequent historical times.

2

Premodern Korea :
Through the Prehistoric Ages to the Dawn of Statehood

The Korean Peninsula in Prehistoric Times

Many millions of years after dinosaurs left their footprints on now fos-
silized beaches in the Korean peninsula, Paleolithic (Old Stone) Age man
appeared in Korea over 30,000 years ago and left his traces. Those crude
tools, made from stone and animal bones unearthed at several Paleolithic
sites in present-day North Hamgyŏng (northeast), South Pʼyŏngan (northwest), Kyŏnggi (central), and North, and South Chʼungchʼŏng (south central) provinces, clearly indicate that tool making people inhabited the
Korean peninsula. Living mostly in caves near water, these early people
gathered fruits, berries, and edible roots while hunting and fishing. Their
stone and bone tools resemble those of the early American Indians. In
the late Paleolithic Age they built round-shaped, deep pit dwellings with a
hearth for warmth and for cooking.

Around 6000 B.C., the Neolithic (New Stone Age) culture emerged
in the Korean peninsula. These people established their habitat along
river banks and sea shores, and made more efficient stone tools. Many
Neolithic sites have been discovered throughout the Korean peninsula.
Evidence shows that the Neolithic people built their dwellings in shallow
pits with a hearth in the center of the floor. They made polished stone
tools and produced pottery with geometric designs (commonly called
comb-marking) in grey color with pointed (V-shaped) bottoms.

Forming clan-centered communal groups, the Neolithic people are believed to have practiced agriculture and domesticated animals, producing new tools such as stone sickles, the bow and spear. They practiced animism, worshiping the heavens, the sun, and the earth; they believed that every object in the natural world possessed a soul or spirit.

Around 3000 B.C., waves of migration brought other clans and tribes from central Asia to Manchuria via Siberia, and some of them moved onto the Korean peninsula. Among them were the people known as the Tungus with the (Ural-) Altaic language, practicing a shaman cult that was associated with spirit worship. At this juncture, painted pottery appeared. Perhaps it was brought to Korea by those who fled from northeastern China. Soon after that, pointed-bottomed vessels were replaced by flat-bottomed vessels with various designs.

The Neolithic period was followed by the Bronze Age some time around 1200 B.C., when the Sytho-Siberian-type Bronze culture developed in Manchuria and slowly spread down into the Korean peninsula. Stone tools gave way to bronze ones, including vessels, daggers, mirrors with geometric designs, and some agricultural and fishing implements.

Living in shallow pit dwellings built on slopes or uplands, the Bronze Age people formed expanded communal units, increasing agricultural life, growing millet and rice, and advancing their metallurgical skills. They produced brownish-red pottery without designs. At the same time, using bronze tools, they cut large stones, erecting menhirs (upright stones) perhaps for heaven worship, and covered burial chambers with large, flat stones called dolmen.

As the bronze culture rapidly replaced the Neolithic culture, those tribes which arrived in Manchuria with their own totems formed tighter political units and expanded their territory. The strength of those tribes who rode horses and possessed bronze weapons of various kinds grew fast. As they subjugated the Neolithic people both in Manchuria and Korea, they built large, walled towns which eventually become city-states. The state which Korean historians call Old Chosŏn was one of those states. It was called Old Chosŏn in order to distinguish it from the kingdom of Chosŏn that emerged in the late 14th century.

Appearance of Early States

Because of the lack of reliable sources, it is difficult to ascertain when Old Chosŏn emerged, who the founders were, or where it was located.

According to a Korean source, *Memorabilia of the Three Kingdoms*, written by a Buddhist monk, Ilyŏn, in the late 13th century, Old Chosŏn was established in 2333 B.C. by Tan'gun (also known as Wanggŏm), the son of a celestial being. He is said to have ruled as king and high priest. While some argue that Old Chosŏn emerged in southwestern Manchuria with its capital at Asadal and its territory covering northwestern Korea as well, others say that Old Chosŏn was in northern Korea with its capital at Waggŏmsŏng, which is modern P'yŏngyang.

Traditionally, the Old Chosŏn period is divided into three sub-periods, namely, the Tangun, the Kija, and the Wiman periods. According to Memorabilia of the Three Kingdoms, around 1120 B.C. Kija, a scion of the fallen Yin (Shang) Dynasty of China fled to Korea with some 2,000 followers and became king of Old Chosŏn, initiating the Kija Chosŏn period. The same source states that around 194 B.C., Wiman, a Chinese military leader who fled to Old Chosŏn, usurped the throne after serving under the king of Old Chosŏn for a few years, beginning the Wiman Chosŏn period. At that time, King Chun of Old Chosŏn was forced to flee to the south where the Chin State is said to have existed.

The validity of the 13th century source is doubtful. Be that as it may, Chinese sources of the 7th century indicate that there existed a strong and arrogant state named Chosŏn in southwestern Manchuria that also controlled northwestern Korea, and it was in conflict with the Chinese states in the north.

By the time the Iron Age began in Korea in the 4th century, other Tugunsic states such as Puyŏ, Ye, and perhaps Koguryŏ emerged in Manchuria, and Imdun and Chinbŏn in the northern part of Korea, while a confederation called Chin of some 78 Han tribes emerged in the region south of the Han River.

Old Chosŏn entered a period of decline after losing its western regions to the Yen State of China at the end of the 4th century and then to other Chinese empires, becoming a smaller kingdom confined to the Korean peninsula. In such a state of flux, Wiman usurped the throne and subjugated Imdun and Chinbŏn. But Wiman Chosŏn was overthrown by Chinese forces of the Han Dynasty in 108 B.C.

After conquering Wiman Chosŏn, Han China established three commanderies in northwestern Korea, taking economic advantage and increasing Chinese cultural influence that had already begun to take root in Korea. A fourth Chinese commandery was established in southern Manchuria where the Ye State had existed. Two of three Chinese commanderies in Korea were overthrown in the 2nd century A.D., and the third commandery named Lolang (Nangnang in Korean) which existed in the Taedong River basin with its capital at Wanggŏmsŏng, was over-thrown by Koguryŏ in 313. As Chinese commanderies collapsed, there emerged two new states of the Tungusic people in eastern Korea—Okchŏ and Tong'ye. The Chinese commanderies that existed in Korea exerted a far reaching impact on the political and cultural history of the people in the Korean peninsula.

As political upheavals unfolded in the north, in the south the Chin State split into three loosely federated states. They were Mahan in the central and southwestern Korea, Chinhan in the southeastern region, and Pyŏnhan in the south central area. Evidence shows that these areas were rapidly influenced by the bronze and iron cultures, as well as a rice cul-ture that developed in the north, while they practiced shamanism and the cult of divination. Like Old Chosŏn, all the rulers of the Han Federations functioned as king and high priest.

3

From the Three Kingdoms to a Unified State

Shortly after the fall of Wiman Chosŏn in 108 B.C. and the establishment of Chinese commanderies in the north, further political transformations took place, ushering in what is known as the Three Kingdoms period.

The Three Kingdoms: Their Rise and Development

Although the founding dates are disputed, traditionally the state of Saro (later renamed Shilla) of six clans is said to have been founded in 57 B.C. in the Chinhan region. Saro State with Pak Hyŏkkŏse as its first king eventually ended the existence of Chinhan by absorbing its other tribal regions.

The Kingdom of Koguryŏ was said to have been established in 37 B.C. by Chumong of the Ko clan who fled from the State of Puyŏ to southern Manchuria and established the new kingdom with the help of five clans which followed him out of Puyŏ. North Korean historians argue that it emerged in 277 B.C. In the 3rd century A.D., Koguryŏ extended its territory in the northern part of Korea, overthrowing Okchŏ and Tong'ye, and in 313 it destroyed the Chinese commandery of Lolang, dominating the entire northern half of the peninsula.

The Kingdom of Paekche is believed to have been established in 18 B.C. in the Mahan region by Onjo, a son of Chumong, with his power base at Hansŏng which was located in the fertile region along the Han River. This kingdom eventually replaced Mahan, controlling the central and southwestern regions of the peninsula. Only Pyŏnhan failed to become a unified kingdom as it remained a federation of several Kaya states. However, one by one, they were taken over by Shilla, and in the second half of the 6th century the Kaya states disappeared.

In Koguryŏ and Paekche, kingship was established in the earlier stages of their national development, but kingdom in Shilla was not firmly established until 500. Up until that time, Shilla rulers used such tribal titles as *kŏsŏgan*, *isagŭm*, or *maripkan*. The founders of these three kingdoms, as well as those of Shilla who established other ruling Dynasties (Kim and Sŏk), claimed divine origin as they consolidated their monarchical legitimacy by copying the Chinese political system. Koguryŏ had a bureaucratic system of twelve ranks, Paekche had sixteen ranks, and Shilla's central bureaucracy had seventeen ranks. All three of them had councils or palatial decision-making bodies.

As monarchical authority became firmer, the rulers of the three kingdoms expanded their national territory in the late fourth and fifth centuries. Kings of Koguryŏ of the period between 371-491, and those of Paekche in the mid-fourth century, and Shilla kings of the 356-576 period and of the mid-6th century were great warriors who built strong kingdoms. As their national ambitions grew, a power struggle among the three kingdoms intensified, particularly after Koguryŏ relocated its capital in 427 from Tonggu (Kungnaesŏng) in the mid-Yalu region to Wanggŏmsŏng (now P'yŏngyang).

As bona fide kingdoms emerged in Korea, social changes took place in each kingdom. In Shilla what is known as the bone quality rank (a bloodline) system was established in the early 6th century. This system had two categories: bone ranks (holy bone and true bone) and the quality ranks. The members of the Pak clan were in the holy-bone rank, and the members of the Sŏk and Kim clans were given the true-bone rank. Members of three other clans of the Saro tribe were graded into six quality ranks.

Shilla's throne was occupied only by the members of the holy-bone rank up to 262, but after that members of the true-bone were able to occupy the throne. Those who were in the quality ranks constituted the Shilla aristocracy and held government posts. Normally, those who were subjugated were made commoners, but some of them were given aristocratic status, while the majority, as well as criminals, were enslaved as the low-born people.

In Koguryŏ, the Ko clan monopolized the throne while those members of the five tribes who participated in the founding of the kingdom constituted the aristocracy. As in Shilla, criminals and those who were conquered were classified either as commoners or low-born people, namely slaves. In Paekche, the Puyŏ clan monopolized the throne as members of the eight prominent clans constituted the aristocracy.

Aristocrats lived in the capital while the peasants tilled the land. The low-born people lived in specially designated areas and were engaged in manufacturing work. A significant social development was the adoption of Chinese-style clan names by certain aristocratic clans in Korea.

The members of the aristocracy provided civil and military leadership. In Shilla, young sons of aristocratic families called *hwarang* (flowery princes) became the backbone of national defense as they practiced what is called *hwarangdo*, or the Way of Flowery Princes, epitomized by chivalry, bravery, fidelity, and righteousness. They may be compared to the knights of Medieval Europe. They contributed much toward the growth of Shilla's military strength, as well as its culture.

The people of the Three Kingdoms worshipped Heaven and Earth, observing spring and autumn festivals. They prayed for a bounteous year in the spring and gave thanks in the late fall, celebrating with several days of singing, dancing, eating, and drinking. Chinese sources said that the people in Korea loved music and dance. They also practiced the shaman cult, seeking harmonious co-existence between spirits and human beings. Shamans, both male and female, played important social as well as religious roles as mediums.

All three kingdoms nurtured economic growth, but Shilla and Paekche became far more prosperous, thanks to the fertile farmlands they possessed, Shilla along the Naktong River and Paekche in the Han, the Kŭm, and other river basins. In addition to rice and millet, hemp was grown in Shilla for textile manufacturing. Koguryŏ's Taedong River region produced much grain, in addition to salt and fish from the eastern regions along the sea. Although hemp cloth was the main textile produced, silk manufacturing also began in Shilla in the 6th century.

While Paekche traded mostly with the Japanese with gold, iron, and other manufactured goods, Koguryŏ exported salt and fish to China. Shillas foreign trade was not developed until much later, in the 9th century.

The three kingdoms nurtured culture and promoted crafts. Using the Chinese writing system that was introduced in the 2nd century B.C., Koguryŏ published the first 100-volume national history called *Extant Records* in its early period. It was re-edited and published as *New Compilation* in 600. Paekche's national history, called *Documentary*

Records, was also published in Chinese in the middle of the 4th century. In 545, National History, written in Chinese, was published in Shilla.

An important cultural contribution by Shilla was the creation and use of the new writing system called *idu* in the 7th century. It introduced the ways to transcribe native words into Chinese according to their phonetic values only.

The arrival of Confucianism in the second century brought about intellectual and educational development as well as political influence. In 372, Koguryŏ had already established the National Confucian Academy and other schools for the sons of aristocrats. In Paekche, Confucian masters promoted studies in the history and literature of China. Some of them went to Japan, introducing Confucian culture there. The national Confucian College, belatedly established in Shilla in 682, brought about the rise of educated leaders and scholars.

Buddhism, believed to have arrived from China in Koguryŏ in 372 and in Paekche in 384, exerted a profound influence, overshadowing the native animism and shaman cult. Shilla accepted Buddhism only in 572 after the martyrdom of Ichadon, but it grew rapidly as Shilla monks went to China to study Buddhism (one of them went as far as India) and brought back various doctrines, and popularized them in Korea. Among the five major sects that developed in Shilla was the *Hwaŏm* (Avatamasaka) sect. This became the most popular sect in the 7th century and took hold as the religion of the masses.

The *Sŏn* (Zen in Japanese) sect which was introduced into Shilla in the 7th century led to the rise of the Nine Mountain Sects of *Sŏn* in the early 9th century. Eventually, two major schools of Buddhism emerged in Korea: the Textual School represented by the Pure Land sect and the Contemplative School represented by the *Sŏn* sect.

With the rise of Buddhism came the construction of temples, pagodas, stone lanterns, production of gold, iron, stone, and wooden statues of Buddha, Bodhisattvas, and Maitreya. Among the temples constructed in the early stage were the Hwang'yong, the Pulguk, and Pŏmŏ temples in Shilla and the Mirŭk Temple in Paekche. The Hwang'yong Temple was destroyed completely by the Mongols in the 13th century and was never rebuilt.

With the growth of Confucian and Buddhist cultures, new rituals, music and dance developed, establishing a new cultural tradition. Buddhist festivals such as *p'algwanhoe* and assemblies for Sutra Recitation by One Hundred Monks and shrine rituals associated with Confucianism enriched cultural life. At the same time, new costumes, new musical instruments such as the five-stringed zither called *kŏmungo* of Koguryŏ and the twelve-stringed zither named *kayagŭm* of Kaya became two major string instruments of Korea.

In the field of fine arts, Chinese studies led to the development of Chinese-style calligraphy. Chinese writing brushes, ink sticks, and stone ink pads became abundant, and renowned calligraphers emerged. Shilla and Paekche left behind very little in painting. Only one, the "Heavenly Horse," painted on tree bark, was found within a Shilla tomb of the early period. Murals which were presumed to have been painted on the walls of Buddhist temples in Paekche and Shilla did not survive fire, war, and natural deterioration. However, Koguryŏ left behind many murals in its tombs which depicted a variety of contemporary scenes.

Metal workers in Paekche and Shilla produced a variety of gilt statues of Buddha, Bodhisattva, and Maitreya. They also produced gold crowns, belts, rings, and earrings in various styles. Evidently, both Paekche and Shilla produced several kinds of earthenware, including roof, wall and floor tiles with symbolic designs, as well as new pottery produced with the potters wheel.

As an increasing number of new Buddhist temples were built after 660, some of the temples which had been destroyed were rebuilt. Among the newly rebuilt temples was the Pulguk Temple. When its reconstruction began in 751, the construction of a grotto temple called Sŏkkuram on the hill behind Kyŏngju, capital of Shilla, was also begun. Those temples constructed in the Chinese architectural style show a high degree of skill on the part of the Shilla workers. Meanwhile, sculptors of Shilla and Paekche built beautiful stone pagodas, stupas, and lanterns. Among those were the Pagoda of Many Treasures, the Pagoda of No Shadow, and stone lanterns currently standing in the inner courtyard of the Pulguk Temple. The large stone statue of Buddha in sitting position placed in the Sŏkkuram grotto temple is among the finest works of the Shilla sculptors. Among the non-religious stone structures that survived is the Star Observation Tower which was built in the mid-8th century in Kyŏngju.

Bronze workers were equally busy, producing large and small bells and statues. Among the large bronze bells which were produced in the mid-8th century and still remain is the Emille's Bell which was installed at the Pongdŏk Temple in 771.

The First Unification and After

Koguryŏ became a threat to Paekche after establishing P'yŏngyang as its new capital and conquering Okchŏ, Eastern Ye, and other areas in the north. Paekche's wars with Koguryŏ were frequent in the late 4th century. Facing this situation, Paekche formed an alliance with Shilla against the aggressive neighbor, but the Paekche-Shilla alliance was broken in the 6th century as Shilla's ambitions in the Kaya region grew, bringing a long period of bloody warfare between the former allies.

As the fortunes of Paekche declined steadily, Koguryŏ, which had already suffered invasions by the Earlier Yen of the Hsienpei in western Manchuria in the 4th century, faced new threats from the Sui Dynasty of China at the end of the 6th century, and then those of the Tang Dynasty in the early 7th century. Koguryŏ was able to defeat the Chinese forces and safeguard its territory, but it too lost much of its vitality, witnessing such interval upheavals as the coup and dictatorial rule of a military leader named Yŏn Kaesomun. The death of Yŏn and its aftermath were even more disastrous to Koguryŏ.

The tables were turned when, in the mid-7th century, Paekche regained her national strength under an able king and launched an aggressive war against Shilla, taking over many of her strategic areas in the western region. At this juncture, Shilla asked Koguryŏ for help, but the territorial concessions it demanded were such that Shilla turned instead to Tang China for assistance.

The war that the Shilla-Tang forces launched against Paekche in 660 brought about the fall of that kingdom despite Paekche's military assistance from the Japanese. After destroying Paekche, the combined forces of Shilla and Tang China attacked Koguryŏ in 661. This war dragged on for several years, but in 668 the vast kingdom of Koguryŏ was defeated and most of the palace buildings in its capital were destroyed.

When Koguryŏ fell, one of its military leaders, who fled to the Manchurian domain of Koguryŏ with many followers, established a new state named Chin in 698 (renamed Parhae in 713), which controlled much of Manchuria and Korea north of the 39th parallel until it fell in 926.

After the destruction of Paekche and Koguryŏ, the Shilla-Tang alliance ended when Tang China attempted to establish its domination in the peninsula, not only in the former Koguryŏ and Paekche areas, but also over Shilla. The two former allies went to war with the survival of Shilla at stake. Shilla's forces were able to defeat Chinese troops in the former Paekche area in 671, and in 676 the Tang forces were driven back beyond the Yalu River. With this victory, Shilla established its hegemony in the Korean peninsula south of the 39th parallel near which P'yŏngyang in the west and Wŏnsan in the east are located.

After unifying the Three Kingdoms, Shilla restructured its administrative and military systems, importing many political ideologies and patterns from China. It promoted industry, including foreign trade, and brought about intellectual and cultural growth. Buddhism reached its golden age in Korea, producing many renowned monks and scholars who wrote important treatises on Buddhism. Many new temples were built and old ones restored. At the same time, Taoist culture and geomancy became popularized, and there was an amalgamation of certain aspects of Buddhism and shamanistic cults. It was during this period that poets and songwriters produced a large number of native songs (*hyang'ga*), both religious and secular in nature, using the idu system of transcribing the language.

However, the very foundation of Unified Shilla was weakened by controversies over succession within the ruling royal house, and unending power struggle among the aristocrats, and between the central bureaucracy and local lords, armed rebellions, and the collapse of trade with China.

The rebellions that broke out in the late 9th century brought about the rise of two states: Later Paekche in the southwestern region in 892, and Later Koguryŏ in the central region in 901, thereby reducing the territory of Shilla and bringing the period of the later Three Kingdoms in Korean history.

The kingship of Later Koguryŏ was taken over by Wang Kŏn, one of the Later Koguryŏ's military leaders, who usurped the throne and, in 918, changed the name of the kingdom to Koryŏ and established its capital at Songak (also known as Kaegyŏng, Songdo, now Kaesŏng). After that, he was engaged in unending warfare against Later Paekche and Shilla to the South and new states that developed in Manchuria. In the end, in 935, he brought about the surrender of the last Shilla king to Koryŏ and the destruction of Later Paekche in 936. At this juncture, the crown prince of Parhae, which was overthrown by the Khitans in 926, fled to Koryŏ, bringing many survivors of Koguryŏ lineage with him. As he had done with the last king of Shilla, Wang Kŏn welcomed him and made him a member of the Wang clan.

4

Korea after Reunification

The reunified Korea was ruled first by the Wang Dynasty which established the Kingdom of Koryǒ (918-1392) from which came the English name for Korea. The kingdom was then ruled by the Yi Dynasty under the name of Chosǒn and lasted until 1910.

Korea's Transformation during the Koryǒ Period

The Kingdom of Koryǒ which was ruled by 34 kings brought about enormous changes in many areas, making it one of the most advanced nations in Asia. Wang Kǒn, whose monarchical title was T'aejo, and his immediate successors initiated various reform programs despite bloody succession disputes. They ended Shilla's bone-rank system, strengthened the kingly authority, adopted the Chinese-style civil service examination system and Chinese laws, and restructured the central bureaucracy between 983 and 1076, installing a bureaucracy patterned after that of China. They also nationalized farm and forest lands, and laws governing the system of land allotment were promulgated.

Although from time to time the structure of the central government was reshaped, on the whole it consisted of a policy deliberation council, an advisory council, an executive organ with six ministries, a censorate, and a military council. Koryǒ also adopted the Chinese system of dividing government officials into nine categories. Each category had senior and junior grades, the total number of ranks being eighteen.

In the beginning, the kingdom was divided into twelve provinces, but in the 11th century it was re-districted into a metropolitan district, five circuits, and two border regions. In addition to the main capital at Songak, two sub-capitals were established, one at P'yǒngyang and the other Kyǒngju. Lower administrative units were provinces, districts, and counties.

Koryǒ's military system initially consisted of two royal guards and six combat divisions, but later on the Extraordinary Military Corps was added. The new unit consisted of a cavalry corps, an infantry corps, and a special corps which included Buddhist monks. Five regional military command headquarters were created, and a large number of garrisons were established throughout the country.

The Koryǒ government established public welfare institutions such as the Bureau of People's Welfare and the East and West Infirmaries to care for the poor and sick. Righteous Granaries were built to care for the poor, and Equalizing Storehouses were established to maintain steady commodity prices.

Koryǒ expanded its territory far north up to the mouth of the Yalu river and constructed six garrison towns in the newly secured area, but it ran into conflict with the Khitans who established the State of Liao in southwestern Manchuria and destroyed the State of Parhae in the late 10th century. Koryǒ successfully met the threats of the Khitans and in the mid-11th century built the Long Wall, linking the northern frontiers near the mouth of the Yalu River with the eastern seacoast near present-day Hamhŭng. This strengthened its defense not only against the Khitans but also against the Jurchens in eastern Manchuria and northeastern Korea.

In the early 12th century, Koryǒ expanded its territory into present-day South Hamgyǒng Province and constructed nine forts in the area adjacent to the Long Wall, this time provoking the Jurchens. Koryǒ withdrew its forces from the occupied territory, but the new leader of the Jurchens who established the State of Chin overthrew the State of Liao in 1125, invaded the Sung capital two years later, and brought heavy pressure on Koryǒ, forcing it to accept its overlordship of Chin.

Early Koryǒ kings brought about the rise of a new social order which was headed by the aristocracy and consisted of those members of the gentry families who helped to found the new dynasty and those Shilla aristocrats who were in the top three grades in the quality rank. In the process of establishing a new social order, such clans as the Kim and the Yi rose to the top, followed by the Yun and Choe clans. Like Kyǒngju,

Songak became the heartland of the aristocracy.

Needless to say, all top civil and military positions in the government were occupied by members of the new aristocracy. Those who passed the civil service examination became members of the aristocracy, but most of them already had their roots in the aristocratic families. The ranked civil officials were collectively called the civil official order, and those ranked military officers were likewise called the military order, initiating the so-called *yangban* (two orders) system. Lesser bureaucrats in the central government formed another order. All members of the peasant families who were enrolled in military service were known as the soldiering order. Members of each order had the hereditary rights and obligations to perform particular functions assigned to them. Petty functionaries in the central and local governments belonged to no particular order, but they also had similar rights and obligations.

The vast number of people belonged to the commoner class which consisted mostly of the peasant population and a small number of free artisans or merchants. Below them were the "low-born people" which included slaves, domestic servants, and manual workers.

Agriculture was the main economic activity, and the land was the major source of income. Following the reunification of the Later Three Kingdoms, the Koryŏ government established national ownership of the land and adopted various methods for land allotments.

The land grants made in the 940s to those who rendered meritorious services before and during the reunification, as well as land allocated under the Stipend Land Law of 976 and other land laws adopted in 998, later created new patterns of land ownership which were characterized by absentee landlordism. Land grants made for meritorious service and to those officials in the top five bureaucratic ranks were given in perpetuity, whereas other officials received land allotments according to their ranks only for the duration of their tenure. Peasant families enrolled in the soldiering order, local government functionaries, and Buddhist temples and monasteries also received land grants. Royal estate land and public agency land, on the other hand, were set aside to raise income to meet the expenses of the royal household and the central and local governments.

Most of the public lands were cultivated by government slaves while other public, private, and stipend lands were cultivated mostly by free peasants.

Rice and hemp cultivation grew, and silk production increased. In 1302 cotton seeds were brought from China to Korea, and cotton cloth production developed rapidly with the use of cotton gins and spinning wheels. A conspicuous trend was privatization of public or stipend lands as the authority of the central government declined. In such a process, large estates of aristocrats emerged while at the same time a growing number of peasants became small farm owners.

Copper coins called *haedong t'ongbo* and other coins were minted, and Chinese coins were imported, but commerce as such grew very slowly. To be sure, like Kyŏngju, Songak witnessed a growing number of shops and traders, but the country as a whole remained agricultural, practicing a barter system.

Due to the collapse of the foreign trade at the end of the Shilla period, trade with Korea was maintained through centers established at the river ports near the capital city of Song'ak by traders from China and the Arab world. Meanwhile, an important aspect of economic growth was the development of the celadon industry.

State schools were established during the reign of T'aejo, but the establishment of the highest state educational institution named Kukchagam in 992 marked the real beginning of educational development of Koryŏ. It was followed by the establishment of six separate colleges in the early 12th century; three for the study of Confucian classics, one for law, one for the study of calligraphy, and one for accounting.

Many private academies emerged following the establishment of the Nine Course Academy by Ch'oe Ch'ung, one of the great Confucian scholars in the second half of the 11th century. Some dozen other private academies of high repute emerged and promoted Confucian studies in competition with state colleges.

Those who were well educated took various types of civil service examinations—classics, composition, and miscellaneous subjects—and after earning appropriate degrees they entered government service. However, under the "protected appointment system," sons of those officials in the fifth rank or above secured official appointment without taking examinations.

The rise of Buddhism as a state religion under the patronage of the royal house was another significant cultural development. The Nine Mountain Sects of *Sŏn* continued to enjoy popularity among the gentry families, but the newly introduced *Ch'ŏnt'ae* was welcomed by intellectuals while another new sect, the *Chogye*, became the religion of the masses. The founder of the *Chogye* sect hoped to bring about reconciliation between the Textual School and the Contemplative School, but such reconciliation was not to occur for a long time. Meanwhile, two types of examination for the monks were instituted along with the system of ranking Buddhist masters.

The printing of a voluminous Chinese-language Buddhist scripture named the *Tripitaka* and other books related to Buddhism was another important development. After the wooden blocks carved in 1087 to print the first set of the *Tripitaka* were destroyed by the first Mongol invasion of Korea in 1231, the carving of the second set of some 8,300 wooden blocks was completed in 1251 in the midst of the Mongol war, and the *Tripitaka Koreana* was printed. These printing blocks are currently preserved at the Haein Temple on Mt. Kaya.

Writing of Shilla-style native songs continued, but in the 13th century new songs, long and secular in nature, were composed. Toward the end of the Koryŏ period, another poetic form known as *shijo*, or occasional verse, emerged.

In the 12th and 13th centuries, renowned literary figures produced prose tales, promoting a new genre in Korean literature. Some of their works personified inanimate objects such as coins, bamboo, oak, and yeast. At the same time, various historical writings, including biographies, were produced. Among them were the *History of the Three Kingdoms* compiled by Kim Pu-shik and others in the 12th century and *Memorabilia of the Three Kingdoms* written by Sŏn monk, Ilyŏn, in the late 13th century. In conjunction with the literary and intellectual growth, master painters and calligraphers emerged, but unfortunately most of their works have been lost.

One of the most outstanding artistic achievements was found in Koryŏ celadon ware that even the Chinese praised as the finest in the world. Although it developed under the influence of Sung celadon, the Koryŏ celadon with its jade-green color became unique. Adapting motifs of plants, animals, and fruits, celadon workers, who utilized secret formulas and techniques, produced a variety of useful ware such as bottles, jars, bowls and plates, teapots and cups, brush holders and water droppers, and incense burners, with incised or inlaid designs of many kinds including flowers, birds, trees, and clouds. Unfortunately, the Mongols who invaded Korea in 1231 destroyed not only the kilns where celadon ware was produced, but the families of craftsmen who kept the secret formulas for Koryŏ celadon.

Koryŏ, whose economy, society, and culture were flourishing, encountered various ills from the 12th century. Following the treason of Yi Cha-gyŏm, father-in-law of the king, who attempted to usurp the monarchical authority in the mid 1120s, a Buddhist monk, Myoch'ŏng, brought about a revolt in the northwest in the 1130s. Meanwhile, the long-standing conflict between civil and military officials (military officials were always subordinated to civil officials) led to a military revolt in 1170, followed by peasant and slave uprisings of the late 12th and early 13th century. This led, in 1198, the house of Ch'oe to establish a military dictatorship that lasted until 1258. Needless to say, these events brought about much property destruction, including palace buildings and Buddhist temples. Meanwhile, Japanese marauders, from their base on Tsushima Island, rampaged along the south coast of the peninsula, causing considerable worry and economic damage.

The Mongol invasions that began in 1231 and their domination over Korea that lasted until the late 1380s sealed the fate of the ruling dynasty. The Mongol invasions brought about the destruction not only of Koryŏ's economic base, including the celadon industry, but also many palace buildings and Buddhist temples. Moreover, after their conquest, the Mongols extracted from Koryŏ an enormous amount of gold, silver, cloth, and other products, as well as agricultural products as tribute goods. Hundreds of thousands of people, including celadon workers, were killed, and a large number of Koreans were taken hostage to China. The Rebellion of the anti-Mongol Three Elite Patrols that began in 1258 against the pro-Mongol government was eventually crushed, leaving no anti-Mongol resistance group.

During the Mongol domination, Mongol culture (language, art, music, hairstyle and costumes) was introduced to Korea. Meanwhile the land distribution system broke down, bringing the rise of large agricultural estates controlled by the powerful families with their private armies. As more lands were taken over by them a large number of the free tenant farmers became enslaved. At the same time, the influence of the aristocrats declined as the power and wealth of educated government bureaucrats called *sadaebu* grew, intensifying the conflict between the aristocrats and bureaucrats.

Attempts made by King Kongmin in the mid-14th century, with the help of the Buddhist monk, Shin Ton, to restore order and national strength failed. Meanwhile, the foreign policy debate related to Koryŏ relations with the Yuan Dynasty of the Mongols created a new crisis. While some officials insisted that Koryŏ should maintain its pro-Mongol policy, others advocated the adoption of a pro-Chinese policy when the Chinese established the Ming Dynasty in 1368 and forced the Mongols out of China.

In the midst of this crisis, the Koryŏ government sent General Yi Sŏng-gye to Manchuria to provide military assistance to the Mongols against the Chinese. However, although Yi did not approve of the intentions of Ming China to establish a Chinese commandery in northern Korea, he believed that to maintain a pro-Mongol policy was not expedient. Therefore, General Yi, who took his troops as far as the Yalu River, brought them back to the capital and carried out a coup in 1388 against the Koryŏ government.

After seizing power, Yi made efforts, in cooperation with the Confucian scholars such as Chŏng To-jŏn, to bring about revitalization of the country by implementing various reforms, including land reform. However, when he encountered opposition to his authority and plans, Yi overthrew Koryŏ in 1392, becoming the founder of a new nation named Chosŏn and its ruling Yi Dynasty.

The Society and Culture of Chosŏn under the Yi Dynasty

Yi Sŏng-gye (King T'aejo) laid the foundation of the new nation of Chosŏn with the adoption of the Administrative Code of Chosŏn and Six Code of Governance. He selected Hanyang (now Seoul) as the capital of the kingdom, built palaces and a new defense system of walls and gates, and the government was relocated in the new capital in 1394. However, after his retirement in 1398, bloody succession disputes within the royal house caused much political instability until the third king, T'aejong, and the fourth king, Sejong, restored order and consolidated the foundation of the new dynasty. T'aejong replaced the Privy Council, which had exercised power since 1392, with a State Council that was a deliberative council with much reduced power, and revised the earlier codes into Basic Six Codes and Supplemental Six Codes. His successor, Sejong, had scholars compile the Orthodox Code, strengthening the legal underpinning. By the time the seventh king, Sejo, took over the throne after deposing his nephew in 1455, the kingly authority was firmly established, and the National Code was promulgated in 1471.

The Kingdom of Chosŏn of the Yi Dynasty, ruled by 27 kings before coming to an end in 1910, bridged the premodern age with the modern era. During this long period of her history, Korea was heavily influenced by Chinese cultures, and a new tradition of the Korean people was shaped.

The Yi Dynasty willingly accepted Korea's vassalage to Ming China with which it maintained amicable yet subservient relations. T'aejo and Sejong expanded the kingdoms territory by conquering the northeastern region of the peninsula where the Jurchens resided, and made the Yalu and the Tumen rivers Korea's northern boundaries. After that the kingdom was redistricted into eight provinces. Each province had sub-districts in descending order.

The State Council of the Three Councilors, with the chief as de facto prime minister, was the highest organ of the State. It was a deliberative body which supervised the affairs of state, including the operation of the Six Boards (ministries) of Personnel, Rites, Taxation, War (Defense), Justice, and Public Works. The Royal Secretariat, the Office of Special Advisers, the Office of Inspectors General, and the Office of Censor-General were other state organs.

Almost all officials in the central and some officials of the local governments were those who passed the civil service examinations and earned appropriate academic degrees. As was the case in Koryŏ, the nine rank-system for top officials was maintained. Those officials in the civil and military branches were collectively referred to as *yangban*, meaning two branches, the term used to denote the upper class in the Yi society.

The Three Armies Headquarters was the supreme military organ. All private armies that had sprung up at the end of the Koryŏ period were abolished by 1400. In 1464, the Three Armies Headquarters was replaced by the Five Military Command Headquarters, which was responsible for the defense of the capital. At the same time, one or more Army Commands were set up in each province, and seven Navy Commands were also established to defend the west and south coasts while a large number of garrisons were set up throughout the country. In the mid-16th century, a defense council was created to improve the defense of the border regions and coastal areas. In order to speed communications between local areas and the capital, a network of beacons and post stations was established. While top military officers came from the upper class, some lower grade officers and soldiers were peasants conscripted into the military on a rotation basis.

The social structure of the Chosŏn period was similar to that of Koryŏ. However, some new features emerged. First of all, the aristocracy of Koryŏ was replaced by the upper class called *yangban*, which consisted of upper civil and military bureaucrats. The *yangban* status was not hereditary, but such a status was maintained by families of *yangban* by producing generation after generation of successful candidates in civil service examinations who received government appointments. The members of this class were exempt from taxation and labor duties. No more than ten percent of the population belonged to this class.

Below the *yangban* class was the "middle people" group which consisted of families of lesser officials who performed technical functions in the government. It included physicians, foreign language specialists, legal experts, and astronomers, geomancers, and diviners.

The vast majority of the population belonged to the commoner class that was called "good people" or "ordinary persons." It included the free peasants, the artisans, and the merchants in descending social order. As before, slaves, domestic servants, executioners, butchers, grave diggers, jail keepers, prostitutes, public entertainers, and leather and wicker workers, were referred to as "lowborn," and were the lowest members of this society.

With the adoption of Neo-Confucianism as a state creed, class distinction between the upper and lower classes was strictly enforced, and intermarriage between the upper and lower class people was forbidden, although upper-class men could have concubines and/or mistresses from the lower class.

The observance of moral, ethical principles and social codes prescribed by Neo-Confucian codes of conduct were required of all upper-class people, particularly by women. All marriages of the upper-class women were arranged, and child-marriage was common. The re-marriage of the widows of the upper class was discouraged or even forbidden, and women's subservience to men was enforced. Women of this class were to be chaste, obedient, and silent. Under the ethical principle known as "three obediences," a woman of the *yangban* class had to obey her father as a child, her husband as a wife, and her first son as a widow.

On the other hand, the lower-class people, being "ordinary," were not expected to understand high moral, ethical and social principles, and therefore they were not required to observe the principles prescribed by Confucianism. Consequently, the commoners enjoyed much more freedom, although they were made subservient to the upper class. Needless to say, the "lowborn" people had neither freedom nor rights.

In such a way, the Yi Dynasty laid the ground for two distinctive social systems and cultures to emerge in Korea, creating a wide gap between the minority *yangban* class and the common people.

The nation's highest educational institution was the national Confucian academy called Sŏnggyun'gwan in Seoul. Also in Seoul were the Four Schools for Confucian studies along with Chinese history and literature. Local schools called *hyanggyo* were established in the provincial capitals and county seats. Many private academies were also established by scholars of high reputation. At the bottom of the educational ladder were primary-level private local schools called *sŏdang* that sprang up in the countryside. Only sons of the upper-class and the "middle people" families had educational opportunity. Their daughters were given some education at home under private tutors. Needless to say, nearly all Korean boys who attended these schools received Confucian education while some were educated at Buddhist monasteries.

Since the Yi government restricted protected appointment to the sons of officials of the top two ranks, the passing of the three-stage civil service examinations became more important if one aspired to secure a government position. As before, although all freemen's sons were eligible to take civil service examinations, only few of them were able to pass.

Those aspiring to military service as officer's took the appropriate military examination consisting of three stages. In addition, four types of examinations in miscellaneous categories were given to select technical specialists in the fields of foreign language, medicine, law, and astronomy, and geomancy.

Although agriculture was the economic foundation of the kingdom, Korea witnessed the growth of crafts and commerce. As was the case during the Koryŏ period, meritorious individuals received land grants in perpetuity, and top officials received land allocation under the Rank Land Law first, and then under Office land and law after 1466. Several other types of land grants were also made to officials widows who did not remarry and to children of officials who lost both of their parents. In 1556, the Office Land Law along with other land grant systems were abolished, and officials were paid salaries in cash or goods. Following the pattern of the Koryŏ period, royal estates and public lands were set aside to defray expenses of the royal house and the central and local government by income from the lands. Military lands were also allocated to junior officers. Eventually all land allocated to individuals became private lands, bringing the rise of a new landlordism of the upper-class families. All farmlands were cultivated by the peasants as tenants and agricultural slaves.

The tenant farmers were required to pay a land tax (the rate was lowered from one-tenth of the harvest in 1444 to one-twentieth). All farmlands were surveyed and were classified into six categories according to the productivity of the land, and the rates of land tax were determined according to fertility. The commoners also paid the tribute tax in goods and the labor tax.

With the construction of reservoirs, the use of more fertilizers, and with better farm implements and methods of farming, some tenants were able to produce more commodities from the farms than they were graded for tax purposes. As a result, economic conditions of some peasant families improved, enabling them to become owner-cultivators by purchasing farms from the *yangban* landlords. Nevertheless, a vast majority of the peasantry was bound to land owned by the *yangban* families, working as serfs in abject poverty. In order to make peasant families mutually responsible for tax payment and security, the government organized five-household units throughout the country. Although rice remained the main food grain produced, millet and barley production increased while the growing of sweet potatoes and cotton became popular after the 16th century.

Most of the artisans and craftsmen were required to produce such items as paper, utensils, weapons, and robes for the government during a designated period each year. Manufacturing of cotton, silk, hemp, and ramie cloth grew vastly in importance, the ramie cloth being mostly for the *yangban* people. Meanwhile, production of paper, brass wares, and furniture increased.

Because the celadon industry of Koryŏ was completely destroyed and its secret formula was totally lost, the ceramic workers of Chosŏn needed to develop a new ceramic industry. Borrowing the technology of Ming China, they produced white porcelain wares. In the early period, they produced ware called "powder-green" (*punchŏng*), a forerunner of white porcelain, in a variety of shapes with blue-color designs of flowers, plants, and birds. While the white porcelain ware was mostly for the upper class, brown-color wares were manufactured for the commoners.

The development of commercial economy was discouraged or hampered by the advocates of Confucian orthodoxy. Nevertheless, as the urban population grew, so did commerce. In order to curtail this trend, the government licensed certain merchants to deal with a particular commodity. Meanwhile, local markets and periodic markets came into being while wholesale merchants and itinerant peddlers promoted commercial economy in the countryside and elsewhere.

A clear sign of the growth of commercial economy was the printing of paper currency in 1401, coining of copper money in 1423, and iron coins in 1464. In 1678, copper coins known as *sangp'yŏng t'ongbo* were minted and circulated. After 1600, taxes could be paid in coins as well as in goods such as rice and cloth. However, Korea's economy remained basically an agricultural one.

With the adoption of Neo-Confucianism as a state creed, Buddhism was discarded by the government, although some members of the royal house and of the upper class still practiced Buddhism, as well as the shaman cult. Under the sponsorship of the government, Neo-Confucianism grew as its adherents gained influence in politics. Among them were Yi Hwang (T'oegye) and Yi I (Yulgok) of the 16th century who created two opposing branches of Neo-Confucianism in Korea.

Perhaps the most significant cultural achievement was the creation and adoption of Korean alphabetical scripts called *han'gŭl* (letters of the Koreans). It was promulgated as Correct Sounds for the Instruction of the People in 1446 by King Sejong, who was given the honorific title of "the Great" because of his many accomplishments and benevolent rule. With the creation of this system, the writing of *shijo* poems and other literary works in *han'gŭl* flourished. However, conservative scholars refused to utilize it and continued to write their works in Chinese.

King Sejong also brought about the development of science and technology, manufacturing such items as the rain gauge, water clocks, and sundials. Manufacturing of metal movable type increased publication of books. Among the important publications in the early Yi period were the annals of kings and the Yi Dynasty, history books, geographic studies, and political guides. The publication of such books as the *Five Rites* of State in 1474 showed the importance attached to observance of proper ritualistic manners and etiquette in all state ceremonies while the publication of the *Conduct of the Three Roads* in the mid-1420s was aimed at the promotion of Confucian ethical and social principles. Several books dealing with science and technology were also published in the mid-1400's.

In the field of fine arts, painters of the 15th century left behind a rich cultural heritage for Korea, promoting Chinese-style literati paintings of landscapes, flowers, plants, birds, and animals. The development of technical skills for the painting of such items as bamboo, orchid, plum blossom, pine, and chrysanthemum was particularly emphasized. These scholar-painters were also engaged in calligraphic arts, and some of them became outstanding calligraphers.

With the rise of Confucian culture, ritual, court music (commonly called *a'ak*), and dance developed. Accompanying this trend, books dealing with music and anthologies of songs were published in and after the 15th century. Meanwhile, in the 16th century, scholar-poets promoted new forms of lyrical songs called *kagok* and *kasa*, while other poets of the late 16th and 17th centuries made *shijo* a major genre of Korean literature.

The successive controversies of the early period subsided in the mid-15th century, but a series of purges of scholars created serious political and social problems. The main causes of the purges were the conflict between the monarchy and Neo-Confucian literati, and the struggle for power between the conservative orthodox Confucian and the reform-minded Neo-Confucian scholars.

The first two bloody purges were carried out in 1498 and 1504 by Yŏnsan'gun, to whom the later historians refused to give the monarchical title of king although he was a legitimate monarch. These bloody purges were followed by others in 1519 and 1545, producing more victims of the power struggle and further decline of the dynastic rule of the house of Yi. To make matters worse, in the 16th century fractional strife began to raise its ugly head, bringing more vicious power struggles of Confucian scholar-bureaucrats in the 17th and early 18th centuries. No less than four factions, which the Koreans called the Four Colors, were engaged in debates aimed at gaining hegemony and power to dominate the government.

The Japanese worsened the situation. They had been troublesome from the late Koryŏ period. Only when a naval expedition sent in 1414 by the Korean government destroyed the bases of Japanese marauders on Tsushima Island did the problem related to piracy of the Japanese subside. However, in 1510 those Japanese who were allowed to reside in the three southern ports open to the Japanese for trade rose up in armed revolt, creating hostilities. Then came the Japanese invasion in 1592.

When the Korean government refused to provide free passage to the troops of a Japanese warlord, Toyotomi Hideyoshi, who vainly hoped to conquer Ming China, he ordered some 150,000 troops belonging to his vassals to invade Korea. Korean resistance, together with military assistance from Ming China, led to peace talks. But when Korea refused to accept unreasonable Japanese demands, in 1597 Hideyoshi renewed the war, dispatching more troops. In a historic encounter a large number of Japanese war and supply vessels were destroyed by iron-clad warships, called turtle boats because of their turtle-shaped hulls, under the command of Admiral Yi Sun-shin. This event, coupled with Hideyoshi's death in mid-1598, brought about withdrawal of Japanese troops from Korea and the end of a seven-year war.

This long war resulted in extensive and devastating property destruction and manpower losses. Not only were hundreds of thousands of people killed, but also many valuable historic buildings such as the Kyŏngbok Palace and the Pulguk Temple were destroyed along with a large number of books. Moreover, thousands of ceramic and skilled workers were taken to Japan as hostages, and books were carried .away by the retreating Japanese troops. It was said that the total acreage of taxable farmlands was reduced by two-thirds. Many dikes and reservoirs were destroyed as agricultural slaves ran away from their bondage, reducing the manpower in rural areas.

As Korea was making efforts to recover from severe wounds inflicted upon her by the Japanese, the Manchu invasion came, creating more havoc in Korea. The Manchus, who established the later Jin state in Manchuria in 1616 (in 1636 Jin was renamed Qing), invaded the pro-Ming Korea in 1627, forcing it to accept a subordinate position. However, when Korea refused to recognize the suzerainty of the Qing State, in 1636 the Qing emperor invaded Korea with a large army, inflicting irreparable damages in northern Korea. When Korea sued for peace, the Manchus took to Manchuria two sons of the Korean king as hostages along with thousands of peasants.

These humiliating and damaging foreign invasions aroused intellectuals with new national consciousness, fresh ideas, and zeal for the reconstruction of their country. They advocated political, economic, and social reform, promoting what is called "Practical Learning" from the early 17th century, criticizing empty, theoretical arguments of the Confucian scholars. They preached practical solutions for the "existing problems" by implementing institutional reforms. Among them was Yi Ik, author of an essay entitled *Discourse on Concerns for the Underprivileged.*

In the late 18th century a new breed of scholars of this reform school emerged, strengthening their movement. Many of them traveled to Beijing, observing changes taking place there as well as becoming acquainted with Western ideas through their personal contacts with the Westerners of China or books written by them. Among them were Pak Chi-wŏn, author of *Jehol Diary*, and Pak Che-ga, author of *Discourse on Northern Learning.* Pak Che-ga was a severe critic of the existing political, economic, and social order. He saw no hope for the future of Korea unless the government and the people brought about many fundamental changes in the way of thinking, doing things, and making a living.

Chŏng Yak-yong (Tasan) of the late 18th and early 19th centuries was another reform advocate. A contemporary of the aforementioned two Paks, Chŏng, who embraced Catholicism, wrote many important essays and books such as *Design for Good Government, Admonition on Governing the People, Treatises on Land*, and *Toward a New Jurisprudence.* He also catalogued fishes near an island while he was in exile, and wrote *Comprehensive Treatise on Smallpox.*

Among the many striking concepts which these "Practical Learning" scholars advocated was the idea that the people were more important than the king, promotion of education was vital for national reconstruction, and the government was responsible for the welfare of the people. Two reform-minded kings of the 1724-1800 period implemented some plans to bring about national unity, end factional strife, and promote economic progress. They reduced the tax rates and changed the method of tax payment under the Equalized Tax law. However, on the whole the conservative scholar-bureaucrats who dominated the government refused to adopt those ideas and plans which the *shilhak* scholars proposed.

Be that as it may, the "Practical Learning" movement stimulated the growth of interest in studies about Korea while broadening their fields of inquiry. As a result, numerous studies on Korean history, geography, language, law, plants, as well as biographies appeared. The first map of Korea was produced in the early 18th century. At the same time, books on astronomy, farming, forestry, animal husbandry, sericulture, and weaponry were published. As cultivation of sweet potatoes grew, books on sweet potato cultivation also appeared. Meanwhile, the knowledge and skills in architecture, machinery, and the solar system increased.

After 1800, less capable kings occupied the throne. Most of them were young boys. In that situation, the wives of the kings on their relatives who were in key government offices played important roles, often misusing political power. In the end what is called "power politics" between powerful families of the queens developed, nullifying much of what had been accomplished in the 18th century.

The power abuse and illegal financial dealings of powerful families and their allies brought about the disarray in the three administrations that were responsible for the management of land tax, military service tax, and the state granary system. As political order deteriorated, new factional disputes of scholars developed, while mismanagement of tax collection became rampant and social welfare systems collapsed, bringing the rise of bandits of all kinds throughout the country. To make matters worse, rebellions and uprisings such as that of Pyŏng'an Province in 1812 and that of Chinju in 1862 erupted, creating a worse social environment. Moreover, frequent floods and famines of the early 19th century added to the hardships of the poverty-stricken masses while bringing about a decrease in the population.

Despite such a sad state of affairs, some positive signs appeared. They included the emergence of new economic and social phenomena and the growth of a new culture. In the economic area, an increasing number of former tenant farmers became full or partial owner-cultivators. At the same time, the number of free artisans grew while the population engaged in commerce also increased.

In the social area, the *yangban*-oriented social structure began to crumble as there was some upward and downward movements in social status. Many fallen *yangban* and those in economic hardships abandoned their status. Some were said to have sold their status to wealthy peasants. Meanwhile, the economic and social status of the middle people (technical and professional bureaucrats) rose while some peasants were able to purchase lower government offices for their sons, gaining semi-*yangban* status.

Another significant social change was the decline of the institution of slavery. Some slaves were able to gain their freedom by serving in the military while others were able to purchase their freedom from their owners. A large number of slaves ran away during the Japanese war, gaining a new social status. As a result, the number of slaves owned by the central government declined from about 350,000 in the 15th century to less than 200,000 in the 17th century. As more free artisans produced more commodities, the need for the government to have slaves was considerably reduced. Thus in 1801 all slaves owned by the central government were freed. Unfortunately, the status of women of the upper class remained unchanged.

A remarkable change occurred in the cultural area. First of all, the introduction of Catholicism, together with the increasing knowledge about the West in the early 17th century, initiated a new intellectual and religious current. Both Catholicism and study about the West were known in Korean as "Western Learning." Catholicism became a new religious force after Yi Sŭng-hun, son of a Korean envoy to China, was baptized in Beijing and organized a Catholic group in Korea at the end of the 18th century, winning converts among young reform-minded Confucian scholars as well as others.

Despite many difficulties, Catholicism grew, and the first Catholic church in Korea was established in Seoul by Koreans themselves. Although it was declared a heresy in 1785, and anti-Catholic persecution began in 1801, the strength of the new religion continued to grow following the arrival of several French priests in the 1830s and a Korean priest who was ordained at Macao in 1840.

The appearance of tales and short stories in the 18th century marked the beginnings of the rise of a popular culture in Korea. Kim Shi-sŭp, a non-conformist Confucian scholar of the 15th century, had already written a tale entitled *The New Stories of the [Mt.] Golden Turtle*, marking the beginning of published fiction in Korea. Following this, Kim Man-jung of the late 17th century wrote a novel entitled *A Dream of Cloud Nine*. After that, a growing number of tales and stories that appealed to popular interest were written in Korean. Some of them were instructive in character, but most were critical of the *yangban* dominated society and the prevailing economic and social injustices.

A popular culture found expression in folk songs, painting, theater, and dance. Various types of mask dances developed. Some mask dances were religious while others were secular in nature. The typically religious ones were the *pyŏlshin* mask dance of the southeastern region and the "lion dance" of Pukch'ŏng of the northeastern region. These dances represent an ancient custom of exorcism, a practice designed to drive away evil spirits from villages and dwellings. Although some were religious in character, most of the mask dances of Pongsan of the northwestern region were for popular entertainment performed during religious or secular festivals. With the development of folk theater, mask dances, puppet plays, dramatic narrative singing called *p'ansori*, along with farmers' music and other forms of popular entertainment, the lives of the common people were enriched.

In such a cultural milieu, in 1860 Ch'oe Che-u founded a new religion called "Eastern Learning" that was renamed in 1906 "Teachings of the Heavenly Way." He preached the unity of god and man, advocating the social gospel of the equality of man, women's rights, and clean living. His teaching, which included a doctrine of social revolution, was declared heresy and Ch'oe was executed in 1864. However, the strength of "Eastern Learning" continued to grow steadily.

Despite the decline of political leadership on the part of the government, factional strife among scholars, and growing tension between the upper class and the commoners, Korea, with its ever changing economic and social conditions and rapidly developing new culture, reached the point in history when the dawn of the modern age was about to break.

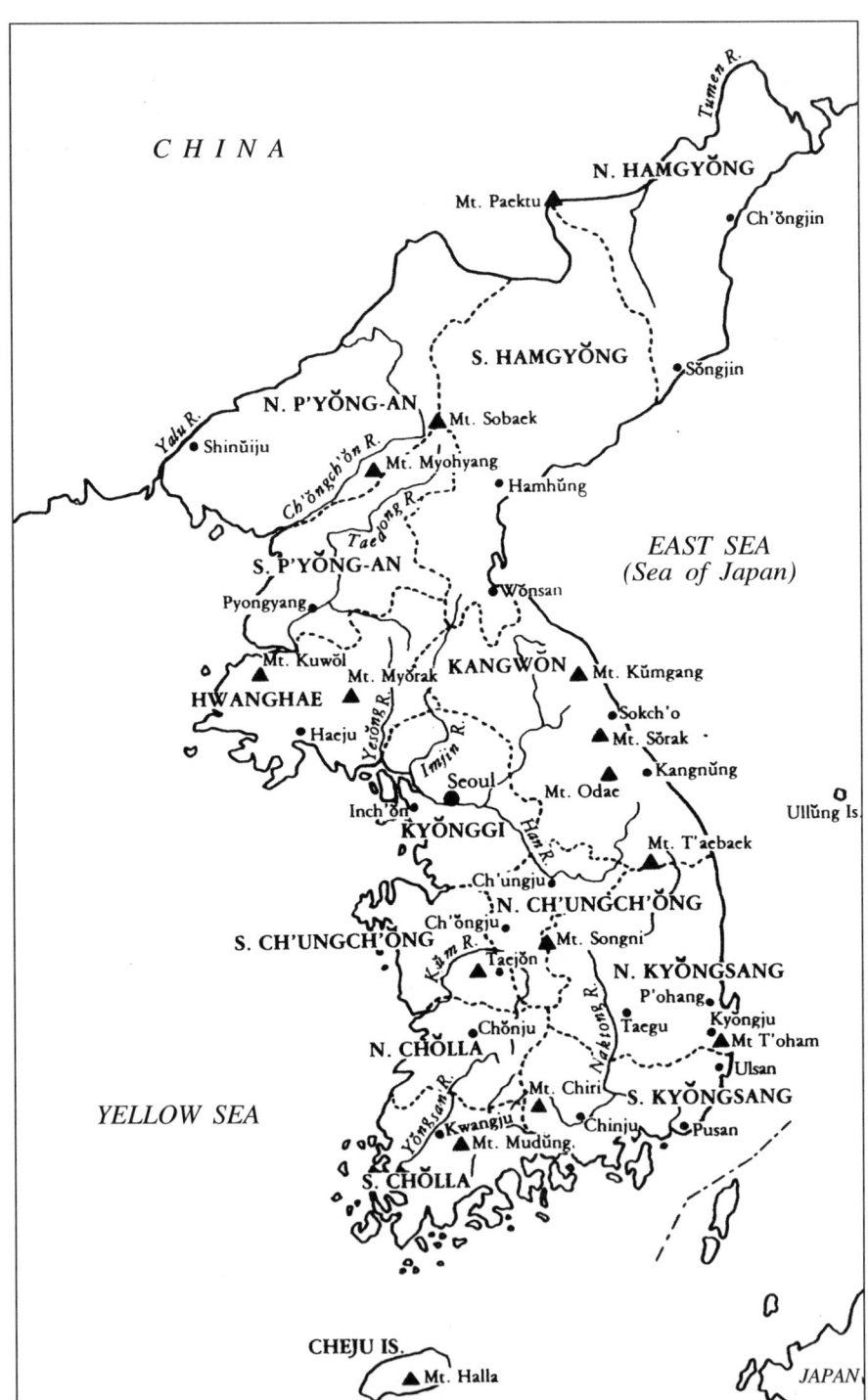

CHINA

N. HAMGYŎNG

Mt. Paektu

• Ch'ŏngjin

S. HAMGYŎNG

• Sŏngjin

N. P'YŎNG-AN   Mt. Sobaek

Yalu R. • Shinŭiju

Ch'ŏngch'ŏn R. Mt. Myohyang

• Hamhŭng

Taedong R.

S. P'YŎNG-AN   *EAST SEA (Sea of Japan)*

Pyongyang   • Wŏnsan

Mt. Kuwŏl

HWANGHAE   Mt. Myŏrak   KANGWŎN   Mt. Kŭmgang

• Haeju   *Yesŏng R.*   • Sokch'o

Imjin R.   Mt. Sŏrak

Seoul   • Kangnŭng

Inch'ŏn   Mt. Odae   *Ullŭng Is.*

KYŎNGGI   *Han R.*

          Mt. T'aebaek

• Ch'ungju

N. CH'UNGCH'ŎNG

Ch'ŏngju

S. CH'UNGCH'ŎNG   Mt. Songni

Kŭm R.   Taejŏn   N. KYŎNGSANG

          P'ohang •

          • Kyŏngju

          Taegu   Mt T'oham

Chŏnju

N. CHŎLLA   • Ulsan

YELLOW SEA   Mt. Chiri   S. KYŎNGSANG

Yŏngsan R.   Kwangju   Chinju   • Pusan

Mt. Mudŭng

S. CHŎLLA

CHEJU IS.

Mt. Halla   *JAPAN*

MAP OF KOREA, 1896–1948

International boundary
National capital
Province-level unit
Province-level
administrative center
Administrative center for
special cities

CHINA

North
Hamgyŏng

Mt. Paektu

Ch'ŏngjin

42

Hyesan

Yanggang

North
Hamgyŏng

Kanggye

Chagang

Kimch'aek

Shinŭiju

North
P'yŏng-an

South Hamgyŏng

40

40

South P'yŏng-an

Hamhŭng

Administrative Center
of Pyongyang

EAST SEA
(Sea of Japan)

Korea Bay

Wŏnsan

Pyongyang

Kangwŏn

Namp'o

Demarcation Line and
Demilitarized Zone

Sariwŏn

North
Hwanghae

South
Hwanghae

Haeju

38

38

Kaesŏng

Paengnyŏng Is.

SOUTH KOREA

Inch'ŏn

Seoul

124

126

128

130

DEMOCRATIC PEOPLE'S REPUBLIC OF KOREA (1992)

Military demarcation line
and demilitarized zone

Provincial boundary
National capital
Provincial capital (special city)
Provincial capital
Special city

NORTH KOREA

38

Kyŏnggi

Ch'unch'ŏn

Kangwŏn

Seoul

Inch'ŏn

Ullŭng Is.

Suwŏn

North
Ch'ungch'ŏng

South
Ch'ungch'ŏng

Ch'ŏngju

EAST SEA
(Sea of Japan)

Taejŏn

North
Kyŏngsang

36

36

YELLOW SEA

Chŏnju

Taegu

North
Chŏlla

South
Kyŏngsang

Kwangju

Pusan

South Chŏlla

Korea Strait

34

34

Cheju

126

128

130

REPUBLIC OF KOREA (1997)

5

Modern Korea :
Twilight of the Kingdom Chosŏn

Korea's modern age began in the late 1800s. In the early phase, Korea encountered many unfamiliar domestic and foreign problems and, despite efforts made, the Yi dynasty fell and the existence of the Kingdom of Chosŏn was terminated by Japan. After witnessing certain modern transformations during the Japanese colonial period, Korea entered into the new phase of change following its liberation.

In 1864, a boy king was enthroned Kojong with his father, the Taewŏn'gun, as regent, to guide the trouble-ridden "hermit kingdom" in its twilight.

New Emerging Patterns

The regency of the Taewŏn'gun that lasted from 1864 to 1873 manifested both positive and negative aspects. Among the positive results were the reassertion of monarchical authority, the reconstruction of the Kyŏngbok Palace that was destroyed by the Japanese during their invasion in 1592, land tax reform, and political reform that included the recruitment of able scholars into the government, regardless of their factional affiliations. Negative aspects included the Taewŏn'gun's method of raising the funds for his palace reconstruction project, the coining of new money, the clos-

ing down of many private academies for the purpose of raising more land
tax, the bloody anti-Catholic persecution, and uncompromising policy of
isolationism.

The Taewŏn'gun's power struggle with Queen Dowager Cho and
Queen Min, the wife of King Kojong, plus the bitter attack of conservative Confucian scholars belonging to certain factions eventually led to his
retirement in 1873, leaving his inexperienced and weak-willed son to manage the ever-growing domestic and foreign problems.

On the domestic front, social conditions were relatively calm following the serious Chinju uprising of 1862, except for the social problems
created by the execution of the founder of the "Eastern Learning" in
1864 and suppression of its followers and the bloody anti-Catholic persecution of 1866 that caused the death of over 7,500 converts, including several French priests.

On the foreign front Korea encountered serious challenges with
which it was not prepared to cope. Had there been no external problems,
the Yi dynasty, despite its weaknesses and the domestic problems it faced,
might have survived longer than it did. However, a series of external
problems eventually brought down the dynastic rule and along with it the
demise of Korean independence.

From 1832 foreign merchant ships and naval vessels appeared in
Korean waters with increasing frequency. Some sought trade with Korea
while military vessels were engaged in marine survey or simple explo-
ration of the Korean coastal areas and islands. Although most of them
were peaceful, some encounters resulted in bloodshed. But the destruction
and killing of crew members of an American schooner, *General Sherman*,
by the Koreans in P'yŏngyang and its vicinity in the summer of 1866
brought Korea face to face with new threats from the West. The same
year the killing of French Catholic priests, who had been in Korea
secretly, put Korea into a serious situation. These two events brought
about the invasions of Korea by a French naval force in 1866 and a U.S.
Naval force in 1871. While the French invasion caused relatively minor
human casualties and property destruction, the invasion by U.S. troops
resulted in a considerable number of Korean troops killed and heavy
damage to coastal defense structures on Kanghwa Island and in the lower
Han River region. These incidents, along with the attempt in 1868 by an
American to rob royal tombs in central Korea, angered the Regent as
well as other Koreans, leading to an official declaration of the policy of
isolation in 1871.

Korea's policy of isolation was seriously challenged in the vastly
altered international environment in East Asia in the mid-19th century,

following the foreign wars in China and the end of Japan's isolation policy.

Korean scholars were split into two groups: those who advocated the policy of isolation and those who favored the opening of Korea to the world. In the second group were young scholar-officials who were strongly influenced by the "Practical Learning" school of thought. While the foreign policy debates continued, in 1876 Japan forced Korea to sign a treaty establishing new diplomatic and commercial relations.

The persistent attempts made by the United States after 1876 brought about the signing of a diplomatic and commercial treaty between Korea and the United States in May 1882, and with other Western powers soon thereafter. While those who had preached the opening of the country to the West rejoiced, the champions of isolationism, including the ex-Regent Taewŏn'gun, were infuriated. Extra territorial rights and tariff privileges granted to foreign powers angered many, including the merchants. A new domestic crisis was inevitable.

Westernization of Korea began with the arrival of diplomats and Christian missionaries. The arrival of Protestant missionaries in 1884 was of particular significance. They not only introduced a new religion, but also a new social gospel which included revolutionary potentials. Christian churches and mission schools which they constructed had an enormous impact on both cultural and social transformation.

The Growing National Problems

Those who had been influenced by "Practical Learning" thoughts were now stimulated by new concepts and systems that were brought into Korea from abroad. The rapidly modernizing Japan and its growing economic and military power under the Meiji government created a new impetus among young Progressive scholar-officials in Korea. Among them were Kim Ok-kyun and Pak Yŏng-hyo. While being antagonistic toward China, they also were concerned with the rapidly rising Japan and growing Western imperialism in East Asia. Such concerns led them to form, in the late 1870s, a group which became known as the "Party of the Progressives (Kaehwadang)," whose aims were to bring about political, economic, social and cultural changes for the strengthening of the nation.

Despite the resistance of the conservatives, modernization took place in the 1880s. New government branches, such as the Foreign Office, were created, fact-finding missions and students were sent to Japan, a palace school was established and foreign teachers were engaged, and a modern military unit (Special Skills Force) was established. However, the "Military Insurrection of the Year of Imo" of July 1882 which brought about Chinese military intervention increased the concerns of the Progressives. This in itself was bad enough for Korea's sovereignty and independence, but the abduction of the ex-Regent to China and the reassertion of China's suzerainty in Korea were intolerable.

Open criticism against the pro-Chinese queen and her supporters, as well as verbal attacks against the Chinese and their advisers in Korea led to a new political warfare between the Progressives and the reactionary conservatives. The Progressives who enjoyed the confidence of the king brought about the publication of a modern gazette (a thrice-monthly called *Hansŏng Sunbo*) and the establishment of a modern postal service. However, they encountered a setback as the queen and her supporters increased their pressure on the Progressives. The Progressives, fearing for their survival, carried out a bloody coup on December 4, 1884 known as the "Political Disturbance of the Year of Kapshin." They overthrew the conservative government and established a new government with the consent of the king. But the military intervention of the Chinese and their Korean collaborators brought the collapse of the reform government three days after it emerged and the death of many of the Progressives. Only a handful of Progressives managed to flee to Japan.

After the fall of the Progressives, the Korean government reverted to the pro-Chinese reactionaries. With this incident, the influence of the queen grew as Chinese interference in the affairs of the Korean government increased. Such development in Korea annoyed many Japanese who agitated for a war with China. However, the leading statesmen of Japan quieted the war cry and signed an agreement with China at Tianjin in April 1885. In this document, both China and Japan agreed to withdraw all their troops from Korea, except legation guards, promised not to send troops to interfere in Korea's domestic affairs, and stated they would notify the other party when a signatory of the agreement dispatched troops to Korea to protect the lives and properties of their nationals. However, China failed to withdraw all its troops from Korea and continued to meddle in Korea's domestic and foreign affairs during the decade from 1885 to 1894, antagonizing not only Japan but also the Western powers.

The new situation that developed in Korea convinced the Japanese that the only way to enhance their own national defense was to remove the Chinese from Korea and assist the Korean government to modernize its society and strengthen its national defense. However, they had to wait for an opportune time to do so. The outbreak of the Tonghak Uprising in 1893 and China's dispatch of army and naval forces to Korea provided a convenient pretext for Japan to start a war in 1894, for although the Chinese sent their troops upon the request of the Korean government, by doing so they violated the 1885 agreement signed in Tianjin.

When Chinese army and naval forces were sent to Korea in June 1894, the Japanese also dispatched their combat-ready military units to Korea to challenge the Chinese hegemony. Immediately after landing in Korea, units of Japanese military forces moved into Seoul and put the city and the royal palace under siege.

Both China and Korea attempted to avert war, but the Sino-Japanese War came in July. The war was fought mainly in Korea, causing much confusion and property damage, particularly around P'yŏngyang where the major land battles were fought. During the war, the Japanese pressured the Korean government to sever its ties with China and implement reform measures that they had formulated, resulting in the Kabo Reform of 1894-95.

The Kabo Reform was carried out under the direction of the newly created Deliberative Council. It was at this time that a modern cabinet system was installed and the Metropolitan Police was established. The kingdom was redivided into thirteen provinces by dividing the large existing five provinces into two. Social reform measures implemented included the elimination of the class distinction between the *yangban* and the commoners, complete abolition of slavery, laws allowing remarriage of widows, and freeing the lowborn people from their traditional hereditary status.

The Japanese who won the war ended Chinese domination in Korea, but Korea's independence became precarious as tragic events unfolded. The Japanese increased their domination in Korea and in October of 1895, in collaboration with some Koreans, assassinated the pro-Chinese Queen Min who had become pro-Russian. This brought about the collapse of the pro-Japanese cabinet, the rise of the pro-Russians, and the king's flight to the Russian Legation in February 1896. The King stayed at the Russian Legation until February 1897, and during this time he made numerous concessions to Russia and other Western powers.

During this momentous period in Korean history, a new group of young reform advocates rose, promoting nationalism, modernism, and cultural progress. In 1896 these nationalists formed the Independence Club under the guidance of Dr. Sŏ Chae-p'il, a former Progressive who had fled to Japan and then to the United States, becoming an American citizen with the Anglicized name of Philip Jaisohn. This group of reformers, while arousing patriotism and reform zeal, launched a new national salvation movement and published the newspaper named The Independent in Korean and English. They also constructed the Independent Gate, and led the king to adopt an imperial title after he left the Russian Legation, renaming Korea the Great Empire of Han in 1897. However, they were unable to change the policy of the stubbornly conservative government, or prevent the coming of a greater threat to Korea's survival as the rivalry between Japan and Russia grew. To make matters worse, the government forced Dr. Jaisohn to return to America and brought about the dissolution of the Independence Club in 1898.

The Russo-Japanese struggle for control over Korea and Manchuria led to war in February 1904. All agreements signed between them in the late 1890s were nullified. The Japanese victory over Russia in the war that ended in September 1905 brought tragic consequences to Korea when the Japanese, with the understanding of Great Britain and the United States, forced the Korean government to accept Japan's protectorate that November. With the establishment of the supervisory agency of Japan called the Residency-General of Korea in 1906, the Japanese took over not only jurisdiction of matters related to foreign relations of Korea but also, step by step, took away the sovereign rights of the Korean emperor and his government.

New groups of patriotic Koreans launched their national salvation movement. They formed patriotic reform societies, adopted a Patriotic Song, wrote new poems and novels, and published magazines and newspapers which advocated nationalism and cultural enlightenment. While the contingents of the Righteous Armies were engaged in armed struggle against the Japanese, Emperor Kojong sent his secret missions to the United States and the Hague, hoping to secure foreign assistance to save his empire from Japanese imperialism. Because of this action, the Japanese forced the emperor to abdicate in 1907, arousing a flood of anti-Japanese sentiments on the part of the Koreans. As a growing number of Koreans became victims of Japanese militarism, in October 1909 a Korean patriot assassinated Ito Hirobumi, who had served as the first Resident-General. He was regarded by the Koreans as an architect of Japanese imperialism.

Korean resistance to Japanese imperialism led the hard-liners in Tokyo to resolve the problem by annexing Korea. Thus, in August 1910, the commander of the Japanese army in Korea mobilized his troops and brought about the signing of the treaty of annexation dated August 22 and abdication of the Emperor Sunjong who had succeeded his father in 1907.

Japanese Colonial Rule and the National Liberation Movement

Instead of uniting the two countries according to the treaty of annexation signed in 1910, the Japanese imposed colonial rule over Korea that lasted until August 1945. During this long, painful period, the Japanese implemented their colonial policies to exploit the natural resources and manpower of Korea for the benefit of their empire.

Dissatisfied and unhappy with Japanese colonialism, the Koreans at home and abroad carried out their struggle for restoration of Korean independence to the end of Japanese colonial rule that came at the end of the Pacific War.

Korea and Japanese Colonial Administration

When the Japanese took over Korea, they called Korea Chōsen (Japanese pronunciation for Chosŏn), and renamed the capital (Hanyang) as Keijo. Korea was regarded as "outer land" (gaichi), a Japanese synonym for colony.

To rule the colony of the thirteen provinces and its adjacent islands, the Japanese established the Government-General of Korea, imposed a military rule, and appointed an army general on active duty as Governor-General in Korea. All but one of the eight governors-general were army generals who were authorized to mobilize the Japanese imperial army units in Korea. They ruled by decrees and ordinances as the Koreans, unlike the Japanese, were given no constitutional rights or protection, and until the very end of the colonial period Koreans had no voting rights.

Needless to say, almost all officials above the lower grade clerks in the Government-General and provincial county, and district governments, as well as police, tax officers and other government agencies were Japanese. Only a handful of Koreans were appointed provincial governors during the entire colonial period. The Japanese military police (kempei, or gendarmes) which also exercised police power over the civilians, was abolished in 1922, but the number of civil police increased after that from 12,000 in 1923 to 21,900 in 1931, and 60,000 in 1941. There was one policeman for every 400 Koreans as of 1941. Nearly all police officers were Japanese while the majority of patrolmen were Koreans. In order to deal with "thought criminals" (anti-Japanese nationalists, socialists, and communists), the High Section was added to the police.

With the establishment of the colonial administration, suppression of the nationalists began. All political organizations were dissolved, political meetings were forbidden, and political discussions, including the discussion of the legality of Japanese colonial rule, were prohibited. All Korean newspapers and magazines which expressed anti-Japanese nationalist sentiments were promptly closed down, and any schools whose teachers uttered words against Japanese policy were shut down. As a result there was not a single Korean newspaper, and the number of schools dropped from 2,250 to about 780. Thousands of Koreans, including Christian leaders, were imprisoned as hundreds of nationalists fled to Russia, China, and the United States. Thus, the voice of the nationalists was silenced as darkness descended upon the land.

The Japanese colonial administration was not only highly bureaucratic, but also oppressive, and the combination of bureaucratism of the traditional period with the more sophisticated and systematized bureaucratism of the Japanese created an impact that made democratization of the country in the post-liberation era more difficult.

Korea's Transition during the Colonial Period

In many ways Korea was transformed. It witnessed the installation of modern communication and transportation systems, and the rise of modern industries, public school education, and urban centers. Telegraph and telephone systems vastly improved communications, and three main railway lines (the Seoul-Pusan, the Seoul-Shinŭiju, and the Seoul-Wŏnsan-Hoeryŏng lines) plus branch railway lines and highways linked all corners of the country to the political and financial center that was Keijo.

New cities such as Shinŭiju in the northwest, Hamhŭng in the northeast, and Taejŏn in the south central region emerged as harbor facilities at Pusan, Inch'ŏn, Wŏnsan, and Kunsan were expanded and modernized. Agricultural and industrial production increased as the commercial economy grew. The population increased from 15 million in 1910 to about 25 million in 1945.

Korea's commercial and industrial development was hampered by such laws as the Company Law of 1910 that restricted economic activities of the Koreans while aiding the rise of Japanese zaibatsu-dominated commerce and industry. When land surveys were concluded in 1918 under the Land Survey Law of 1910, some 21.9 million acres, or 40% of farm and forest lands, were taken over by the Japanese colonial government. As a result, hundreds of thousands of former Korean landowners became tenant farmers. Thousands of Japanese farmers were imported, and they were given farmland freely or were allowed to purchase farmlands at low prices. The Japanese civilian population in Korea grew from 171,000 in 1910 to 750,000 in 1945.

Education and cultural development were retarded by Japanese policy. On the one hand, they did not allow the rise of highly educated Koreans. On the other, their policies aimed at destroying the cultural heritage and ethnic consciousness of the Koreans in a number of ways. The study of Korean history was prohibited at the beginning of Japanese colonial rule; the Japanese language was made the "national language" for the Koreans, and the Korean language instruction that was allowed at lower level schools was terminated in 1938 when all public transactions and gatherings were conducted in Japanese. Educational progress was restricted by an inadequate number of schools of both lower and high levels. It is true that the establishment of public schools increased the number of students from 110,800 in 1910 to 1,776,078 in 1943. In 1943 there were only about 3,000 college students in Korea. Due to lack of opportunity for higher education at home, thousands of Korean students attended private universities in Japan. For all practical purposes, the only university, which had a student body of just 650, and a half dozen professional colleges established by the Japanese were for Japanese students. Had there been no colleges, high schools, or primary schools established by foreign mission boards and some Korean private citizens, the number of Koreans receiving a modern education would have been much smaller. It was not until 1920 that a handful of Korean language newspapers were allowed to be published.

One of the important social changes was the disappearance of the yangban class as such. As modern transformation took place, and under a deliberate policy of the Japanese, new Korean leaders emerged from the former "middle people" group, as well as the commoner class. Another significant change was the rise of urban population and industrial workers. Very little change took place in the social status of women although more young girls received modern education, including college education.

With the introduction of modern agricultural implements and application of chemical fertilizers, there was a significant increase in agricultural products, particularly rice. However, some 40% of the rice produced in Korea was exported to Japan, creating a chronic food shortage in Korea.

The National Liberation Movement

These modern transformation trends notwithstanding, the Korean people whose land had been stolen and their opportunities limited, coupled with the humiliation of the harsh colonial rule, sought in various ways to liberate their fatherland from the Japanese yoke. While their compatriots in Siberia and Manchuria organized nationalist and socialist societies, those who stayed at home formed various secret societies despite laws against such movements, in order to struggle for the restoration of Korean independence, if not to preserve their ethnic heritage and improve the people's living conditions.

The Korean leaders came to the realization that the restoration of Korean independence was imperative for the preservation of the Korean people and their heritage and for the enjoyment of freedom, equality, and human rights. In 1918, they learned about the principle of self-determination of colonial people the American president Woodrow Wilson advocated. Such principle and the direction of general trends in the world convinced the Korean leaders that the time had come for them to take a positive step to restore Korea's independence. Thus, they wrote the Declaration of Independence and selected the First of March, 1919, to be the day that Koreans should rise up and express their desires to be free from Japan.

What is known as the March First Movement of 1919 was a peaceful expression of the Koreans for freedom and national independence. The Declaration of Independence stated so, and the majority of some two million participants in nationwide and peaceful demonstrations expressed their desires to be free. The demonstrations for independence lasted several months. The participants in the demonstrations shouted "Long Live Korea" or "Long Live Independence" as they waved the hitherto forbidden national flag of Korea. But the demonstrators were crushed by Japanese military and police, producing over 2,000 casualties (553 killed and 1,409 wounded) according to the official Japanese account. Over 12,000 Koreans were arrested. The figures differ drastically from those of a Korean nationalist report which indicated that some 7,500 were killed, 15,000 were injured, and 45,000 were arrested.

In April, 1919, those Korean nationalists who were in China established in Shanghai the Provisional Government of Korea in cooperation with those nationalists who fled from Korea to China after the March First demonstrations took place. Dr. Syngman Rhee who was in the United States was elected premier and later president.

The March First Movement failed to restore Korea's independence, but it made the Japanese revise their colonial policy and schemes in Korea. As a result, a retired Japanese admiral, Saito Makoto, was appointed as Governor-General in 1919 (he served between 1919-27 and 1929-31), and he implemented the policy of appeasement that he called "the civilized rule." During his administration, the Company Law was revised, allowing the rise of commercial and industrial enterprises owned by Koreans. The publication of Korean-language magazines and newspapers was also allowed, with the appearance in 1920 of such daily papers as Dong-a Ilbo and Chosŏn Ilbo which promoted ethnic consciousness on the one hand and maintained the Korean cultural heritage on the other. Saito also abolished the military police system as he increased the number of civilian police. He allowed the establishment of a few private schools, including colleges of both foreign mission boards and Korean private citizens.

While the Provisional Government of Korea sustained the independence movement of the Koreans, many new organizations of the nationalists and socialists emerged in Siberia, Manchuria, and China. Whether they were rightists or leftists, these overseas societies formed military units, combating the Japanese. In Korea, some 5,728 societies of all types registered with the colonial government by September 1922. The two largest groups of these societies were religious and youth organizations. Among them were women's societies of both rightist and leftist ideologies. No political party was allowed to be formed, but some 50 of them were societies with political aims. In 1924 and after, many underground socialist organizations were formed, including the Korean Communist Party in 1925. Meanwhile, the newly established national daily newspapers, along with many newly introduced magazines, played a significant role in promoting national and ethnic consciousness. The attempt made in the early 1920s by Korean leaders to establish a Korean university failed, but the number of private schools steadily grew.

While communist and socialist organizations were engaged in underground revolutionary activities, the nationalist intellectuals established such societies as the Korean Language Research Society in 1921, later renamed the Korean Linguistics Society, and the Chindan Academic Society to promote studies of Korean language and history. Actors and actresses formed drama societies and counteracted the Japanese policy of cultural assimilation and registered their protest against economic and social injustices. Poets, writers, musicians, composers, and playwrights also played an active role in promoting new Korean culture by writing patriotic poems, lyric songs, and novels and plays. The united front movement of the nationalists of all colors was launched by a men's organization (Shin'ganhoe), formed in 1927, and a women's society (Kunuhoe), formed in 1928, but it failed to sustain its movement, which collapsed under heavy pressure of the Japanese and dissension within its own ranks.

During the 1920s, high school and college students of both sexes carried out school strikes, and in June 1926 those students in Seoul carried out what became known as the Second March First Movement, demonstrating against the Japanese. Some students expressed socialist revolutionary ideologies. In November 1929, a nationwide student strike spread all over Korea in the aftermath of bloody fighting between Korean and Japanese students in the city of Kwangju.

The Manchurian invasion of the Japanese, known as the Mukden Incident, which occurred in September 1931, and the commencement of the China War in July 1937, brought about what the Japanese called the "critical situation." The "darkest period" in Korean history came as the Japanese intensified their policy of suppression and assimilation. In 1931 more Korean youths were mobilized into Japanese industries, and after 1937 they were mobilized into the military. Thought control and suppression of "subversive Koreans" were vigorously pursued, producing many victims. Intellectuals, including the writers, suffered greatly as the use of the Korean language in public was prohibited and the Korean language instruction abolished.

As farm youths were taken away to Japanese mines, factories, and war fronts, the so-called Patriotic Neighborhood Units were formed and various programs were launched by the Government-General to "Japanize" the Koreans and make them contribute more to Japan's ambitious empire-building schemes. Thousands of young girls were taken away to perform sexual duties for Japanese soldiers. By 1940, all private Korean language dailies, along with many journals and magazines, had lost their publication rights and were shut down. In 1941, in the name of assimilation, Koreans were forced to abandon their names and adopt Japanese-style surnames and given names.

When the Pacific War began in December 1941, the Provisional Government of Korea declared war against Japan and joined the Allies in fighting with its Korean Restoration Army in China. The Korean Communist, both in China and Manchuria, joined the Chinese Communists military forces, combating both the Japanese and the Chinese Nationalists. Dr. Rhee and other Korean nationalists in America unsuccessfully attempted to win the recognition of the Provisional Government of Korea by the United States and other Allies. Meanwhile, in Korea, Yŏ Un-hyŏng, a moderate leftist, formed in 1944 an underground organization named the Alliance for Korean Independence, anticipating the eventual defeat of Japan by the Allies. In July 1945, a member of the Korean Patriotic Youth Society, displaying the persistent anti-Japanese sentiment, threw bombs into the Citizen's Hall where a pro-Japanese organization was holding an oratorical event.

7

Liberation and Partition

The long awaited liberation of Korea came when Japan accepted the Potsdam ultimatum of the Allies and surrendered on August 15, 1945. However, Korea was first divided into two zones of Allied occupation, and then it was partitioned into two states, bringing about tragic consequences, including a devastating war.

The Allied Occupation

When Japan surrendered to the Allies sooner than they had expected, the United States hastily proposed to the Soviet Union the division of Korea along the 38th parallel into two zones of Allied occupation. Moscow agreed. The Soviet forces had already invaded the northeastern corner of Korea and swiftly defeated the Japanese following the declaration of war against Japan on August 8. If the United States had not proposed the division of Korea, Soviet troops might have occupied the entire Korean peninsula because U.S. troops were still six hundred miles away, fighting Japanese troops on Okinawa. U.S. troops arrived in Korea in early September.

When it became clear that his country was about to accept the ultimatum of the Allies, the Japanese governor-general of Korea asked a Korean nationalist to form a committee to take the reins of power from the Japanese and to maintain law and order upon the surrender of Japan. He was aware that the Allies (U.S., England, and China) had agreed in November 1943 at Cairo, Egypt to free Korea from Japan and re-establish its independence "in due course." When he failed to enlist the help of this nationalist, he turned to another Korean, Yŏ Un-hyŏng, who the Japanese had in prison.

Upon the acceptance by the Japanese of the conditions Yŏ offered, Yŏ was released from prison, and on August 15 he formed the Committee for the Preparation of National Reconstruction (CPNR) in cooperation with others, including moderate nationalists and socialists. The CPNR established its branches throughout the country, functioning as the central authority in Korea.

On September 6, after learning that Korea would be occupied by the Allies, Yŏ established the People's Republic of Korea and its government, choosing as its president Dr. Syngman Rhee, who was waiting to return to Korea from the United States.

With the establishment of the People's Republic, cities and local areas formed people's committees as local governments, and the Five Provinces Administrative Bureau was established in P'yŏngyang as the North Korean Branch of the Government of the People's Republic. The coalition government included many rightist and a few leftist ministers. Many Koreans wondered why they should be under Allied occupation instead of being allowed to establish their own government in a free and independent Korea. Be that as it may, the Allies divided Korea into two occupation zones along the 38th parallel with the north being the Russian zone and the south that of the United States.

The occupation forces quickly disarmed the Japanese troops, and they were repatriated to Japan along with some 750,000 Japanese civilians who were living in Korea. The two occupation authorities governed their respective zones differently. Whereas the Soviets allowed the existing people's committees under the Five Provinces Administrative Bureau of the CPNR to maintain law and order and manage their own affairs under the supervision of the Soviets, the U.S. occupation authorities in the south outlawed the CPNR and established the United Stated Army Military Government in Korea (USAMGIK), antagonizing the Koreans who had just been liberated from Japanese military rule.

Because the Allies had no plans for Korea other than their expressed intentions stated in the Cairo Declaration, foreign ministers of the United States, England, and the Soviet Union met in Moscow in late December 1945, and agreed (Moscow Agreement) to form a U.S.-U.S.S.R. Joint Commission and to establish a Korean national government in consultation with "democratic Korean people." Furthermore, they agreed to put Korea under the trusteeship of the Allies for up to five years. The decision to impose the Allied trusteeship over Korea dismayed and angered the Korean people in both zones.

Despite vehement opposition to the trusteeship plan and nationwide anti-trusteeship demonstrations and labor strikes, in January 1946 the occupation authorities formed the U.S.-U.S.S.R. Joint Commission and proceeded to implement the Moscow Agreement in March. Although some minor agreements were reached, they failed to achieve the main goals of the Joint Commission. In the end, the United States abandoned any hope for the settlement of the Korean issue by the Joint Commission. In July 1947 the U.S. asked the United Nations to deal with the Korean question.

While the Joint Commission was making its futile efforts, the U.S. occupation authorities proceeded to Koreanize the USAMGIK in order to secure more cooperation from the Koreans, particularly that of nationalists who had returned to Korea from China and the United States in the fall of 1945. Thus, the South Korean Interim Legislative Assembly (SKILA) was established in November 1946 and the South Korean Interim Government (SKIG) in February 1947 following the establishment in January 1946 of the Constabulary and the Coast Guard in order to train the Koreans to maintain their own security. The American military government and the new National Police it created maintained law and order as they prevented mass starvation and epidemics with relief goods supplied by the U.N. and by the U.S. government agencies. Freedom of the press, assembly, and speech, as well as religion, were allowed. This brought about the mushrooming of presses and political parties and social organizations of all political orientations. However, these changes failed to foster a democratic system. Soldiers were poor teachers of democracy, and internal conditions often led the American military government to resort to undemocratic measures.

The Emergence of the Two Korean States

At the request of the United States in November 1947, the U.N. General Assembly adopted a resolution to take up the Korean issue, and established the U.N. Temporary Commission on Korea (UNTCOK), mandating it to implement the U.N. resolution of 1947. When the UNTCOK representatives went to Korea, they encountered the opposition of the

Soviets in the north. They failed to even visit that region. After a series of meetings, UNTCOK agreed with South Korean leaders such as Dr. Rhee, who insisted that two-thirds of the Koreans (20 million) residing in the south had the right to establish a Korean government, and decided to conduct general elections to elect two-thirds of the Constituent Assembly of 310 members.

Many prominent South Korean leaders objected to the decision made by UNTCOK, fearing that the establishment of a government in the south would lead to a permanent division of the country. Thereupon, they made efforts to settle the Korean question without outside mediation. But they were betrayed by the North Koreans who broke the agreement reached at the conference of Korean leaders held in P'yŏngyang in February 1948.

On May 10, 1948, general elections were held in the south under U.N. supervision, and members were elected for the constituent Assembly. In June, the assembly adopted a democratic constitution, establishing the Republic of Korea (ROK), commonly called South Korea, and elected Dr. Rhee as its first president. It designated the former capital of Chosŏn as the new national capital, officially naming it Seoul. On August 15, 1948 the government of the ROK was inaugurated, and in December the U.N. General Assembly declared that it was "the only legal government in Korea."

In the north, preparations to set up a socialist republic were in progress from 1946 when the Communists under Kim Il-sung demolished the nationalists and their organizations. Kim and some 300 partisan Communist soldiers who arrived in Korea with Soviet troops had formed a new powerful communist group while eliminating the indigenous communist leaders in late 1945. After that the Soviets groomed Kim to be the new leader as they put down the nationalists, including Cho Man-shik, a Christian elder and a staunch nationalist who had served as head of the Five Provinces Administrative Bureau of the CPNR. Meanwhile, the Soviets allowed some 22,000 seasoned Korean communist soldiers, veterans of the Chinese communist military campaigns in north China, to enter the north.

By March 1946, the fall of the nationalists in the north was complete as Cho was put under house arrest and most of the nationalists fled to the south. With little opposition, Kim Il-sung emerged as the strong man, becoming head of the People's Committee, which replaced the Five Provinces Administrative Bureau, and the co-chairman of the North Korean Workers' Party which in 1949, with the help of the Soviets, became the Korean Workers' Party. Meanwhile in 1946 socialization of economy, including land reform, was carried out. At the same time, socialist trade unions and social organizations such as the Korean Young Pioneers, the Communist Youth League, and the North Korean Democratic Women's League came into being. In the spring of 1947, the North Korean People's Assembly was established, and in February 1948 the People's Army was created with military aid given by the Soviets.

When the ROK was established in the south, the north Korean Communists carried out their own general elections, electing in August 1948 the Supreme People's Assembly which ratified the constitution of the Democratic People's Republic of Korea (DPRK), commonly called North Korea. They claimed that secret elections had been held in the South to elect its representatives to the Supreme People's Assembly. On September 9, the communist state of the DPRK was inaugurated, claiming that the whole of Korea was its territory and P'yŏngyang was a temporary capital. Designating Seoul as its capital in the constitution, the north Koreans referred to South Korea as "the southern half of the republic." Thus the two Korean states emerged, making the 38th parallel the national boundary.

8

The Korean War and After

Soon after the two states with mutually antagonistic ideologies and systems emerges, a war was launched by the north Korean communists. That inconclusive war lasted three years.

After the armistice was signed by the belligerents, except South Korea, both republics reconstructed their war-ravaged economics and societies while promoting two different cultures, making the two Korean states increasingly dissimilar.

The War

Both North and South Korea claimed that the entire Korean peninsula was their national territory. While South Korea claimed that Seoul was the capital of Korea, North Korea also named Seoul as its capital and P'yŏngyang as its temporary capital. Both Koreas indicated their strong desire to unify the country, and sporadic border clashes along the 38th parallel took place.

As early as April 1948, underground members of the South Korean Workers' Party instigated a rebellion of Cheju Island, and in October of that year the communists within the South Korean defense forces brought about the military insurrection known the Yŏsu-Sunch'ŏn Rebellion, hoping to bring down the South Korean government. Meanwhile, a sizeable number of communist troops infiltrated into South Korea, establishing their base in the mountainous region. When the Yŏsu-Sunch'ŏn Rebellion was subjugated, the North Koreans and the remnants of the rebels fled into mountainous regions of south-central Korea and formed the so-called Southern Army. However, by the spring of 1949, all the rebels had been either captured or killed.

Kim Il-sung became convinced that only a war could destroy the southern republic. Before launching a war, he conferred with Stalin in Moscow in late December 1949 and early 1950 and explained his plans to Mao Zedong of China during his meeting with him in Beijing in April 1950. In the spring of 1950, China allowed some 50 to 70 thousand seasoned Korean solders in the Chinese Communist Fourth Army to go to Korea while a large number of Chinese People's Liberation Army troops were mobilized in Manchuria under Commander Chu De to defend the border and if necessary cross the Yalu River to help North Korea.

When Kim Il-sung received Stalin's approval to launch the war and new Soviet military advisers replaced old ones, final preparations for aggression were completed. Kim Il-sung was certain that the United States would not intervene since the U.S. Secretary of State had indicated publicly in January 1950 that Korea was not within the U.S. defense perimeter in the Pacific region. Relying on assurances given by his foreign minister, Pak Hŏn-yŏng, Kim was confident that when North Korean troops took over Seoul, the communists and their sympathizers in the south would rise up and overthrow the South Korean government, bringing about the unification of Korea. He had already received assurances for military assistance from both Stalin and Mao.

On June 25, 1950, the well-trained and better equipped North Korean troops invaded South Korea across the 38th parallel, forcing the poorly trained and ill-prepared South Korean troops to retreat southward. Three days later, Seoul fell as the South Korean government fled to a southern city. Taken by surprise, the U.S. government immediately mobilized its troops in Japan, sending them to Korea to halt the advance of the invaders, but they too were unable to stem the tide of war. By early August, North Korean troops captured all but a small area in the southeastern corner of Korea east the Naktong River known as the Pusan perimeter. The fall of South Korea seemed imminent and inevitable.

Facing this unhappy prospect, the U.S. government led the Security Council of the United Nations to condemn North Korea as an aggressor. The U.N. created an international Military force consisting of troops from sixteen U.N. member nations under the command of General Douglas MacArthur of the United States.

After U.N. forces arrived, Gen. MacArthur launched a counter-attack, making a successful amphibious landing at Inch'ŏn and retaking Seoul on September 25. With this maneuver, North Korean troops were trapped and destroyed. In early October, the U.N. and South Korean troops crossed the 38th parallel in pursuit of the fleeing communist troops. After capturing P'yŏngyang on October 20, U.N. troops reached the Yalu River region. It seemed that the destruction of North Korea was at hand. However, U.N. troops encountered a new enemy. Some 260,000 Chinese communist troops had crossed the Yalu River on October 19 and joined the badly deteriorated North Korean force. Northern troop size increased until over one million Chinese troops were fighting in the Korean war. The "entirely new war" as Gen. MacArthur called it had begun. Soviet pilots had been flying Soviet planes given to North Korea, but the intervention of such a large number of Chinese communist troops made the Korean conflict an international war. During the harsh winter months, U.N. troops retreated from the north suffering tremendous casualties. Seoul was retaken by the communist in January 1951, but a stalemate developed as battle lines were stabilized.

In early 1951, the United States initiated secret talks with the Chinese for a truce. However, the deadlock remained as more see-saw battles were fought. Lack of progress in the truce talks ended only with Stalin's death in March 1953, and Mao's adoption of a new Korean strategy because of domestic problems. Serious truce talks were carried out following a proposal made by the Soviet Union in June.

Despite vehement opposition to the truce by South Korea, the Korean armistice was signed on July 27, 1953 at P'anmunjŏm by the U.N. Command and Chinese and North Korean representatives, establishing the four-kilometer-wide demilitarized zone (DMZ) along the new boundary line. P'anmunjŏm was designated as a neutral zone where the U.N. Neutral Nations Commission then established its headquarters. Although South Korea refused to sign the armistice, it agreed to honor the agreements, and the United States signed the mutual defense treaty with South Korea in October 1954.

The Korean War was a tragic event for both North and South Korea. To be sure, North Korea's ambition to unify Korea did not materialize. The war only brought devastation to both North and South. The toll of human lives was enormous. In the south, the number of soldiers killed or wounded, and the civilians killed, executed by the communists, wounded, abducted to the north, or missing was about 1.3 million. The war resulted in some one million orphans and 600,000 war-widows. The capital city of Seoul was badly damaged as one half of South Korea's industrial establishments and one-third of the housing were destroyed.

In the north, the combined military and civilian casualties were estimated at around 1.5 million. Most of the industrial facilities were
destroyed or badly damaged, and the capital city of P'yŏngyang was
reduced to ashes. North Korea's population was reduced to 8.5 million in
1953 from 11 million in June 1950, while in the South the population
grew to over 22 million with refugees from the north. The bitter sentiments created by the war made peaceful unification of Korea only more
difficult.

Korea After the War

Soon after the end of the war, both Korean states carried out their reconstruction schemes. North Korea was recovering and developing faster than
South Korea up until the mid-1960s. After that, South Korea picked up
speed, making more rapid progress in many areas, including economic
growth, despite its internal instability. Eventually, South Korea became a
modern, industrial nation while North Korea under a totalitarian rule of
the communists remained a closed society with sagging economy.

North Korea. With the assistance provided by the Soviet Union,
China, and other Communist countries, North Korea rebuilt its economic
foundation, concentrating on the development of heavy industries under
the reconstructed party and government apparatus. Kim Il-sung's power
was vastly increased after the war as his personality cult grew with the
adoption of his *Juche* ideology, a state creed. *Juche* implied such notions
as self-orientedness, autonomy, and independence.

As before, the Korean Workers' Party with Kim as its head, exercised an absolute monopoly of political power. The reconstituted Supreme
People's Assembly and the People's Army provided strong support for
Kim's dictatorial rule. The Administrative Council (cabinet) was the executive organ of the Central People's Committee whose head was Kim Il-
sung. The constitution which was revised in 1972 created the presidency
of the nation which was occupied by Kim after that time. At no time did
he relinquish his secretary-generalship of the Korean Workers' Party and
supreme commandership of the People's Army. All trade unions, including
professional societies, and social organizations which were reconstructed in
the mid-1950s gave Kim undisputed loyal support.

With the so-called "Heavenly Horse" or ch'ŏllima movement that
was launched in the mid-1950s and under the Taean method for industrial

development and the Ch'ŏngsan-ri method for agricultural development, North Korea's economic development under several planners was rapid. Both commerce and industry had been nationalized, and private owner-ship of property had been abolished. However, the dwindling economic aid from China and the Soviet Union after the mid-1960s slowed down North Korea's economic growth, bringing shortages of food, capital, and raw materials. Its economic situation worsened in the 1980s. North Korea's GNP growth rate was actually a shrinkage of 3.7% in 1990 and 5.2% in 1991. The joint venture plan implemented in 1984 made little impact. Thus its GNP in 1991 was only $22.9 billion with per capita GNP of $1,038. Its population grew to 22.5 million in 1991 despite measures attempting population control.

The development of Kim Il-sung's personality cult and socialization of culture make North Korea increasingly different from the south. It had discarded the use of Chinese characters before 1950 and after abandoning traditional social customs and culture, North Korea's monolithic culture for socialist revolution emerged. All songs, movies, and musical plays of North Korea were aimed at glorification of Kim Il-sung, his family mem-bers, deceased as well as living, and other Communist revolutionaries.

In 1980, Kim Jong-il, son of Kim Il-sung, emerged as undisputed heir to his father's power, and in the early 1990s as a member of key party and military establishments, he played an increasingly influential role. Meanwhile, North Korea's intention to "liberate the southern half (South Korea) of the republic" with its 900,000 men armed forces remained its supreme national objective. Several attempts made by North Koreans to assassinate South Korean presidents and its subversive activi-ties to overthrow the South Korean government failed. Meanwhile, even after the fall of the Communists in Eastern Europe in the late 1980s and in the former Soviet Union in 1991, North Korea insisted on keeping its socialist revolutionary ideology and scheme.

South Korea. During forty-five years after the end of World War II, South Korea underwent painful processes for democratization and eco-nomic development. Its First Republic of President Rhee, whose auto-cratic rule and dubious means used for constitutional amendments in 1952 and 1954 led to the Student Uprising of April 1960, was overthrown after making a modest economic recovery. The Second Republic followed and attempted to instill democracy, but it was overthrown by the May Military Revolution of 1961. After the period of junta rule, in 1963 the Third Republic emerged, followed by the Fourth Republic in 1971, the Fifth Republic in 1981, and the Sixth Republic in 1988. The Seventh Republic has succeeded in 1993.

The struggle of the people for democracy gained its initial success in 1987, and during the Sixth Republic period, democracy grew as freedom of speech and the press vastly increased. In 1992, South Korea elected by direct vote, for the first time since 1954, a president with no military connections.

South Korea's economy, which made only modest growth before 1963, expanded rapidly during the Park administration of the Third and Fourth Republic, although his autocratic rule brought about persistent anti-government and pro-democracy demonstrations during the 1960s and 1970s until his assassination by the director of the Korean Central Intelligence Agency in October 1979. After 1964, particularly in the 1970s, South Korea became a modern and industrial nation as its GNP increased more than 10% annually with the completion of four five-year national development plans. With the nation's growing economy and rapidly changing social and cultural aspects, Seoul was able to host the Summer Olympics in 1988.

South Korea's economic growth slowed down after 1979, with a still high average growth of 8.8% GNP in the 1980-91 period. In 1961, its GNP and per capita GNP were $12.7 billion and $74 respectively. In 1991, which was the last year of the sixth five-year plan, its GNP grew by 8.6% to $274.8 billion with per capita GNP of $6,340. The seventh five-year plan began in 1992.

During the four and a half decades of struggle for democracy, the South Korean people of all walks of life demonstrated their unbending spirit and desires for freedom and rights. While promoting Western culture, South Korea made serious efforts not only to preserve its cultural heritage, but also to promote and modernize its traditional culture. South Korea, like North Korea, was the land of illiterate people, with a literacy rate in 1945 of only 25%. However, after the war the government implemented various plans to promote education, bringing the rate of literacy to 99.5% by 1990. Initially, primary education was made compulsory, later all children were mandated to obtain education up to the ninth grade. Adult education and other systems for the promotion of culture and education were highly successful. In 1991, the total number of students was 10.5 million; 4.4 million in primary schools, 4.7 million in middle and high schools, and 1.4 million in colleges.

While the population grew to 43 million by 1991, social modernization also took place. As the number of female graduates of high schools and colleges increased, social status of South Korean women improved vastly as they gained both legal and social rights. The birth rate decreased to 1.2% by 1991, reducing the size of the average family as nuclear families increased in number. The average life span increased to 70 in 1991. Urbanization of the South Korean nation was rapid.

While promoting democracy at home, the Sixth Republic struck a diplomatic coup, implementing what is called Nordpolitik or "Northern Policy." Following the guideline set in 1973 by then President Park, who established normal relations with Japan in 1965, President Roh Tae-woo established diplomatic relations with former Socialist countries of Eastern Europe in 1989. Following this, in 1990 South Korea established diplomatic relations with the Soviet Union and with the People's Republic of China and Vietnam in 1992.

The two rival Korean states signed agreements in December 1991 to establish friendly relations and bring about peaceful unification of Korea. But like the agreement in July 1972, the new agreements signed failed to produce any appreciable results. The unification of the divided Korea remains as remote as it was before 1991.

No matter what progress the people of the two Korean states may make in economy or culture, so long as Korea remains divided, their ultimate national aspirations will remain unfulfilled.

Suggested Further Reading

Eckert, Carter J. et al. 1990. *Korea Old and New: A History*. Seoul: Ilchokak Publishers.

Lee, Chong-sik. 1965. *The Politics of Korean Nationalism*. Berkley: University of California Press.

Lee, Ki-baik. 1984. *A New History of Korea* (translated. by Edward W. Wagner with Edward J. Shultz). Cambridge, Massachusetts: Harvard University Press.

Nahm, Andrew C. 1993. *Introduction to Korean History and Culture*. Seoul and Elizabeth, New Jersey: Hollym Corporation Publishers.

_____. 1988. *Korea: Tradition & Transformation – A History of the Korean People*. Seoul and Elizabeth, New Jersey: Hollym Corporation Publishers.

_____. 1973. *Korea Under Japanese Colonial Rule – Studies of Policy and Techniques of Japanese Colonialism*. Kalamazoo, Michigan: Center for Korean Studies,Western Michigan University.

Palais, James B. 1975. *Politics and Policy of Traditional Korea*. Cambridge, Massachusetts: Harvard University Press.

3

Language
by John H. Koo

1

Introduction

Korean is one of the top twenty languages in the world in terms of number of speakers. It is spoken by about 70,000,000 people worldwide: 22,028,100 in North Korea, 43,268,000 in South Korea, 1,922,097 in China, 730,901 in Japan, 437,680 in the former U.S.S.R., 1,516,763 in the United States and Canada, 53,460 in Europe, 89,892 in Central and South America, 15,068 in the Middle East, and 2,614 in Africa (according to the information provided by the Ministry of Foreign Affairs, South Korea in 1991).

The linguistic affiliation of Korean is uncertain, though it is considered by many linguists as belonging to the Tungusic branch of the Altaic language family, which includes Turkish, Mongolian, and Tungus, or Tungus-Manchu. The similarities between Korean and the other Altaic languages are not striking; nonetheless Korean displays some important Altaic linguistic features. Korean and Japanese are often regarded as related and are sometimes included in the Altaic group, because the grammatical (or syntactical) structure of Korean is strikingly similar to that of Japanese.

2

Korean Writing

Koreans did not have their own writing system until 1446. For much of their history Koreans were under the heavy influence of Chinese culture. Their early attempts to develop their own writing system were not successful. Instead, they adopted Chinese characters (i.e., ideograms) as the medium of their writing. Koreans were the first foreigners to learn and use Chinese characters, the oldest writing in East Asia. In the 8th century, a system of transcribing Korean sounds by means of Chinese characters was perfected, which was known as idu, and by a royal decree an anthology of Korean native songs (or *hyang'ga*) was compiled in idu.

The Korean alphabet was created by a royal commission of linguists and philologists during the enlightened reign of King Sejong (1418-1450), the fourth king of the Yi Dynasty (1392-1910). The Korean writing is alphabetical in which symbols represent sound units or phonemes of the language. The alphabet *han'gŭl* is made of 28 symbols (19 consonants and 9 vowels). It is known as one of the simplest, most concise, efficient means of writing in the world. With this alphabet Koreans were able to write their own language.

Korean may be written entirely in *han'gŭl* or in mixed script (i.e., *han'gŭl* and Chinese characters). The language can be written vertically or horizontally. Traditionally, it is written in vertical fashion from the right to the left. Today, the horizontal writing from the left to the right is more commonly practised.

During the Japanese occupation of Korea (1910-1945), the use of *han'gŭl* was banned. With the defeat of the Japanese in 1945, the alphabet was once again in use. October 9 is *Han'gŭl* Day when Koreans celebrate the anniversary of the first promulgation of the writing system in 1446. Korea is possibly the only nation in the world to commemorate the invention of the writing system.

The language and literature of Korean have been greatly influenced by China. According to *K'ŭn sajŏn*, (Great Dictionary) compiled by the Korean Language Society, Korean vocabulary of Chinese origin accounts for more than half (54%) of the words in use today. This is due to the long predominance of Chinese learning in the past. Nearly all the technical terms in law, economy, social science, and natural science are of Chinese origin. Korean governments have periodically launched efforts to limit the use of difficult Chinese characters and to expand the use of the *han'gŭl* alphabet, but these attempts have not been successful.

3

Dialects

One of the most difficult theoretical issues in linguistics is how to draw a satisfactory distinction between language and dialect. Mutual intelligibility is the most commonly used criterion in deciding the two forms. One common problem with this criterion is, however, that dialects of the same language are not always mutually understandable in their spoken form (e.g., Mandarin Chinese and Cantonese) and are not the same in the degree of intelligibility. In the case of the latter, for instance, it can be more difficult for someone from Seoul to understand someone from Cheju Island than from Ch'ungch'ŏng Province. The degree of comprehension can be even worse when Seoulites attempt to communicate with Koreans living in Yanbian (Manchuria), since there had been few contacts between the populations until recently.

Korean dialects have traditionally been classified according to the administrative regions (e.g., Hamgyŏng dialect, P'yŏng'an dialect, Kang'wŏn dialect, Chŏllado dialect, Kyŏngsangdo dialect, Seoul dialect, etc.). The standard language of Korea is generally defined as the dialect spoken by middle-class people living in Seoul and vicinity.

The social, economic, and cultural changes of some thirty years in the past including industrialization, the propagation of schooling and the rapid spread of radio and television in the country, have greatly accelerated the disappearance of distinctive dialectal features. South Korea shows a tendency towards widespread use of the standard language.

4

Honorifics

Korean has highly developed and elaborate honorific or polite forms which require speakers to show their relationship to the addressee by lexically (or morphologically) and grammatically distinct forms. As Brown and Levinson argue, most aspects of social deixis are relational and have to do with speaker-addressee or speaker-referent relationships. They are closely related to the dimensions of power and solidarity. In other words, the addressee, or the referent, is placed in a position higher or lower, or stronger or weaker than the speaker, judged along the axis of power, and is evaluated on the axis of solidarity to determine his group membership. Honorifics are called for when the relationship between the speaker and the addressee is asymmetrical.

The traditional Korean society is vertically structured with interpersonal relationships strongly affected by differences in relative social strata. Due to these vertical relationships, honorific expressions have been highly developed.

The development of honorifics in Korean is indicative of a long-established culture in which interpersonal communication is judged more by how one says something than by what one says. In traditional Korean culture the linguistic mannerism is so firmly held that any deviation, even if unintentional, is susceptible to being judged as an insult or an act of rude and uncivilized behavior. A wrong term of address, for instance, is invariably the cause of embarrassment not only for the addressee but also for the speaker. One characteristic of the Korean honorific system is nonreciprocity. The superior can use either formal or informal speech forms, whereas the inferior can only use formal, honorific (or deferential). Some examples of lexical items that show distinction between honorific and plain are:

PLAIN   HONORIFIC
chip   *taek* (house)
chada   *chumushida* (to sleep)
it'ta   *kyeshida* (to stay)
mŏkta   *chapsushida* (to eat)

Consider the following variants of verb endings. They may be added to a verb stem to exhibit different speech levels.

1. -(ŭ)shipsiyo (e.g., *anch-ŭshipshiyo* 'Please sit down')
2. -(ŭ)seyo
3. -ayo/-ŏyo
4. -(ŭ)shiyo
5. -a/-ŏ
6. -chi

The choice of an appropriate ending is made by such factors as age, sex, and intimacy. For instance, one may use the ending -(ŭ)shipshiyo (l), which is formal and deferential in addressing an elderly person. A husband will not use the same ending in addressing his wife; instead he will use either -*ayo/-ŏyo* (3), or -*a*/-ŏ (5) if his relationship with his wife is very close. It is noted here that the selection between the vowels *a* and *o* in (3) and (5) is determined by the quality of the verb stem final vowel. That is, the suffix vowel a is to be used when the stem vowel is *a* or *o*, and the suffix vowel ŏ is to be used if the stem vowel is other than *a* or *o*. This phonological feature has to do with vowel harmony in the Korean language.

Another characteristic of the honorific system is that in Korean, personal pronouns are in the minority, and there are many other words or expressions that are used in place of the second personal pronoun. There is no generic term for "you" in Korean. For instance, the second person pronoun *tangshin* is not neutral with regard to socio-cultural features. The connotation varies depending on such factors as the addressee's age and sex. The word may signify power and superiority if it is used by a male speaker to address his male inferior, whereas it may indicate intimacy if it is used by a female to address her spouse. If it is used by a detective or policeman in interrogating a suspect, it may connote threat or condemnation. Further, the speaker never addresses a superior with a personal pronoun such as *tangshin*, *chane*, or *nŏ*. A lower-status person is socially prohibited from using pronouns to address a higher-status person. The Korean language is rich in grammatical and lexical means of showing various levels of politeness and deference. Respective social status and age differences are amply represented in the linguistic forms. Thus one has to adjust to the relatively higher, lower, or equal degree of personal intimacy or power of the conversants.

However, the modernization process that South Korea has experienced since the 1960s has heavily impacted the language. One of the most noticeable linguistic changes is the widespread adoption of an egalitarian speech pattern by younger Koreans. This trend has reduced the significance of differing speech levels (such as honorific speech) and address terms, which traditionally played important roles in Korean society.

5

Onomatopoetic Words

Onomatopoetic words are those which imitate natural sounds. In Korean these words not only imitate natural sounds, but also describe a certain action or condition. There are literally hundreds of these words in Korean. The language has perhaps the richest and most extensive system of sound symbolism in the world. Such a highly developed system of phonetic symbolism expresses subtle and structured differences in connotation (Kim, 1980). The words which represent sounds are called *ŭisŏngŏ* (sound imitating words) and the words which describe actions are called *ŭit'aeŏ*. Frequently, the use of *ŭisŏngŏ* or *ŭit'aeŏ* is the only way to accurately describe a certain action or condition. For instance, the verb usta can be 'to smile' or 'to laugh' depending on which *ŭisŏngŏ* is used. See the examples below:

> *shinggŭl-shinggŭl utta* (to smile)
> *k'ŏl-k'ŏl utta* (to laugh boisterously)
> *pŏnggŭl-pŏnggŭl utta* (to smile happily)
> *k'il-k'il utta* (to giggle, to chuckle)

The following expressions each describe a different sort of flowing water from the drizzling to the pouring of rain, from the murmur of a gentle brook to the breaking of ocean waves, from the trickling of sweat to the spurting of blood (Kim, 1980).

*chol-chol, chul-chul, chŏl-chŏl, chwal-chwal, chil-chil, chal-chal,
chuluk-chuluk, ch'ullŏng-ch'ullŏng, chilkŭm-chilkŭm, ch'alsak-ch'alsak,
ppŏl-ppŏl, ttok-ttok, ttuk-ttuk*

6

Dual System of Native and Sino-Korean Words

A dual system of native Korean (NK) and Sino-Korean (SK) words pervades the Korean lexicon. They are interchangeably used in some cases but are mutually exclusive in others. One good example is the two sets of numerals that occur with measure words (such as sheet, bottle, cupful).

> han shi '1 o'clock' ; il pun '1 minute' ; se chang '3 sheets' ;
> NK SK   SK SK   NK SK
> han chu / il chu '1 week' ; se   chan '3 cupfuls' ;
> NK SK   SK SK   NK SK
> han hae / il nyon '1 year'
> NK NK   SK SK

Although native Korean and Sino-Korean words have co-existed, the Sino-Korean words have dominated over the native words to such an extent that many native words have been completely replaced by Sino-Korean words (Kim, 1988). It is quite interesting to note that Sino-Korean words are generally regarded as more respectful than native Korean words.

7

Some Grammatical Features

Phonological Level:

1. No consonant clusters occur word initially.
2. Consonant stops are regularly nasalized before a nasal.
   Examples: chimmadang (chip + matang) 'house yard' ; pannunda
   (pat + nunda) 'he receives' ; kungmul (kuk + mul)
   'soup'
3. The sounds l and r are in complementary distribution; the l
occurs word finally or preceding a consonant, and the r occurs elsewhere.
   Examples: tool 'stone' ; tooldari 'stone bridge' ; sori 'sound' ;
   maru 'floor'
4. Vowel length is linguistically important (i.e., phonemic), since it
changes the meaning.
   Examples: *tol* 'year' /tool 'stone'; nun 'eye' /nuun 'snow';
   kul 'oyster' /kuul 'tunnel';
   pam 'night' /paam 'chestnut';
   mal 'horse' /maal 'language'; il 'one' /iil 'work'
The long vowel appears to occur only in the mono syllable words.

5. In Korean, vowel harmony plays an important role. Vowel harmony is a phonological feature of a language where all the vowels of a
polysyllable word share certain features (e.g., frontness, backness, round-
ness). The vowel harmony in Korean is, however, not as fully developed

as, for instance, in Turkish and Finnish or as rigidly regulated as was 15th century Korean. One area where the vowel harmony is well revealed is the past tense forms of verbs, in which the vowel quality of the past tense suffix is determined by that of the preceding syllable of the verb stem with which it occurs. That is, the choice of the variants of -ass, -ŏss, -yŏss is made by the quality of the stem-final vowel. If the stem vowel is a or o, the past suffix is -ass, and if it is other than a or o, the past affix is -ŏss. The -yŏss occurs only with the special verb stem ha- 'to do.'

Examples:

-ass: padatta (pat-ass-ta) 'received' ; poatta (po-ass-ta) 'saw' ;
-oss: masyŏtta (masi-oss-ta) 'drank' ; midŏtta (mit-ŏss-ta)
        'believed' ; paewŏtta (paewu-ŏss-ta) 'learned' ; mŏkŏtta
        (mŏk-ŏss-ta) 'ate' ; sokyŏtta (soki-ŏss-ta) 'cheated'
-yŏss: hayŏtta (ha-yŏss-ta) 'did' ; choyonghayŏt'ta (choyong
        ha-yŏss-ta) 'was quiet'

Syntactic Level:

1. The basic (or preferred) word order of a transitive sentence is Subject-Object-Verb (SOV). The word order in Korean is relatively free as long as the verb is fixed as the last constituent of the sentence. All of the following word orders are thus acceptable.

(1) Maeil kŭpun-ŭn sul- ŭl mashinda.
     everyday he TM liquor OM drink
(2) Maeil sul-ŭl kŭpun-ŭn mashinda.
(3) Kŭpun-ŭn maeil sul-ŭl mashinda.
(4) Kŭpun-ŭn sul-ŭl maeil mashinda.
(5) Sul-ŭl kŭpun-ŭn maeil mashinta.
(6) Sul-ŭl maeil kŭpun-ŭn mashinda.
     TM = topic marker; OM = object marker

Notice, however, that certain orders are somewhat unnatural and are not preferably used. For instance, in sentences (2), (5), and (6) the objects of the sentences precede the subjects. In most languages, the object follows the subject.

2. Korean is an agglutinative language in which grammatical ele-

ments (i.e., morphemes) are shown by addition of suffixes to a word stem (particularly verb stems), thus forming a single word. The English sentence "(he) did not come," for example, can be manifested as follows:

(Kupun-i) oshichianhasssŭmnida (o- 'to come' , -shi HON,- chianh NEG, -ass PAST, -pni POL, -ta DCL)
SM = subject marker; HON = honorific; NEG = negative; POL = polite; DCL = declarative

3. Noun modifiers always come before the nouns they modify.
pissan ch' aek 'expensive book' ; Hankuk ŭi suto 'the capital of Korea' ; kŭ haksaeng-i ilkŭn ch'aek 'the book that the student read'
Notice that Korean has no relative pronouns.
4. Korean is postpositional (as opposed to prepositional). Grammatical relations that would be represented by prepositions or word order (e.g., in English) are expressed by postpositions (i.e., grammatical particles that follow the noun or its equivalent).
Kupun-i ch'inku-wa kich'a-ro Seoul-e kat'ta.
     SM   with   by   to
(The person went to Seoul with his friend by train.)
5. A subordinate clause always precedes its main clause, and the conjunction is always placed at the end of the subordinate clause.
Naeil ka-myŏn, kŭpun-ŭl mannamnida.
tomorrow go-if, he-OM will meet
(If you go tomorrow, you will meet him.)
Pissa-chiman sakessŭmnida.
expensive-although I will buy
(Although it is expensive, I will buy.)
6. The plural marker may be attached to almost any constituent. That is, the plural maker -tŭl may be used not only with nominals but also with adverbs and adverbial phrases (with particles). In general, the plural ending may be omitted if it is clear by the context. Consider the following examples.

With nominals:
    (1) Ai-tŭl-i nonda. (The children are playing.)
        child-PL-SM are playing
    (2) Haksaeng-tŭl-i sul-ŭl mashinda.
        student-PL-SM liquor-OM drink
        (Students are drinking liquor.)
    (3) Sul-tŭl-ŭl mashinta. (They are drinking liquor.)
        liquor-PL-OM drink.

With adverbials:
(4) Chal-tŭl kashipshiyo. (Goodbye, lit. Go well.)
(5) Manhi-tŭl chapsushipshiyo. (Eat much.)
(6) Kongpu yŏlshimhi-tul hayŏssŭmnikka? (Did you study hard?)

With adverbial phrases:
(7) Hankukmal-lo-tŭl malhashipshiyo. (Please say in Korean.)
(8) Chip-esŏ-tŭl muŏsŭl hashimnikka? (What do you do at home?)
(9) Hakyo-e-tŭl kapshita. (Let's go to school.)

Notice that the plural endings attached to the adverb, the adverbial phrase, and even the object, for instance in sentence (3) above, refer to the subject, thus making the subject plural. The plural ending-tŭl is uniquely "versatile" (Martin and Lee, 1968). In Korean, the plural marking is optional when numerals and quantifiers are present as seen in the examples below.

se haksaeng(tŭl) 'three students'

Haksaeng(tŭl)-i mant'a.   (There are many students.)
students)-SM   are many

7. Adverbs always precede verbs.

8. The subject in a Korean sentence is normally omitted if evident from the context. See some examples above.

Hangŭl (Korean Alphabet)

In Korean there are 19 consonants and 9 vowels. The following are the basic symbols that are combined to form various letters.

    1. Consonant Symbols

ㄱ (k)	ㅋ (k')
ㄴ (n)	ㅌ (t')
ㄷ (t)	ㅍ (p')
ㄹ (1,r)	ㅎ (h)
ㅁ (m)	ㄲ (kk)
ㅂ (p)	ㄸ (tt)
ㅅ (s)	ㅃ (pp)
ㅇ (ng)	ㅆ (ss)
ㅈ (ch)	ㅉ (cch)
ㅊ (ch')	

    2. Vowels

ㅏ(a), ㅓ(ŏ), ㅗ(o), ㅜ(u), ㅡ(ŭ), ㅣ(i), ㅔ(e), ㅐ(ae), ㅚ(oe)

    3. Semi−Vowels

      (a) y−group   (b) w−group

ㅑ (ya as in English yard)	ㅘ (wa as in English Washington)
ㅕ (yŏ as in English young)	ㅙ (wae as in English wagon)
ㅛ (yo as in English york)	ㅝ (wŏ as in English was)
ㅠ (yu as in English you)	ㅟ (wi as in English queen)
ㅖ (ye as in English yes)	ㅞ (we as in English western)
ㅒ (yae as in English yam)	

(For explanation of the symbols above, see the section on Pronunciation of Korean in the front.)

    The writing of a letters is from top to bottom and from left to right. Some examples are:

가 (ㄱ + ㅏ)	(ka)
무 (ㅁ + ㅜ)	(mu)
손 (ㅅ + ㅗ + ㄴ)	(son)
목 (ㅁ + ㅗ + ㄱ + ㅅ)	(moks)

As noticed above, the final consonant or consonants of a syllable are always placed below a vowel letter, and the final consonant is read together with the following vowel. See the examples:

먹읍시다	(mŏ-kŭp-shi-ta)	Let's eat.
앉았다	(an-chass-ta)	I sat.
미국은 크다	(mi-kŭ-kŭn-k'u-ta)	America is big.

Suggested Further Reading

Brown, Penelope and Stephen Levinson. 1987. *Politeness*. Cambridge University Press.

Huh, Woong. 1983. "Development of the Korean Language," *The Korean Language*. Seoul: Si-sa-yong-o-sa, Inc.

Kim, Chin-W. 1980. "Language and Linguistics," *Studies on Korea: A Scholar's Guide*. Han-Kyo Kim (ed.). University of Hawaii Press.

Kim, Nam-Kil. 1988. "Korean," *The World's Major Languages*. Bernard Comrie (Ed.). New York: Oxford University Press.

Koo, John H. 1992. "The Term of Address 'You' in South Korea Today," *Korean Journal*. Vol. 32, No. l.

Lee, Ki-moon. 1983. "Foundations of Hunminchongum," *The Korean Language*.Seoul: Si-sa-yong-o-sa, Inc.

Poppe, Nicholas. 1965. *Introduction to Altaic Linguistics*. Wiesbaden: Otto Harrassowitz.

Ramstedt, Gustaf. 1957 *Einfuehrung in die altaische Sprachwissenshaft: I Lautlehre*. Helsinki: Suomalais-Ugrilainen Seura.

Shibatani, Masayoshi. 1990. *The Languages of Japan*. New York: Cambridge University Press.

4

Folk Beliefs and Shamanism
by Kwang Kyu Lee

1

Introduction

Religion is important in all cultures. Religions deal with spirits, gods, and other worlds, and they reflect the covert culture and the innate values or world views of the people. In Korea, the study of religion can be used to explain not only the group subconsciousness but also the history of Koreans. Generally, foreign religions were adopted by the elite, and the indigenous religions in Korea have survived in a purer form among the populace. A good example in this respect is Korean shamanism, which has been preserved in a very pure and highly developed form. In Korea, shamanism has not only preserved its original structure, but it has developed its own ways of thinking through the stimulus of contact with foreign religions.

Religions in Korea include worship of house gods, village gods, and natural gods by housewives and ordinary villagers. The worship of these gods differs from shamanism, even though shamanism has incorporated some of these gods. Sometimes it is difficult to determine where these two indigenous religions, shamanism and god worship, have intermixed or developed independently.

Folk Beliefs

As do all primitive religions, Korean indigenous religion includes a variety of folk beliefs regarding things unknown or supernatural, as well as those of the natural world that affected Koreans lives. These folk beliefs accompany many forms of religious practices, creating a particular religious cult.

1. House Gods

Ancestor God. The ancestor god, along with other spirits, is the oldest known god with the Koreans worshiped from the earliest times in history. There are many different names for this god depending on locality, but one well-known name is the jar of ancestors, or *chosang tanji.*

The "jar of ancestors" is a small jar in which rice is stored, and the mouth of the jar is covered with white paper. Without exception, this jar is located on a high shelf in one corner of the inner room. In some localities, this god is referred to as "grandmother." It is connected with the fertility of agricultural land and with child bearing. In some areas, people put white papers in a small box, called the ancestor box, next to the jar. As with other gods in the house, the ancestor spirit in the jar is served by the housewife during an annual ritual held each 10th lunar month. The housewife sets in front of the god a steaming jar of rice cakes, a bowl of fresh water, and a dried pollack. After that, the housewife rubs her hands together and prays for several minutes, wishing for her family's good fortune and well being. Then she takes the same offering table to the other gods in the house and repeats the ritual.

The House Master God. On a shelf in one corner of the wooden floor room (*maru*) there is another jar which is called the master god (*sŏngju*). Rice or barley is put into this jar. In the central part of the Korean peninsula and in some regions of Kyŏngsang Province, the master god is represented by a piece of paper. A white piece of paper is hung in the corner of the wooden floor room or on the upper part of a post. In some houses, an old coin or some rice is put in the paper.

This house master god is supposed to protect the family head. The housewife pays homage to this god on the same day when the ritual service for ancestor spirits is performed. Particularly devoted women dedicate a separate table to this god on seasonal holidays or on the birthdays of the family members. Whenever special foods are received from neighbors, they are placed in front of the house master god before being touched by the housewife. During shaman rituals there is one stage dedicated to this house master god.

The Fire God. The fire god (*chowang*) is located in the kitchen. A small white bowl containing fresh water is placed on the platform of cooking pots as the symbol of the fire god. An especially devoted woman will change this water every morning, but most wives change the water once a month on the first day of the month. Without exception, the fire god is called grandmother. She protects the housewife. The housewife can prepare a special place at home to dedicate herself to this god. Even in such a case, the god is represented merely by a bowl of fresh water. On a day when ritual is performed for the house gods, the fire god receives the same table of offerings that is dedicated to the other gods. Shaman rituals include a stage dedicated to this fire god. The fire god is worshiped as an important god in Chŏlla provinces and parts of Chungchŏng Province.

The House Site God. In the backyard, near the platform of various storage jars, the house site god (*tŏju*) and the god of wealth (*ŭp*) are placed side by side. The house site god is represented by a bundle of straw bound at the top. Inside the straw is a jar which contains rice. Next to it, there is a straw heap laid flat which stands for the god of wealth. As the name implies, the house site god protects the house site, and the god of wealth preserves the wealth of the house. The inside of the straw heap representing the god of wealth is empty, but it is believed that a snake resides within. If a snake is seen coming out from beneath the straw heap, it is believed that the family's fortune will decline. As do other gods of the house, both of these gods receive a special dedication by the housewife once a year. The house site god and the god of wealth are honored in Kyŏnggi Province more than in other provinces.

Other Gods. Among other house gods are the gate god who is regarded as a general god and resides at the main entrance, and the toilet god who is regarded as a young woman with a perverse character.

The house gods in Korean families have their own particular functions in protecting the family. There is no hierarchical connection among them, and they have no functional connections with one another. They stand on equal footing with equal status, and they have a strongly individualistic character. Appeasing domestic gods is primarily a housewife's responsibility. Ritual services for the house gods are performed by the housewife. Men engage in ancestor worship, but never concern themselves with the house gods, except in Kangwŏn Province. Sexual segregation in household management extends even to ritual performances for the gods. Many of the house gods are called grandmother, and they are mild in character. Several of them are represented by jars of rice and are connected with abundant crops, offspring, and wealth.

2. Village God

The Character of the God. As has been mentioned already, every village has its own tutelary god who protects the inhabitants of the village. Even though the worship of the village gods has weakened due to the recent New Community Movement, many villages still preserve the concept of a village god.

The village god is easily identified in the southern parts of the Korean peninsula because there is usually a large old tree in front of the village or in the center of the village, which is considered the tutelary god. In the middle part of the Korean peninsula, the village god is usually located underneath old tall trees on a hill near the village. In these villages, the trees themselves are not considered to be the god; rather, the god is supposed to reside in these trees. Therefore, the trees are considered sacred and cannot be cut down. In such a case, there is no object which can be identified with the god itself. The village god may also take the form of a stone. Generally, the stone is not big, but in some special cases it is. The stone representing the god is housed in a small shrine, which is built with wood and tile in the rear of the village, on a hillside or under a large old tree. In many places, the shrine itself is considered to be the god. Sometimes a shrine contains a piece of folded white paper, a small iron horse, or a tablet on which the name of the god is written. In some cases, the shrine contains a painting or a wooden statue of the god. The god is normally a god of nature, but there are special cases in which historical persons are worshiped as village gods.

The Ritual Process. The ritual service for the village god is usually performed on the 15th of the first month according to the lunar calendar. In a few places, it is performed on New Year's Day, or on a day in the second month. The time for the ritual is midnight when all is quiet.

A master is selected from among the villagers. The old men of the village decide whether or not they will perform a service. If there has been a funeral in the recent past, the ritual service is canceled or postponed. When the village decides to perform a ritual service, the villagers select one from a number of candidates for the ritual master. Horoscopes are cast to see if the masters and the vice-masters ages are in harmony with the current year. If found satisfactory, these masters supervise the ritual process.

The master and the vice-master prepare food in front of the village god. They perform the ritual service for the village god in the same way as the ancestor ritual service is prepared at home. After this, the master burns as many pieces of paper as there are families living in the village. The master dedicates each piece of paper, reciting each time the family name and the family's wishes. When this is finished, the participants place food and wine in front of the god.

The next day, all the villagers come together to the masters house. During this meeting, they partake of food, and the vice-master presents a report about the income and the expenses for the ritual service. The master reports on the entire process of the ritual service and explains the conditions of burning each paper. If the village has a farmers band, it performs at this time.

There are several kinds of village god worship which differ according to the localities. One of the interesting types of worship is found in south Chŏlla Province, near the sea coast. In one village there are 12 gods (*dangsan*) who are members of the same family. The ritual service is performed only for the grandfather god.

In the southeastern provinces, particularly along the sea coast, the village god is called *kolmaegi*. Each village has one or two *kolmaegi* who are referred to as the grandmother or grandfather of such-and-such, using the family name of an earlier settler of the village. In other words, the founder of the village later becomes the village god.

In mountainous areas of Kangwŏn Province, the village god is called sŏnhwang. There are sŏnhwang individual families, sections of the village, and the entire village.

In Cheju Island, there are several different gods: the god of the village, the god of illness, the god of snakes, and the god of woman divers. Each of these gods is worshiped only by women. The men have separate village gods. The men perform Confucian rites, whereas the women perform their own rites.

The most important element in communal religious activities is its function as a unifier of the villagers. The villagers have the feeling of being we through participating in communal rituals.

2

Shamanism

Shamanism is one of the oldest religions and is found around the world. North Asia, in particular, is famous for its shamanism. Korea is one of the important places where shamanism has been clearly preserved until today. Shamanism is centered around shamans, who make contact with gods or evil spirits through special ecstatic techniques. About 200,000 shamans registered with the Ministry of Culture and Information in 1990. Most of them are illiterate, and their practices are loosely organized, so it is hard to estimate the exact number of believers in shamanism. Nonetheless, it is known that the number of shamans in Korea is significantly large.

The shaman is usually a priestess in shamanism who officiates rituals. A shaman must have at least three qualifications. The most important qualification is that the shaman has experienced the so-called "shaman illness." Around the time of her adolescence, or sometimes later in life, a woman will suffer from an unknown illness, having bodily pain and mental exhaustion. She will often dream of demons or gods, and she will experience hallucinations and illusions even during the day. She may take a variety of medications, but there is nothing which makes her feel better. Consequently, she goes to a shaman who knows about shaman illnesses. The shaman becomes the godmother of the younger woman, who, in turn, becomes the shaman's assistant and a novice shaman. The novice takes the god who appeared in her dream as her guardian deity. When the novice has spent about five years in training and when it is acknowl-

edged that she has learned enough skills and techniques, she herself con-
ducts a large ceremony, after which she is considered a new shaman.
Many shamans who are friends of the godmother are invited to attend
this ritual.

A shaman has a shrine in which her guardian deity and other
instruments for her ritual services are kept. The shrine belongs to the
individual shaman. It is usually a small separate building, but it is sometimes kept in the corner of the shaman's room when she has no extra
space. The shrine is a holy place, sometimes decorated with flowers, burning incense, and fruit. Naturally, the most important function of the
shaman is the performance of rituals.

The main duty of a shaman is to perform shamanistic ritual services
which usually occur over a two-day period. One person cannot perform a
long continuous ceremony of two days by herself, so there is usually a
group of shamans and musicians who perform the ritual together. Four or
five shamans are a good number for such a ritual, although two or three
shamans can constitute a group. The number of musicians depends on the
size and budget of the ritual, but at least five musicians are needed. The
essential musical instruments in the ritual are the Korean drum, or
changgo, a large drum, a fiddle, a gong, and pipes. The Korean drum is
the most important musical instrument for the singing and dancing of the
shaman. It is used to give the shaman signals and to accompany her
singing.

The ritual service is performed for the purpose of securing good
luck, for effecting a cure for physical or mental illness, or for pacifying a
deceased spirit. The first function, that of securing good fortune, has
become popular in recent times. Without exception, the owner of a ship
performs a shamanistic ritual before going out to sea. Rich merchants and
taxi owners in urban areas have the rituals performed regularly. Even in
big textile factories it is thought that the best way to pacify workers is by
having a shamanistic ritual once a year. But the other two functions, curing illness and pleasing the deceased, have long been part of shamanism
and are also practiced today.

When a shaman is famous and has abilities in singing and dancing,
she has many patrons; however, the number of patrons is generally fixed.
The shaman and her patrons are bound together by a special relationship.
This is not only in the ritual service but also in daily life. Patrons give the
shaman presents on signal holidays and on her birthday. Patrons sometimes create a special relationship between the shaman and a young son
who is considered weak. The mother of such a son gives a cloth to the
shaman on which is written the name and the birth date of the son. It is

called the "life" of the child, and the shaman keeps it until the child's death.

A patron requests the shaman to perform a ritual service, and the shaman sets the date and the amount of money it will require. With the money, the shaman prepares different kinds of paper flowers for decorating the altar, and she prepares food for the dedication. Most importantly, she contracts the services of other shamans and musicians who will participate in the ritual.

The shaman ritual consists of four elements: shaman clothes, music, dance, and song. In general, there are twelve stages in shaman ritual. At each stage, the shaman wears different clothes in various forms and colors, which may include official dress, a military uniform, a monk's costume, etc. Shaman music is intended to accompany the singing and the dancing of the shaman, and it has a special rhythm called *dŏngdŏkkung*. The shaman dance begins with slow motions, which invoke the spirit and make things pleasurable for the god. Later, the dance changes to a quick tempo, which symbolizes the ecstasy of making contact with the spirit. Thereafter, all of the singing and speech is assumed to be coming from the god through his medium, the shaman. The long singing and speaking stages of the ritual performance may require several hours altogether. The performance includes myths about the cosmos and people, the sorrows and joys of humans, the rules of the universe, the rise and fall of societies, and people's future.

In general, there are twelve stages (*kŏri*) in shamanistic ritual called kut. The length of each stage depends on the particular audience that will participate in the ritual. A single stage can continue for several hours.

The first stage is called *pujŏng*, which literally means "cleansing." The shaman wears normal dress while singing and dancing around the area of the performance. This is a ritual to purify the stage, the food, and the instruments.

The second stage is *kamang* stage. During this stage, the shaman wears normal dress, but also wears an overcoat. Nobody can clearly explain the meaning of this second stage. However, it seems to be a greeting to all the gods or the main god who will be served during the ritual service.

The third stage is called *malmyŏng* stage, which is dedicated to deceased spirits. The shaman wears a yellow coat and holds a large shaman fan made with yellow cloth and bells. This symbolizes gratitude for the protection of deceased spirits.

The fourth stage is for General Choe Young, and it is called *sanbang* stage. General Choe Young was assassinated by General Yi, who founded the Chosŏn Dynasty. General Choe is honored as a tragic hero, and he is honored as the highest god by shamans in the Kyŏnggi area. This stage is performed by the main shaman who wears the military uniform of a general and a red hat. In some instances, the shaman climbs on the blade of a sword with naked feet and demonstrates thereby the supernatural powers of a shaman.

The fifth stage called *sŏngju maji* is for the house master god, who protects the family and brings good luck to the house. This god is considered to be the protector of the family head. The shaman wears a red coat and puts on a red hat.

The sixth stage is called *pyŏlsŏng* stage, which is dedicated to the god of smallpox. During this stage, the shaman wears a sleeveless robe and a soldier's hat.

The seventh stage is called the *taegam* stage. The shaman wears military uniform or a sleeveless robe and pays respect to the tutelary gods.

The eighth stage is named for *chesŏk*, who was originally considered to be a god in Buddhism, but now functions in relationship to births, maintaining longevity and prosperity in farming. The shaman wears a white coat and a flowered hat. Dishes containing meat are removed while this stage is being performed.

The ninth stage is called *hogwi* stage. He is the god of measles, which was a most dangerous illness in the past. The shaman wears a baggy dress and small crown.

The tenth stage is called *kunung* stage. The shaman again wears a military uniform and a red hat during this stage. The god is an ancestor spirit who protects the family.

The eleventh stage is called *ch'angbu* stage. The name *ch'angbu* derives from an actor, and he is considered to be the god of public entertainers. However, the shaman prays to him for protection against evil, and she again wears a military uniform for this stage.

The twelfth is the final stage. The shaman wears normal dress and bows several hundred times to greet all of the gods and all the good and evil spirits who participated in the ritual. She drops off pieces of food and wine as offerings to the demons, bidding farewell to them.

Of the twelve stages, the first two and the last two stages are considered to be greetings and farewells to the gods. The third and the fourth, and the ninth and the tenth stages are dedicated for protection against calamities. The essential core of the ritual service consists of the fifth through the eighth stages, in which the shaman petitions for good fortune, health, wealth, and longevity. These four things are the most highly valued concepts of the Korean people.

Shamanistic rituals for securing good luck and for curing illness follow the same twelve stage processes. The shaman changes the wording of desires and the god's speech according to the purpose of the ritual service. In the case of the ritual for pacification of a dead spirit, there is one more stage added, called chinoguy, between the eighth and the ninth stage. This is a long stage which contains an epic about Princess Pari. The princess was born as the seventh daughter of a king who wanted a son. The king was angry with the birth of this princess and abandoned her. During her childhood, she was raised by a humble old couple. Thereafter, she experienced the lowest kind of life in society, she got married, and she had six sons. One day she was told the news that her father had died. None of the other six princesses could help their father, but this seventh princess dedicated herself to find a medicine to cure him. During this time, she underwent unbelievable horrors and trials. When she finally brought the medicine, her dead father was being carried out of the palace on his bier. However, the king returned to life because of the medicine. The king repented of his behavior toward this seventh princess, and he offered to give her his kingdom. But she rejected the offer and went to heaven, becoming the guardian of shamans. When the shaman performs this stage, there are many women who cry endlessly. The epic of the seventh princess is a favorite story for Korean women.

3

Variations of Shamanism

Throughout its long history, shamanism in Korea has developed several regional variations. The Korean shamanism may be divided into two large groups: the northern and the southern. The demarcation line between the two types is found around the middle part of the Korean peninsula in the southern part of Kyŏnggi Province in central Korea. Shamanism of the northern type is characterized by ecstasy, dress, singing, and dancing in the ritual service. The southern type, however, has no ecstasy and no dance, and the shamans of the southern type are monotonous. Moreover, most southern shamans perform their rituals in sitting position, and they do not change their clothes.

Shamans in Ch'ungch'ŏng Province. The shamanism of Ch'ungch'ŏng Province belongs to the southern type, but it has its own characteristics which are similar in some features to those in Kyŏnggi Province. In Ch'ungch'ŏng Province there are five categories of shamans. The two prominent ones are shamans who are called diviners and shamans who are called legal masters. They are usually middle-aged women who suffer after being possessed by spirits. They establish altars in their homes. Such women are said to be possessed by a spirit, but they experience no shaman illness.

The diviners perform shamanistic ritual of the southern type by reading divine sentences and telling fortunes. In particular, they give directions to their clients as to whether they should go to the mountain or temple to offer prayer. When necessary, a diviner herself performs a ritual service for a god at the patrons home, and in such a case she may try to cure an illness or try to bring good fortune to the family.

The legal masters are male shamans. In other provinces, the legal master is a word used for a blind man who recites divine books, but in this province they are not necessarily blind. They consult books for the selection of dates and for reading faces and palms. When they are invited to a shamanistic ritual, they read special selections for good luck, for curing illness, for house gods, for dead spirits, or for calming the mentally disturbed. These male shamans are highly trained for reading, but they are subordinate to the female shamans, the diviners.

Shamans in Chŏlla Province. A typical southern type of shamanism is that found in Chŏlla Province. This type of shamanism does not involve ecstasy, and shamans do not experience shaman illness. A daughter-in-law learns all of the shamanistic techniques from her mother-in-law. The most interesting phenomenon in the shamanism in Chŏlla Province is its parish organization. One shaman has one fixed territory under her influence. In Kyŏnggi Province, patrons of a shaman have personal relationships with the shaman, but these relationships can be broken; they are not determined by territory. However, the parish organization in Chŏlla cannot be broken by an individual. If someone should want to break his relationship with the shaman, he has to move out of the village. The parish is considered to be the shaman's territory. If someone should invite another shaman without the permission of his own shaman, the invited shaman must pay a penalty. A shaman can invite other shamans by contract. The parish cannot be inherited by a shaman, or it can be sold by one shaman to another.

The ritual service in Chŏlla is much simpler than that of the northern type. There is no change of dress. There is no dance, even though the shaman stands and walks around the stage. The most important difference from the ritual service of the northern type is that the southern type does not include divine words spoken through the shaman. What is spoken and sung by the shaman is mainly intended to honor the gods and to please the gods.

Shamans in Kangwŏn Province. Especially on the east coast of Kangwŏn and Kyŏngsang provinces, there are several groups of shamans who go wandering from village to village. They have no permanent residence or organization. Each time a ritual is performed, a shaman leader brings together several shamans and musicians for the purpose.

The most important characteristic of shamanism in this area is its style of performance. Since it belongs to the southern type, there is no change of dress and no divine speech, but the ritual of the shaman is connected with village god worship and is often amusing. During the ritual service for the village god, there are several stages for the household gods, the dragon god, the water god, and other gods. Among the several stages, there is one stage for reading a classical epic. The last stage is for amusement only. During various stages, the shaman brings several men or women from the audience for different proposes. The shaman does satirical skits on teachers, state examinations, initiation rites, women divers, and military service. She also imitates the delivery of a child in a dramatic form.

Shamans on Cheju Island. The shamans in Cheju Island belong to the southern type, but they have peculiar features. Shamans in Cheju are called shinbang. They become shamans by passing through three stages. After the first rite, they become a novices. Through the second rite they become assistants, and through the third rite, they become real shamans, but there is no ecstasy experience. The shamans in Cheju Province perform ritual services for individual families as well as for village gods. There are special village gods who are worshiped and protected by the shaman alone. There are no divine words in this shaman ritual, as with other shamanistic rituals in the south. One interesting aspect of Cheju shamanism is the so-called "large ritual" which continues for three days. During this ritual performance, the shaman provides for the happiness of 18,000 gods.

There are several varieties of shaman ritual performances and functions in Korean shamanism. However, the main object of shamanistic ritual performance is the expulsion of misfortune and the calling for happiness, which includes good fortune, longevity, and wealth for family members. It may be that the main reason for the continued existence of shamanism in Korea has been due to the sincere desires of the people, especially those who are suffering from poverty and anxiety. Throughout their long history in Korea, shamans have had a role as entertainers to the people in addition to their religious functions.

Suggested Further Reading

Ch'oe, Kil-song. 1982. "Community Ritual and Social Structure in Village Korea," *Asian Folklore Studies*. Vol. 41.1.

Harvey, Youngsook Kim. 1979. *Six Korean Women: The Socialization of Shamans*. St. Paul: West Publishing Co.

Janelli, Roger L. and Dawnhee Yim. 1982. *Ancestor Worship and Korean Society*. Stanford: Stanford University Press.

Kendall, Laurel M. 1985. *Shamans, Housewives and Other Restless Spirits*. University of Hawaii Press.

_____. 1988. *The Life and Hard Times of Korean Shaman*. University of Hawaii Press.

Kendall, Laurel and Peterson M. (eds.) 1983. *Korean Women: View From the Inner Room*. New Haven: East Rock Press.

Lee, Kwang-Kyu. 1984. "The Concept of Ancestors and Ancestor Worship in Korea," *Asian Folklore Studies*. Vol. 43.2.

5

Confucianism
by Mark Peterson

1
Introduction

Confucianism has had more influence on Korean life than any other religion or philosophy, yet that influence is subtle and even hidden when compared to Buddhism, Christianity or shamanism. Buddhist temples abound in Korea and are ornate and beautiful. Christian churches are found throughout the country in both cities and the countryside. Even shaman ceremonies are filmed or photographed for television and magazines. Yet few visitors to Korea see a Confucian shrine. Large percentages of Koreans claim to be Buddhist or Christian or followers of shamanism, but everyone in Korea, to one degree or another, is Confucian. Even those who practice other religions (including those who openly criticize Confucianism) perform Confucian rituals on a regular basis and adhere other Confucian values in their everyday life.

One interesting measure of the impact that Confucianism has had on Korea is found on the money. Three units of paper currency feature a king, and two Confucian scholars. King Sejong is on the ₩10,000 note. (A fourth unit, ₩500, featuring a naval hero is no longer in circulation.) Putting a king on the money is common in any culture, but what of the two Confucian scholars ? They held government offices as well, but that was not the reason they are honored on modern money. It was because they wrote commentaries on Neo-Confucian texts and other explanations of Confucianism that made them cultural heroes.

Korea's last dynasty was the most Confucian of all Korean dynasties. After the Korean Yi dynasty (1392-1910), or state of Chosŏn, decided to implement Confucian principles, the impact was felt throughout the society. If Confucius himself were to return to earth and wanted to live in the time and place where his principles were practiced to the highest degree, he would probably choose to live in the last centuries of the Chosŏn period.

2

Historical Setting

Confucianism first entered Korea in the Three Kingdoms period (around the 4th century), but made a greater impact during the Koryŏ period, when a "new" Confucianism began spreading in Korea. This Neo-Confucianism became the official ideology of the dynasty established by the Yi household in 1392. Confucianism was regarded as the perfect ideology in setting up a good government.

Confucius himself was a political consultant who traveled from kingdom to kingdom teaching a system of ethics and benevolence in a world dominated by power-hungry warlords who believed that might made right. On the other hand, the ideas prized by Confucius were *ch'ung* (loyalty), *hyo* (filial piety), *in* (benevolence or human heartedness), and *shin* (trust). An article of faith taught in the most basic Confucian texts was the concept that "never has there been a man who was filial at home who was not loyal to his king."

Interest in Confucianism grew throughout the centuries of the Chosŏn period. The first century saw the political transformation of the government. The second century was marked by advent of the greatest philosophers of Korean Confucianism. The third century saw changes in the lineage and family with the emphasis on the eldest son and the development of the patrilineal lineage system. The fourth century saw kings and other officials seeking perfection as Confucian sages. The fifth century was marked by Confucian traditionalists trying to hold on to the past while the changes in the outside world were starting to overwhelm them.

Looking back on Korean history, there are those who criticize Confucianism for embodying blind conservatism that led to the loss of the country at the hands of the Japanese (from 1910 to 1945). But there are others who point out that the stability of the Chosŏn period, one of the longest lived dynasties in the history of the world, was due to Confucianism. Modern Koreans are divided in their opinions about Confucianism, and yet even those who criticize Confucianism will often observe Confucian protocol in social relations and participate in Confucian style rituals at times of funerals or wedding.

3

Confucian Ideology

What is Confucianism ? At root, it is the teachings of a man who lived in ancient China named Kong Chiu (551-479B.C), but who was known as Master Kong, or Kong Fuzi. The equivalent of that name is expressed in the Roman alphabet as Confucius. His teachings are sometimes called religious, but at other times are called non-religious philosophy. The best appraisal might be to call Confucianism a "this worldly" religion. Unlike Buddhism, which can be called "other worldly" — concerned with the next life — Confucianism is concerned with this life and this world. When a disciple asked Confucius about spirits, he responded that one should stay away from spirits; when asked about the next life, he responded that it was difficult enough to understand this life, how can one even ask about the next life.

Confucianism, the way Confucius taught it, and the way it was practiced in Korea were somewhat different, however. In the centuries after Confucius' time the philosophy became more sophisticated, although it never strayed too far from its roots. The biggest changes took place in the 12th and 13th century when Zhu Xi and other philosophers of the Sung dynasty began a revival and a refurbishing of the ancient beliefs, which later came to be known as Neo-Confucianism. They were concerned with broader questions than those answered in the Confucian classics; not questions of "other world" but questions of the metaphysics of this world. The roots of all life were found in *li* and *chi* (*i* and *ki* in Korean); *li* is translated as principle, and *ki* is often translated as "material force." Each creation has its own shape and form because of its *li*, and each comes into being through *ki*. The ramifications of the philosophy are extremely complicated and have their manifestations throughout the natural world, even in personality and emotions.

Underpinning the principles of government taught by Confucianism were a set of principles that defined social relationships. The formula for expressing these is called the *samgang oryun*, "the three bonds and the five cardinal relationships." The three bonds (unchangeable relationships) are:

1. Sovereign to subject
2. Parent to child
3. Husband to wife.

The five cardinal relationships are expressed as a formula that repeats the three bonds as it defines each in terms of the quality of the relationship and then adds two others. They are:

1. Between sovereign and subject there is justice.
2. Between father and son there is closeness.
3. Between husband and wife there is separation of duties.
4. Between senior and junior there is order.
5. Between friend and friend there is trust.

The relationship between ruler and subject is at times described by the term loyalty, and that between father and son is at times described by the term filial piety (an obscure term limited to translations of the Chinese character that means a faithful and attentive attitude of a child toward the parents).

In other contexts, filial piety is listed first (as in the quotation above, that all who are filial are also loyal), and loyalty follows close behind. Citizens in countries with Confucian traditions often tolerate autocratic governments for long periods because change is equivalent to disloyalty, and thus, is worse than patiently suffering through with bad leaders. Confucianism, however, also calls for goodness and virtue on the part of the leader. The rivals of Confucius in his day were those who believed in power. By comparison, the teachings of Confucius were ethereal and abstract. Yet he taught there was greater power in morality and virtue. In fact, most of the rulers of his day rejected his teachings, and only in later centuries did Confucius become recognized as a sage.

4

Monuments

One of the hallmarks of Confucianism is the setting up of monuments. Confucian architecture is fairly simple, and there is not an iconography as in Buddhism. Monuments were erected to commemorate the contributions of those men who exemplified the values mentioned above—for filial sons (*hyoja*) and for loyal subjects (*ch'ungshin*). But monuments were also set up for outstanding women—faithful wives or widows (*yŏllyŏ*). These monuments were inscribed stone tablets that were several feet tall. Some monuments had little pavilions built over them. The decisions to build such a monument was not a private or even family decision. Only with the permission of the king could a monument be set up.

Monuments erected for loyal subjects were usually to commemorate the contributions of war heroes and high government officials. Those erected for filial sons were to commemorate remarkable acts of sons, usually for those who mourned for the prescribed three years at the grave side of a deceased parent. Monuments for faithful wives and widows were erected for those women who sacrificed for a husband or parents-in-law. There are many stories of heroic women who went to extreme measures to find medicine for an ailing husband or father-in-law. These episodes are recorded in books, primarily collected essays (*munjip*) of prominent men as well as on the monuments. These were serious matters, and important actions of a Confucian government—a government concerned with morality in action.

Other important concepts in Confucianism include a concept that is expressed simply in a Chinese character pronounced *in*. The Chinese character is made of two elements, the symbol for man, and the symbol for the number two. It means the proper or ideal relationship between two people. It is hard to translate, but the terms benevolence, goodness, and human heartedness are often used. If you were to ask a scholar of Confucianism which is the first important concept, some would say *in*, and some would say *hyo* (filial piety).

5

Education

Propriety (*ŭi*), etiquette or ceremony (*ye*), knowledge (*chi*), and trust (*shin*) are also important and have impact on the daily lives of Koreans. These values are acquired through education, which has a striking impact on Korea and other East Asian societies. Today parents make tremendous sacrifices for the sake of educating their children, and children make their own sacrifices to study long hours during their high school years. The value of education has more than abstract underpinnings. Historically, education was the key to social success.

In traditional times, officials were recruited to serve in the government on the basis of passing an examination. The assumption was that good men made good government and that good educations (in the Confucian classics) made men good. Therefore, there was an extensive education and examination system in traditional Korea. It is important to note that the only source of prestige as well as wealth in traditional times was government service. Businessmen were looked down upon. Lawyers, accountants, doctors, scientists, and engineers all served the government officials and were considered members of an inferior social class.

The Confucian classics speak specifically of education: "What is more enjoyable than studying?" And indeed, education was the key to passing state civil service examinations and achieving success in traditional times, and it is today. In today's society, rapid economic development is the hallmark of the day, and again, education is the key to success. It has been said that Korea's education miracle preceded its economic miracle.

The first line of the Analects, one of the Confucian classics, says, "What is more pleasurable than greeting guests who have come from afar!" And just as implied by that passage, Koreans are wonderful hosts. Foreigners are given royal treatment in homes and in restaurants in Korea today.

6
Ceremonies

Not all the statements of the classics translate into action. In spite of the fact that Confucius himself warned people to stay away from spirits, the most important ceremony in Confucianism is the ancestor ceremony. Almost all Koreans perform Confucian-style ceremonies for the dead. There are some who perform Buddhist-style funerals, but many of them perform Confucian-style commemorative ceremonies on the anniversary dates of the death. The ceremonies include the funeral ceremony and annual worship ceremonies, sometimes on an anniversary date (either a birthday or death day) and sometimes on public holidays, at which tables are elaborately set with all kinds of food that is first offered to the dead and then becomes the feast partaken by all the living relatives who attend.

In spite of the fact that Confucius said people ought to only pay attention to this life because we can know nothing of the next life, the ancestor ceremony is offered to the spirits of those who have gone on to that next life. Buddhist temples often have paintings depicting either the punishment or the bliss of the next life, but for Confucianism, where the central ceremony deals with the spirits of the departed, there are no explanations of life in the next world at all, let alone any paintings. The dead live on and their spirits partake of the food offerings that are part of every ancestor ceremony, yet there is no tradition of explaining anything of the conditions or organization of that spirit world. It is a kind of agnosticism. We know the spirits exist, but we don't know anything specific about their existence.

Confucian ceremonies are performed at the family level, at the lineage level, at the county level, and at the national level. The most frequent are those at the family level where family members maintain the memory of elders who have died. The lineage, or segments of the lineage, commemorate remote ancestors who are the apex of a pyramid of descendants that can number from dozens to thousands. Such rituals are usually held once a year at an ancestral hall built for that purpose or at grave side of the deceased.

The county level ceremonies are held at either the *hyanggyo*, the county school of pre-modern times, or at various *sŏwŏn*, private Confucian academies that developed during the latter half of the Chosŏn period. Both the hyanggyo and the *sŏwŏn* served the dual function of a school and a ritual center. The dead who are honored at each hyanggyo include Confucius himself and the eighteen Korean sages—those prominent scholars who have been formally inducted into the National Confucian shrine. The *sŏwŏn* honored a prominent scholar from the area, and at times several of that man's disciples were also enshrined. There were several hundred *sŏwŏn* by the end of the Chosŏn period. Only 47 of them were allowed to remain open but hundreds of them were ordered torn down by the king's regent in the 1860s. In modern times, with greater affluence in Korea, most of those that were torn down have been rebuilt; and each of them is the site for ceremonies honoring the spirits of those enshrined there. The ceremonies at the county level are held twice a month, when there is a full moon and when there is a new moon, and twice a year, with a major ceremony in the spring and one in the fall.

National Confucian ceremonies are held at the National Confucian Academy, the Songgyungwan, in Seoul. There, like the *hyanggyo*, the spirit tablet of Confucius is enshrined together with tablets for the eighteen Korean sages. But in addition there are also tablets for the four disciples of Confucius and sixteen other Chinese who were enshrined in the Chinese shrine to Confucius. The ceremony has a special name, the *sŏkchŏnje*, and is the most elaborate of all the Confucian ceremonies. The *sŏkchŏnje* is held twice a year, once in the spring and once in the fall. There are also minor ceremonies twice a month, but the semi-annual ceremony is by far the most elaborate of the rituals found in all of Korean Confucianism. Today many local dignitaries and many foreign ambassadors attend the ceremony.

The ceremony for the royalty of the Chosŏn period, the Yi Dynasty, is a national ceremony similar to the *sŏkchŏnje* but held only once a year on May First. The site is the shrine to the royal family (Chongmyo) near the fourth section of Chongno in downtown Seoul.

7

Confucianism in the Modern World

Twenty or thirty years ago, before Korea became an economic success story, many people thought Confucianism was one of the factors that was holding Korea back from developing. As they looked at other underdeveloped countries of Asia, their conclusion was reinforced. Confucianism seemed to be an ideology that prevented economic growth as well as other aspects of modernization. Today, however, the opposite interpretation is heard—the miracle economies of East Asia (Korea, Taiwan, Hong Kong, and Singapore), at times called the "four Dragons," are all said to have been successful because of the influence of Confucianism that is common to all four. Religion (or philosophy) can, at times, be interpreted in ways that are polar opposites and such is the case with Confucianism in the modern world.

When Confucianism was blamed for holding Korea back from development, it was the more conservative aspects of the doctrine that were quoted. Now that it is given some of the credit for the development of Korea, it is the orderliness and hierarchical order that is quoted as the reason why people work hard and follow directions. Education is also given as the reason for the development of technology an management skills that are part of the modernization movements in Korea and elsewhere in Asia.

What will Confucianism be like in the future? It is probably safe to say that Confucianism will continue to play an important role in Korea. As society changes, Confucianism makes some adjustments to the new situation, but more importantly, it will probably be one of the constants that people can look to in an ever-changing world.

In recent years, as Koreans have become more affluent, young people have become more nationalistic and have begun looking for old values to cling to as they find themselves awash in a sea of Western ideas and modern economic innovations. Confucianism as a philosophy, as a basis for important ceremonies, as a voice of the ancestors speaking to people today, will continue to play a major role.

Suggested Further Reading

Ching, Julia. 1977. *Confucianism and Christianity*. Tokyo, New York, and San Francisco: Kodansha International.

Janelli, Roger. 1982. *Ancestor Worship in Korean Society*. Stanford: Stanford University Press.

Kim, Kwang-ok. 1988. "A Study on the Political Manipulation of Elite Culture: Confucian Culture in Local Level Politics," *Korea Journal*. Vol. 28, No. ll.

Palmer, Spencer J. 1986. *Confucian Rituals in Korea*. Berkeley, CA: Asian Humanities Press.

Yang, Key P. and Gregory Henderson. 1958-59. "An Outline History of Korean Confucianism," *Journal of Asian Studies*. Part I and Part II.

6

Buddhism
by Donald Baker

1

Introduction

A first-time visitor to the Republic of Korea could be forgiven for mistakenly assuming that South Korea is a Christian country. The hundreds of church steeples which pierce the sky over Seoul encourage such a misperception. Especially since those churches far outnumber the relatively few Buddhist temples in that capital city which a tourist would be likely to notice. Even a sight-seeing tour of the countryside would be unlikely to alter this misleading first impression, since, more often than not, the largest building in Korea's many small villages is a Christian church, not a Buddhist temple.

Yet there are more Koreans who call themselves Buddhists than there are Koreans who call themselves Christians. Moreover, Buddhism has been a part of Korean life much longer than Christianity has. In fact, the history of Buddhism on the Korean peninsula is almost as long as the recorded history of the Korean people themselves. Buddhism has contributed so much for so long to the way Koreans have viewed the world around them, and to the ways Koreans have expressed that vision through literature and the arts, that it is impossible to discuss Korean culture and traditions without mentioning Buddhism.

Buddhism has become an integral part of Korean civilization, despite the fact that it originated in a land so far removed from Korea both geographically and culturally that it took centuries for Buddhist teachings to reach Korea. Sākamuni, the man now known as the Buddha, began preaching his pessimistic insights into the causes of human suffering and his optimistic suggestions for overcoming it, around 2,500 years ago, in the northern corner of the Indian sub-continent.

2

The Teachings of the Buddha

Sometimes during the 5th or 6th century B.C., the Buddha (a title which means the enlightened one and was conferred on him by later generations) began asking why human beings suffer. He wanted to know why it appeared to be impossible for him, and for everyone he knew, to go through life without experiencing pain and unhappiness. After years of wrestling with this problem, he decided it is life itself which is responsible. In other words, to live is to suffer.

He did not mean that people are unhappy from the moment they are born until the moment they die. He recognized that there are times when our lives are trouble free and we are glad to be alive. However, there are also times when we are disappointed and unhappy and even times when we feel physical pain. Such moments, ironically, are the inevitable consequence of our desire for pleasure and happiness. It is only because we seek pleasure that we are disappointed when we fail to obtain it. It is only because we want to feel strong and healthy that an injury or an illness feels so painful. In short, our desires are our downfall.

The Buddha shared the belief in reincarnation which dominated thinking in South Asia 2,500 years ago. This made his conclusion, that life seemed to inevitably lead to suffering, particularly unsettling. As the Buddha saw it, human beings were doomed to be born, suffer, die, and then be born again to repeat that whole cycle once more. They would remain on that wheel of birth and rebirth forever, forced to endure periods of pain and suffering over and over again, unless some way could be found to release them from that cycle once and for all.

The Buddha believed that he found a way. Since it was the desire for pleasure which caused unhappiness, if human beings could only eliminate their desires, they would no longer suffer. That meant eliminating not only the desire to feel good and avoid pain but also the deeper, underlying human craving for permanency. Men want their moments of pleasure, as well as those objects and activities which give them those moments of pleasure, to last forever. In fact, since human beings realize that it is only because they are alive that they are able to enjoy life, they want to live forever. It is this desire for eternal existence which causes reincarnation: human beings are so attached to life that they tie themselves to the wheel of birth and rebirth, and that forces them to submit repeatedly to the pain, suffering, and unhappiness which living inevitably entails.

How could human beings still all their desires, including the desire for life itself, and thus gain release from an eternity spent alternating between pain and pleasure ? The Buddha's answer was that they have to stop taking life and the material world too seriously. They have to develop an attitude of detachment, in which they observe the world around them, with its trials and tribulations as well as its delights and gratifications, without demanding that it provide them with a consistency and a permanency it cannot provide. They have to realize that ultimately the world is not real.

By "real," the Buddha meant "unchanging and unchangeable." Since everything in the world we live in, including ourselves, is constantly changing, it is not real, as the Buddha defined real. It is precisely this unreality which causes pain and suffering, since we feel disappointed and even hurt when something we have grown attached to changes and becomes something else, whether it is a young healthy body turning old and frail or a loved one passing away. If we can keep our minds focused on the ultimate unreality of the world we live in, then we will not be surprised by the inevitable changes in it, and therefore those changes will not disappoint us. In particular, if we remember that we, too, are constantly changing and therefore we, too, are ultimately unreal, we will realize that there is no "we" to feel happy or feel sad. Thus, happiness and unhappiness, pleasure and pain, are equally unreal and thus equally of no real consequence.

This is the basic message of Buddhism. However, in the centuries between the Buddha's sermons and the arrival of Buddhist missionaries in Korea eight centuries later, much was added. As Buddha's followers gradually spread his message throughout India, up into Central Asia and over

into China, they elaborated on the theoretical, philosophical, and psychological ramifications of his musings on the causes of, and solutions to,
human suffering. For example, intricate philosophical schools of thought
developed within Buddhism, all attempting to explain how it is that the
world can be unreal and yet present significant obstacles to our attempts
to escape the suffering it inflicts.

Some believers in Buddhism began to gather together in monastic
communities, hoping that by living together they could help each other
understand the Buddha's teachings better and cultivate the attitude of
detachment he encouraged. Others, looking for supernatural assistance to
supplement their own feeble human efforts to overcome desire, deified
the Buddha so that he became more than just a simple mortal. He came
to be depicted as a historical human manifestation of ultimate reality,
sharing Buddhahood with such others as Vairocana, the primordial
Buddha and Lord of the Cosmos, and Amitabha, the Lord of Paradise.

By the time the Buddha's teaching reached China around five centuries after the Buddha's death, the various buddha's were accompanied
by bodhisattvas, analogous to saints in the Christian tradition. Bodhisattvas
are beings who have earned release from the realm of suffering but, out
of compassion for the less advanced, have postponed their own final
emancipation in order to offer assistance to others who wish to reach that
same goal. Avalokitśvara (*Kwanŭm* or *Kwanseŭm* in Korea), the bodhisattva of unlimited compassion in the here and now, and Maitreya, the
bodhisattva who promised a better world in the future, were objects of
particularly strong popular devotion.

3

The Korean Adoption of State-centered Buddhism

This is the Buddhism which reached Korea at the end of the fourth century. It was a Buddhism which taught a sophisticated and elaborate body of doctrine and worshipped a panopoly of supernatural beings. Moreover, it was a Buddhism which was associated with the advanced civilization of China which the various rival states on the Korean peninsula were just beginning to adopt.

One conspicuous feature of the adoption of Buddhism in Korea is that it was initiated by the highest levels of government. Buddhism was seen as one more tool in the strengthening of royal authority and was not treated at first as a religion for the masses. Only after the rulers of Koguryŏ in 372, Paekche in 384, and Shilla in 572 (these are the traditional dates and may not be accurate) welcomed Buddhist missionaries from China and Central Asia and provided official support for Buddhist temples within their kingdoms did Buddhist slowly begin to penetrate the religious world of the lower-levels of the aristocracy and then the common people. This early state-sponsorship of Buddhism in Korea has meant that Korea Buddhism has often been nationalistic, despite its international origins, and has been characterized as *hoguk* ("protect the nation") Buddhism.

It is this focus on the power of the Buddha to protect Korea that lay behind one of the most well-known contributions of Korea to world Buddhism. In the 11th century, when Korea was threatened by Khitan invasions from Manchuria, the Koryŏ Dynasty spent seventy years carving a complete set of important Buddhist scriptures on printing woodblocks in the hope that the Buddha would be so pleased by this show of respect for his teachings that he would use his divine power to protect Korea. When that set of woodblocks was destroyed two centuries later by Mongol invaders, the Koryŏ court had another set of woodblocks carved. This set, totalling over 81,000 pages, each carved on its own individual printing block, survived the Mongols and subsequent invaders and can be seen today at Hein temple not far from the city of Taegu. This Koryŏ *Tripitaka* is the most comprehensive collection of Chinese-language Buddhist scriptures found anywhere and continues to attract the attention of scholars of Buddhism from all over the world.

Another sign of the nationalist orientation of Korean Buddhism is the *Samguk yusa* (Memorabilia of the Three Kingdoms), one of the oldest surviving histories of early Korea. Written by the monk Ilyŏn (1206-1289), this account of the formation of the Korean nation places much more emphasis on native Korean elements in Korean civilization than does the only earlier history available to us today, the *Samguk sagi* (History of the Three Kingdoms) by the Confucian scholar Kim Pu-sik (1075-1151). For example, it is Ilyŏn, not Kim Pu-sik, who recorded the oldest examples of Korean language poetry, the *hyangga* ("native songs") of Unified Shilla and early Koryŏ, most of them Buddhist in theme and authorship. Ilyŏn also provides the earliest surviving written account of the myth of Tan'gun, giving the people of Korea an ancestry as ancient as that of the Chinese, as well as independent of them.

The relationship between Buddhism and the state was so close during the Koryŏ Dynasty that the government administered a civil service examination for monks, paralleling that used to select bureaucrats, and awarded official titles to those monks who passed those examinations. Those official clerical examinations continued to be held during the 1st century of the following dynasty, even though that Chosŏn Dynasty defined itself as much more Neo-Confucian than Buddhist.

Over the five centuries of the Chosŏn Dynasty, Buddhism lost much of the official patronage it had earlier enjoyed. The examinations for the official appointment of monks were abolished in 1508, for example. Moreover, temples lost most of their tax-free land and monks were no longer welcome as advisors to the king. In fact, both temples and monks in clerical robes were formally barred from Seoul, the capital city, for most of the five hundred years the Chosŏn Dynasty ruled over the Korean peninsula.

Buddhism did not disappear, however. Monks continued to practice and preach Buddhism in temples and monasteries outside of the capital, particularly those situated in mountain valleys and foothills far from government administrative centers. Buddhist beliefs and practices, dismissed as products of superstition and ignorance by the new Neo-Confucian ruling elite, penetrated Korea's villages instead and were incorporated into the folk religion which prevailed among the majority of the Korean population at that time.

Though the Neo-Confucian scholars who ran the Chosŏn Dynasty looked down on Buddhism and Buddhist, they did not hesitate to call upon monks when the nation needed their help. Monk-physicians, for example, were sometimes dispatched by the Chosŏn government to fight regional outbreaks of epidemics. And when the Japanese under Hideyoshi invaded Korea at the end of the 16th century, monks took up arms in defense of their homeland, winning some of Korea's few victories on land in that war. Monks, at royal request, also built Namhan *sansŏng*, the fortress in which the king took brief refuge during the Manchu invasion of 1636.

Despite the contributions they had made to shaping Korean civilization and defending Korean territory in the past, monks and Buddhism have generally not been major players in the 20th century drive to build a modern, strong, and prosperous independent Korean nation. For the last hundred years, both politics and culture on the peninsula have been dominated by representatives of newer religions, such as Christianity.

Buddhism and Korean Culture

Two exceptions stand out, however. Han yong-un (1879-1944) is one of those exceptions. Han was one of only two Buddhists to sign the March First, 1919, Declaration of Independence. (16 Christians and 15 followers of the indigenous *chŏndogyo* religion made up the rest of the 33 signers.) He was both a Buddhist monk, active in the reform and modernization of Korean Buddhism, and a tireless fighter against Korea's Japanese colonial overlords. He was also one of the most important Korean poets of the 20th century. Selections from his 1926 collection of free verse, entitled *Nimŭi ch'immuk* (The Silence of My Beloved), are still widely read and admired today. Han helped both shape the structure and determine the themes of contemporary Korean poetry.

Another well-known Buddhist poet, novelist, and political activist is Ko Ŭn (b. 1933). Ko was a monk for only ten years from 1953 to 1962, but Buddhist themes continue to inspire his prolific writing, including his best-selling novel, *Hwaŏmgyŏng* (Flower Garland Sutra). Since the 1970s he has also been inspired by a passion for democracy and was one of the few with a Buddhist background in the front ranks of those fighting for democracy against the Park Chung-hee and Chun Doo-hwan dictatorships in the 1970s and 1980s.

Despite the high visibility of Han and Ko in both political and literary circles this century, many Koreans today continue to identify Buddhist monks primarily with their contributors to Korean culture in centuries past. It was Buddhist monks who, in the Three Kingdoms periods, first introduced Koreans to the sophisticated painting and architecture of China. Moreover, the history of Korean sculpture was, until this century, primarily a history of Buddhist sculpture. That is why one-third of those objects officially recognized by the Korean government as important cultural treasures today are paintings, statues, pagodas, bronze bell or worship halls found in Buddhist temples or created by Buddhist monks. The famous Sŏkkuram grotto, carved out of the side of a mountain near Kyŏngju in the eighth century to house stone images of the Buddha and thirty-eight of his bodhisattvas, attendants, and guardians, is only one example of how Buddhism inspired many of the greatest products of Korean artistic genius.

Much of the literature and philosophy produced during the Shilla and Koryŏ dynasties was also inspired by Buddhism and written by Buddhist monks. That changed in the Neo-Confucian Chosŏn dynasty, when education came to mean an education in the Confucian classics rather than in the Buddhist scriptures. Though, prior to the 14th century, most of the best writers and best thinkers on the Korean peninsula tended to be Buddhist monks, that has not been the case since.

When Neo-Confucianism lost its control over the intellectual life of Korea at the end of the 19th century, secularism and Christianity, not Buddhism, replaced it. There is only one Buddhist university, Dongguk University, in the Republic of Korea today, and it has to compete with dozens of Christian, private, and government-run universities to attract the brightest students to its campus. Though there have been some active Buddhists among those Koreans who have gone overseas to pursue an advanced education and then have returned home to write books about their experience and what it has taught them. Christian and other non-Buddhist scholars and intellectuals far outnumber them.

Even when a Buddhist scholar did obtain the educational credentials which modern society expects of its writers and thinkers, he would often find that he did not have as many channels for communicating his views to the general population as some others did. Some of the largest bookstores in Korea, including the influential Chongno Sŏjŏk in Seoul, began as Christian enterprise. And until 1990, when the Buddhist Broadcasting System radio station began operation in Seoul, Christians had had a monopoly on religious broadcasting for almost four decades. The result has been that Buddhist voices, with such rare exceptions as Han Yong-un and Ko Ŭn, have been silent or ignored on some of the more important intellectual, political, and cultural issues which have been debated on campuses and in the media as Koreans have sought to redefine Korean culture and Korean identity in the modern age.

5

Modern Buddhism Confronts the Christian Challenge

The problem Buddhist intellectuals and Buddhist monks alike have faced in the 20th century is that contemporary Koreans tend to identify Christianity with modernity, and Buddhism with tradition. Buddhism is seen by many, particularly the urban and the educated, as belonging to traditional Korean culture, and thus more of a museum piece to be admired than as a living religion with values and beliefs relevant in the modern world. Many Buddhist laypeople and clergy are aware of this problem and have tried to clothe Buddhism in a more modern dress. Often this has meant borrowing terminology and techniques from Christians.

In the 1980s, following the painful experience of the Kwangju incident of May 1980, and the political radicalization of the university student population which followed, some Buddhist thinkers began portraying Buddhist doctrine as an activist philosophy concerned for the poor and oppressed and highly critical of unjust and unlawful authority. For the first time in modern Korean history, in 1986 and 1987 young monks in their clerical robes were clearly visible in the ranks of those demonstrating in the streets of Seoul for democratic reforms. At the same time, some older Buddhist intellectuals began talking about *minjung* Buddhism.

The term *minjung* has become a popular way in recent decades in South Korea to refer to the masses who have paid the brunt of the costs of modernization, urbanization, and industrialization. In the 1970s, many progressive Christian professors and pastors preached what they called *"minjung* theology," in which Christ was depicted as one of the poor and oppressed. Christian *minjung* theologians argued that it was therefore the duty of Christians to show their love for Christ by siding with the poor and oppressed against their oppressors. *Minjung* Buddhism did not talk of Christ, of course. Instead progressive Buddhist thinkers wrote that the venerable Bodhisattva tradition of placing the needs of those less fortunate ahead of our own needs should motivate Buddhists to become involved in political issues on behalf of those who have suffered the most at the hands of politicians and the existing socio-economic system.

Just as in Christian circles, minjung activists have been highly visible and vocal but they have not had much influence on the majority of their fellow believers. Those who have focused more on how the Buddhist message is presented, rather than on what that message is, have had more impact.

When Buddhism first began to take roots in Korea over 1,700 years ago, Korea was overwhelmingly rural and agricultural. It remained that way well into this century. As recently as the 1960s, South Korea had almost three times more people living in its villages and small towns than living in its large cities. However, the rapid industrialization and urbanization which began after the Korean War transformed Korean society. By the early 1990s, less than a quarter of the South Korean population earned its living through agriculture and over three-quarters of the South Korean people lived in its cities. Yet the dominant Korean Buddhist denomination, the Chogye order, remained institutionally anchored in the countryside. Over two-thirds of Chogye-run temples are situated in the mountains of South Korea, compared to the less than one out of five located in the large cities where most South Koreans now live.

This traditional rural orientation has made it difficult for Buddhism to compete successfully with Christianity for the allegiance of city dwellers. As a result, Christians outnumber Buddhists in Seoul and its suburbs, though Buddhists outnumber Christians in most of the rest of the country. Buddhists have responded by opening proselytizing centers and small meditation halls in condominium complexes and office buildings to provide places for urban Buddhists to meet, mediate, and discuss Buddhist teachings. Since the 1970s they have also encouraged the formation of lay societies, some of them under the guidance of rural temples, others organized and managed by lay Buddhists themselves without any formal ties to any clerical or monastic bodies. Whether formally affiliated with a mountain temple or not, these lay societies all have one goal in common. They provide a chance for urban Buddhists to meet in small groups and create the social networks, artificial villages of friends in the middle of an impersonal urban environment, which have played such an important role in the rapid spread of Christianity in South Korea in the latter half of the 20th century.

Urban lay Buddhists have also pioneered the modernization of Buddhist music. Koreans are known for their love of song, and some have argued, only half in jest, that one reason Koreans have flocked to Christian churches is that they enjoy the choral singing that is a part of many Christian services. Buddhism has had its own music traditions in Korea, but it has been a monastic, rather than a lay tradition. Moreover, the monks usually chant, rather than sing, in a ponderous style which is quite different from the livelier way popular music is usually sung in modern Korea. Rather than try to imitate traditional chanting, in the 1970s lay Buddhists began taking the words of traditional Buddhist rituals and singing them to melodies borrowed from popular Christian hymns. The piano, which can often be seen along a side wall of the main worship hall in many Korean Buddhist temples today, attests to the growing popularity of this modernization of Buddhist music in response to the Christian challenge.

The publication of a Buddhist Bible in 1972 is further evidence that Buddhists are borrowing Christian tools to counter the popular impression that Christianity is the religion of the future and Buddhism is a religion of the past. Buddhists traditionally did not believe that all of the fundamental doctrines of their religion could be found in just one book. There are a number of ancient revered texts, called sutras, which Buddhists treat as scripture, though those sutras seem at times to contradict each other in what they say about what the Buddha taught, what rules Buddhists should follow, and what practices they should adopt. Some of those sutras emphasize intellectual understanding of the nature of ultimate reality as the best path to the detachment which gives release from suffering. Others stress ritual and prayers as the best way to overcome the problems that life inevitably brings. There are also sutras which offer the hope that faith in the Buddha will be rewarded with rebirth in a paradise free of the suffering and pain found in this world.

These differing presentations of Buddhist doctrine have been viewed as more complementary than contradictory, with each sutra seen as pointing to only one of many ways the teachings of the Buddha can be interpreted. Buddhists have been taught to believe that the eternal truths of Buddhism are to be found in the totality of Buddhist scripture, rather than any specific text. That is why, when the Koryŏ Dynasty wanted to preserve the most important scriptures of the Buddhist religion in a more permanent form than paper, they felt compelled to transfer over 81,000 separate pages of text onto wooden printing blocks. That is also why monks in Korea's Buddhist seminaries are required to study intensively not just one but many different sutras as well as other Buddhist writings from centuries past.

Lay believers with families to take care of and work to attend to do not have the time to read all those Buddhist scriptures, especially since they are written in classical Chinese, a language no more easy for most contemporary Koreans to read than Latin is for most Americans. The Buddhist Bible takes the most important and most popular sections of that massive Buddhist canon, translate them into the modern Korean language, and puts them together in one volume of just a few hundred pages. The final product resembles, both in its size and its binding, Korean versions of the Christian Bible, allowing devout Buddhists to carry their Buddhist Bibles with them and read them on the subway as they ride to work just as many Christians do with their Christian Bibles.

6

The Monastic Core of Korean Buddhism

The Buddhism of the lay urban intellectual, with its resemblance to Christianity in some of its modern elements, is not the Buddhism of most practicing Korean Buddhists, however. Monks and nuns, the most visible active Buddhists and those whom most Koreans thinks of first when they think of Buddhism, continue for the most part to live the way Korean Buddhist monks have lived for centuries. They withdraw from society into isolated monasteries, where they mediate, study the sutras, perform Buddhist ceremonies, and engage in the ritual chanting.

Korean monks and nuns are no different from their fellow monks and nuns in China and Japan in that the ultimate aim of all of their activities is enlightenment, the realization of that state of detachment which will win them release from the world of desires and the suffering those desires cause. What does set Korean monastics apart is the greater inclusiveness of Korean Buddhism. Korean Buddhism appears less sectarian than Buddhism in Japan or traditional China. Korean monastics see nothing incongruous in demanding that meditative monks receive rigorous academic training in technical Buddhist philosophy or in having a hall for the recitation of the Buddha Amitabha's name within the grounds of a doctrinally-oriented monastery.

This respect for the many different paths believers may take to reach the same Buddhist goal contrasts sharply with the rigid divisions Korean Christians have erected among themselves. Korean Buddhists often point with pride to what they call their unique ecumenical spirit of syncretism, which they ascribe primarily to the legacy of two outstanding Korean Buddhist monks: Wŏnhyo (617-686) of the Shilla Dynasty and Chinul (1158-1210) of the Koryŏ Dynasty.

Wŏnhyo was one of the few leading monks of Shilla times who never visited China. Because he spent his whole life in Korea and never met any of the leading Chinese Buddhist thinkers of his day, no ties of personal friendship or discipleship forced him to support any one particular approach to Buddhist teaching over another. That left him free to read the sutras and commentaries of all the competing Chinese interpretations of Buddhist doctrine. He found something of value in all of them, arguing that, despite their apparent contradictions, they were all essentially nothing more than different manifestations of the same underlying One Mind. Moreover, when he was not writing treatises harmonizing the arguments of the various philosophical schools of Buddhist philosophy, Wŏnhyo wandered through the villages of Korea, encouraging illiterate peasants to adopt the Pure Land tradition of reciting the name of the Amitābha Buddha, the Lord of Paradise. He believed that those who could not follow the cerebral arguments of Buddhist metaphysics should be provided less intellectual means to advance toward enlightenment.

By the time of Chinul, in the 12th century, Wŏnhyo's preference for inclusiveness in both doctrine and practice dominated scholastic Buddhism on the peninsula. However, by then that intellectual approach to enlightenment had a challenger. Meditative Buddhism, known as Sŏn in Korea but better known in the West by its Japanese name of Zen argued that an overreliance on the written word of the sutras made it more difficult to go beyond the sutras to the worldless state of enlightenment. Sŏn advocates criticized the emphasis doctrinal schools placed on obtaining an intellectual grasp of obscure points of Buddhist philosophy, insisting that monastics should spend less time studying and spend more time in meditation instead, stilling their desires by stilling their mind.

Chinul brought the two approaches together. He believed that the lengthy and intensive study of Buddhist sutras was an essential preparation for successful meditative practice. he insisted that monks and nuns had to be well-versed in the verbal teachings of Buddhist tradition before they could move beyond them into the non-verbal realm of enlightenment. Chinul's two step approach to Buddhist practice has become the dominant model for monastic life in Korea. The largest Buddhist denomination in Korea today, the Chogye order, borrows its name from the mountain where Chinul established his first community of practitioners. In the spirit of Chinul, the Chogye order embraces both doctrinal and meditative traditions, as does the T'aego order, the second largest. The only major difference between those two denominations, which together claim the allegiance of well over half the Buddhists in Korea, is that the T'aego order allows its monks to marry while the Chogye order insists on celibacy.

7

The Buddhist Faithful

Despite the monastic image of Buddhism in Korea, lay believers far out-number monks and nuns. There are only around 25,000 Buddhist monks and nuns in South Korea, compared to between 12 million (according to a government survey in 1991) and 20 million (according to the membership figures reported by Buddhist denominations in 1990) lay followers. Some of these lay Buddhists, like the monks and nuns they admire, are primarily interested in the spiritual message of Buddhism. They share the monastic goal of detaching themselves from the things of this world, though they recognize that as lay people immersed in mundane affairs of this world they cannot expect to make as much progress as those who have retreated to a monastery.

Others, and it is impossible to estimate how large a percentage of the total Buddhist population they are, look upon Buddhism much as the kings of the ancient Three Kingdoms did. They look to buddhas and bodhisattvas for supernatural assistance in obtaining more material blessings in this world as well as for help in protecting those blessings they already have. In particular, they pray and make offerings at temples in the hope that they will thereby be assured of both wealth and health for themselves and for their family members. These are the Buddhists, for example, who make monetary donations to a temple in return for a promise that a monk will pray for one hundred consecutive days that their eldest son will be accepted into one of Korea's top universities. These are the Buddhists who hike up a mountain to bow repeatedly before a statue of Kwanŭm carved into the summit and pray that the first child of their newly-married daughter will be a boy. And these are the Buddhists who place pebbles on the top of small mounds of pebbles in and around temple grounds as a sign of their faith that the buddhas and bodhisattvas will grant their requests.

A typical Buddhist temple compound in Korea addresses both the spiritual and pragmatic concerns of the faithful. Along with a main hall, where religious services are held before a statue of a major Buddhist figure such as Sākamuni or Vairocana, there will often be one or two smaller worship halls off to the side for those who have specific requests to make of Kwanum, the Bodhisattva of Compassion, or Yaksa Yŏrae, the Buddha of Healing. Behind the main buildings, but still within the temple grounds, most major temples will have an additional small building or two where prayers can be addressed to the local mountain god or to the Big Dipper Deity (the spirit of good fortune).

When questioned, monks will often dismiss those shrines as intrusions of Korea's worldly folk religion into a pure Buddhism which teaches detachment from such worldly concerns as the sex of a grandchild or the ranking of a son's university. Nonetheless, the large number of devout visitors to those temples who also visit those shrines and pray before them, indicates that many practicing Korean lay Buddhists turn to Buddhism for help in fulfilling desires, not eliminating them.

In fact, Buddhism is so widely viewed as a useful tool for obtaining those things necessary for a better life in this world that at times it is difficult to tell where Buddhism ends and shamanism begins. Many shamans call themselves bodhisattvas (*posal*) these days and a Buddhist symbol on the gate of a house often means that a shaman lives within and is available for fortune-telling and relaying requests to spirits and ghosts. Since shamans and their clients usually answer "Buddhism" when asked which religion they believe in, it is unclear how many of the millions of Koreans listed in government figures as Buddhist actually would qualify as Buddhist if adherence to Buddha's teachings was the criterion.

What we do know is that many more Koreans are willing to call themselves Buddhists now than were seventy, thirty, or even ten years ago. We also know something about who those self-proclaimed Buddhists are, compared to those who identify themselves as Christians.

In the 1920s and the 1930s, when Korea was under Japanese rule, less than 200,000 Koreans in the entire peninsula were willing to identify themselves publicly as Buddhist. After liberation from Japanese rule and the Korean war, that number rose dramatically. In 1962 Buddhist denominations claimed almost 700,000 followers in South Korea alone, a little more than half of the more than 1.3 million Christians in South Korea. As the number of Christians grew, the number of Buddhists grew even faster. In 1985 a government census found a little more than 8 million Buddhists in South Korea, compared to 8.3 million Christians. A more recent survey, in 1991, found that the number of self-proclaimed Buddhists had surpassed the number of Christians for the first time in modern Korean history. Of the 54% of the entire South Korean population which claimed a religious affiliation, over half (51.2%) called themselves Buddhists, compared to the 45% who said they were Catholic or Protestant. That means that, as Korea nears the end of the 20th century, over one out of every four South Koreans proudly proclaims him or herself a follower of the Buddha. Korean Buddhism clearly can no longer be dismissed as a religious relic of Korea's past, doomed to disappear into irrelevancy as Korea modernizes.

This does not mean, however, that Buddhism will replace Christianity any time soon as the most active and most visible organized religious force in South Korea, despite its apparent rise to numerical superiority. It is not clear why there are so many more people calling themselves Buddhists now than there were twenty, forty, or sixty years ago. It could mean that modern Buddhist hymns and the vernacular Buddhist Bible have proven to be powerful proselytizing tools and that those numbers reflect a genuine rise in Buddhist devotees. However, it could also mean that more Koreans have simply adopted the Western practice, introduced into Korea by Christians, of identifying with a specific religious orientation.

It is possible that many of those new Buddhists may have been Buddhists all along but never saw themselves as such nor bothered to proclaim themselves as such until the last couple of decades. As Buddhism has modernized its image in South Korea, there may be less of a stigma attached to calling oneself a Buddhist. A rise in Korean national pride may be another reason for that rise in the number of Buddhists found by Korean census takers. When Korea was an undeveloped nation, many Koreans felt somewhat ashamed of their traditional culture. That is no longer the case. Growing economic strength has led to a growing pride in things Korean. A public assertion of a belief in Buddhism may be another way to assert a pride in a Korean heritage.

Though we cannot say for certain why there has been such a rapid increase in the number of South Koreans willing to call themselves Buddhists over the last three decades, we can say that those who proclaim they are Buddhist do not appear, on the average, to be as fervent or as active in their faith as Korean Christians are. Though over 90% of

Christians say they contribute financially to their churches several times a year, over half of all Buddhists say they make such donations only twice a year or even less often. That could be because they do not attend Buddhist services very often. Over half of all Buddhists said they seldom, if at all, attend a Buddhist service, though 76% of all Protestants and 67% of all Catholics claim that they attend Christian worship services at least once a week. Moreover, 55% of all Korean Buddhists say they never read the sacred scriptures of their faith, compared to the 67% of Protestants and 47% of Catholics, who read their Bible at least once a week. Korean Buddhism clearly does not demand as much money, time, or fervor from its followers as Christianity does.

We also know that Korean Buddhists, in general, tend to be female rather than male, though the leadership (except in the Pomun order which is run by and for nuns) is overwhelmingly male. The T'aego order, for example, claims almost three times as many woman followers as males. Buddhists are also more likely than Christians to live in rural areas, where they outnumber Christians almost two to one. In what is probably a related phenomenon, they are also less educated, on the average. Almost one out of every three university graduates in South Korea is Christian, but only 7% of university graduates say they are Buddhists. The reverse is true of those who never went beyond elementary school. Almost 29% of them are Buddhists, versus only 16% who are Christians. The fact that Korean Buddhists tend to be less educated and more rural may be reflection of the fact that they are also older. Over 28% of Koreans over 40 are Buddhists, compared to less than 10% of those between 18 and 24. Christianity, on the other hand, claims the allegiance of 25% of those between 18 and 24 but drops to less than 20% of those over 40.

Does this mean that as the older generation dies off and is replaced by the newer, less Buddhist generation, and as more and more Koreans move to the cities and receive more and more education, Buddhism will disappear from the Korean peninsula? That is highly unlikely. Korean Buddhism has shown amazing resiliency since the Korean war, and there are now more Korean Buddhists than at any previous time in Korean history. Even North Korea, which is officially atheist, has been forced to concede that Buddhism cannot be eliminated from the peninsula. P'yŏngyang hosts the headquarters of an official Korean Buddhist Federation, with a membership of several thousands in the Democratic People's Republic of Korea.

Korean Buddhism will surely change in the years ahead, just as it has changed in the past, but those changes will not be so great that they threaten the essential Buddhist values, beliefs, and practices at its core. Nor will it change so much that it will no longer attract a substantial number of Korean believers. As long as there are Koreans, there will be some Koreans who are Buddhists. And as long as there are Korean Buddhists, Buddhism will remain an integral part of a proud and vibrant Korean tradition and culture.

Suggested Further Reading

Buswell, Robert. 1983. *The Korean Approach to Zen: The Collected Works of Chinul.* Honolulu: University of Hawaii Press

_____. 1989. *The Formation of Ch'an Ideology in China and Korea: The Vajrasamadhi-Sutra, A Buddhist Apocryphon.* Princeton: Princeton University Press.

_____. 1992. *The Zen Monastic Experience.* Princeton: Princeton University Press.

Ch'en, Keneth. 1964. *Buddhism in China: A Historical Survey.* Princeton: Princeton University Press.

Grayson, James H. 1989. *Korea: A Religious History.* Oxford, England: Clarendon Press

Harvey, Peter. 1990. *An Introduction to Buddhism.* Cambridge, England: Cambridge Press.

Keel, Hee-sung. 1984. *Chinul: The Founder of Korea Sŏn Buddhism.* Berkeley, California: Institute of South and Southeast Asian Studies.

Korean Buddhist Research Institute (ed.) 1933. *The History and Culture of Buddhism in Korea.* Seoul: Dongguk University Press.

Pak, Sung Bae. 1983. *Buddhist Faith and Sudden Enlightenment.* Albany: State University of New York Press

7

Christianity
by Donald Baker

1

Introduction

In 1991 the government of the Republic of Korea, as part of a broader survey to obtain a statistical snapshot of its citizenry, asked its citizens what their religious beliefs were. It had asked such questions before and had noticed that the number of people professing a specific religious orientation was steadily rising. That trend continued in 1991. For the first time in the history of the Republic of Korea, a majority of South Koreans proclaimed an allegiance to a specific religious tradition.

In 1985, 57.5% of South Koreans told census takers that they had no particular religious affiliation, compared with 42.5% who identified themselves as Buddhists, Christians, or members of other, smaller religious communities. Over the next six years, that ratio was almost reversed. In 1991, 54% of the South Korean population proudly proclaimed a specific religious orientation, compared with 46% who still answered none when asked which religion they believed in. Sometime toward the end of the 1980s, South Korea had become a nation with a religious majority.

Actually, this change may be more apparent than real. Koreans have always been a highly religious people. The rituals and spirits of the folk religion, including shamanism, have probably been a part of Korean village life for as long as there have been Korean villages. Moreover, Neo-Confucianism served as the functional equivalent of religion for Korea's ruling elite for most of the five centuries of the Chosŏn Dynasty. However, until relatively recently, Koreans usually did not identify with one particular religious tradition at the exclusion of others.

That is the reason Japanese records from the colonial period (1910-1945) identify only a small percentage of the Korean population as religious. When the Japanese, who kept detailed records on all aspects of Korean life and society when they controlled Korea from 1910 to 1945, asked Koreans for their religious affiliation, they found that most Koreans said they had none. Out of a population for the entire peninsula of 23.5 million, less than a million told their Japanese questioners that they had any specific religious preference. And of those, over half proclaimed themselves Christians.

It is no accident that Japanese statistics show more Christians than adherents of any other religion in Korea during the colonial period. Christians were the ones who introduced to Korea the notion of separate and distinct communities of faith, in which belief in one religion prohibits belief in another religion or even participation in its rituals. Until Christianity came to Korea, most Koreans did not think of themselves as Buddhists rather than Confucians, or of Buddhism and shamanism as mutually exclusive. It has been primarily in response to Christians proudly proclaiming that they are Christians that other Koreans have chosen religious labels for themselves.

That is why, as the number of Christians in South Korea has grown, so has the number of self-proclaimed Buddhists. Of the self-consciously religious population in 1991, approximately 12 million call themselves Buddhists, affirming allegiance to a Korean religious tradition over 1,500 years old. However, almost as many South Koreans (10.5 million) call themselves Christians, a remarkable phenomenon in a nation which had no Christians at all until a couple of centuries ago and still had only a half million Christians as recently as 1940.

The large number of Christians in South Korea, over 24% of the population, is particularly surprising, considering the neighborhood Korea is in. In neither China nor Japan do Christians make up more than 1% of the population. The only other nations in that part of the world which have substantial Christian populations are either populated chiefly by immigrants from historically Christian nations of Europe or are former colonies of such Christian nations. Unlike Australia and New Zealand, Korea does not have a large number of citizens of European descent. Nor was Korea colonized by a European power, like Vietnam and the Philippines were. Korea's colonizer was the non-Christian nation of Japan and the Korean people are a homogeneous people, with little immigration into their peninsula since the beginning of the Christian era. Nonetheless, there have been Korean Christians on the peninsula for a little more than two hundred years and, in the 20th century, they have became a significant part of the Korean population.

2

The First Christians

The first Christians in Korea were Roman Catholics. In 1784 a young Confucian scholar named Yi Sŭng-hun (1756-1801) returned from Beijing, where he had accompanied his father on a diplomatic mission, and announced to his friends that he had been baptized a Catholic by a French priest who lived in that Chinese capital. At that point there were no Catholic missionaries in Korea, so Yi Sŭng-hun began preaching his new faith on his own. Yi quickly converted quite a few other Confucian scholars. That was when his troubles began.

Male members of the Confucian scholarly elite during the Chosŏn Dynasty were required to perform Confucian mourning rituals when their parents died. Catholics, however, were forbidden to perform or participate in such rituals, since authorities in Rome had ruled that such rituals were a form of ancestor worship and thus were forbidden as idolatrous. When the mother of Yun Chi-chung (1759-1791) died, and that Korean convert to Catholicism did not perform a proper Confucian memorial service for her, he and his fellow Korean Catholics were immediately attacked as perverted followers of an immoral religion. Yun was sentenced to death by the Neo-Confucian government in Seoul for his violation of Confucian moral principles, becoming Korea's first Christian martyr.

He was not to be the last. Thousands more were martyred over the next century. The king at the time of Yun's execution, King Chŏngjo (r.1776-1800), tried to minimize the persecution of Christians, hoping that those Catholics would soon come to see the error of their ways on their own. His successor was not as patient, particularly when it was discovered that the infant Catholic community had grown to almost 10,000 strong by 1800. Whats more, those Catholics had further defied the government ban on Christianity by smuggling a Chinese priest into Korea to serve as their pastor.

Soon after King Chŏngjo died and a new king assumed the throne in 1800, government officials learned that Fr. Zhou Wen-mo (1752-1801) had been secretly ministering to Catholics on the peninsula for almost six years. They began interrogating and executing those who had helped that Chinese priest enter Korea and aided him in carrying out his underground pastoral activities. One young convert escaped into the mountains, where he composed a letter to the French bishop of Beijing, asking that bishop to send the French navy to Korea to force the Korean government to grant religious freedom to Catholics. Unfortunately for Hwang Sa-yŏng (1755-1801), his letter was intercepted. After the government read his plea for foreign military assistance, the persecution intensified. Catholics were hunted down not just for being immoral but for being subversive as well.

Hundreds of Koreas first Christians were executed in 1801. The government was not able to capture all of the Catholics at that time, however, and there were more major persecutions in 1839, 1846, and 1866 through 1869. The number of Catholics executed by the Chosŏn Dynasty government reached into the thousands by the end of the 19th century. Of that number, 103 were singled out for particular piety and steadfastness under persecution and were canonized by Pope John Paul II when he visited Korea in 1984. Of those 103 canonized saints, ten were French priests who had begun smuggling themselves into Korea in 1836. Together with the 93 Korean martyrs who joined them in sainthood, they allow Koreans to brag that Korea has more officially recognized Catholic saints than any other nation outside of Western Europe.

During these decades of persecution in the 19th century, Korean Catholics retreated into remote mountain valleys where they established Catholic villages in which they grew tobacco or made the earthenware pots in which Korean housewives stored food before the advent of refrigerators. Their main contacts with non-Catholic Koreans came from the infrequent trips they made out of their Catholic villages down to rural market towns to sell their goods. Otherwise, they tried to ignore the larger world around them. Consequently, when winds of change began to blow across the Korean peninsula in the last quarter of the 19th century, the Catholic community had its sails down.

3

The Arrival of Protestantism

Though the first Protestant missionaries did not arrive in Korea until 1884, a hundred years after the first conversions to Catholicism, those Protestants were the ones who established Koreas first modern medical facilities and first modern schools. Horace Allen (1858-1932), an American Presbyterian, opened the first hospital in Seoul in 1885. The next year Methodist missionaries from the US opened two modern schools in the capital city. One of those schools, the first school in Korea to provide formal education for women, later grew into Ehwa Womans University, regarded as one of the best universities in Korea today and one of the largest all-womans universities in the world.

Protestant missionaries were able to operate openly in Seoul, though Catholics were still hiding out in the countryside, because they arrived at a time when the Korean government was beginning to recognize the need for modernization. The Protestant missionaries, from the U.S., Canada, Australia, and the United Kingdom, presented themselves more as modernizers than as missionaries. A beleaguered government, under unprecedented pressure from both China and Japan, turned a blind eye to their proselytizing activities in order to take advantage of their knowledge of the modern world and modern technology.

The Korean government was forced by pressure from Western governments to openly recognize religious freedom in 1898, allowing Catholics and Protestants alike to move and preach freely throughout the peninsula. Nonetheless, Protestant converts continued to be much more visible in politics, in education, and in the media than were Korean Catholics, reinforcing this early identification of Protestant Christianity with modernity. Though there were more Catholics than Protestants in Korea until early in the 20th century, Koreas Catholics remained concentrated in the countryside and relatively inactive in the public affairs. Unlike the Protestants, the Catholics did not open many highly visible urban medical clinics or schools. Under the guidance of conservative priests from France, Koreas Catholic community, over 40,000 in number in 1900, focused most of its attention on spiritual matters, leaving matters of this world to others.

That may be one reason many Koreans in the early part of the 20th century thought that Catholicism and Protestantism were two separate religions, rather than merely two different versions of Christianity. Protestants built schools and hospitals and prayed to a God they called either *hananim*, a term meaning the one true God coined by the first Protestant missionaries from native Korean elements, or *hanŭlnim*, a colloquial Korean term for the lord of heaven. Catholics, on the other hand, made clay pots, built brick churches rather than hospitals or schools, and prayed to a God they called ch'ŏnju, the less colloquial, Sino-Korean equivalent of the Protestant term *hanŭlnim*.

Moreover, Catholic priests were celibate, spoke French (over half of the foreign priests in Korea in the first part of this century came from France) and intoned their ritual prayers in Latin. Protestant missionaries, on the other hand, were married, spoke English (over half of them came from the U.S.), and baptized and prayed in Korean. They seemed as different from each other as Buddhist monks were from shamans.

Even though Catholics and Protestants now use the same Korean translation of the Bible, the Catholic mass is now said in Korean rather than in Latin, and Catholics and Protestants now share the term *Hanŭlnim*, many Korean's continue to think of them as quite different. When Koreans talk of "Christians," usually they mean Protestants. Catholics are called *kat'ollik* instead.

4

Christianity, Nationalism, and Modernization

Superficial differences of language and terminology were reinforced by differences in behavior, particularly when Korea was struggling to establish itself as a modern independent nation. Many of those converted by the first Protestant missionaries were converted to more than the religion from the West. They were also converted to many of the secular values, beliefs, and assumptions of the modern world which those missionaries also brought to Korea. Early reformers such as Yun Ch'i-ho (1865-1945) and Sŏ Chae-p'il (1866-1951), who joined forces in 1896 to establish the *Independent*, Korea's first modern newspaper, argued explicitly that Christianity, modernization, and national independence went hand in hand. They were thinking in particular of the United States, where they had both studied and where they had both noticed a large Protestant population.

As well-known Protestants who also actively promoted the adoption of the latest institutions and technology from the West in order to preserve Korea's independence from foreign control, Yun and Sŏ created an image of Protestants as modernizers and nationalists. Drawn by their example and their rhetoric, many more reformers, modernizers, and nationalists were attracted to the Presbyterian and Methodist churches which missionaries were erecting all over Korea by the end of the 19th century. By contrast, Catholics were mostly quiet during this critical period in Korea's history. That could be because, in contrast to the Protestant reformers, there were then no Korean Catholics with a modern education acquired in the West.

Another reason Catholicism failed to forge a link with nationalism and political reform is that the Korean Catholic Church was under foreign control. In 1900, Korea had twelve Korean priests (all of them ordained in 1898), compared to forty foreign priests. That ratio became somewhat more favorable over the next few decades but foreign missionaries continued to outnumber Korean-born priests. As late as 1940, when the number of Korean priests had risen to 139, the number of foreign priests had risen as well, to 169. Moreover, from 1891 until 1933, the head of the Korean Catholic Church was Bishop Gustav Charles Mutel of France. There was not one single Korean bishop in the Korean Catholic Church until 1942, after the Japanese had expelled most of the foreigners, including foreign bishops. And it was not until 1965 that the local church hierarchy was firmly in Korean hands, with seven Korean bishops outnumbering five foreign bishops. Only three years earlier, in 1962, the Korean Catholic Church had finally been granted self-rule by the Vatican and given independent dioceses and archdioceses, after more than a century and a half of direct oversight by Rome.

Protestant churches in Korea were much more independent. Soon after they arrived on the peninsula, Presbyterian missionaries, the largest Protestant contingent, decided to make the Korean church self-supporting, self-governing, and self-propagating as soon as possible. In accordance with that plan, in 1901 missionaries opened a Presbyterian seminary in P'yŏngyang to train Korean ministers. They took the next step toward self-governance in 1907, when an independent Presbytery of the Presbyterian Church in Korea was established by thirty-three foreign missionaries and thirty-six Korean elders.

Perhaps because so much of the responsibility for promoting Protestantism in Korea had been turned over to the Koreans so quickly, Protestantism grew at a very rapid rate and the number of Protestants quickly surpassed the number of Catholics. A revival meeting in P'yŏngyang in 1907 sparked an explosion of religious fervor which led to a doubling of Church membership over the figures for 1905. By 1910 Protestant churches in Korea claimed to have over 100,000 members, with two-thirds of those Korean Christians attending Presbyterian churches and the rest in Methodist congregations.

This rapid expansion of Christianity was occurring at the same time that the nation of Korea was rapidly losing its independence to Japanese imperialism. Despite the misgivings of foreign missionaries, many Korean Christians became involved in nationalistic, anti-Japanese politics. In 1907 many leading Christians joined with a few non-Christians to form the

Shinminhoe (New Peoples Association), an organization dedicated to working publicly to strengthen Korean education and the Korean economy while planning privately for an armed struggle against the Japanese takeover of Korea. Soon after the Japanese completed their annexation of Korea in 1910, Japanese colonial authorities attacked the Shinminhoe.

In 1911, Japanese police charged that the Shinminhoe had conspired to assassinate Governor-General Terauchi Masatake at a town in northern Korea which was over half Christian. Colonial authorities arrested almost seven hundred Koreans and eventually brought 105 of them to trial. Most of those indicted were Protestants (one was Catholic) and during the trial the prosecution claimed that the accused had conspired with the Methodist Bishop M.C. Harris and with the Presbyterian missionaries Horace Underwood and Samuel Moffett. Though some of the Christian political activists ensnared in this conspiracy trial, such as Yun Ch'i-ho, were so frightened by the experience that they shied away from politics once they were released from prison, Protestant Christianity came away from this trial with an even stronger nationalist image.

That image was further strengthened in the independence movement of 1919. On March 1st of that year, 33 prominent Koreans issued a public statement denouncing Japanese colonial rule and asserting the Korean people's desire for independence. Sixteen of those signers were Christian. (Two Buddhists also signed, as did 15 followers of the indigenous religion ch'ŏndogyo.) Of the thousands who were arrested in nationwide demonstrations in the weeks following that declaration, almost 20% were Protestants, though at that time Protestants made up only about 1% of the overall population. Catholics, too, were arrested in those nationalistic protests, though in much smaller numbers. Only 54 of those arrested declared themselves Catholics, about one-quarter the number of Buddhists arrested, compared to over 2,700 Presbyterians and Methodists.

The next opportunity for Christians to display their nationalistic fervor came in 1935. That was when Japanese officials began demanding that Korean students, teachers, and government employees participate in regular rituals honoring the Japanese emperor at Shintō shrines in Korea. Catholics were spared the painful dilemma of having to choose between the commands of their church and the demands of their government when Rome ruled, in 1936, that Shintō ceremonies were political, not religious, and therefore Catholics could take part in them. By acceding to Japanese demands, Catholics lost a chance to acquire an aura of nationalistic resistance to colonial oppression.

Protestants, on the other hand, did resist the Japanese demands at first and many were imprisoned for doing so, polishing their nationalistic credentials in the process. However, in 1938, under strong pressure from the Government-General, the Presbyterian General Assembly joined the Vatican in declaring Shintō rituals non-religious in nature. That surrender to Japanese pressure created rifts which simmered for years before exploding after liberation in 1945 and fracturing Korean Protestantism.

5

Growth and Division after Liberation

Liberation in 1945, and the subsequent division of the peninsula into a Communist-controlled North and an anti-Communist South, presented Christianity in Korea with an additional challenge: the loss of a substantial number of churches along with much of their congregations. For Catholics, that meant the loss of South P'yŏngan Province, which in 1945 had the second largest concentration of Catholics in all Korea, second only to Kyŏnggi Province in which Seoul was located. In all, over one-third of all the Catholics in Korea in 1945 lived north of the 38th parallel, an area soon severed from any formal association with religious organizations in the south.

The threat to Protestant organizations was even more severe. Almost three out of five Protestants lived in that part of Korea which came under Communist control. South P'yŏngan province alone, where P'yŏngyang was located, had 30,000 more Protestants than lived in and around Seoul, and North P'yŏngan province had even more. Many pastors and lay people were able to flee south, however, preferring a government run by the Methodist Syngman Rhee to one run by Kim Il-sung, who had a Christian education but had since become a dedicated Communist.

That influx of refugees, combined with disputes between those who had given in to Japanese demands for participation in Shintō ritual and those who had gone to prison for refusing to do so, led to a Protestant church in disarray. In addition, the social disruption caused by the Korean

War in 1950 and then the rapid migration from villages to cities which followed the end of the war in 1953, dissolved traditional community ties as well as the trust and mutual respect they fostered. The result was factionalism and a fragmentation of Korean Protestantism which continues today.

In 1951 a group of Presbyterians centered around Korea Theological Seminary in Pusan broke away from the General Assembly of the Presbyterian Church in Korea to form the General Assembly of the Presbyterian Church in Korea, Korea Seminary faction. They were upset at the refusal of their fellow Presbyterians to declare that the Presbyterian Church in Korea should publicly repent its failure to successfully resist Japanese demands for participation in Shintō rituals. They also disagreed with the theology taught in the main Presbyterian seminary in Seoul, which they considered too liberal. They remain a separate Korean Presbyterian sub-denomination today, with almost 200,000 men and women attending their over 1,300 churches.

Despite the departure of their most conservative adversaries, the professors at that seminary continued to come under attack for teaching a somewhat more liberal theology than was usual among Korean Presbyterians. Refusing to be intimidated by such condemnation, in 1952 they and those who shared their theological orientation broke away to form their own General Assembly of the Presbyterian Church in the Republic of Korea. That group is commonly known as the Christ Presbyterian Church of Korea and claims the allegiance of approximately 330,000 of Koreas Presbyterians.

After the departure of both its left and right wings, the mainstream Presbyterian General Assembly, commonly known as the Jesus Presbyterian Church of Korea, itself broke up in 1959 into two rival general assemblies. The main issue this time was whether or not to affiliate with the World Council of Churches. Those in favor of affiliation became the more liberal General Assembly of Presbyterian Churches in Korea, Ecumenical. Those who opposed such an affiliation, on the grounds that the World Council of Churches appeared to be a Communist front, formed a more conservative General Assembly of Presbyterian Churches in Korea, Non-ecumenical. That dispute split Korean Presbyterian roughly in half, with each side now claiming the allegiance of approximately 2 million members attending around 5,000 different churches.

These are only the major divisions dividing Korean Presbyterians. In 1992, Presbyterians in South Korea, who comprised almost 60% of all Protestants, could choose from 74 different groups, each claiming to represent true Korean Presbyterianism. At least 8 of those groups claimed over

100,000 followers in their camp. The other denominations are not as divided. Most Methodists belong to one unified Korean Methodist Church The Korea Evangelical Church is only a little larger than its rival, the Jesus Korea Holiness Church. And the Korea Baptist Convention embraces a majority of South Korean Baptists, though the Southern Baptist Convention of Korea and the Korean Evangelical Baptist Church each claim over 100,000 members.

A number of other Protestant organizations are represented in South Korea as well, from Anglicans and Lutherans to the Assemblies of God and the Salvation Army. Korean Christians trying to decide which brand of Protestantism they prefer have a dazzling array of denominations and sub-denominations to choose from. Competition among all these varieties of Christianity has fueled much of the remarkable growth of Protestant Christianity since 1960, from less than 500,000 baptized Christians in 1962 to over 2 million Protestants in 1970, over 5 million in 1980, and a little more than 8 million in 1991.

The proselytizing fervor of Korea's Protestants is one reason why almost one out of five South Koreans is now Protestant. Another reason may be the rapid urbanization and industrialization of the Republic of Korea, which has ripped millions of Koreans out of villages where they had been surrounded by family and friends and placed them in an impersonal urban environment. Churches can provide an oasis of friendship and community in a desert of strangers, which could be the reason there have been many more conversions to Christianity in the cities than in the countryside, and why the rate of growth for Protestant churches has slowed as urbanization has slowed. A third factor could be that Christianity has been identified in Korea with the West, and with the modernization and nationalism which interaction with the West has brought Korea this century. Since Christianity is often seen by South Koreans as part and parcel of the modern world, a modern world which is often indistinguishable in their eyes from the Western world, the more education South Koreans receive, and the more modern or Western ideas and values they are likely to hold, the more likely they are to be Protestant.

Many of the same factors which have fueled Protestant growth since the end of the Korean War have ignited a rapid increase in the number of Korean Catholics as well. Korean Catholicism is no longer the quiet, rural, withdrawn and isolated church it once was. It now shares the aura of modernity.

Unhindered by denominational fission and energized by a growing number of Korean priests and bishops, after the Korean War the Korean

Catholic Church began to show more concern for the material as well as the spiritual needs of the Korean people. Catholic welfare services were some of the most effective organizations helping war refugees with food, clothing, and housing in the 1950s. In gratitude, many Koreans began to take the Catholic version of Christianity more seriously. By 1962, according to one government survey, there were more baptized Catholics than baptized Protestants in Korea.

Protestants soon retook the lead they had held since the early part of the century. However, Catholicism has continued to grow at a steady rate, reaching the one million mark in 1974 and then doubling to two million by 1986. Spurred on by two visits by Pope John Paul II (in 1984 and 1989), growth accelerated in the 1980s. By 1993 there were three million Catholics in South Korea, almost 6% of the population, up from 2% in 1962.

One reason the Catholic Church in Korea has become more visible and has attracted more adherents is that, after the Korean War, it became an urban church erecting modern urban institutions. In 1956 less than 18% of Korea's Catholics lived in Seoul and only 35% lived in South Koreas five largest cities combined. By 1990 the figure had risen to over 35% for Seoul alone. When the Catholics in the neighboring city of Inchŏn and in the densely populated Kyŏnggi Province which surrounds Seoul are added in, the percentage of Korea's Catholic population which is concentrated in and around the capital city rises to over 53% in the early 1990s.

In order to minister to that rapidly growing urban community, the Catholic church began building hospitals in the 1950s and 1960s (a project Protestant churches had embarked on decades earlier), so many that by the 1990s more than 10% of South Korea's hospital beds were in Catholic hospitals. The Catholic church also started establishing colleges and universities, including Sŏgang University, which opened in Seoul in 1960, allowing it to compete with Protestants, who had been attracting some of the best young minds in the nation to such well-established Protestant universities as Yonsei University and Ehwa Womans University.

Both Catholic and Protestant churches further heightened their visibility and their reputation for modernity by assuming a leadership role in the democratization battles of the 1970s and the 1980s. The Presbyterian ministers Pak Hyŏng-gyu and Mun Ik-hwan and the Catholic Bishop Chi Hak-sun, among others, spoke out against Park Chung-hee's dictatorial *yushin* system, as well as against corruption, injustice, and the exploitation of workers and farmers which fueled Korea's extraordinary economic growth during the Park years. They, and many other Christian activists who shared their belief in the social gospel, were jailed for their non-violent expressions of concern for the rights of the underprivileged. Just as Christian protesters against Japanese colonial rule had done before them, through their moral courage they gained respect and admiration not only for themselves but also for the religious beliefs which motivated them.

6

Korean Characteristics of Korean Christianity

Not all Christian pastors espouse the social gospel, and not all Christians are drawn to Church pews by political concerns. For many, personal happiness is more important than what kind of government they live under. These apolitical Christians, who in the past would have probably turned to shamanism for otherworldly assistance in obtaining the good things of this world, choose Christianity instead as a more appropriate, effective, and modern tool to the same end. They provide the constituency for such pastors as Rev. Paul Yonggi Cho, who preaches prosperity rather than politics. He proclaims that faith in Jesus will be rewarded with a richness of material possessions as well as a richness of spirit. His message is so popular that his church, the Yŏŭido Full Gospel Church in Seoul, claims to have the largest congregation of any single church in the entire world, over 700,000.

The pursuit of health, the number one concern of South Koreans according to a 1983 survey, also brings people into Korea's churches. Just as many Koreans resort to shamanistic rituals to supplement medical treatment they or a family member are receiving, others pray loudly, fervently, and repeatedly in churches and in Christian prayer groups in the belief that prayer will make their doctors prescriptions more effective. Faith healing, especially when combined with more secular forms of medical treatment, is not considered unusual in either Catholic or Protestant churches in Korea. In fact, most large urban Protestant churches in Korea operate their own *kidowŏn* (retreat center) in a nearby mountain or rural county to provide believers with a place they can go to fast or stay up all night in prayer in search of a divine cure for whatever illness afflicts them.

The shamanistic pursuit of wealth and health through supernatural means are not the only signs that Korean Christianity has been influenced by the culture in which it has been transplanted. Confucianism has left its mark as well. Korean Christianity tends to be much more patriarchal than North American or Western European Christianity. Although women make up approximately two-thirds of active church members, there are very few women in leadership positions or serving as ordained ministers. In 1984, for example, if the Salvation Army (which treats men and women equally) is not included in the figures, there were 19,591 male ministers, compared to only 123 who were women. The situation has not changed much since then. Most major Protestant organizations still have no women ministers at all. And, of course, the Korean Catholic Church, just like the Catholic Church elsewhere, still has no ordained women priests.

Another Korean feature of Korean Christianity is a focus on individual charismatic pastors more than on denominational ties. In what may be an echo of the private Confucian academies organized around the teachings of charismatic Confucian scholars during the Chosŏn Dynasty, Protestant denominations tend to splinter and regroup around personalities. If a pastor disagrees with his denominational superiors and leaves to establish his own church, his congregation will often follow him. Moreover, Christians who are members of the same denomination but attend different churches will often compete for converts, trying to convince even other Christians to attend their church rather than that of a rival pastor from the same denomination.

In another sign of more respect for personalities than denominations, Korean Christians do not necessarily attend the church nearest their home. Especially if they are upper-middle class and have easy access to transportation, they may travel half-way across town to attend a church with a particularly well-known and respected minister instead, even though there may be a church of the same denomination within walking distance of their home. This tendency to gather around famous preachers has given birth to a number of churches in Korea with congregations which are unusually large by world standards. The Yŏŭido Full Gospel Church may be the largest, but it is not the only church in Korea to claim a congregation numbering in the tens of thousands. Those who attend the Yŏngnak Presbyterian church in Seoul, for example, proudly proclaim that their church is the largest single Presbyterian church in the world, with over 60,000 members. Such large churches often establish branch churches in other neighborhoods of Seoul or even in other South Korean cities, creating what are in effect sub-denominations within the sub-denominations which form the major denominations of Korean Protestantism.

Besides shamanistic influence on church sermons and services and Confucian influence on church hierarchies and structure, there is other evidence that Korean Christianity has become truly Korean. Korean theologians, particularly Protestant theologians, have begun producing Korean theologies.

For decades, Korean theology was primarily a reiteration of the theology of the American missionaries who first brought Protestant teachings to Korea. That has changed, starting in the 1960s. That was when Yun Sŏng-bŏm (1916-1980), among others, began trying to reshape Christian theology into a theology more distinctively Korean. Yun argued for an indigenized theology which incorporated foreshadowings of Christian doctrines which he claimed to have found in the ancient myths of Korea and in the virtues of Confucianism. Most Korean Christians, however, have rejected his suggestion that Hwanin, Hwanung, and Tangun are really the Trinity in Korean disguise or that Confucian sincerity can provide a foundation for Christian ethics.

The *minjung* theology of the 1970s and 1980s has not had much more success in winning the support of mainstream Korean Christianity. Minjung theologians, such as David Kwang-sun Suh, argue that Christ died to save the *minjung*, a politically loaded Korean term for the oppressed and underprivileged members of society. *Minjung* theology is essentially a Korean version of Latin American liberation theology, without its Marxist underpinnings. It represents a theological assertion of resistance to dictatorship and unbridled capitalism and, as such, is more popular in the faculty clubs of theological seminaries than in the pulpits of churches.

In the 1990s, it is the feminist theology of Professor Chung Hyun-kyung, of Ehwa Womans University's department of theology, which has attracted the most attention. In 1991, at an assembly of the World Council of Churches in Canberra, Australia, Professor Chung prayed for the souls of those who suffer political, economic, and sexist oppression. As she prayed, she was accompanied by shamanistic and Australian aboriginal dance and music, offending many of the more conservative Christians in her audience.

Despite the often harsh criticism she has received for her use of non-Christian elements in her prayers and rituals, Chung continues with her project of creating an Asian feminist liberation theology. She focuses on the suffering of Asian women and the lingering resentment, *han* in Korean, that suffering engenders. She incorporates shamanistic elements into her rituals and prayers because, she says, shamanism is primarily a woman's religion and has been used by women for centuries for *hanpuri*, resolving their grievances. Chung insists that women's lives have to be incorporated into theology, which should become a theological articulation of the life experiences of Asian women, in which those women's lives provide the text and the Bible the context.

Korean Protestants in the pews and pulpits are generally more con-servative than those theologians in university and seminary classrooms who have attracted so much attention outside of Korea. Korean Presbyterians and Methodists, who together make up over two-thirds of all Korean Protestants, have preserved the beliefs, values, and theology of the missionaries of one hundred years ago, resembling more the Pentecostals than the Presbyterians of modern North America.

For example, Korea's Protestants regularly affirm the inspired inerrancy of the Bible, rejecting the stance adopted by so many North American theologians who emphasize the Bibles overall spiritual message over a literal reading of its every word. The Protestant churches of Korea also continue to stress the utter sinfulness of human nature and the need to be born again. And much of the preaching from Korean pulpits can be accurately described as pre-millenarian. Few are as specific as the Seoul pastor who predicted that the world would end on October 28, 1992, but many predict that the end will come soon, in a matter of years rather than centuries.

Moreover, mainstream Korean Protestant churches exhibit an emo-tional intensity that in North America is usually associated with evangeli-cal churches. Protestant church services in Korea are often filled with loud, fervent praying and confessions of faith and with exuberant joyful singing and praise for the Lord. Perhaps remembering their ancestors experiences with shamanistic possession, Korean Christians often look for, and expect, concrete signs that they or their follow worshipers have been filled with the Holy Spirit. In addition, many of them, especially women believers, attend church not only on Sundays but on weekdays as well. Most churches provide weekday pre-dawn services for those who wish to sing the praises of the Lord and ask for His help before they begin the day's work.

Some Koreans look at how much more enthusiastic they are about Christianity than most of their Christian neighbors around the world are and come to the conclusion that Korea is destined to become the next center for world Christianity, the new Israel, as many Koreans call it, the home of the latest chosen people of God. Few would go as far as Moon Sun-myung, leader of the Holy Spirit Association for the Unification of World Christianity (the Unification Church), who says that a new messiah has been born in Korea. (Many of his followers believe that he is that messiah.) However, many do believe that the torch of faith which passed from the Middle East into Europe and then into America has now crossed the Pacific Ocean into Korea. Only a little more than a century after the first Protestant missionary arrived in Korea, not only is Korea no longer the object of foreign missionary endeavors, Korean churches, both Catholic and Protestant, now send their own missionaries overseas. And many Korean Protestants believe that it is time for North American Christians, and Christians from the rest of the world as well, to start learning from Korea how to be true Christians.

One nation South Korean Christians have not been able to dispatch missionaries to, though they are prepared to do so at any time, is North Korea. There has been a revival, of sorts, of Christianity in the Democratic People's Republic of Korea in the 1980s. North Korea opened two churches in P'yŏngyang in 1988, one for Protestants and one for Catholics, after having no open churches for decades. Two years earlier, North Korea had announced the existence of a Korean Christian (Protestant) Federation, with around 10,000 active members, out of a population of over 21 million. In 1988 they proclaimed the existence of a Korean Catholic Federation as well, and said it had around 1,000 members. There has been some limited contact between North and South Korean Christians, primarily at international religious gatherings or through visits to the North by South Korean priests and ministers living in the U.S. or in Europe. As yet, however, South Korean Christian organizations have not been able to establish any formal ties with North Korean Christians, and it is not clear who the Protestants and Catholics of North Korea really are.

Much more information is available on the Christians of South Korea, of course. It is known that they tend to be female, as are most of the religiously active population of South Korea. However, they also tend to be younger, better-educated, more likely to live in a city, and to have a higher income than followers of other religions in Korea. For example, a recent study of an upper-middle class neighborhood in Seoul found that almost 85% of the residents surveyed were religious, compared to 54% of the national population. Moreover, though there are more Buddhists than Christians in the Republic of Korea, over 30% of this neighborhood was Protestant and almost 22% Catholic, compared to only 21% who called themselves Buddhists. Another survey of the entire nation in 1991 found that South Koreans between the ages of 15 and 19 are more than twice as likely to be Protestant than to be Buddhist, though those who are over 60 years of age are twice as likely to be Buddhist than to be Christian, either Protestant or Catholic.

There is no doubt that Christianity has established a formidable and permanent presence in Korea, though the amazing growth rates of earlier years seem to have slowed somewhat and Buddhism seems to be growing stronger lately. If current trends continue, it is unlikely that South Korea will become a Christian nation (with over half of its population Christian) any time soon. However, it is certain that Christianity, both in its Protestant and its Catholic varieties, will continue to play an important role in the religious, political, and cultural life of the Republic of Korea, so much so that anyone who wishes to understand contemporary Korea must first understand Korean Christianity.

Suggested Further Reading

Clark, Donald. 1986. *Christianity in Modern Korea*. Lanham, Maryland: University Press of America.

Commission on Theological Concerns of the Christian Conference of Asia (ed.). 1983. *Minjung Theology: People as the Subject of History*. Maryknoll, New York: Orbis Books.

Grayson, James H. 1989. *Korea: A Religious History*. Oxford, England: Clarendon Press.

_____. 1985. *Early Buddhism and Christianity in Korea*. Leiden: E.J. Brill.

Huntley, Martha. 1984. *Caring, Growing, Changing: A History of the Protestant Mission in Korea*. New York: Friendship Press.

Kang, Wi Jo. 1987. *Religion and Politics in Korea Under Japanese Rule*. New York Edwin Mellen Press.

Kim, Joseph Chang-mun and John Jae-sun Chung (eds.). 1964. *Catholic Korea Yesterday and Today*. Seoul: Catholic Press.

Suh, David Kwang-sun. 1983. *Theology, Ideology and Culture*. Hong Kong: World Student Christian Federation.

_____. 1991. *The Korean Minjung in Christ*. Hong Kong: Christian Conference of Asia.

Wells, Kenneth M. 1990. *New Nation: Protestants and Self-Reconstruction Nationalism in Korea 1896-1937*. Honolulu: University of Hawaii Press.

8

Korean Culture and Worldview
by Won Sul Lee

1

Introduction

A culture is the product of a myriad of factors climatic, topographical, social, political, economical, educational, and ethical in interplay. Korean culture has not been an exception. To understand the uniqueness of Korean culture, one has to delve into the interplay of all these factors, and much more.

One cardinal factor underlying Korean culture that one is apt to overlook is worldview. In a broad sense, culture is a product of human spirituality. Some animals and insects notably monkeys, bees, wasps ants, and termites live gregariously, achieving a certain degree of social stratification, but this social phenomenon is instinctive rather than acquired, and for the most part transmitted genetically not through tradition. Culture is a uniquely human phenomenon, independent of the laws of biology. Culture is acquired, not innate, and habitual in character rather than instinctive. It rests on man's mental capacity to form habits under the influence of his natural and social environment.

In *Dynamics of World History*, Christopher Dawson, a British historian, maintains that "a culture, even the most primitive kind, is never simply a material unity; it involves a continuous and conscious physic discipline (1957: 112)." Emil Brunner, a Swiss theologian, echoes Dawson by saying that the arts, literature, and sociopolitical institutions have their origins "not in mere biological necessity but in spiritual impulses; whenever spirit, transcending the physical urge, enters the scene of life as a formative force, there culture comes into existence (1949: 127)."

What then is the basic conceptual framework by which members of a society order their impulses; impressions, interpretations, and activities ?

Scholars on the study of culture generally agree that the worldview is the central systematization of a culture from which stems its values and systems (Kraft, 1980: 5153). As early as 1790, the word *Weltanschanung* was found in Kant's *Kritik der Urteilskraft*, but Soren Kierkegaarg was the first philosopher to give the term technical meaning: "a set of ultimate beliefs." Reflecting the stream of German philosophy, Welhelm Dilthey called it "a conception of reality that solves the mystery or riddle of life." Today, Robert Redfield, an American scholar, defines it as "the way a man in a particular culture sees himself in relation to everything around him" (1952: 1-90). In his *The Universe Next Door*, James Sire says that "a worldview is a set of presuppositions (or assumptions) which we hold, consciously or subconsciously, about the basic makeup of our world. Going one step further, he maintains that a worldview includes basic answers to (a) what is prime reality, (b) who is man, (c) what happens to man after death, (d) what is the basis of morality, and (e) what is the meaning of human history" (1976: 9-10).

2

Shamanistic Worldview

The fundamental worldview, the oldest, that lies underneath all other kinds of world in the Korean psyche seems to be a shamanistic worldview.

Shamanism is part of a nature-centric worldview: Since his advent on earth, man has felt a close bond with nature, the source of his food, clothes, and shelter. Nature is beautiful, but nature can also turn ugly and ferocious. It is frightening to see nature rage, roar, and destroy what we value. Whether nature is good or bad, we cannot live even one day without interacting with it.

As in all other primitive societies, Koreans in the prehistoric era had close relations with nature. Awed by natural phenomena, primitive people tried to understand what nature was, but it was beyond their comprehension. So they personified, deified, and worshiped the forces of nature.

In shamanistic beliefs, the world is full of gods the sky god, the earth god, the mountain gods, the thunder gods, the sea gods, the tree gods, the rock gods, the dragon gods, the kitchen gods, the gate gods, and the toilet gods. These "nature gods" are in control of human affairs, individually and collectively (Eliads, 1974: 24-25). How can people conciliate these gods to ward off impending evils and open ways for getting blessings ?

Through performing a ritual, called *kut* (a form of auto-hypnotism) in Korean, a shaman (a Tungus name for the priest) can communicate the wishes of a person to the world of spirit, beseeching the god's blessing on the distressed. The shaman uses magic to cure the sick, to divine the hidden, and to control future events.

In the case of Korean shamanism, the *mudang*, the shaman, is not a priest comparable to a Buddhist monk. A *mudang*, usually female, is a medium. But she does not live in a special type of dwelling. She does not practice meditation. Nor does she read any cannons. The office of shaman may be hereditary or acquired. Although no formal education is needed, one indispensable qualification for shamanship is a predisposition to fits and trances. Every shaman is supposedly given authority over certain spirits.

So long as people are trapped by this belief system, they cannot liberate themselves from superstition. On the other hand, shamanism has played some positive roles priestly, oracular, and medicinal in Korean history. In time of crisis, people felt relieved when the kut was performed by a *mudang* to comfort their troubled souls. Even after the introduction of new worldviews such as Confucianism and Buddhism, shamanism in Korea has survived as a folk religion. It has become more sophisticated by the absorption of many Confucian, Taoistic, and Buddhistic elements, and it has continued to exert an influence on Korean culture, especially on music, dance, and paintings.

3

Buddhistic Worldview

Around the 4th century A.D., Buddhism was introduced to Korea. An offshoot of Hinduism, Buddhism was not totally disinterested in the cosmological thoughts expressed by the Vedas and the Upanishads, but Siddhartha, instead of entangling himself in an endless argument of the nature of gods and the universe, paid primary attention to material reality. The doctrine of the "middle way" steers between theism and atheism, and Buddhist teachings are more psychological than cosmological. Buddhism is both a way of life and a way of deliverance (Theodore, 1972).

In Buddhist thought, man is made of five components: (a) form and matter (*rupa*), (b) sensation (*vendana*), (c) perception (*sanna*), (d) all the various psychological constructions such as emotions and propensities, and (e) consciousness. With these five components man tries to find the happiness, which can never be obtained in the transitory world. As a consequence, his life is full of sorrow (Whitehead, 1926: 49-52).

The Four Noble Truths of Sorrow teach that birth, aging, disease, and death are man's major sorrows. The four minor sorrows are contact with the unpleasant, separation from the pleasant, every wish unfulfilled, and living with all the five components of the individual.

How can a man escape sorrow? Buddha taught that a man must get rid of ignorance the chain of causation which rules the universe and human life—because rebirth takes place according to the law of karma. He should know that sorrow is due to craving and that it can be stopped only if craving stops. A man is chained by six cognitive faculties—the sense of vision, audition, smell, taste, and the faculty of intellect and of consciousness and by—six corresponding objects of cognition—color, shape, sound, order, savors, and tangibles. Without liberating himself from these chains, he can never find or regain himself, and without recovering his self, he is enslaved by ignorance, instincts, propensities, senses, sense-contact, impressions, and consciousness—all of which are subject to momentary change.

Buddhism was introduced to Korea around 372 A.D. Among the three kingdoms—Koguryŏ, Shilla, and Paekche—the kingdom of Koguryŏ was the first to embrace the new teachings of Buddhism. A Chinese monk brought images of Buddha and Buddhist sutras. Twelve years later, another Chinese monk introduced Buddhism to Paekche. In both cases, the royal houses welcomed Buddhism as part of their overall receptivity to Chinese culture. Before long, a number of Buddhist temples were erected in the two kingdoms.

But the case of Shilla was somewhat different. Buddhism was brought to Shilla late in the fifth century, but the Shilla aristocrats strenuously opposed it. It was not until the mid-sixth century after the martyrdom of a devout, Ichadon, that Buddhism secured the official acceptance of the kingdom. But after that, Buddhism flourished in Shilla, more so than in the other two kingdoms. Even today, the Pulguk temple in the old Shilla capital of Kyŏngju stands as an exemplar of Shilla Buddhism.

It appears that Buddhism was readily accepted by the people in all these three kingdoms largely because of its humanistic tenants. Buddhism gave them a more practical and pragmatic way for deliverance from human sufferings. The royal houses favored it as a well-suited religion, undergirding the governing structure centered on the authority of the throne. The aristocrats of these kingdoms especially liked the doctrine of karma, which justified their privileged positions (Eckert et al, 1990: 35-38).

Buddhism taught Koreans principles of life far higher than shamanism. According to its precepts life is ephemeral. In the flow of time, nothing can remain unchanged; everything is transient. Man's suffering is caused mainly by his desires. His salvation from the miseries of life is through exterminating desire.

Immeasurable influence has been exerted by Buddhism upon Korean culture. In literature, the *hyangga*, a genre of religious poetry, has become popular. In scripture, the Sŏkkuram grotto is famous. The Pagoda of Many Treasures and the Pagoda That Casts No Shadow in the Pulguk temple compound are exquisite. Especially, Buddhism was the spiritual backbone of the "five injunctions" of *Hwarang* (flower of youth) warrior of youth. Disciplined in the Buddhist precepts of loyalty to the king and the practice of fidelity in friendship, the youth of Shilla grew to be capable of uniting the three kingdoms.

After the establishment of the Yi Chosŏn in 1932, however, Buddhism suffered a great deal. The Yi Dynasty accepted Confucianism as its political ideology and suppressed Buddhism. King T'aejo himself instituted a registration system to prevent the monk population from increasing. King T'aejong demolished many Buddhist temples. But among the ordinary people, Buddhism has many adherents because of humane worldview. Even today, Buddhism has more followers than any other religions in Korean society.

4

Confucian Worldview

Although Chinese cosmological thought is vast and diverse, it has displayed sufficient homogeneity to constitute a single worldview. One common denominator uniting all Chinese philosophical inquiry has been the absence of even the idea of a personal creator. Derk Bodde, an American sinologist, writes that the idea of the creator only appeared in popular religion (1967: 19-20).

In many ways, both Lao Tzu and Confucius, founders respectively of Taoism and Confucianism, were synthesizers of already existing worldviews rather than progenitors of new ones. It seems that Confucius regarded Heaven as an immanent, directive principle of the universe. Heaven is an abstract, moral principle governing the order of human society—a spontaneous principle of nature. Lao Tzu, on the other hand, was more interested in the origin of the universe and made his cosmology the basis of his teaching. The Taoist scripture states, "There was something undifferentiated and yet complete, which existed before the heavens and the earth. Soundless and formless, it depends on nothing and does not change. Tao produced Oneness, Oneness produced Duality. Duality evolved into Trinity, and Trinity evolved into the myriad of things."

It is safe to assume that both Taoism and Confucianism are basically nature-centric. The universe is the result of a naturalistic process of development, starting from a first cause, but the first cause does not have a will of its own. So all things are self-produced. Everything creates itself. In due course, Confucianism came to have a more systematic worldview. In

An Explanation of the Diagram of the Great Ultimate, Chou Tung-yi, a foremost thinker of the Neo-Confucian school in the Sung Dynasty, held that before the creation of the universe, something else existed. "Silent, empty, self-sufficient, and unchanging, revolving without cease and without fail, it acted as the mother of the world." He called this nebulous source the "Great Ultimate." The Great Ultimate, through movement, generates the *yang* (the positive cosmic force). As tranquillity reaches its limit, the *yang* becomes tranquil. Through tranquillity, the Great Ultimate generates the yin (the negative cosmic force). As tranquillity reaches its limit, activity begins anew. In the endless oscillation of these two seemingly opposite but mutually complementary cosmic forces all things in the universe have been created and maintained (Theodore, 1969: 56, 458).

In this Confucian worldview, man was viewed as a part of nature—a microcosm, a reflection of nature's organization. About the human body, Huai-nan-tzu writes: "heaven has four seasons, five elements, nine divisions, and three hundred and sixty days. Man likewise has four limbs, five viscera, nine orifices, three hundred and sixty joints. Heaven has wind, rain, cold, and heat; and men likewise have the qualities of accepting and giving, joy and anger. Therefore, the gall corresponds to the clouds, the lungs to vapor, the spleen to wind, the kidneys to rain, and the liver to thunder."

In the same way, society was understood to correspond to the principles of nature. Every man had his place in society. According to Confucianism, society consists of a large number of small units of people such as the family, the village, the sib, each of which has leaders and followers according to their seniority and ability. It is natural for a society to have different classes, because human beings are not inherently equal. However, if a society is to be stable, there must be harmony between the different subgroups, and this harmonious cooperation is the major concern of statecraft.

In nature, all things are grouped in five. There are five directions —east, west, north, south, and center; five colors—green, red, yellow, white, and black; five tastes—sour, bitter, sweet, acrid, salty; five organs in the human body—kidney, lung, heart, liver, stomach; and five smells— goatish, burning, fragrant, rank, rotten. Therefore, it is essential for human being to have five precepts of social relations: loyalty between the king and his subject, filial piety between the father and the son, distinction between the husband and the wife, faith between friends, and order between the old and the young. Confucius added: "If the prince is not the prince, the minister not minister, the father not father, the son not son, when with all the grains in my possessions shall I ever get to eat any ? "

In fact, Confucianism was introduced to the three kingdoms of Korea in the fourth century about the same time Buddhism was introduced. All these kingdoms laid great stress on inculcating the Confucian worldview as a means of maintaining their stratified social orders and cementing the solidarity of their societies. In time, many Confucian educational institutions were established and Confucian teachings were inculcated in the minds of the people.

Especially after the Yi Dynasty took up Confucianism as its state ideology, Confucianism took a form of religion in Korea by incorporating the rite of ancestral worship into it. The king was regarded as the father of the state, and filial piety in every family was regarded as the key for social stability.

In literature, the arts, architecture, drama, calligraphy, and poetry, the nature-centric worldview of Confucianism expressed itself powerfully. The dominant motif of traditional Korean painting is nature, its mystified power. The high mountain peaks shrouded with clouds, exuberant pine trees on cliffs, winding rivers, and deep gorges are not realistic portrayals but symbolic representations of the individuality, but by making use of space, stillness, and time in a symbolic fashion, it aims expressing the collectivity of human beings living in harmony with nature.

5

Christian Worldview

As mentioned previously, all the diversified worldviews that had existed in Korea before the arrival of Christianity were basically nature-centric. Even primitive Buddhism was not theistic, for Buddha was basically interested in resolving the problems of human suffering rather than expounding the nature of deities. All of them regarded nature as the source of everything, including man. Their teachings were by and large derived from the observation of nature.

In contrast, the biblical worldview of Christianity was entirely different. In his book, James Sire points out that God is not a mere force or energy. He specifies the uniqueness of God as follows: (a) God has personality with self-reflection and self-determination; (b) God is transcendent in which He is not part of nature, but at the same time, He is immanent; (c) God is omniscient and all-knowing; (d) God is sovereign in that nothing is beyond His interest; (e) God is good, surpassing all goodness, and God is the creator of nature and man (1976: 24-26).

The Bible clearly tells us that nature is the manifestation of God's power, glory, and goodness. Psalm 19 praises God: "The heavens declare the glory of God; and the firmament showeth His handiwork." According to the Bible, God created the universe from "*ex nihilo*" (the state of nothingness). No other worldview in the ancient world could speak of a real creation, not even Greek philosophy. Nothing would come from nothing (*el nihilo*). The Greek gods, even including Zeus, were not omnipotent because their power was constantly checked by Anangke and

Moira (blind fate). In sharp contrast, no power in the universe could stand against Yahweh, the Creator. To the Judeo Christian mind, nature is, therefore, not an object of worship. It is an object of understanding.

Likewise, man is a being created in God's image, capable of subduing the earth. "So God created man in his own image, in the image of God he created him; male and female he created them. God blessed them and said to them, 'Be fruitful and increase in number; fill the earth and subdue it'" (Genesis 1: 27-28). God must be at the very center of a man's worldview. Emil Brunner says that the Judeo-Christian worldview alone sees man as a spiritual-bodily unit whose powers and impulses, originating from his physical nature and from his spiritual disposition, are all coordinated in such a way that they are subordinate to a human destiny which transcends the natural and spiritual life, and is directive of both.

The mystery of man's spirituality comes from the fact that among all the living beings, man alone thinks, feels, hopes, fears, expects, humors, judges, and intends. As an embodied spirit, man is also a relational being. Creatureliness means dependency. A man is dependent not only on God but also on nature and on his fellow human beings. He has to perform his duties as a societal being.

This God-centric worldview of Christianity was totally different from the traditional worldviews, of Korea—Shamanistic, Buddhistic, and Confucian—which were basically nature-centric. Because of this, Christians were severely persecuted in Korea in the past.

In fact, the introduction of Christianity to Korea was quite unusual in Church history. In the latter part of the 18th century, Yi Sung-hun, who had accompanied his father in a "tributary mission" to China, was so impressed to hear the Christian gospel that he immediately embraced it. He gathered as many Christian tracts as possible in China, and upon his return, he translated them into Korean. Since many Korean literati who belonged to the *Nam'in* (the southern faction estranged from power) were disgruntled with Confucianism, Yi was able to convert a good number of *yangban* (the upper class) youth into Christian faith and baptized them. When the Vatican heard the news, a good number of French Catholic missionaries arrived in Korea from China, and the church grew fast.

To this introduction of a new worldview, the government reacted violently. Since Christianity preached the "inalienable human rights" such as liberty and equality, the ruling cliques in the government felt seriously threatened. On the pretext that Christians defied the Confucian teaching of ancestral worship, the government killed thousands of Christians in the early part of the 19th century.

Toward the latter part of the 19th century, Protestantism was introduced to Korea by a group of American missionaries. In the wake of the signing of the Treaty of Amity and Commerce between the United States and Korea in 1882, Horace N. Allen and Horace G. Underwood arrived in Korea. By building modern schools and hospitals, the missionaries played an important role in arousing a sense of national identity among the Koreans. When Japan forcefully annexed Korea as its colony in 1910, the Korean church served as a hotbed of Korean nationalism. Many key leaders of the Korean Provisional Government in China during the Japanese colonial period (1910-1945) were devoted Christians. The governor-general persecuted Christians and forced the Korean people to worship Japanese *shinto* gods. To maintain Christian faith under Japanese rule was by no means easy.

In 1945 when Korea was liberated from Japanese colonial yoke, the total Christian population was less than half a million. Then, the northern half of the Korean peninsula became Sovietized. But in South Korea, the growth of the Christian church has been phenomenal. It finds no historical parallel. Today, the combined figure of Protestants and Catholics in the Republic of Korea reportedly exceeds 12 million. This means that one out of four is a Christian.

6

Symbiosis of Divergent Worldviews in Korea

In the wake of modernization, no one worldview dominates today's Korea. Not a few people still stick to a shamanistic worldview. The majority of the people honor ancestral worship and practice Confucian precepts. Buddhists claim that there are over 15 million believers of Buddha. The Christian church is growing fast, and some expect to see over half of the Korean population coming into the fold of Christ at the early part of the coming century.

Korean society has become, therefore, pluralistic not only in terms of its social strata but also in terms of worldview. All sorts of worldviews should learn how to live symbiotically. Especially after the demise of Communism, it is necessary for everyone to have a worldview that will respect human rights. To treasure one's own worldview is important, but to respect other people to have different worldviews is equally important in this pluralistic, democratic society.

Suggested Further Reading

Bodde, Derk. 1967. Harmony and Conflict in Chineses Philosophy. *Studies in Chinese Thought.* (Edited by Arthur Wright) Chicago: The University of Chicago Press.

Brunner, Emil. 1949. *Christianity and Civilization.* London: Nisbet and Co.

Dawson, Christopher. 1957. *Dynamics of World History.* New York: Sheed and Ward.

de Bary, William Theodore. 1972. *The Buddhist Tradition.* New York: Vintage Books.

de Bary, William Theodore, ed. 1969. *Sources of Chinese Tradition.* New York: Columbia University Press.

Eckert, Carter J. & others. 1990. *Korea Old and New: A History.* Seoul: Ilchokak Publishers.

Holms, Arthur. 1983. *The Contours of a Worldview.* Grand Rapids, Michigan: William B. Eerdmans.

Kraft, Charles. 1980. *Christianity in Culture.* Maryknoll, New York: Orbis Books.

9

Political Tradition and Contemporary Politics and Government
by John Kie-chiang Oh

1

Traditional Political Culture

Elite Structures. Until 1910, Korea had monarchical systems of government with some variations in elite structures and nomenclatures. Kings ruled the country with the assistance of well-entrenched, elite groups who administered the nation. In the Shilla Dynasty that unified Korea in 668 A.D., most nobles came from stratified aristocratic families. The court and the aristocracy established a tightly centralized government, and they enjoyed vast privileges and wealth while the common people were increasingly impoverished and some of them were reduced to slavery.

The Koryŏ Dynasty (918-1392) largely remained an aristocratic society with a centralized power structure. While the Koryŏ elite subscribed to Confucianism as the orthodox doctrine for governance, they also accepted Buddhism for their spiritual tranquillity and salvation after death. Buddhist monasteries gradually became large and powerful landowners during the Koryŏ period, thanks to donations of tax-free lands by the royal court and aristocratic families.

The Yi Dynasty, or the last Korean kingdom (also known as Chosŏn), was established in 1392 by a military commander, Yi Sŏng-gye, following over a century of Mongol domination. Yi was effectively supported by Neo-Confucian literati in inaugurating a new dynasty. Without the military, Yi could not have seized the power, and without the civil literati, he could not have established legitimacy for his new regime. The question of legitimacy was important then and has remained so in most Korean minds. Once the regime was consolidated, Neo-Confucianism became the state creed, and Confucian civil groups became paramount in the Yi Dynasty. Buddhism was quickly discredited. The temple lands were seized in sweeping land reforms launched by the new regime.

The Yangban (Two Groups) System. From the 10th century, the concept and the system of *yangban* (two groups) of officials had existed in Korea. It was in the Yi period, however, that the *yangban* system was formalized. Two separate groups of officials, civil on one side and the military on the other, lined up before the throne. Initially, beginning in the Shilla period, some Korean officials attained their positions through the merit system at state examinations administered at various levels, as was usually the case in China, where the system originated. Subsequently, however, some Korean monarchs began arbitrarily appointing men of their choice without the benefit of examinations, and during the Yi period the eligibility for state examinations was legally limited to *yangban* descendants as the *yangban* system became a recognized structure. Both of these modifications negated important aspects of open competition and social mobility based on merit, making the system of recruiting government officials increasingly more arbitrary, manipulative, and ascriptive.

Those attaining the *yangban* membership, a tiny proportion of the population, monopolized power and wealth. In a society that had remained predominantly agrarian and largely stable if not always peaceful, joining the civil officialdom represented the ultimate attainment of manhood. In their official lives, the highest ranking officials had a constituency of one, viz., the monarch, and those in lower ranks in the bureaucracy were accountable only to their superiors. The monarch and the court officials were insulated, distant, and aloof from the people.

Middle and Lower Strata. Below the aristocracy of those actually attaining government positions and their family members and relatives who claimed aristocratic status were the *chung'in* (ideographically, "middle men"). They were originally the permanent professional-clerical staff of ministries and offices in Seoul. Along with clerks in some 350 counties which constituted local administrative units and professional military officers, the *chung'in* constituted the middle layer of the population. They were mostly from humble social origins and performed practical functions such as clerical assistance in the central government, tax collection, assessing and supervising corvée, and performing skilled work in dam constructions and disaster relief projects. Most members of this social stratum received some book learning.

While members of the *yangban* class mastered Confucian classics and argued endlessly about them, the "middle people," slightly larger in number than the *yangban*, acquired practical and professional knowledge and skills. Not being bound to the Confucian orthodoxy during nearly 500 years of the Yi Dynasty and tightly prescribed social order, some members of this stratum were more open than aristocrats to non-orthodox teachings such as Catholicism when it was introduced through China in the early 17th century until it was ruthlessly suppressed by the beginning of the 19th century. While intense, high-level controversies regarding the "Western Learning" subsequently raged among the *yangban* factions, some "middle people" had an early exposure to rudimentary forms of Western astronomy, calendars, commerce, mathematics, science, and technology.

When the Yi Dynasty along with its rigidly aristocratic class was dying out toward the end of the 19th century, it was the middle stratum that proved pragmatic and aggressive. Despite the prevailing view that merchants were in the lowest social stratum in the old Korea, the pragmatic "middle people" became important middlemen in emerging commercial activities. Some became adaptive and entrepreneurial as Japan colonized Korea. Taking advantage of *yangban* and the Japanese ignorance of local and property conditions, some former local tax collectors soon became the largest landlords. On the strength of the wealth that landholding produced, these men later became successful entrepreneurs during the colonial period. More importantly, since World War II, democracy provided a highly favorable setting for their skill and connections. Running enthusiastically in countless elections, they became probably the single most significant political class in contemporary Korea, according to Gregory Henderson.

Below the middle layer was a vast number of commoners, including farmers, artisans, merchants, and the *ch'ŏnmin*, or the despised people. Farmers undoubtedly constituted the largest segment of the population, probably more than three-fourths of Yi Dynasty Korea. In the traditional hierarchical view, farmers came next only to the *yangban*-official class, as farming was said to be the foundation of the society. A fair number of handicraftsmen, potters, carpenters, and the like produced useful items largely with their hands, something that scholar-officials would never do. As daily commodities, ranging from cloth and woven baskets to earthenware, proliferated, a large number of peddlers became the forerunners of the businessmen of contemporary Korea. Still below these commoners, butchers, grave-diggers, and leather workers constituted the bulk of the *ch'ŏnmin*, the despised people, while a relatively small number of slaves existed until the end of the Yi period.

Throughout the era, the court and the *yangban* constituted a tiny minority of the population, while the middle stratum probably fluctuated but was never large in number. Commoners, including a larger number of farmers, probably constituted over four-fifths of the population that toiled and supported the *yangban* officials and those who directly served them. Since the five centuries of Yi rule in Korea were largely settled and stable, the class distinctions also remained fixed and usually unbreachable. Some social mobility existed, but it was the exception rather than the rule. For about five centuries, most Koreans accepted their social status with apparent resignation and fatalism.

Some Legacies of Confucianism. Paradoxically, the lives of the monarch, the court officials, and yangban scholars were hardly stable or relaxed. This was largely due to the prescriptions and proscriptions of Confucianism. It prescribed the "three bonds" (*samgang*) and "five relationships" (*oryun*) in all human relationships. The latter dealt with the relationships between ruler and subject, father and son, husband and wife, elder and younger brother, friend and friend. The first three and most important of these relationships, the "three bonds," were vertical, hierarchical, unequal relationships of loyalty, filial duty, and submission. Even the fourth relationship between elder and younger brothers prescribed order (*sŏ*), and only the fifth dealt with trust (*shin*) between friends. Unquestionably, the "three bonds" were authoritarian, and that suited the monarchists fine. There was nothing even proto-democratic in this tradition.

In the early Yi period, the Neo-Confucian doctrines of Chu Hsi (Chuja in Korean) became dominant and maintained that "behind the Universe stood the Supreme Ultimate which controlled the operation of two universal elements of yin and yang which manifest their 'will' through the five elements of fire, water, wood, metal, and earth." In Neo-Confucian Korea, the monarch was at the epicenter of such a relatively small, centralized, and tightly controllable universe. He was not only the temporal ruler but was also the chief sage who was responsible to Heaven for the political, moral, and ethical tone of his realm.

In this setting, the doctrines of the Chu Hsi of the sŏngni school of Confucianism were made the basis of curriculum in the National Confucian Academy, the center of Confucian orthodoxy. One of the key tenets of Chu Hsi-ism was the mutual interaction of the inseparable universal principles of *i* (or li) which is often translated as "reason" and *ki* (or ch'i) that is often translated as "vital force." These could be viewed as opposing principles, with *i* representing intangibles such as logic or moral principles, and *ki* including activity or substance.

Clearly, these were highly abstract concepts that were beyond concrete or scientific proofs. Because other various elements of Neo-

Confucianism were also capable of engendering widely different interpretations, and more importantly because the outcomes of these interpretations were directly tied to *yangban* scholars' appointments to governmental positions and thus to their fortunes, factionalism was inevitable, rampant, and bitter. Various factions formed alliances and counter-alliances in utterly intolerant and uncompromising struggles. When the monarch himself was directly involved in these controversies, factionalism became a life-or-death struggle among *yangban* scholars and officials.

Social Unrest and the "Eastern Learning" (Tonghak). While the court and the yangban officials were preoccupied with philosophical controversies, factional struggles, and palace intrigues, it was not surprising that governance of the country was neglected. Furthermore, as politics became faction-ridden and seldom merit based, corruption was rampant from the very top down to the level of local tax collectors, usually at the expense of the powerless and the poor. Worse still, a series of natural disasters including famines, floods, and epidemics swept across the peninsula, and by about 1800 the country was racked with revolts large and small.

The peasants, who had been paying increasingly higher taxes in kind to many corrupt local officials, often starved by the time of ch'ungongi, the spring starvation periods, when they ran out of food after paying such heavy taxes. One of the most bloody revolts occurred in 1812, led by Hong Kyŏng-nae, a disgruntled or "fallen" *yangban*. The revolt was joined by peasants, merchants, and even some discontented local government officials. The government was still capable of mobilizing a large force that outnumbered the 3,000-strong rebels and decimated them. In desperation, the peasants and other lower-class people often turned to new religions. However, Catholics were ruthlessly eliminated by 1866.

At this juncture, it was a revolutionary native cult called Tonghak, or Eastern Learning, that attracted a large following among the downtrodden. Tonghak left an indelible mark on modern Korean history and played a decisive role in the demise of the Yi Dynasty. Mostly because aspects of Tonghak tenets had what might be called proto-democratic ideas which were relevant to contemporary politics in Korea, this teaching deserves a brief study. Tonghak originated in 1860 with Ch'oe Che-u (1824-1864), an illegitimate son of a local squire, thus a person destined never to be a *yangban* official.

The Eastern Learning was a syncretic, revealed religion that incorporated elements of Catholicism, Confucianism, Buddhism, Taoism, and Shamanism. What was revolutionary about the teaching were four closely interrelated articles of faith: *shi ch'ŭnju* (serve heavenly master), *in nae ch'ŏn* (man and heaven are one), *sa in yŏch'ŏn* (treat people as though they are heaven), and *tongwi ilch'e* (all revert to one body). Toward the end of the decaying Yi Dynasty, these propositions logically and explicitly dictated the political principle of *poguk anmin* (protecting the nation and securing the well-being of the people).

The Tonghak incantation begins with the term, *shi ch'ŏnju* that has been interpreted in various ways by Tonghak leaders themselves, although *shi* literally means "to serve." *Ch'ŏnju*, or Heavenly Master, was a term used by Korean Catholics; Catholicism was, and still is, known as *ch'ŏnjugyo* (literally, the Teaching of the Heavenly Lord). Before the advent of Catholicism, however, Koreans had long been familiar with the seldom-defined concept of Heaven, as in China, but the Korean vernacular for Heaven was hanŭl, also meaning the sky. It is likely that the Tonghak founder was exposed to Catholic terminologies.

In any case, the Tonghak founder declared that *shi ch'ŏnju* for him meant not just helpless man serving omnipotent heaven. He declared that a human person, man or woman, possessed "he divine spirit within and infinite energy without." It was a concept that a human person embodied the essential element of the divine and that a human person bore heaven within himself. This startling and revolutionary concept of the founder subsequently led to that *of in nae ch'ŏn* (man and heaven are one), a dictum that had already appeared in 1888 when the second Tonghak leader, Ch'oe Si-hyŏng, had the *Tonggyŏng taejŏn* (The Canon of Eastern Scriptures) published. The concept boldly declared that a human person equals heaven.

Though the Koreans had used the term heaven from the dawn of time, until this Tonghak declaration, heaven had been infinitely above and beyond earth and man. By this three-character declaration of *in nae ch'ŏn*, Tonghak leaders equated heaven and man without even positing a single intermediary, e.g., a son of heaven, a monk, or a shaman. By unqualifiedly equating man with heaven, this Tonghak concept elevated man to a heavenly value and dignity for the first time in Korean history. The concept totally negated all the class distinctions that had condemned the peasants and the other low-level people to lives of worthlessness and indignity for untold generations.

Because a man is heaven, it naturally followed that each and every man, regardless of one's parentage or position, had to be treated as though he were heaven itself, or *sa in yŏch'ŏn*, with respect and dignity. With this view of man, it was further declared that all men ultimately fused into one eternal body, or the hanŭlnim, meaning "one universal being." With the tenet of *tongwi ilch'e*, Ch'oe Che-u rejected the idea that some ascended into heaven while others descended to hell. Instead, every human would find happiness within the one universal and "egalitarian being." Further, this was not to be a remote and uncertain heaven. It was to be the actual dwelling place of all men, the human society. It was not other-worldly. It was definitely this-worldly, aimed at the attainment of a "heaven on earth." It was a startling good news to lowly people who had fatalistically accepted their hopeless lives.

"Righteous" People. In order to achieve a heaven on earth, the first task had to be the practical and political stage of protecting the Korean nation which was threatened internally by greedy and oppressive officials and externally by marauding Western aggressors as well as Japan. Thus poguk anmin (protecting the nation and securing the well-being of the people) was necessary. Tonghak leaders were thoroughly convinced that politics and ethics in dynastic Korea were corrupt beyond redemption, and external menaces could not be countered by the court and yangban officials. In the fifth passage of his *Kwŏnhakka* (Songs to Prompt Learning), Ch'oe wrote that "righteous people should firmly unite to achieve the goal of *poguk anmin.*" The message was clear: that the people of the nation had to overthrow the old monarchical and elite-dominated order and establish a new government that would be capable of protecting the nation and establishing a new order. Ch'oe apparently could not detail his political programs at the time, fearing the authorities would persecute him and his followers for doing so.

Peasant Rebellions and the Fall of the Dynasty. If that was the case, Ch'oe's caution was to no avail. As Ch'oe's teaching gained popularity, three southeastern provinces became engulfed in peasant rebellions. Some of Tonghak teachings were written in *han'gŭl,* the Korean alphabet readily understood by the commoners and women, while Chinese characters were used in the court and yangban circles. Beginning in the spring of 1862, several thousand peasants wearing white headbands swarmed through many southern villages and cities, killing not only government officials but local landlords and wealthy merchants in a month-long rampage. Before the much superior government forces wiped out the ragtag Tonghak rebels, the rebellion had swept through dozens of cities and villages.

Ch'oe was arrested in the following year. He was specifically charged with preaching the existence of an ultimate being superior to the king. His doctrine was identical with illegal Catholicism, which believed in ch'ŏnju (Heavenly Lord). Ch'oe was executed in April 1864 as a subversive. Ch'oe's martyrdom, however, did not stop the spread of Tonghak among the poor and downtrodden, who were incensed at the execution of their leader. Another abortive revolt was launched in 1871.

Meanwhile, the Korean government's treasury emptied because of the breakdown of the taxation system in a country racked with unrest. As the taxation base shrank, those still effectively under government control were taxed to the utmost.

Under these circumstances, it was the historic Kabo Tonghak Rebellion of 1894 that had nationwide and international consequences. Tens of thousands of rebels engaged in a full-scale rebellion, mostly in the southwestern provinces of Ch'ungch'ŏng and Chŏlla. Unable to crush the tidal waves of Tonghak rebels who threatened to topple the central government, the government requested Chinese assistance for its survival. Subsequent dispatches of Chinese troops and the landing of uninvited Japanese troops in Korea to counter the Chinese led to the Sino-Japanese War that culminated in the Japanese annexation of Korea in 1910. From another perspective, the common people of Korea had a dramatic if bloody and abortive initiation into grassroots politics.

In Korean history, there were some small-scale and isolated rice riots or other anti-government disturbances. However, they were quite unlike the massive, though intermittent, mobilization of the "righteous" people for over 30 years from 1862 to 1894. In the past, ethical-religious and ideological justifications had been the monopoly of the elite, never affecting the lives of the masses. For the first time, Tonghak provided the motivating force to the "righteous people." It may not be claimed that Tonghak founders were the first democrats of Korea, but it cannot be denied that Tonghak teachings contained the first embryos of populist concepts advanced by their Korean cult leaders. These concepts included revolutionary views on human dignity for all, essential equality among men and women, social justice for the lower class, and national commonwealth for all.

The March First Movement. In 1905, Tonghak was renamed Ch'ŏndogyo (the Teaching of the Heavenly Way). Just as the massive Tonghak Rebellion of 1894 proved casus belli for the Sino-Japanese War and the Japanese colonization of Korea, Ch'ŏndogyo leaders and followers unquestionably provided the key leadership, financial sources, and nationwide organization and mobilization for the massive March First Independence Movement of 1919. The third "supreme leader" of Ch'ŏndogyo, Son Pyong-hui, a man of considerable charisma and stature, was a central figure in forging a coalition among Ch'ŏndogyo, Christian churches in Korea, Korean Buddhist, and others to organize the massive, nationwide demonstration for Korean independence. Clearly, the leadership for the March First Movement came from nationalist elites of various backgrounds, but it was the people who demonstrated across the country.

Thirty-three "national representatives" signed the declaration, and following some arguments among these representatives, Son was the first one to sign and affix his seal on the Declaration of Independence to be followed by Christians, Buddhists, and others.

By 1919, Ch'ŏndogyo organizations were apparently solvent enough to lend 5,000 won a sizable amount then to Christian groups to encourage their leaders to agitate and mobilize Christians in the nationwide demonstrations. According to Ch'ŏndogyo records, Son also sent 30,000 won to Korean nationalist groups in Shanghai and 60,000 won to those in Manchuria. Such financial strength was based on the over 3 million Ch'ŏndogyo members who made regular donations to the organization through the practice of sŏngmi (sincerity rice) whereby each family daily set aside a tablespoonful of rice for each member to contribute to Ch'ŏndogyo activities. This indicated that the numerous followers, presumably motivated lower-class people, had actively participated in the financial support of the organization.

According to various statistics of the Koreans arrested by the Japanese troops and police from March to December 1919, it is also clear that Ch'ŏndogyo believers participated in demonstrations in large numbers and constituted some 11.7 percent of those arrested second only to Presbyterians who constituted 12.7 percent. Son was one of those arrested, and following lengthy trials, along with the national representatives and other notable demonstration leaders, Son was sentenced by the Japanese authorities to a three-year prison term that was suspended because he suffered a brain hemorrhage and severe complications.

When Son died at age 62 in 1922, Ch'ŏndogyo ceased to be a unified and effective religious-political entity, partly due to factional struggles among its leaders after the passing of a charismatic and towering supreme leader. For a brief period, Ch'ŏndogyo also provided an outlet to nationalist literary expressions in the *Kaebyŏk* (The Creation), a magazine affiliated with Ch'ŏndogyo. Articles were heavily censored by the Japanese between 1920 and 1926. It was suspended 32 times before it was ordered to cease publication altogether. The Ch'ŏndogyo Ch'ŏng'udang (The Young Friends Party) was organized in September 1923, under the doctrinal concepts of *sa in yŏch'ŏn* (treat people as though they are heaven) and *chisang ch'ŏn'guk kŏnsŏl* (establishment of heaven and earth). This party was quickly paralyzed due to factional strife and was driven underground with the arrest of several hundred members by the Japanese authorities in 1934. Since 1945, Ch'ŏndogyo reemerged in both parts of Korea, but largely as feeble appendages to ruling groups.

2

Contemporary Politics and Government

A Quantum Leap. It was on these traditional political-cultural foundations that contemporary Korean politics unfolded following the Second World War. A "republican" government was established in 1948 with the termination of the American military occupation of South Korea. Anticipating an early end to the American occupation, the U.S. Army Military Government in Korea (USAMGIK) established the South Korean Interim Government in May 1947, and the interim government gave birth to the Constitution Drafting Subcommittee. It was this subcommittee, composed of six prominent Korean members of political and intellectual elites and an American advisor, that set about to define the fundamental character of a new Korean government.

For most South Korean elites, including the members of the subcommittee, the occasion of state building was seen as a golden opportunity to make a quantum leap toward modernization of Korea's polity. Returning to the discredited dynastic form was utterly unthinkable. It was clearly repugnant to emulate the imperial Japanese model. By 1947 Japan, too, had a startlingly modern and democratic constitution drafted by a group of Americans in the name of "We, the Japanese people."

Sharing the democratizing drives of the MacArthur headquarters in Japan, Lt. Gen. John R. Hodge, who commanded the U.S. military forces in Korea, issued a "Declaration on the rights of the Korean People" on April 7, 1947. With the stroke of a pen, General Hodge declared that the basic rights of the Korean people included the equality of all Koreans before the law, the freedoms of assembly, association, press, speech, and religion. All Korean women were decreed to be free and equal with men, just as the "MacArthur Constitution" did for Japanese women. South Korean opinion leaders, regardless of their views on General Hodge's performances in Korea, apparently welcomed such a declaration. The full text of General Hodge's declaration was highlighted in all major daily papers in South Korea and had the effect of setting the direction of a new South Korean polity yet to be determined in a new constitution.

In any case, to the drafters of the Korean constitution, it was clear that they should adopt a system that would be compatible with the wave of the future. To these drafters and to many Korean intelligentsia who learned about Western democratic politics, the victory of the democratic coalition in two world wars indicated that democracy represented the wave of the future. Establishing a democratic government might also demonstrate Korea's or the elites cultural equality with advanced nations of the West and make Korea acceptable to democratic states. More concretely, the intensifying rivalry with the authority in the north that was fast becoming a Communist state dictated that South Korea establish an anti-Communist, and ergo, a democratic state.

The Governmental Framework. The first written constitution of Korea was adopted by the very first National Assembly in Korean history on July 12, 1948. The preamble to the constitution boldly declared that the newly independent republic was determined

To establish a democratic system of government eliminating evil social customs of all kinds, and to afford equal opportunities to every person and to provide for the fullest development of the capacity of each individual in all the fields of political, economic, social and cultural life.

The General Provisions in Chapter I declared that the Republic of Korea "shall be a democratic and republican state" and that "the sovereignty of the Republic of Korea shall reside in the people from whom all state authority emanates." Article 5 also stated that the republic "shall be responsible for respecting and guaranteeing the liberty, equality and initiative of each individual and for protecting and adjusting these for the purpose of promoting the general welfare." Chapter II of the Constitution then enumerated specific rights of the citizen guaranteed in the first chapter. Indeed, little fault could be found with the liberal-democratic orientation of the fundamental law.

However, Article 28 qualified all the preceding provisions by stipulating that "laws imposing restrictions upon the liberties and right of citizens shall be enacted only when necessary for the maintenance of public order or welfare of the community." The freedoms mentioned in preceding articles were supposedly guaranteed, but with such qualifications and escape clauses as "except as specified by law," "except in accordance with the law," and "with the provisions of the law." Thus, when deemed "necessary" by the ruling powers, all these liberties could be restricted. Further, Article 57 contained the familiar emergency clause:

When in time of civil war, in a dangerous situation arising from foreign relations, in case of natural calamity or on account of a grave economic or financial crisis, it is necessary to take urgent measures for the maintenance of public order and security, the President shall have the power to issue orders having the effect of law or take necessary financial disposition, provided, however, that the President shall exclusively exercise such power if time is lacking for convening of the National Assembly.

Though the constitutional framework, at the first glance, appeared to establish legislative supremacy by the National Assembly that was to exercise legislative power, and initially, to elect the president, close examination disclosed many opportunities for it to become a strong presidential form. As to the judicial branch of the new government, Chapter V of the Constitution stated that judges should be free from executive and legislative interference. Theoretically, the judiciary was to have check on the executive and the legislature. In practice, however, the chief justice of the Supreme Court, appointed by the president with the ratification of the National Assembly, and judges of other courts appointed for a relatively short term of five years, were also made amenable to presidential direction. Questions involving the constitutionality of laws were to be decided by a constitutional committee presided over by the vice president of the republic and composed of five justices of the Supreme Court and five members of the National Assembly.

For the new Korean republic to face the future without some provisions for decisive executive actions would have been ignoring the realities in a divided peninsula where a hostile regime was almost simultaneously being established in the north. However, whether the emergency and the other escape clauses in the constitution would destroy the democratic system, only time could tell. More importantly from a historical-cultural perspective, whether the democratic superstructure could be sustainable on the political soil that Korea had inherited from her past remained to be seen.

The Republic in Operation. Under these circumstances, much was dependent on the very first president of the republic, Syngman Rhee, in interpreting and applying the constitutional provisions, shaping the government, and setting precedents in the operation of the government. It was apparently hoped by many that Rhee, who had spent some 33 years as a political exile mostly in the United States, where he received political science degrees including his Ph.D. from Princeton, would lead the first republic to realize democracy. Such a hope in the euphoric days of the inauguration of the republic, however, tended to ignore the weight of the traditional political culture, Rhee's origins and personality, and the realities that Korea then faced. It was no exaggeration that the Korean nation was only a few wobbly steps away from her indigenous national past, i.e., the dynastic culture. From the perspective of realizing democratic politics, the colonial period under the Japanese was of little help. If anything, the Japanese era had tended to accentuate the negative aspects of the traditional culture, even perpetuating superstitions, since the colonial masters encouraged them as they made Korea easier to rule.

As to Rhee, when he began to govern South Korea with myriad accumulated problems, the American-educated septuagenarian's behaviors evidently reverted to traditionally Korean patterns. It was recalled that Rhee (Yi) was allegedly a scion of a princely family of the Yi Dynasty. Even as the elected president of Korea, his behaviors tended to be those of a haughty yangban aristocrat who demanded obeisance and loyalty from his appointed ministers, lawmakers, or judges. The central criterion for appointing and abruptly removing his cabinet members appeared to be personal loyalty to himself, and the tenure of ministers was often a few months. Also, being an heir to a well-to-do family of traditional Korea, Rhee knew or cared little about the economic life of the common people who were in desperate conditions.

The Crisis Government. According to Clinton L. Rossiter there are three types of crises in the life of a democratic nation. They are economic depression, rebellions, and wars. The infant republic headed by Rhee faced all three crises within the first three years of the establishment of the government. The economy in South Korea was one of endless despair, despite sizable American and other economic aids. The agrarian half of the divided peninsula could not produce enough food for South Koreans and the millions of refugees from the north.

The infant republic also faced a number of bloody rebellions. The rebellion on Cheju Island that began in April, 1948, was getting worse. Then came the Yŏsu-Sunch'ŏn incidents in October, 1948, barely a month after the inauguration of the government. The South Korean police and the constabulary had to engage in exhausting subjugation campaigns against largely Communist-inspired rebels. In these campaigns, the civil liberties elegantly enumerated in the constitution were often ignored. Frequently, hapless villagers suspected of aiding guerrillas were summarily executed. Then came the Korean War, less than two years after the inauguration of the Rhee government, a total war for the Koreans who lost a million lives among civilians alone and suffered damage estimated at three billion dollars.

By the time the truce agreement was signed in July 1953, President Rhee had become the undisputed autocrat of South Korea. Some of his potential rivals who were not eliminated earlier by terrorists were taken to the north by the retreating Communist army. In the wartime capital of Pusan, operating under martial law, Rhee had rammed a constitutional amendment through the besieged National Assembly to have the president elected by direct vote of the people who still held him in awe instead of by the National Assembly that was becoming increasingly hostile to him.

It set a precedent of manipulating the constitution for political expediency of a ruler instead of the fundamental law regulating the ruler and the government. While Rhee's role as the unifying symbol of South Korea in the darkest hours of the Korean War could not be underestimated, Rhee crassly took advantage of the crisis of the Communist aggression to make himself an unchallengeable autocrat. Toward the end of his regime, Rhee and his government of obsequious ministers resembled an old dynastic court of a king and his yangban officials. As Rhee became absolutely powerful, his regime turned into an arrogant and corrupt clique that was aloof from the people whose livelihood had hardly improved during the 12-year rule by Rhee. The per-capita annual income was $67 in 1953 when the Korean War ended, and it was $79 in 1960, when Rhee decided to run for his fourth presidential term.

Enthusiasm for Education. At the same time, it is noteworthy that the traditional obsession with education of the young, probably attributable to the Confucian emphasis on learning, was reflected in the constitution that provided: "All citizens shall have the right to receive an equal education correspondent to their abilities ... Compulsory education shall be free." The Education Law was legislated and promulgated in 1949, and a compulsory education system was inaugurated in the very first years of the republic. The education of the young continued even during the Korean War in makeshift barracks and sometimes outdoor classrooms. Education opportunities were rapidly expanded on higher levels also, driven by the people's traditional and sustained interest in education. In due time, these drives were to have far-reaching impact on political development as well as economic growth.

"Righteous" Uprising of Students. If it was astonishing that Rhee, now 85, was running in 1960 for another four-year term, it was not surprising that the ruling clique was determined to ensure his election victory

and particularly that of his Vice President Yi Ki-bung, who would succeed him should Rhee die during the term. Instead of seeking a "democratic" mandate through a fair election held on March 15, 1969, the rigging of the election was complete throughout South Korea. Specific instructions were sent out by the Home Ministry to police chiefs throughout the nation, stipulating the exact majority by which Rhee and Yi were to be "elected." When votes were "counted," it was announced that the Rhee-Yi team had won a lopsided victory. The country was seized with a sullen mood of bewilderment and resentment.

Few persons outside the small port city of Masan knew that a riot had broken out there on election day when the public became convinced that the election was being stolen by the ruling clique. The people of Masan felt suffocating fury, but they were helpless against the reinforced police power. When a fisherman discovered, on April 11, 1960, the body of a high-school boy with a tear-gas shell imbedded in one eye, however, all Masan went out of control. The people's anger finally reached an exploding point.

The Masan riot triggered a rapid succession of massive student demonstrations in Seoul and other major cities beginning on April 16. Owing to the people's abiding interest in education, there were some 903,000 middle and high school as well as college-level students in 1960, while the comparable figure was approximately 128,000 in 1945. Nearly a million students could potentially demonstrate against the Rhee government, and they were soon joined by their teachers and other members of the citizenry.

Characteristically, President Rhee declared martial law, and heavily armed soldiers were brought into Seoul. By then, the police force was demoralized, and when the soldiers showed no intention of shooting at demonstration students, Rhee in his besieged mansion had no choice but to resign. A seemingly formidable regime was swept away by the waves of spontaneous protesters. This was the "April Student Revolution" or the "Righteous Uprising of Students" of 1960 that spread like an uncontrollable prairie fire not unlike the Tonghak rebellion of 1894 that could not be contained by the soldiers of the Yi Dynasty and led, in time, to the demise of the dynasty.

The Second Republic. The Second Republic was the direct result of the almost unexpectedly sudden fall of the First Republic. Premier Chang Myŏn attempted to run a democratic republic, true to a constitution that was once again revised to adopt a responsible cabinet system to prevent a repeat of the presidential form of government that had become autocratic under Rhee. The elaborate cabinet system of government of the Second

Republic included a ceremonial president, a prime minister who was to be chief executive, and a bi-cameral legislature. However, the factional struggles among Confucian scholar-officials of yore, and this fact alone, in a responsible cabinet system, meant accumulated political gridlock at a time when accumulated problems in South Korea demanded effective government that was capable of addressing the socio-economic problems.

To its credit, the Second Republic made an early attempt to launch the first five-year economic development plan, which was to be implemented from the spring of 1961. Instead, what was swiftly implemented in May, 1961, was a military coup d'etat led by then Major General Park Chung-hee. Just as the First Republic died a sudden death about a year earlier, the Second Republic quickly evaporated like mirage, largely because it lacked a political soil to root the institutional superstructures.

A Son of a Tonghak Rebel. From May, 1961 to December, 1963, the military ruled the country directly through what was grandiosely called the Supreme Council for National Reconstruction (SCNR), headed by General Park. Unlike the two chief executives before him, Rhee and Chang, Park was born in the 20th century. Further, Park's origin could not have been more different from those of well-born and well-educated Rhee and Chang, particularly Rhee, who belonged to an aristocratic elite. Park was the eighth child two of whom died in infancy of an impoverished farmer who joined the Tonghak rebels, as Park himself asserted to followers of Ch'ŏndogyo, the modern reincarnation of Tonghak. The desperate circumstances of Park's birth are reflected in a story that his mother, upon learning that she was pregnant again, reportedly drank a large quantity of soy sauce and repeatedly jumped from a large soy sauce pot in a pathetic attempt to abort him.

His career up to 1960 was one of continuous struggles to survive. He reportedly began plotting a military coup as early as the early 1950s when Rhee was turning autocratic during the Korean War. Park led an austere life, cultivated a wide-ranging network of anti-status quo, coup-minded young officers, and attained the rank of a major general by 1961. However, his military career was then being threatened with involuntary, early retirement. He was assigned to no less than nine posts in a six-year span ending in 1961, when he decided to take the risk of leading a military coup.

The Military and Economic Growth. In a society with a lasting Confucian tradition that held legitimacy to be essential for a government, Park was keenly aware that his military junta lacked legitimacy. Also, in traditional Korea, military officials were seen as inferior to the civilian group of the yangban. With his impoverished origins and life experience as an incorruptible army officer, he also knew the desperate economic deprivation of the common people in the appallingly underdeveloped economy of Korea. The per capita annual income in 1961 in South Korea (still largely agrarian) was $82. Under these circumstances, the coup had to be quickly justified to the legitimacy-conscious people who had experienced several general elections by 1961.

On January 1, 1962, barely half a year after the military takeover, General Park, in his capacity as Chairman of the Supreme Council for National Reconstruction, announced with great fanfare the First Five-Year Economic Development Plan, 1962-66. Park evidently decided once again to risk his own future. He hoped to justify his military coup and legitimate his regime. Park quickly committed the full weight of his unchallengeable power and that of his military junta in support of the unprecedented economic plan, the "marching order" given by General Park. It was an audacious politics of justification by economic growth.

It was indicative of this soldier's orientation that Park first created the Korean Central Intelligence Agency (KCIA) shortly before he launched the Economic Planning Board (EPB) on July 21, 1961. KCIA was far more than an intelligence gathering organization. It quickly became a powerful and pervasive force of coercion and control for the Park regime, not only in the political arena but also in the economic sector, subsequently including labor control. EPB, headed by a vice premier to coordinate economy-related ministries, was to be the central organ to plan, coordinate, and execute economic growth activities under the overall supervision and often hands-on involvement of General Park himself.

Thus was created a central headquarters for rapid economic growth. Park was at the controls, commanding the twin engines of KCIA and EPB. All of South Korea was soon mobilized by the powerful military regime that co-opted groups of economists, scientists, engineers, managers, entrepreneurs, and others who could embrace the concrete goals of rapid economic growth. It was not difficult to mobilize the common people who still led subsistence-level lives some one-third of whom were unemployed or underemployed in early 1960s to follow the marching orders that promised them jobs and liberation from poverty.

There remained uncompromising intellectuals, like principled literati of yore, who clung to a belief that democracy should not be sacrificed on the altar of uncertain economic growth championed by a military junta. Their voices persisted throughout the military-dominated era and grew increasingly louder, and indeed thunderous, toward the end of the period as the military-dominated authoritarian regime became dictatorial. However, in the early 1960s, a majority of the South Koreans shed no tears in abandoning the seemingly confusing, corrupt and bankrupt "phantom republics." After all, most people then were more familiar with an authoritarian regime than with governments that parroted democratic jargons but were, in fact, autocratic or incompetent.

A frenzy of activity was to follow the announcement of the first five-year plan. The people were given the impression that their economic life would soon improve. It was in this milieu that the military, which was the only group that clandestinely organized a well-financed political party while all civilians were barred from any political activities, suddenly called for presidential election on October 15, 1963. The constitution was once again revised to make the presidency stronger than ever, overshadowing the cabinet, legislative, and judicial branches. Immediately before the elections, General Park retired from active military status and became the presidential candidate, supported by a political party that was throbbing with youthful energy.

Predictably, Park was the winner over Yun Po-sŏn, the ceremonial president of the Second Republic, but with a thin margin, 42.6% vs. 41.2%. Thus began the military-dominated, but elected, Third Republic. The government regained legitimacy, but on a very narrow base. Thus the need to enlarge the base of legitimacy through rapid economic growth clearly remained. Park's marching orders in the form of successive five-year economic plans issued forth, and South Korea was transformed into a mobilized and regimented workplace. A "Korea, Inc." was born. Slowly and then noticeably some say miraculously the Korean economy took off by the mid-1960s, partly thanks to favorable external conditions, and gathered momentum into the 1970s. The per capita GNP skyrocketed from $82 in 1961, the year of the initial coup, to $1,544 in 1979, when Park was shot to death.

A Transforming Nation. Though the economy continued to grow spectacularly under another general-turned-president Chun Doo-hwan, his bloody suppression of demonstrators in Kwangju in May 1980 and his heavy-handed, authoritarian rule caused increasing resentments among the people who were changing gradually but significantly, at least in three ways. First, thanks to the traditional Korean eagerness for education, a large number of South Koreans were educated well beyond the compulsory level. The number of middle and high school enrollees, for instance, jumped from about 802,000 in 1960 to 4,169,000 in 1980 a five-fold increase in 20 years. The college-level enrollment also skyrocketed from approximately 101,000 in 1960 to 602,000 in 1980, to far surpass a million mark less than a decade later a ten-fold explosion in about 30 years. These records were truly unprecedented in Korean history as well as in comparison with other nations.

Secondly, a significant majority of South Koreans were economically comfortable by Korean standards by the end of the Chun era in 1987, the per capita GNP being over $3,000. In the Korean setting, they were no longer poor, and this fact further fueled the enthusiasm for higher education. Consequently, and thirdly, a large number of South Koreans joined the educated "middle class" with some of the traditional middle class values, including relatively liberal political values. Both private and government-sponsored surveys indicated that some 75% of South Koreans by the late 1980s identified themselves with the middle class.

A Peaceful Transfer of Power. These developments meant that a significant majority of South Koreans became economically secure and politically assertive. The economic and political soil in Korea had been transforming and pressures for liberalization was building up. However, President Chun failed to take cognizance of these changes. In the spring of 1987, he attempted to dictate his personal choice of former General Roh Tae-woo, his former classmate at the Korean Military Academy, as the presidential candidate of the ruling party, to be elected through a "rubber stamp" organization, but the people rejected the approach resoundingly in yet another massive popular protest. Hundreds of thousands of people demonstrated for months in most urban centers against Chun's imperious moves, and the police began to run out of tear gas shells by early July.

Characteristically, Chun was about to move troops to enforce his dictates in mid-July. But he faced the overwhelming "people power" of an unending sea of demonstrators who packed all highways and byways around the capital city. This time, demonstrators included not only students and workers, but significantly, large numbers of the middle class. Apparently recalling the futility of Rhee's imposition of martial law in 1960 and the bitter experience with the Kwangju massacre of May 1980, Chun's advisors, including his prime minister, urged caution. The U.S. government also advised Chun against the use of troops against the people. When Roh adroitly decided, on June 29, 1987, to accept a direct presidential election, the people subsequently elected him over the divided opposition, though Roh garnered only 36.6% of votes cast. However, a peaceful transfer of power was accomplished for the first time in 27 years.

Thus, President Roh had to democratize Korean politics and liberalize economic controls by the government. Understandably, the Roh regime, a democratic government headed by a former general, often appeared schizophrenic and to lack clear policy orientations. In the era of liberalization in most sectors of the society, corruption was rampant and degeneration of moral codes became glaringly visible. At the same time, the economy went through a rocky period of large-scale adjustments, partly in response to pent-up demands by workers for equitable wages and other benefits, and externally against tougher competitions in a widely depressed world economy.

A Civilian President. As Roh's single-term presidency was ending, there was no longer any question about duly electing another president in 1992. No threat of another military takeover was made. All three major presidential candidates were bona fide civilians with no military background. One was an industrial tycoon, a Ross Perot of Korea, reflecting the spectacular economic growth in South Korea. The real contest was between Kim Young-sam and Kim Dae-jung, both erstwhile opposition leaders.

In January, 1990, Kim Young-sam had merged his party with the ruling party of President Roh whom Kim Young-sam had previously denounced as a military dictator. Having in time become the head of the powerful ruling party through his adroit political maneuvers, Kim Young-sam enjoyed all the benefits of his new position in the 1992 election. While he championed political and economic stability with incremental reforms, including the eradication of corruption, Kim Dae-jung represented forces of rapid political and socio-economic reforms and bold approaches to the north-south reunification.

The electorate in the transforming South Korea opted for Kim Young-sam, who advocated "reform amidst stability," by a substantial margin of 42% to 43%. It was clear that Kim Young-sam also benefitted from deeply rooted regionalism among voters, many of whom disliked Kim Dae-jung from the Chŏlla province. In any case, Kim Dae-jung conceded his defeat promptly and gracefully. A peaceful transfer of power to a duly elected civilian president took place in February, 1993, for the first time in 32 years.

3

Conclusions

Traditionally, Korea had a monarchical system with relatively well-defined ruling elites, the *yangban*. Until 1910, the political tradition of Korea was harshly authoritarian, mitigated somewhat by Buddhist influences and the Confucian scholar-officials' adhesion to the concepts of legitimacy and meritocracy. Politics had been the monopoly of the often dogmatic and fractious ruling groups until the late 19th century when the "righteous" followers of Tonghak were thrown into the crucible of short-lived populist politics. Further, the authoritarian tradition was subsequently subjected to the militarist imprints of Japanese colonialism for over a generation.

The Korean political system took a quantum leap following the Second World War when South Korea was occupied by American military authorities with democratizing zeal. On the authoritarian political soil that contained some seeds of populism was erected a democratic superstructure when South Korea hurriedly established a republic with the blessing of the departing American occupation forces. However, when faced with economic chaos, internal rebellions, and the Korean War, the democratic structure quickly evaporated, and politics reverted to authoritarianism. Meanwhile, the Korean enthusiasm for education, partly attributable to the traditional Confucian emphasis on learning, was creating a well-educated populace. When the authoritarianism of President Rhee lost legitimacy by massively rigging presidential elections, the spontaneous but massive "righteous" uprising of students and some citizenry toppled the autocratic regime.

After a briefest interregnum of a democratic but chaotic Second Republic, the military forcibly inserted itself in Korean politics. As the military lack political legitimacy, and in view of the impoverished Korean economy, the military leaders decided to gain legitimacy by triggering and sustaining rapid economic development. Soon a "Korea, Inc." was forged, and the government, business, and workers created an economic miracle that has made South Korea relatively well-to-do. In time, coupled with sustained educational efforts on all levels, the economic growth created a well-educated middle class with some liberal political values. The military regimes, whose contribution to the rapid economic growth could not be minimized, had sown the seeds of its destruction. When the military dictatorship attempted to perpetuate itself, a massive popular resistance, now swelled by a growing middle class, triggered the process of revival of a civilian rule that was finally accomplished in 1992-93.

The political culture of Korea has been transforming. From the authoritarian-elites past that was superseded by militarist rule, it has been gradually evolving to a civil and democratic one. With the emergence of a well-educated and growing middle class, there might now be a stable base for this transformation to continue.

Suggested Further Reading

Eckert. Carter J. et al. 1990. *Korea Old and New: A History*. Seoul: Ilchokak Publishers.

Henderson, Gregory. 1968. *Korea: The Politics of the Vortex*. Cambridge: Harvard University Press.

Nahm, Andrew C. 1988. *Korea: Tradition and Transformation*. Seoul and Elizabeth, N.J.: Hollym International Corp.

Oh, John Kie-chiang. 1968. *Korea: Democracy on Trial*. Ithaca: Cornell University Press.

Palais, James B. 1991. *Politics and Policy in Traditional Korea*. Cambridge. Council on East Asian Studies, Harvard University.

10

Politics in South Korea since 1993
by Han-Kyo Kim

1
Introduction

The year 1993 marked a major milestone in postwar South Korea's political history. For the first time since the 1961 military coup, a civilian politician was installed as president of the Republic of Korea (ROK), thereby ending 32 years of rule by army generals. The newly-elected President Kim Young-sam (1993-1998) vowed to create a "New Korea" that would be democratic and corruption-free. His efforts took many forms, some of which were more successful than others. On balance, they helped Korea take an important step forward.

2

Civilian Government

Political Neutrality of the Military

Kim Young-sam, a long-time opposition leader who, at times, had been subjected to political persecution by Presidents Park Chung-hee (1961-79) and Chun Doo-hwan (1980-1988), was elected president by direct popular vote in December 1992 as the standard bearer of the Democratic Liberal Party, a party created in 1990 through a merger of Kim's own Democratic Party with the ruling Democratic Justice Party. Kim took his oath of office as his predecessors, Chun Doo-hwan and Roh Tae-woo (1988-1993), both ex-army generals, looked on.

Within two weeks after his inauguration, Kim replaced key military leaders, including the powerful army chief-of-staff, all of whom had been appointed by Roh, with generals who had been known to be non-political officers. The newly-elevated generals took oaths forswearing any interference in politics. A secret organization of politically-oriented military officers called *Hanahoe* (One Mind), which included ex-presidents Chun and Roh as charter members, was ordered to disband. Civilian control of the military was reestablished for the first time since 1961.

Trial and Punishment of Former Military Leaders

Grievance over the brutal suppression of pro-democracy riots in the city of Kwangju (in South Chŏlla province) in 1980, had long been a political time bomb, but it did not receive a proper hearing until after those responsible for the use of excessive military force had left their government posts. At the heart of the Kwangju problem was not only the issue of democracy versus military authoritarianism but also that of regionalism that tended to drive a wedge between the people of the southwestern province of Chŏlla and their neighbors in the southeastern province of Kyŏngsang. President Kim, a native of Kyŏngsang, was unwilling, at first, to initiate a formal inquiry, saying that history should be the ultimate judge. The state prosecutors obliged by declaring that there were no cases of indictable offenses.

In late 1995, however, Kim changed his mind under mounting pressure from the families of the victims and their allies in the opposition parties and elsewhere, and the full force of judicial proceedings was unleashed against those implicated in the Kwangju case, many of whom were also charged with corruption. First, ex-president Roh was arrested on charges of having accepted several hundred million dollars in bribes; charges of collaboration in the Kwangju incident were added later. Within weeks, Roh's predecessor and former army colleague, Chun, was arrested and indicted on multiple charges including the Kwangju case, extortion of "political contributions" that surpassed in value those received by Roh, and mutiny arising from the arrest of the then army chief-of-staff by Chun's men on December 12, 1979, in the first stage of his rapid climb to power. Also investigated were dozens of former high-ranking military officers who occupied key government posts under Chun and Roh, as well as a score of business magnates who allegedly had offered bribes. After months of trial that was open to the public, Chun was sentenced to death, Roh to twenty-two and a half years in prison, and twenty-five others to lesser punishment. Chun's sentence has since been commuted to life imprisonment. The extraordinary spectacle of rows of former high-ranking military officials, including ex-presidents, dressed in prison uniform and standing at attention in the court room, was a visual testimony to the end of an era of military rule in South Korea.

3

Anti-Corruption Reforms

Purge of Corrupt Officials

The former military leaders were not alone nor were they the first to be implicated in bribery scandals. It was an open secret that corruption was wide-spread and existed at virtually all levels of bureaucracy and at other public organizations. At the outset of his 5-year term, President Kim told the nation that he would not accept any offer of political funds from anyone, and proceeded vigorously to punish corrupt officials irrespective of what offices they held. The Board of Audit and Inspection conducted investigations that led to the prosecution and punishment of many, including cabinet-level officials. A new code of ethics was enacted, requiring everyone in public service to disclose and register their assets. Kim set the example by making public his and his family's assets, and other high officials and members of the National Assembly followed suit. Publicity forced those who were found with excessive but unexplained wealth to resign. The public cheered the anti-corruption campaign and gave the president an unprecedented 81% approval rating toward the end of his first year in office.

Disclosure of a series of other bribery scandals in the succeeding years, besides the cases of Chun and Roh, proved once again that corruption was a deep-rooted social malady that could not be cured overnight. The age-old custom of gift-giving provided fertile ground for the seeds of corruption to grow. Despite the continued emphasis on punishing errant bureaucrats, politicians, bankers, businessmen, or even educators for accepting gifts in return for special favors, corruption persisted. The reform campaign lost much of its popular support when a high ranking member of the Presidential Secretariat and long-time aide to Kim Young-sam was indicted early in 1996 for accepting a large bribe; the president was forced to issue a public apology. In the meantime, his popularity rating steadily declined in 1995 and 1996, partly due to the perceived lack of success in his anti-corruption campaign.

The Real Name System in Banking and Real Estate Ownership

For years, South Koreans could open bank accounts under names other than their own, and they also could register real estate under fictitious or borrowed names. Those who wanted to shield their wealth from the tax office or any other probing eyes had found the system very helpful. However, tax officials, law enforcement agencies, and some economic planners thought otherwise and proposed to require the use of the owners real name. On the other hand, some feared that the real name system would dry up the supply of capital for Korea's expanding economy by scaring away potential savers and depositors. There also were concerns over the political repercussions of stepping on the toes of the wealthy and the powerful.

In August 1993 President Kim surprised virtually everyone by announcing the mandatory use of the real names on bank accounts. When the two-month grace period was up, 95% of the false-name accounts had been converted to real-name accounts. Two years later, a similar change was decreed in real estate ownership registration. Again, despite initial misgivings, the real name system prevailed without any meaningful opposition. Discontinuation of the fictitious name system, which had certainly contributed to clandestine or illicit fund transfers and tax evasion, marked another step in modernizing Korea's economic system. It is no surprise, therefore, that many consider the change to the real name system a part of Kim's anti-corruption campaign and a positive accomplishment of his administration.

4

Democratization

Toward a Kinder and Gentler Government

Throughout the years of his political career as an opposition leader, Kim Young-sam appeared to be a fighter for democratic principles. His triumphant entry into the Blue House (presidential mansion), therefore, seemed to promise a dramatic turn toward democracy after decades of authoritarian military rule. In the first weeks of his administration, such anticipation was seemingly borne out in his selection of top aides and in his public statements. Appointed as one of the two deputy prime ministers was an academic who had been imprisoned and blacklisted by the preceding regimes for his activities against military rule. Another academic was appointed to head the Agency for National Security Planning, the former Korean C.I.A., and he proceeded to end the agency's role as a secret police that monitored the activities of government officials, politicians, journalists, the intellectuals, and everybody else. President Kim also used his office as a pulpit from which to preach that the bureaucrats were indeed public servants and that every effort should be made to make them more responsive and courteous to their clients. In order to highlight his populist image, as well as to eliminate unnecessary inconvenience to the citizens of Seoul, President Kim opened to civilian traffic the streets leading to the Blue House for the first time in many years.

As months and years passed, however, the initial thrust for democratic reforms appeared to lose steam. Former pro-democracy activists did not stay in their government jobs long enough to introduce much reform in their agencies. Above all, the authoritarian bureaucratic culture was too deeply rooted for a quick solution. President Kim certainly initiated a process of change toward a "kinder and gentler government," but the process turned out to be slow and full of unexpected twists and turns.

Local Autonomy

One of the lasting legacies that President Kim will have left behind when he steps down in 1998 may be the long-awaited implementation of local elections. Direct popular elections of provincial governors, city mayors, county chiefs, heads of city wards, and the members of assemblies at various levels of local government took place in June 1995, for the first time since 1960. Election contests were conducted in an atmosphere that allowed, by and large, free and fair competition. The ruling Democratic Liberal Party suffered major setbacks, particularly in the city of Seoul. A former university professor, new to partisan politics, won a decisive victory over a former prime minister to head the government of the capital city. Equally surprising was the sweep of the offices of ward chiefs in Seoul; 23 out of 25 wards elected Democratic Party-endorsed candidates. The ruling party fared better in other races but the psychological impact of its defeat in Seoul was disheartening to say the least. Viewed from a larger perspective, however, the voters at long last could and did exercise their constitutionally-guaranteed right to select the administrative heads and councilmen at the grass-roots level. Belatedly, South Korea took another major step towards the democratic transformation of its politics.

Realignment of Political Parties

An important sequel to the local elections was a restructuring of the opposition camp. Buoyed by the Democratic Party's successes in Seoul and in Chŏlla provinces, its elder statesman and three-time presidential contender, Kim Dae-jung, decided to end his self-imposed retirement and reenter politics. A rival of President Kim since the early 1970s when they competed for a chance to run as an opposition candidate against President Park, Kim Dae-jung promptly set to organize a new party of his own, the National Congress for New Politics (NCNP). The emergence of the NCNP gutted the opposition Democratic Party which, however, continued to exist, albeit reduced to being only a minor group.

Within the ruling party, the three-way merger that had created the Democratic Liberal Party (DLP) in 1990, came unraveled. Kim Jong-pil, the leader of one of the three merged parties, left the DLP under pressure in early 1995, and promptly restructured his group into the United Liberal Democrats (ULD). The ULD survived the electoral tests in 1995 and 1996 as a credible third party with strong showings in Ch'ungch'ŏng provinces, Kim Jong-pil's home base. As for the DLP, it decided to strengthen President Kim's control of party affairs by appointing his long-time supporters to key posts replacing some of the erstwhile supporters of the previous Chun and Roh regimes. In order to distance himself from the two disgraced former presidents, President Kim also changed the name of his party to New Korea Party (NKP), four months before the National Assembly elections scheduled for April 11, 1996.

The NKP won a comfortable plurality, 46 percent, of the assembly seats, while the NCNP took only 26 percent; due to faulty pre-election calculations regarding the distribution of the "at-large" seats that were assigned to each party, Kim Dae-jung himself failed to retain his seat in the assembly. The ULD did better than expected by taking 17 percent.

While the party realignment in 1995 and 1996 was essentially a reprise of the previous pattern with only new names and new faces, there was one noticeably new development, namely, the rise of a new generation of politicians. Many well-known veterans of party politics lost their seats in the 1996 National Assembly elections to political newcomers many of whom were relatively young. This is a trend that, according to some observers, may bring about an end of the era of the Three Kims when President Kim leaves the Blue House in early 1998. It appeared probable that, in the last years of the Twentieth Century, a generational change in South Korean politics was in progress although nobody could spell out all the ramifications of such change. It was, nevertheless, a good bet that the process of democratization would continue.

5

Relations with North Korea

The Nuclear Issue

President Kim's inaugural message contained a strong reaffirmation of his commitment to the reunification of his homeland despite ideological differences between North and South Korea. A civilian president replacing a military rule in the South was also expected to be in a better position to pursue a conciliatory policy toward the North who, in turn, might soften its hostile stance toward the South. Events proved otherwise.

Soon after Kim's assumption of power in Seoul, Pyŏngyang challenged and eventually announced its withdrawal from the international regime regarding nuclear non-proliferation. The United States, the chief sponsor of the non-proliferation treaty (NPT), became alarmed and entered into a series of intensive bilateral negotiations with North Korea, which finally agreed to suspend its renunciation of the NPT and further consented, in October 1994, to freeze its existing nuclear projects in return for international assistance for new, "safer," light-water reactors to be built in North Korea. As Washington and Pyŏngyang talked, Seoul stood on the sideline, although about 70 percent of the fund for the international project was to come from South Korea. Seoul acquiesced in the nuclear accord in the hope that Pyŏngyang would honor its pledge to resume the North-South dialogue that had been suspended for over two years.

Earlier in 1994, when the tension over the nuclear issue reached a critical stage, North Korea's Kim Il-sung met with former U.S. president

Jimmy Carter in search of a breakthrough for the seemingly deadlocked nuclear negotiations then in progress. That was when Kim Il-sung made a surprise proposal for a conference with President Kim of South Korea. Seoul promptly accepted the proposal. Twenty days later, however, the "Supreme Leader" in Pyŏngyang suddenly died and the plan for a historic inter-Korean summit died with him. North-South relations quickly returned to the status quo ante—or worse. Seoul's refusal to send condolences to Pyŏngyang was greatly resented and North Korea has since insisted on Seoul's apology as a precondition for any North-South dialogue.

Economic Exchanges with the North

Despite the frigid political relations between Pyŏngyang and Seoul, the fledgling pattern of economic exchanges managed to stay on course—at least until the second half of 1996. Included in the economic package were South Korea's participation in the Korean Peninsula Energy Development Organization (KEDO) to build South Korean-type light-water reactors in the North, in a UN-sponsored project for a free trade zone in Rajin-Sŏnbong area on North Korea's east coast, and in the development of another free trade zone near Namp'o on the west coast. There also were a small number of North-South joint ventures in various stages of planning or operation.

Commodity trade between the two Koreas had slowly grown since 1988 when the two-way trade was less than $19 million, and it reached $287 million by 1995. South Korea became the third largest trade partner, and the second largest export market for the North. Furthermore, South Korea provided 150,000 tons of rice free of charge in 1995 to relieve an acute food shortage in the North which was aggravated by damage from summer-time floods. North Korea's unfriendly treatment of South Korean seamen who delivered the relief grain, however, hardened Seoul's position on economic exchange with Pyŏngyang: no further aid or economic cooperation without the resumption of political talks between the two Koreas.

Intrusion of a North Korean Submarine

The inter-Korean relations reached its lowest point in years when a North

Korean submarine was found abandoned on the rocky shore near the South Korean city of Kangnŭng in September 1996. The crew and passengers, who were specially-trained commandos, escaped into the mountains nearby, but all except one died either in gunfights with the pursuing South Korean troops or by their own action (suicide pact?). The South Korean casualties which included innocent civilians were not light in the two-month-long manhunt. Confronted with such an unmistakable act of intrusion in violation of the armistice agreement, the people in the South experienced shock and anxiety over their safety and their nation's security; they also felt anger at North Korea which deliberately sent the submarine, probably not for the first time, and then refused to admit its culpability and apologize. Any hopes for better inter-Korean relations were dashed, and the future of all existing cooperative projects, including that of the KEDO, became uncertain as 1996 drew to a close.

Suggested Further Reading

Kim, Han-Kyo. 1994. Korea. *The Americana Annual.* Yearbook of the
    Encyclopedia Americana (n.p.: Grolier, 1994). pp. 307-310.

_____. Korea. 1995. *The Americana Annual.* Yearbook of the
    Encyclopedia Americana (n.p.: Grolier, 1995). pp. 297-301.

_____. Korea. 1966. *The Americana Annual,* Yearbook of the
    Encyclopedia Americana (n.p.: Grolier, 1996). pp. 305-309.

_____. Korea. 1997. *The Americana Annual.* Yearbook of the
    Encyclopedia Americana. forthcoming.

Koh, B.C. 1996. "South Korea in 1995," *Asian Survey* XXXVI:1. pp. 53-
    60.

Lee, Chong-Sik and Hyuk-Sang Sohn. 1994. "South Korea in 1993,"*Asian
    Survey.* XXXIV:1. pp. 1-9.

_____. 1995. "South Korea in 1994," *Asian Survey.* XXXV:l. pp. 28-36.

Id. and id. "South Korea in 1994," *Asian Survey.* XXXV:1 (January 1995),
    28-36.

11

Traditional Culture and Society
by *Nancy Abelmann*

1

Introduction

In this chapter we will focus on Korean families, lineages, and villages as the most important contexts for understanding pre-20th century, particularly the late Chosŏn period (17th-19th century), Korean social life. Broadly, we will explore Korean traditional society as patrilineal (a kinship principle), patriarchal (the organization of power within families), and familistic (the broader social, political, and economic distribution of power is intimately tied to kinship ideologies and the family system). "Traditional" families associated with agricultural villages are not remote features in the contemporary, largely urban industrial, South Korean landscape. Indeed, it is easy to forget that many of South Korea's urbanites are first generation migrants, the sons and daughters of farmers. Many South Koreans continue to be connected, although increasingly more loosely, to a rural homeland or *kohyang* where they periodically visit relatives and grave sites.

Beyond personal ties to rural homelands, widely shared images portray "traditional" Korean society and life-style; at the mere mention of "tradition," an array of social practices and cultural symbols come to mind. These images are in large part promulgated through widespread public education, nearly universal exposure to mass media images including historical films and soap-operas, and even advertisements. Further, contemporary official and popular discourse posits social transformation in relation to these images; there is broad consensus that many features of late 20th century Korean life represent a radical break with the past, and also that rapid social flux is an ongoing feature of contemporary life. The consensus shatters, however, when it comes to the evaluation of these changes: some assert that the shackles of traditional society thwart progressive social and political reform, while others champion a renaissance of past life styles, mores, and practices to reinstate moral and meaningful family and social life. Indeed, contemporary South Korean "culture" emerges above all as an ongoing debate over what Korean culture was, is, and should be.

Thus constructions of the past sketch the self-conscious legacies with which contemporary society engages in ongoing dialogue The lens of history always works—self-consciously or unconsciously—through such a dialogue, and Korea's particular historical circumstances render this particularly obvious. Intensive foreign social-cultural, ideological, and political-economic intrusions over the century have forced Koreans in popular, scholarly, and political circles to ask: what are the Korean indigenous patterns? Pre-modern Chinese influences, Japanese colonial intrusion (1910-1945), and U.S. cultural and ideological penetration in the post-Liberation period (1945-) pose enormous scholarly and political challenges to consideration of enduring Korean social life and culture. One cannot peel away historical layers to resuscitate an original, something pure or enduring. The task is impossible, both because historical transformation is not a neat or simple process of layering in which one pattern of social life replaces another and because there is never a static or enduring original. In this sense we must be wary of portraits of tradition which are fixed, those that are fabricated in the present.

Nevertheless, we will proceed by first sketching the broad contours of late Chosŏn period family and kinship ideology and social relations, understanding that these were never fixed or enduring, and that this portrayal most closely depicts the lives of elites. Following this somewhat static portrait we will consider formation in a stratified society in flux. It is in this context that this cultural portrait will emerge as an ideological system developed in and maintained by particular political arrangements. We will see that culture and power must always be considered together-in the past, the present, and the present memory of the past. By the end of this chapters discussion, we hope that it will be difficult to maintain a static portrait of pre-modern Korean "tradition." We must, however, appreciate that the following configuration of ideology and concomitant social practices is still today the most widely shared image of traditional society—what we might call a dominant social or cultural memory.

Confucianism and Patrilineal Ideology, Institutions, and Practices

The widely shared sense of the traditional family cannot be wrested from the ideologies and images of Confucianism. While Americans seldom talk about a "family system," South Koreans understand the ideologies and requirements of extended family organization as a somewhat rule-bound system, specifically the practice of Confucianism. While there is a tendency to assume that all that is traditional is Confucian, it is in practice difficult to suggest a simple one-to-one relationship between what we might call features of Korean social organization and Confucian ideology. Ideological systems are flexible, lending themselves potentially to the rationalization of any number of social forms and practices. This distinction becomes even more complicated when we understand that Confucianism itself was a foreign ideological system that both refashioned Korea and was itself refashioned on Korean soil, effecting what one scholar calls a "Confucian revolution."

Confucianism is an ideological system in two senses. First, it is a set of ideas which prescribes ideal social behavior and human values. Second, Confucianism in the late Chosŏn period was a set of ideas employed by the ruling classes to legitimate, rationalize, and perpetuate their status and power. In this sense, Confucianism in the pre-modern Korean social historical context was both a prescription for an ideal social life and a cultural system used to perpetuate relations of inequality.

We begin by taking Confucianism and most particularly its Korean kinship corollary, patrilineal ideology, as systems of ideas governing individual and family behavior.

3

Filial Piety and the Separation of the Sexes

Confucianism prescribes ideal human social relations across age, generation, gender, and status, establishing clear hierarchies between elder and
younger, male and female, and ruler and ruled. The superiority and submission implied in these linked pairs is at the heart of late Chosŏn period
Korean kinship ideology. While these basic relationships could lead to an
array of social practices and ideologies, we will see that the primary social
values can be considered an extension of these basic relationships.

The primary generational and gender ideologies were filial piety and
the separation of the sexes. Filial piety assumes the enormous debt of
children to their parents and by extension of people to their ancestors. It
demands strict obedience, respect of authority, and careful care of parents
and ancestors by offspring—effectively, economically, and ritually.

The separation of and inequality between the sexes is the literal
practice of this gender ideology, suggesting that women are secondary to
men and that they should remain separate from them. These principles
are captured in the spirit of two popular Chinese ideogram phrases: *nam-
nyŏ-yubyŏl* (sex-difference) and *namjon-yŏbi* (honored men, lowly
women). One of the most popular and still widely cited Confucian
metaphors proclaims men the heavens, and women the earth, who are
thus destined to follow. Young women were not to have any contact with
men, and even homes were divided into gender spaces: outer rooms or
sarangbang for men and inner rooms or *anbang* for women.
Prescriptions for women's behavior, movement, and even clothing made

women invisible.

Keeping these basic gender and generational principles in mind, let us turn to patrilineal kinship ideology. By kinship ideology we can think simply of the principles governing the relations between individuals and groups of individuals understood to be kin. While at first glance, kinship can appear to be something biological or natural—simply the entire set of people related to a person by blood—the process through which people are recognized and organized as kin is a social system which varies enormously across space and time. While kinship ideologies and organizations have diminished importance in capitalist, industrial society, in pre-capitalist societies such as pre-20th century Korea they were central to social, political, and economic organization, and to daily life and ritual practice. In practical terms, then, more aspects and more time of more lives were tied up in relations that were understood to be family or kinship relations.

The central axiom of patrilineal kinship ideology is that families are not independent, timeless entities, but rather nodes of a large and historically deep entity: a line or lineage of people linked through male kin. If we imagine a family tree, a patrilineage refers to those branches that trace through male kin; this does not mean that women cannot be part of a patrilineage, but that they are only part of it through a male link. While potentially almost infinite, patrilineages are limited because they are imagined as the progeny of a single ancestor rendered through generations of male descendants. In this sense, patrilineages can split to continue to produce new patrilineages or patrilineal branches. Thus for example the great-great-great-great grandchildren of two brothers can consider themselves members of distinct patrilineages, namely those descended from different great-great-great-great grandfathers. This social concept of descent takes on life in several ways, most centrally via ancestral worship.

At the heart of the reproduction or continuity of a patrilineage is the birth of a son; daughters, who marry into another man's patrilineage, are therefore incidental. A common prescription in Korea is that women follow three men over their lifetimes: their father, their husband, and finally their son. Whether male or female, the children of a woman are not members of her father's patrilineage. A patrilineage dies if there are no sons to continue the line and thrives if it can accrue property and status through the careful care of its elders and its ancestors.

Korean patrilineal ideology maintains strict hierarchy among men according to generation, birth order, and age. While lineage is traced through men generally, the most important man is the oldest son, and the most important family is his family, the senior family. Primogeniture refers to kinship systems which in this fashion stress the importance of the eldest son. Within patrilineages, then, whatever their depth, it is the descendant of the deepest ancestor's oldest son—the oldest son of the oldest son of the oldest son—who is the most important. Indeed there were even names for the individual who occupies this privileged position and for his wife. The "houses" or families of eldest sons become "big houses" or *k'ŭn chip* in relation to the younger sons' *chagŭn chip* or "small houses."

Kinship terminology follows the principles of age, generation, and genealogy. While in the United States, "grandfather" can refer to one's maternal or paternal grandfather, in Korean it generally refers to a person's paternal grandfather, the father of one's father. While people may have important social relationships with their maternal grandfathers, they are not members of one's patrilineage. To indicate maternal grandfather, the Chinese ideogram for "outside," *oe*, is affixed to the word grandfather. Unless she specifies otherwise, a married woman will use "grandfather" to refer to her husband's father. Many kinship terms, including those for uncle, aunt, great uncle, and great aunt, distinguish between maternal and paternal relatives; that is, there are distinct terms for one's mother's brother, father's brother, mother's sister, and father's sisters. We can also recognize the principle of age, for example, as uncles on both one's mother's and father's side are carefully distinguished by age: "small uncles" if they are younger than one's father, and "large" if they are older. Further they are often numbered as the second uncle, third uncle, and so on.

These hierarchies are observed not only through kinship terminology but also through language use generally. The Korean language observes age hierarchy; verbs, forms of address, and even vocabulary vary depending on who you are speaking to, such that a casual eavesdropper can immediately gauge social distance and age difference between speakers. It is easy, however, to imagine cases where hierarchical principles of age, generation, and status are conflicting, such as the case of an uncle who is younger than his nephew, a not uncommon arrangement in families with many children. We mention this example to recall that these are principles, sets of social ideas, that lend meaning to social life rather than rules which uniformly govern behavior.

4

Patrilineal Corollaries:
Marriage, Inheritance, Adoption, and Widowhood

Thus patrilineal ideology embodies the Confucian principles: males are accorded more value than females, seniors more value than juniors. Indeed, women are to defer to men, juniors to seniors, junior generations to senior generations, and the ruled to rulers. The primary corollaries of the Korean patrilineal system all follow these age and gender hierarchies. We will examine a number of corollaries of patrilineal ideology and social organization, including inheritance, lineage exogamy, patrilocal marriage practice, adoption, and widowhood.

Integral to patrilineal social organization and the particular principle of primogeniture in Korea is inheritance. Property was ideally divided among male offspring disproportionately such that eldest sons were given more and daughters were excluded entirely.

Lineage exogamy, another corollary of patrilineage, dictates that people not marry descendants of the same ancestors or members of the same lineage. Simply, a marriage between kin is considered incestuous. Such a group can in theory be large or small, but in the Korean case it is often very large. Although most people's identifications in daily life are with what we might call proximate patrilineages, those of several generations, people can also be considered members of very deep patrilineages. The deep patrilineages might, for example, refer to all the people who have the same last name, or to a subset of all the people who have the same last name. Indeed, in Korea's patrilineal exogamy, marriages between people with the same last name or the same branch of the same last name (such as the "Kims from Andong") are neither socially nor legally recognized. In spite of concerted popular calls to change this practice in Korea today, and although the legal system has abolished many other patrilineal features, these marriages remain prohibited. Because there are relatively few surnames in Korea, and because an even smaller number of surnames or surname branches account for a majority of the population, large numbers of people are out of bounds for marriage. However, considerable numbers of people do fall in love and co-reside with people of the same surname or surname branch. While legally these marriages cannot be registered, the state addresses this problem by periodically sanctioning these unions.

A third corollary of patrilineage is patrilocal marriage in which women marry into their husband's families and reside—at least for a period—with their husband's families. The bride is expected to leave her family behind as she enters her husband's patrilineage, taking on the duties to first and foremost give birth to the male descendants of that patrilineage and to serve its elders and ancestors. This is particularly the case for the so-called "oldest daughter-in-law," the wife of the oldest son. Although the wives of secondary sons will live with their in-laws for a period of time, eventually they tend to branch off, taking up their own residences as nuclear families. Interestingly, the Korean historical record suggests that in spite of strong patrilineal ideology, most families were in fact stem families, units of parents and their children. Eldest sons, however, continued to reside with their parents, exercising their duties as the primary male offspring. Patrilineages, however, can take social form beyond the confines of a single home or village, even in an urban industrial setting.

The young bride then is considered to marry "into a family." Indeed, people's identities are intimately tied with patrilineages and patrilineal groups of kin. It is still a commonplace in contemporary South Korea that marriage is a union, often political, of families, not of individuals. Even today the most generally used word for a woman's marriage is "to go to one's husband's family"; to herald South Korea's changing social tides, a 1993 advertisement for a new marriage journal proclaimed: "Now we don't 'go to our husband's family' we 'get married.'" In traditional marriages, the relationship between the bride and the groom, the husband and wife is secondary; rather, the relations between parents and sons, particularly fathers and sons, are central to the patrilineage. In most cases the young couple are strangers at the wedding, and sexual relations between husband and wife are not considered the consummation of romantic love but the requirement of patrilineages to produce male offspring. In this sense, marriage can be broadly considered an arrangement whereby a woman arrives to fulfill duties to her husbands patrilineage. Often couples did not sleep in the same quarters, and occasions for sex were determined and arranged by the older generation members of the household. This does not, however, mean that romantic love or sexual passion were absent in pre-modern Korea. Rather, to a large extent, they were strangers to formal upper-class marital relations. Beyond marriage there were important relations with concubines and prostitutes, and there were formally registered secondary wives.

It is no surprise that the young bride's position was, and in some circles still is today, delicate and difficult. Most vulnerable of all was a young bride unable to fulfill her greatest duty: the birth of a male offspring. One need not look far in Korea today for the tragic stories of ancestresses who were barren or could not bear sons. Indeed, until they produced a son, young brides were quite expendable. As a 94 year-old woman told me in 1993, "I bore no sons, my life has no value—I should have died long ago."

For women, the relations to sons and mothers-in-law were the central axes of social life. The mother-in-law and daughter-in-law relationship was and still is often conflictual where women vie for attention from and control over the same man, son and husband respectively. Even today this is a theme played out in endless proverbs, literary genres, and popular media. It is, for example, commonplace to warn against marrying the eldest son so as to avoid the most direct link to a husband's patrilineage, to the hardships of dealing directly with a mother-in-law, and the often arduous duties of caring for a family's elders and ancestors.

It is revealing to examine adoption—one of the solutions for son-less families as a window on patrilineal ideology. Even in the East Asian Confucian context, Korea stands out for its rigid principle of consanguinity—enormous importance accorded to blood relationships. Where a couple is childless, the adoption of a non-relative will not satisfactorily perpetuate the patrilineage. Indeed, the common pre-modern practice was to adopt members of the same patrilineage. If, for example, the "big house" could not bear a son, ideally one of the younger brother's secondary sons would be adopted. In this way even the adopted son's generation was consistent with patrilineal hierarchy. The lack of a son constituted legal grounds for divorce and was also solved by taking on secondary wives to bear a son; this strategy, however, became less ideal over the Chosŏn period because increasingly gender norms privileged the first wife. Although we find increasing adoption of non-affines in South Korea today, it remains largely taboo, and frequently adoption is hidden from the larger society and even from the adoptee.

Widowhood, and particularly early widowhood, became in Korea perhaps one of the most symbolic arenas for the practice of Confucian ideology and the patrilineal principle. The virtuous widow was to remain faithful to her husbands patrilineage till death, particularly if she had already become the mother of that patrilineage's male descendent. Should she decide to leave, however, her children—especially sons—would remain with her deceased husband's family. In the case of any dissolution of marriage, the children remained with the father's family. The faithful widow was a cultural icon, a credit to her family and patrilineage.

5

Patrilineal Groups and Institutions

If patrilineage is an idea or socially created cultural system—remembering that there is nothing natural or biological about it—how does it take form in broader social life and organization? In pre-modern Korean society one of the ways in which patrilineages took form was in *chokpo*, Korean family registers, books which recorded the family tree. In addition to such registers, we can also examine who was and was not included in family rituals, particularly those reserved for the deceased members of a family: the ancestors. We can also consider the flow of goods, time, and property, examining who shares what with whom, who inherits what, and who spends time with whom.

As Confucian patrilineal ideology casts lineages of people descended from the same ancestor, it also identifies groups of kin which can be mobilized in ritual and economic activities of daily life. In the case of distant ancestors these are indeed large groups, who practice ancestral worship together but are less involved in each others day-to-day lives. What links small groups is the common descent from a relatively close ancestor, perhaps a great or great-great grandfather. Depending on the extent or depth of the lineage affiliation, this can translate into nothing other than a group of first and second affinal cousins among whom to share farmwork or farm tools, or alternatively an affiliation that allows or aids a man in his efforts to hold public office and accrue social benefits and material wealth. Both proximate and deeper lineages can collectively own and administer property, but most importantly they accord members symbolic and human capital: rights to a particular lineage status—the claim of a particular heritage—and networks of relatives who extend various favors to one another. The link between larger groups who ritually observe a more distant ancestor is the status of the group as the descendants of typically a man of great Confucian learning who has held an official state position.

Villages were themselves often clusters of households of affinal kin. Even today it is not uncommon for middle-aged urbanites to recall their childhood living in close proximity to second, third, or even fourth cousins. In so-called kinship villages, those where the vast majority of residents are agnates, the village social relations accord with the patrilineal principle and hierarchy. Systems, for example, of control and of distribution—keeping order and sharing wealth—follow patrilineal hierarchy. Still today in the South Korean rural landscape one can feel the kinship primacy in villages through the impressive grave sites that are nestled in the most auspicious spots of villages.

Graves are a palpable reminder that lineages are tied to locales, the places where the ancestors are buried, where periodically the group of mourners must gather. Ideally, the oldest male descendent remains to care for the grave, tends to the ancestors, and hence perpetuates the lineage and the village. By now, of course, the history of the highest rural exodus rates in the world and considerable emigration have fated transgressions: homelands and graveyards to be tended to by distant affines or non-relatives, or worse yet to be untended entirely. More amazing still from the gaze of this ideological universe are the elderly who live alone in the countryside. Naturally, as villages have stopped reproducing themselves, so too have a broad array of practices.

It is nearly impossible, however, to speak of "traditional" villages as homogeneous units across space or time. Casual travel in the Korean countryside immediately reveals that clusters of homes can be large or small, that the homes can be nearly one on top of another or generously scattered, that they can be nestled in foothills or dispersed on open plains and so on.

For our consideration the more relevant aspect of this diversity is the nature of village social relations. Status or class distribution in the village was particularly determining of social relations. In villages where a single *yangban* lineage dominated numerically, the village social organization—including the distribution of power, the organization of labor, and ritual and recreational—life tended to follow the lines of hierarchy of Korean patrilineal ideology. That is primary lineages and ages seniors tended to dominate, and much of social life was caught up in the more formal exercise of above reviewed ideologies. Many villages, however, were composed entirely of commoners, and others still of a mixture of commoner and *yangban* lineages.

20th century village ethnographies (in-depth studies of single villages) have shown that in villages where a single *yangban* lineage does not obviously dominate, social ties are far more egalitarian, and kinship principles and ideologies of gender and age hierarchies do not exert an absolute control over social life. Instead, mutual cooperation in economic activities, and more informal and even unruly social exchange in leisure activities guide the tenor of social life. Village studies reveal, for example, that even lineage rituals can become occasions for open village gathering in which non-kin participate as well. One ethnographer contrasted the "anarchic egalitarianism" of non-lineage social relations, observing that personal charisma, leadership skills, and generosity win respect and local authority in contrast with the ascribed attributes of age and kinship position which reign in *yangban*-dominated villages or social situations.

In recent years in South Korea, social activists have taken a great interest in counter-Confucian ideologies or practices; they are interested in the legacies of egalitarian human relations, labor cooperation, communal activities, and rich and informal social life and cultural expression. Of particular interest to some contemporary scholars and activists are horizontal social organizations unmediated by kinship or power hierarchies. These include primarily *ture*, cooperative labor organizations, and *kye*, rotating credit organizations. Exciting new research has begun to document the nature and social life of such organizations. While the documents are scarce, creative consideration of such social domains challenges long-standing understandings of dominant ideologies and their social controls.

In villages, competing status and power hierarchies made for complex social organization, conflict, and enormous local variation.. The Chosŏn period, and particularly its final centuries, were years of political tumult, economic restructuring, and social mobility, such that in practice *yangban* lineages were comprised of branches and families spanning the status hierarchy. There were lower and higher ranked segments, and poorer and richer segments. In turn, increasingly influential and well-to-do commoners emerged, so that wealth and personal achievement cut across *yangban* status. By the end of the Chosŏn period, birthright alone could only go so far in governing the local distribution of wealth and power.

To further appreciate late Chosŏn conflicting hierarchies and social flux, let us now turn to a consideration of Confucianism as an ideological and political transformation. This examination will help us consider the complex interplay between culture and power such that traditional social life emerges as a contest and a process rather than a static or homogeneous entity. We will see that patrilineal ideology and its social practices together effected an enormous social transformation. Turning to the politics of this transformation, we must remember that regardless of the size or social composition of villages, they are largely face-to-face communities with few secrets and extensive informal social controls. Day-to-day gossip and social censure go far in regulating the exercise of social and ethical values. Vincent Brandt notes, for example, that any transgression of filial piety invited village scorn and the loss of prestige.

6
Confucianization as a Political and Ideological Process

We need to examine Confucianization as a process in order to query the limits of the reach of these ideologies which seem to dominate so much of social life and relations. At both the state and local levels, Confucianism was employed as a rationalizing philosophy for rule, a body of knowledge for mastery in academies that flourished over the Chosŏn Dynasty, and finally as prescriptions governing family organizations and daily social life and cultural values. The strict adherence to the cultural values and organizational principles outlined above—be it the observance of filial piety, the practice of ancestral worship, or the seclusion and subordination of women—was central to maintaining social standing and legitimizing political control. In other words Confucianism as a social and cultural system was integral to the expression of class standing and political and economic privilege.

7

Confucianism and Social Stratification

Late Chosŏn period society was dominated by *yangban*, a literati class of civil and military officials who passed the civil service examination and comprised the state bureaucracy. These Chinese-inspired examinations tested for the mastery of Confucian texts and learning. By the Chosŏn Dynasty, and even today, *yangban* families or patrilineages were ideally those which could claim ancestors who passed the state examinations and served in official positions. Although in principle officialdom was open to all who could achieve a certain rank in the state examinations, in practice it was principally *yangban* who sat for these exams. There is thus no way to disassociate the exercise of Confucian ideologies and social prescripts from these two matters: educational achievement as the mastery of Confucian texts and official positions in the centralized state bureaucracy. Over the Chosŏn period new families made claims to *yangban* status and privilege, and it even became possible to purchase *yangban* status. If we consider these avenues and the frequency of social mobility, lineage and Confucian ideologies become the criteria through which status was asserted. In *Ch'unhyangjŏn*, one of the most famous Korean stories which dates back to the Chosŏn era, for example, we find a mother who, although once a public entertainer (*kisaeng*), is determined to raise her daughter as a *yangban* to be able to assert her social status in spite of her mother's humble birth.

The job of *yangban* was to study in Confucian academies or *sŏwŏn* which proliferated all over the country over the Chosŏn period, to sit for the state examinations, and to hold office. *Yangban* were not to engage in other pursuits including crafts, business, and agriculture. The province of local government through so-called Local Agencies was administered by local yangban. While land was officially state-owned, it was increasingly over the Chosŏn period effectively accrued and managed by *yangban* officials. At the village level *hyang'yak*, the village contracts and its corollary social organization of all villages across the class spectrum was also directed by the *yangban*. While some *yangban* scholars have written of the egalitarian social relations in these apparently horizontal organizations, their democratic egalitarian character is somewhat dubious as they were in effect controlled by local elites. Rather, their proliferation suggests avenues for the widespread indoctrination of Confucian elite values among the wider populace.

While numerical estimates of the extent of *yangban* vary—some estimate 10%, others suggest that the figure is much higher in the late Chosŏn period—it is quite certain they represent a minority in contrast with the laboring, largely farming sector of the population. Beyond *yangban*, freeborn commoners (*sangmin*) tilled *yangban* land, and *ch'ŏnmin* or "low borns" which included outresident slaves were also largely agriculturists. Slaves—public and private—often had independent households but could technically be bought and sold. Some have estimated that slaves comprised as much as one third of the population over the Chosŏn period. Finally there were the outcast *paekchŏng* whose activities were limited to several abased occupations, including butchering and tanning.

The Chosŏn landscape was quite literally colored by status or station distinction. State decrees and local practices regulated the design, fabric, color, and extent of adornment of clothes, shoes, and hats. Even coiffures were controlled in this fashion. The body was thus a site for inscribing class and social position. Similarly stratified was the material expression at ancestral services; the government, for example, went so far as to regulate the nature and extent to which commoners could adopt these practices.

While *yangban* exercised local political authority and ideological power, their ties with the center assured their local power and status. Although considerable local autonomy allowed local elites to exercise local control and to censor the agents and agencies of central control, they were accorded this authority and status through ties to Korea's center: Seoul. Local lineages, for example, were often linked via kinship or marriage ties to powerful officials in Seoul. Also, local elites were often those who had served in the capital and were returning to their home areas. Indeed, Korea remains remarkably centralized in Seoul, demographically, politically, educationally, and economically.

For *yangban* elites, marriage was the way to secure relations between powerful families. Although marriage was lineage exogamous, it was class endogamous. These social networks were thus at once political networks because of the extent to which regional *yangban* controlled local areas politically and economically. It is still relevant in South Korea to examine the way in which family ties, lineages, and groups united through marriage intersect with economic and political lines of power. While the cultural exercise of status has been challenged on many fronts in contemporary South Korea, there is no question that kinship, lineage, and symbolic *yangban* class alliances continue to have some social life, albeit diminishing. It is in this sense that people pay attention to the marriage alliances between today's major corporations or to the patterns of regional and lineage affiliation of powerful politicians and bureaucrats.

Some scholars classify societies where family and lineage are the central units of social status and political control as familistic, or such a state as a family-state. The deep ancestral lineages we discussed above took on social life because they celebrate the status of the lineage, the fame and political achievement of a distant forbear. As such, lineages were agents in the preservation and continual reproduction of social status. Some scholars have noted that *yangban* was a cultural rather than a legal concept such that the criteria for *yangban* identification were subjective and flexible; the race for *yangban* status prescribed an array of social and moral practices. Of course, families aimed to produce male offspring who could achieve status themselves through education and official employment, but the very exercise of Confucianism through daily life and rituals—the careful maintenance of the above-outlined hierarchies—was itself the production of status, that is the display of a set of behaviors that when carefully executed marked one and one's family and lineage as members of an elite.

We must not, however, forget that for large numbers of Koreans social mobility was next to impossible, that they barely survived and had little economic margin to afford much of the ritual expression or exercise of Confucianism or patrilineal ideologies. For example, the principle of separation of women and men, and the seclusion of women assumes that women do not labor in the fields and that homes have multiple rooms surrounding yards—conditions foreign to the majority of Koreans. Further, these ideologies assume the recording of family pedigrees, resources for ancestral services, and literacy in order to fully exercise ritual practices. The majority of Koreans did not share pedigrees that identified with a great ancestor, often did not even have surnames and had little access to or ability to read written Confucian texts.

8

Confucianization as a Cultural and Social Process

We must also consider pre-Confucian cultural and social organizational principles in order to appreciate the drastic social change which Confucianism required in theory and to imagine the likely areas of resistance and cultural tension. The 16th and 17th centuries comprise the era in which Confucian social and cultural life was intensively legislated and to some extent popularized. JaHyun Haboush, for example, speaks of a normalized Confucian society by the 17th century. Extraordinarily revealing are the numerous ways in which social life was legislated and regulated, from marriage and inheritance to adoption, funerary practices, and widowhood. This social legislation reminds us that the basic lineage and Confucian hierarchies we discussed above—of gender, age and generation—were to an extent against the indigenous grain of the time.

Let us review several of the pre-Confucian social and organizational structures and cultural practices that were most at odds with the Confucian transformation. First and foremost, patrilineage was neither the primary social organizational or cultural principle; daughters and their offspring, for example, were considered integral members of family lineages. Accordingly, daughters and their offspring were listed in local registers and could inherit family property. Indeed women had property rights, and inheritance was divided equally among sons and daughters. Not surprisingly, ancestral services were conducted by women as well, and maternal kin were commemorated equally alongside male ancestors. These practices suggest the enormous transformation effected by the patrilineal and gender hierarchical principles of Confucianized Chosŏn society. Considering other social and cultural corollaries, we find that women's remarriage was neither discouraged nor unusual, that adoption was rare and that when practiced it did not accord with patrilineal principles. Additionally, uxorilcoal marriage was common whereby grooms would at least for a period come and live with the bride's family; also marriage among relatives was common, and marriages were easily dissolved.

What emerges is a bilateral kinship system, in which the kinship net cast according to both the maternal and paternal lines, and a society in which gender hierarchies were somewhat relaxed. It is thus not surprising that several aspects and practices of even late Chosŏn society strictly adhere to a more bilateral pattern. In this regard, marriage ceremonies and arrangements are most notable. Even by the end of the Chosŏn era many women returned to their natal homes after marriage, staying there several years, often until a child was born. One historian suggests that the wedding rite represents the institution that most "persistently resisted Confucianism."

We should not, however, jump to conclusions that pre-Chosŏn society was neither hierarchical nor class stratified—it was both. Nor should we hastily conclude that pre-Confucian society had achieved egalitarian gender relations—this was not the case. However, we do need to recognize this tidal wave of social change and the social engineering that Confucianism required. Various aspects and practices of social life were legally regulated and socially sanctioned. Funerary practice, for example, had to be severely legislated in order for people to discontinue Buddhist practices of cremation and to assume ancestral worship; in 1474 the state decreed that people who cremated their parents would be punished. Also, the spatial and body seclusion of women were legislated. In 1412, for example, it was decreed that women should not show their faces in public.

9

Confucianism and Cultural Resistance

The sense we get of Chosŏn society—contrary to many popular stereotypes—is of a rapidly changing society in which social flux and class mobility necessitated the constant exercise of cultural superiority and status. Here for example, the careful keeping of genealogies, the impeccable performance of ancestral services, the record of chaste widows, and virtuous wives were at least in part the gist of status expression. Cho Haejoang argues that in this cultural matrix women were ironically "powerful"—although lacking authority—as mothers, indispensable to the social assertion of power and integral to the social practice of Confucian ideology. In their role as bearers and chief managers of male offspring who should succeed to become educated and political elites, and in their role as purveyors of the feminine virtue making a *yangban* family, they were crucial to the exercise of those attributes that afforded prestige and thus the exercise of economic and political privilege. Beyond social mobility strategies and state or elite controlled social engineering, we must look both to those people entirely excluded from these efforts and to those social practices resisting these processes.

Difficult to recuperate are the hearts and minds of people: when economic and cultural resources barred landless peasants or slaves from participating in the Confucian practices of patrilineal lineages did they resist, mock, or make light of these ideologies? Where formal expressions such as song, dance, or story-telling, in which elites were often parodied. Where there are important records of anti-elite movements, particularly the struggles of tenant farmers against their landlords and state officials in the 18th, 19th, and early 20th centuries, it is difficult to assess to what extent these embodied deep-seated cultural rejections of the dominant ideologies of their times. An integrated look at Confucian and patrilineal ideologies as a ruling ideology forces us to shift any simple images of Korean tradition.

Many of the corollaries of these ideologies perhaps did not extend very far in pre-modern Korean society. Many of the values and practices were moot for those with few economic resources or little social pedigree. Beneath and beyond these ideologies and their requisite social structures and practices lie entirely other models of social interaction, group formation, and even cultural value. It has, however, been easier to preserve the ruling ideological universe as "tradition" precisely because it was invested with power and because it was and remains documented.

By today there are two contrasting images of this Confucian ideological and organizational principle: first as agents of social order, propriety in Korea as "the country of manners," an often-repeated phrase, and second as forces which over the last century in particular—over the crucial era of early contact with the Western world—have perpetuated resistance to progressive social change for a less authoritarian, less stratified, and less sexist society. The later portrait depicts effete aristocrats wholly engaged in the production and reproduction of their social status through the exercise of rigid Confucian rules and practices and thus unable to initiate enlightened social transformation or to prevent the eventual colonization by Japan. Increasingly, scholarly research suggests that this tension—the simultaneous embrace and rejection of the ruling ideological system—is not a late twentieth century invention but itself a tradition legacy.

One fruitful consideration of expression beyond the tenets and practice of Confucianism has been shamanism. In shamanistic rituals, typically conducted by shamans or *mudang*, a pantheon of deities as well as ancestors come to life via the shaman to respond to individual, family, or even village misfortune, trouble or sickness. Shamans and shamanism have been largely a female domain. Laurel Kendall suggests that the primary unit of shamanistic ritual is the household—those co-residing in a single abode, not the lineage, and that as the household is primarily the domain where women officiate, it is not surprising to find their primary ritual responsibility.

While the ancestors of ancestor worship are largely benevolent or at least non frightening characters, those in shamanistic ritual are often menacing or even malevolent. Some scholars offer that this reflects the ambivalent, conflict-ridden relationship of women with their husbands family. Also revealing is the bilateral character of the ancestors of shamanistic rituals; that is, women's natal kin appear alongside the kin of their patrilineages by marriage. Many of the tragedies and troubles which call for shamanistic rituals or *kut* can be related to the ideological sway of neo-Confucianism, including the inability to bear sons or problems with the achievement or maintenance of family wealth and status. While Confucian rituals are staid and tightly staged, *kut* are often unruly, humorous, and even bawdy. Confucianism and shamanism are, however, by no means mutually exclusive practices or systems. Nor are *yangban* and *non-yangban* lifestyles discrete. When we examine culture itself as a field of ideological and political struggle in times of tumultuous social transformation, we appreciate that such dichotomies—including "traditional" and "modern"—make little sense.

10
Conclusion

Consideration of traditional Korean society requires an understanding not of fixed social reforms or practices, but rather of transformative processes and historical contests in a stratified society. The ideological tenets of Confucianism have had enormous sway over family and social life. Confucianism considered as a political system and historical process, however, challenges the limits of elite ideological idioms and social forms. Korean traditional culture or social life emerges as a meaningful contemporary contest over the nature of historical legacies and agenda for social transformation.

Suggested Further Reading

Brandt, Vincent. 1971. A *Korean Village: Between Farm and Sea.* Cambridge: Harvard University Press.

Cho, Haejoang. Male Dominance and Mother Power: The Two Sides of Confucian Patriarchy in Korea. Unpublished manuscript.

Deuchler, Martina. 1977. "The Tradition: Women during the Yi Dynasty," *Virtues in Conflict: Tradition and the Korean Woman Today.* Sandra Mattielli (ed.). Seoul: Samhwa Publishing Co.

Haboush, JaHyunn Kim. 1991. "The Confucianization of Korean Society," *The East Asian Region: Confucian Heritage and its Modern Adaptation.* Gilbert Rozman (ed.). Princeton: Princeton University Press.

Janelli, Roger L. and Dawnhee Yim Janelli. 1982. *Ancestor Worship and Korean Society.* Stanford: Stanford University Press.

Kendall, Laurel. 1985. *Shamans, Housewives, and Other Resless Spirits: Women in Korean Ritual Life.* Honolulu: University of Hawaii Press.

Yi, Kim Eunhee. 1993. *From Gentry to the Middle Class: The Transformation of Family, Community and Gender in Korea.* Ph.D. Dis., University of Chicago.

12

Education
by Robert H. C. Kim

1

Introduction

Korea has a long history. It is alleged that Tan'gun, Korea's legendary founder, established a kingdom on the Korean peninsula sometime in 2333 B.C. Even if we were to dismiss this legend, it is nonetheless known that the indigenous people had left significant marks of their well developed culture on the peninsula long before people on the European continent established settled communities. Education was then, as it is now, an essential component of culture. People living in groups had to devise ways of teaching the young how to hunt and fish for their food, to till the land, to build fires, to protect themselves against dangerous enemies, and to co-exist with other members. In order to maintain social harmony, primitive laws developed in Old Chosŏn as early as the 12th century B.C. These laws prohibited killing people, stealing property, and doing harm to other people. It is said that the aboriginal tribal people had an educational philosophy based on the concept of *hongik in'gan*, or broad service for the benefit of mankind.

The recorded history of education for the Korean people does not start until after the founding of the Three Kingdoms in the peninsula. The first kingdom to be established was the Shilla Dynasty in 57 B.C., to be followed by Koguryŏ in 37 B.C. The last Dynasty, Paekche, came into being in 18 B.C. For a number of reasons, formal education probably did not begin until after these kingdoms had been well established. First, there had to be organizations capable of disseminating skills and information. This meant that people had to wait for organizations to develop.

Second, means of communication, both verbal and written, had to be invented or imported so that the young could be taught. Third, educational contents had to be developed. Fourth, there had to be mature adults who were able to teach the young. These and other pertinent factors seemed to have been satisfied to a certain extent in these kingdoms by the time Buddhism and Confucianism were introduced to them. Introduction of these two religions into Korea played a major role in developing educational institutions.

Remarkably, Confucian men, their ideas, and their institutions withstood challenges of time for change during the following twenty centuries until modernity began to assault them with science and technology. Americans and Europeans rushed into Korea with their new methods of education as well as Christianity toward the end of the 19th century. They established schools and churches to teach the young and the old. They taught them new values and new beliefs and began to change Korea's traditional values and institutions. Before these efforts were able to bear fruit, however, Japan took over Korea in 1905 and finally made Korea its colony in 1910. Japanese colonial policy was to assimilate the Korean people into Japanese culture. Education for Koreans was devoted to that singular political goal, and the Japanese colonial administration in Korea pursued it rigorously between 1910 and 1945. Japans continued territorial expansion touched off a major war in the Pacific in 1941, and Japan was finally defeated by the combined forces of the Allied Nations in 1945. The Korean peninsula was, however divided into two areas along the 38th parallel, according to the secret agreement made between the United States and the then Soviet Union. In August 1945, North Korea was occupied by the military forces of the Soviet Union, while America established its military rule in South Korea. North and South Korea still remain divided by the Demilitarized Zone, a by-product of the war that was fought from 1950 to 1953. Since the end of World War II North Korea has pursued educational goals of socialism and of *Juche* ideology. In contrast to North Korea's Communist educational goals, South Korea has strived for "anti-Communist, democratic goals" in education.

In presenting a short historical survey of educational achievements and current developments in both Koreas, it is necessary to identity four major strains of educational philosophy and practice that are uniquely characteristic of Korean culture and civilization. The first of these is the classical approach to education deeply embedded in religious teachings of Buddhism and Confucianism. The second is the Japanese colonial educational policy to Japanize all Koreans. The third is the Christian educational approach to education with emphasis on science and technology.

The fourth could be identified in North Korea as *Juche* ideology, or national self-identity, which has been the guiding educational philosophy since the early 1970s. In South Korea, however, the prevailing educational philosophy has been that of "anti-communist, democratic education."

2

Education in Traditional Korea

What constitutes traditional Korea? This question would certainly invite a great deal of debate from many scholars who have different views on the historical development of Korea. But, for the present purpose, the period that spans between the Three Kingdoms period and the third quarter of the 19th century may be appropriate. The aboriginal people on the peninsula practiced shamanism, and worshiped the sun, the moon, and heavenly gods as well as earthly objects. Their shamanistic beliefs were incorporated into both the religious concerns of Buddhism and the ethical behavior of Confucianism. The Buddhism that had been brought to the Koguryŏ kingdom in 372 A.D. spread rapidly and gained popularity among common people. Buddhism enjoyed the support of royal families during the Three Kingdoms period as well as during the Koryŏ period.

The first institution of higher learning in the long history of Korea was established in 372 A. D. This state-operated school known as *t'aehak*, or Great Learning, admitted upper-class male youths, who were taught the Chinese classical literature, history, and the art of archery. Private schools known as *kyŏngdang* were also established in cities and provinces after the dynasty had moved its capital to P'yŏngyang in 427 A.D. These schools were comparable to the cathedral schools operated in Europe during the later Middle Ages. They admitted youths from both the common classes and well-to-do farmers. They taught the Chinese classics, history, and the art of archery. *Kyŏngdang* was different from *t'aehak* in their organization. The former included grades from elementary to the higher levels, while the latter was strictly an institution of higher learning.

During the reign of King Chinhŭng (540-575 A.D.) of the Shilla Dynasty, there developed an educational institution called *hwarangdo*, or The Way of the Flowery Princes, a unique system of training and educating young men in academic subjects and military skills. The goals of this state institution were articulated well by Buddhist priest *Wŏn'gang* in the Five Morals: loyalty to king, filial piety to parents, trustworthiness towards friends, valor in time of war, and careful selection in the act of killing.

The principal educational institution of the post-unification period of the Shilla Dynasty, known as the "Unified Shilla," was *kukhak*, or State education, established in 682 A.D. It was a nine year course primarily designed to teach Confucian classics. The ages of students ranged from fifteen to thirty years of age. *Kukhak* had three departments, all teaching the *Analects of Confucius* and *Hsiao-ching*, or *Dialogue on Filial Piety*, but each offering different sets of additional classics. Each department had a major professor and several assistant professors. There was also an optional course in mathematics which was taught by a professor or an assistant professor.

In 788 A.D., a system of public service examinations was created to select government officials on the basis of scholarship. This system was called the "Three Standards System." The high standard required mastery of *Tsochuan Annals*, the *Book of Rites*, the *Analects*, and *Hsiao-ching*. The middle standard was attained when students achieved mastery of the *Analects, Hsiao-ching,* and the etiquette chapter of the *Book of Rites*. The low standard called for a mastery of *Hsiao-chinc* and the etiquette chapter of the *Book of Rites*. A scholar who had a mastery of the five classics, three histories, and the writings of the "One Hundred Scholars" was considered to have reached a superior standard and was given a high position in government.

Throughout the Three Kingdoms and the Unified Shilla periods, the latter lasting until 935 A.D., Buddhism played a major role in shaping the fundamental religious orientation of common people on the Korean peninsula. Confucianism certainly dominated formal education during these periods, but it was rather limited to the socially privileged elite class. As far as common people were concerned, Buddhism had a pervasive influence upon their basic attitude towards daily life. Consequently, Buddhist monks had profound influence on informal education, as they engaged in teaching Korean youth in reading, writing, and other arts.

Koryŏ Dynasty, from which the present English name Korea originated, was established in 918 A.D., and it lasted until 1392, when it was overthrown by General Yi Sŏng-gye, the founder of the Yi Dynasty.

During the earlier period of the dynasty, there developed three state institutions of learning: *kukchagam, tongsŏ haktang,* and *hyanggyo.* The first two were established in the capital, while the last was instituted in provinces. *Kukchagam* was founded in 992 A.D., but it was revised to include three *t'aehak* departments: *kukchahak, t'aehak,* and *samunhak,* each accommodating three hundred students. Only sons of noble birth were allowed to enter these schools. *Kukchahak* consisted of seven major faculties called *che,* and all of them taught the *Book of Change,* the *Writings of Old,* the *Book of Poetry, Chou-li, Book of Rites,* the *Annals,* and military science. Little is known about the nature of instruction and organization of *tongsŏ haktang,* or East-West school. It was said that the school was founded in 1272 A.D.

Hyanggyo, sometimes called *hyanghak* or provincial school, was also a state-supported institution established throughout the country during the reign of King Injong (1123-1146 A.D.). Students registered in these schools were from families of low-ranking government officials or local gentry. Good students of these schools were selected and given the opportunity to study at *kukchagam.*

There were two types of private institutions of education: *sahak* and *sŏdang. Sahak,* or private learning, was established by prominent Confucian scholars in their villages and towns. Many graduates from these private schools passed the state examination which had been introduced to recruit young men for government services. *Sŏdang,* or hall of books, was instituted to teach youths of low birth the rudiments of the basic Confucian classics. This type of institution was passed down to the following dynasty in terms of its instructional practice and lasted even after the Japanese annexation of Korea in 1910.

As stated earlier, Buddhism had been a major religious influence upon the lives of common people in Korea throughout the Three Kingdoms and the Koryŏ period. The influence of Buddhism on Korean traditional education may be seen in terms of how eminent Buddhist teachers thought of human development and character formation. First, Korean Buddhist teachers did not think of character as something to be molded, nurtured, or developed; rather, character is inherent in being a human being. The task of the individual is to seek self-actualization in his own way in accordance with his own light. Second, Buddhist teachers thought of character as that which has to be self-realized. Only after a person achieved self-realization, could the individual relate with other people, the local community, and the larger society in an attempt to realize harmonious relations in the world. Third, Buddhist teachers thought of man's character as that which comes naturally through self-learning. All learning should be self-motivated, self-learned; all other types of learning are considered training and indoctrination.

Yi Dynasty adopted Confucianism as its governing ideology, and repressed Buddhism for a number of reasons. Certainly, the new regime was in need of an ideology that could justify its overthrow of the old regime. But it also wanted to set the nation on a different ideological course that was more concerned with ethical and moral issues than with other-worldly problems. After all, the people who overthrew the old dynasty were military men who were more practically minded towards the affairs of daily life than Buddhist priests. Confucianism was considered a very proper worldly ideological system, because it not only prescribed appropriate conduct in daily life, but also proscribed what was considered improper human conduct in maintaining harmonious interpersonal relations in family and community life.

Confucianism was established in China and developed as a dynamic ethical system that prescribed appropriate human conduct for social harmony. But it lost its original vitality by the end of the 6th century. Consequently, in an attempt to revitalize the teachings of Confucius, many Chinese philosophers developed their own ideas on the natures of universe and of man between the 6th and 12th centuries. These philosophers contributed to the development of what is now called Neo-Confucianism. Prominent among these philosophers was Chu Hsi (1130-1200) who initiated a school of thought known as Ch'eng-Chu school, or *Li hsüeh* (School of Principles). Sometimes it is simply called Chu Hsi-ism. This particular school of Neo-Confucianism was introduced to Korea by An Yu (1243-1306) sometime during the reign of King Ch'ung'yŏl (1275-1308), the 25th King of Koryŏ Dynasty, and it grew to become a dominant political ideology throughout the Yi Dynasty.

Many ideas have been taught by Neo-Confucian scholars. Of all their ideas, the following two are the most significant in terms of their impact on the later development of philosophy in Korea: the concept of *i*(*li* in Chinese), or reason, and that of *ki* (*ch'i* in Chinese), or matter or energy. According to the Neo-Confucian cosmological view of universe, everything exists in duality: *i* and *ki*. *I* is the essence of anything and everything. But *i* does not bring matter into existence. If there is only *i* in the universe, then there would be no matter or action. *I* cannot be captured into a shape; *i* stands above shape. *Ki* gives form to matter, and through it matter is produced.

I and *ki* are inherent in human beings. Because of *i*, human beings are endowed with sympathy, righteousness, humbleness, and wisdom, all of which, in turn, help them to discern what is right from what is wrong.

Thus, principle is critical in the education of man. The *ki* side of human beings is related to human desires and emotion. Because of man's tendency to become self-centered, Neo-Confucian scholars emphasized the importance of *ye* (*li* in Chinese), or proper ritual behavior. *Ye* became an indispensable component of Confucian education, because it provided a philosophical framework within which socialization of the young could be undertaken and understood. Included in *ye* were *samgang oryun*, or Three Principles and Five Rules. These were considered indispensable in transforming natural man into a social being. The three principles referred to the proper relationship between king and his subjects, between father and son, and between husband and wife. Five rules referred to righteousness between king and his subjects, closeness between father and son, separateness between husband and wife, proper order between the old and the young, and faithfulness between friends.

Immediately after the founding of the dynasty, an institution of higher education, Sŏngkyunkwan, was established in 1398 with two departments; *munmyo* and *myŏnggyŏngdang*. The former was a shrine honoring Confucius and other leading Korean scholars of the Confucian tradition. The latter was the school building itself. This state-supported institution annually enrolled 200 students of fifteen years of age and above. The students of the institution enjoyed privileges which allowed them to send memorials to the king for policy recommendations or criticism against government policies.

Hyanggyo, founded during Koryŏ Dynasty, increased in number during the Yi Dynasty. It was founded in every county throughout the country, but its educational function was reduced rather considerably after the emergence of the *sŏwŏn* system. *Sŏwŏn*, a new type of educational institution established in 1543, was a private school where Confucian classics were taught for fees. They also held Confucian rites twice a year. Through private contributions and royal grants, *sŏwŏn* developed into a financially and politically influential institution. Some of these schools educated young people for government service.

Sŏdang, or Hall of Books, was the only elementary school that was available for children of the common people at the time when the Yi Dynasty was established. During the dynasty, *sŏdang* increased in number as various groups of private citizens established them in order to educate their children. At *sŏdang*, children were taught by a teacher and one monitor. Their curriculum included the reading and writing of the *One Thousand Character Classics* in which Chinese ideographs which were arranged in a particular way to reflect the belief in the Confucian cosmology. *Sŏdang* was also known as "loud school," because each child would read the book aloud until he learned its content by heart. Recitation of Chinese classics was the principal method of instruction in *sŏdang*.

3

Christian Mission Education in Korea

The first European to step onto Korean soil was perhaps a Portuguese cleric, Father Gregorie de Cespedes, who came to Korea with the Hideyoshi's army that invaded the country in 1593. But he had little opportunity to proselytize among local people. It was only after 1884, when Horace N. Allen came to Korea as a missionary dispatched by the Presbyterian Board of Foreign Missions that Christianity, particularly its Protestant version, began to spread in Korea. During the earlier years of mission work, many Christian missions were reluctant to get involved in establishing formal educational institutions. They put more emphasis on general evangelism than on education. After 1893, however, the Council of Missions in Korea adopted a resolution that encouraged primary education to be organized, managed, and serviced by Christian missions.

It is said that the first primary school was established by Horace G. Underwood, who named the school "Jesus Doctrine School." It had a humble beginning, as it started as no more than an orphanage for boys. This school became a template for other Christian missions to follow, and by 1908, there were thirty primary schools in Seoul alone. It was reported that there were 766 primary schools established by missions in 1926. They had 24,170 boys and 13,576 girls who were taught by a total of 1,188 teachers. In addition, there were 313 one-room schools which taught han'gŭl (Korean alphabet) and Chinese characters. They had a total enrollment of 12,923 students with 722 teachers. The number of school years varied widely, although most primary schools required a four-year course of study before graduation.

Secondary education in any modern sense of the term was introduced to Korea by Christian missionaries. In 1886, a secondary school for girls, Ehwa Haktang, was established in Seoul by Mrs. M.F. Scranton, who was lucky enough to recruit one student. The student was reported to have been a concubine sent to learn English by her patron. During the same year a secondary school for boys, Paechae Haktang, was founded in the same city by H. G. Appenzeller, whose educational philosophy did not depart much from that of Mrs. Scranton. Students enrolled in the school were taught Chinese characters, English, astronomy, geography, biology, mathematics, handicrafts, and lessons from the Bible. Modern organized group sports were introduced to Korea during this period. Students learned Western sports such as baseball, soccer, and tennis. School discipline was also patterned after rules and regulations enforced in Western schools. Students were strongly admonished to comply with and show respect for the laws of the country. They were to abstain from using alcoholic beverages and obscene language. Secondary schools were also established in provinces. One school, established in 1905 in a small town located north of P'yŏngyang, was called Sinmyŏng High School. It also had an English name, Hugh O'Neil Jr. Boys' Academy. Its founder wanted to cast the school in the mold of Park College of Parkville, Missouri. The curriculum of the school offered chemistry, physics, and other subjects which were then taught in American high schools. By the end of 1937, a total of thirty-seven secondary schools—four for boys, six for girls, three industrial schools, and twenty—four non-standardized schools were operated by various foreign missions. Most of these secondary schools offered a four to five-year courses of study before graduation.

Higher education in any modern sense of the word was also developed in Korea by foreign missions. Through the combined efforts of all foreign missions six major institutions of higher learning were established during the first decade of this century. These were Severance Medical College, Union Christian College, Chosŏn Christian College, Ehwa College, Presbyterian Theological Seminary, and Union Methodist Seminary. Chosŏn Christian College, founded in 1915, is now called Yonsei University, which is one of the finest universities in South Korea today. Ehwa College established in 1915, is now called Ehwa Womans University, and it has the largest enrollment of women in the world.

4

Education under Japanese Colonialism

Japan took over Korea as a protectorate in 1905, and subsequently annexed Korea in 1910, thus depriving the Koreans of their nationality. Soon after the annexation Japan issued the first of its four major educational reform laws enacted between 1911 and 1943 concerning colonial education in Korea. The first came in 1911, followed by the second reform law in 1922. The second reform was designed to accommodate Korean resistance against Japan's harsh treatment of Koreans during the first ten years of its colonial administration. Beginning on March 1, 1917, Koreans peacefully demonstrated against the Japanese colonial administration, demanding their political independence. Japan used overt military force to put down Koreans' peaceful demand for their political independence. As part of Japan's policy of appeasement towards Korean resistance against its colonial policy, Japan enacted the 1922 educational reform law. Under this reform law, five different types of educational institutions were to be established. First, common schools were to be created to accommodate children of six years of age, and they were to offer a six-year course of study before graduation. Second, high common schools were established to receive graduates from common schools. These schools were to be five-year schools of study. The same type of school girls was, however, a four year curriculum. Third, normal schools were also created to train teachers, and they were six-year schools. Fourth, specialized schools and one university were created by the law. Specialized schools were for three- to five-year courses of study, although local conditions sometimes dictated it to be a two-year course. Within the university system a two-year preparatory course of study was created to prepare students for university education, and the university was to be three-to four-year courses of study before graduation.

Although various schools were created by this reform law, the opportunity for advanced education for Koreans was rather limited, and most Koreans did not advance beyond the common school. This school system was maintained with little change until Japan was defeated in the Pacific War. But there were two other educational reform laws. The third one came in 1938, dropping the Korean language from the compulsory study requirements. This was part of the war-time measures adopted after Japan had invaded China in 1937. The last educational reform was issued in 1943 during the Pacific War.

The purpose of the colonial education enforced by Japan in Korea was clearly articulated by the Chief of the Bureau of Education under the Governor-General, Minami Jiro. He stated that the educational ideal of the colonial education was the Japanization of Koreans. He believed that the Japanization of Koreans was possible through education. Education, therefore, should be focused on making Koreans Japanese.

The limited educational opportunity at various level of education for Koreans could be seen in terms of Koreans enrolled at these institutions in comparison with the total school age population. For instance, in 1935, only 25 percent of the school age Korean children were enrolled in primary schools, while over 91 per cent of the school age Japanese children were already in primary schools by 1919. The number of Korean students in middle schools in 1939 was 1.31 per 1,000 of the Korean population, while the same figure for the Japanese population in Korea was 32.7. In higher education offered by the Keijo Imperial University, Korean students were outnumbered by Japanese students. In 1942, there were 422 Japanese students in regular course of study, while the same department had only 361 Korean students.

5

Current Education in North Korea

The educational system in North Korea has gone through four major stages of systemic and curricular changes before reaching their present practice: (1) the formative period of introducing the Marxist-Leninist principle and practice in education (1945-1955); (2) the period of implementation and dissemination of Communist education (1956-1962); (3) the formative period of establishing education based on *Juche* ideology (1963-1971); and (4) the period of implementing, disseminating, and strengthening education grounded in *Juche* ideology (1972-present). During the first period, "democratic principles" of education based on the Marxist-Leninist ideology were emphasized. Textbooks were re-written to eliminate Japanese cultural influence from formal education. They introduced students to fundamental principles of Marxism-Leninism. Primary school facilities were expanded to accommodate primary school age children. Also, more secondary educational institutions were established across North Korea. A new university named after Kim Il-sung was created. During the second period, after the end of the Korean War (1950-1953), North Korea launched a campaign for collectivization in agriculture and industry. Education followed suit by teaching students to live their lives under the collective slogan, "One for All, and All for One." During the third period, more emphasis was placed in education on the "anti-Japanese guerilla experience" of Kim Il-sung than on the principles of Marxism-Leninism. Students were admonished to follow the footsteps of the great leader Kim Il-sung. The fourth period saw the elimination of the Marxist-Leninist principles in all aspects of education. They were replaced by educational principles based on *Juche* ideology.

There are four major components in *Juche* ideology; self-identity in ideology; national independence in politics, self-defense in national security, and self-reliance in national economy. According to Kim Il-sung, North Korea has to go through three major revolutions by means of *Juche* in order to achieve these goals of national identity, political independence, self-defense, and self-reliance. They are revolutions in ideology, science and technology, and culture. But the revolution in ideology and in culture cannot be achieved, unless North Korean citizens are re-educated and reformed in accordance to *Juche* ideology, which was elaborated upon in his "Theses on the Socialist Education," issued in September 1977. According to Kim, the alleged author of this educational treatise, *Juche* ideology places man in the center of universe, making him the master of his destiny. Man is a conscious; independent, and creative social being who wants to better his life by controlling and improving his environment. Education is a necessary tool for him to have, because it enables him to accomplish these goals.

When the *Juche* ideology is translated into educational purposes and goals, they focus on indoctrinating North Korean youth to support the North Korean political system. Generalissmo Kim Il-sung is portrayed as the greatest leader the Korean people have ever had in history, and his entire family is now worshiped by North Korean people as the revolutionary family to be emulated by them. The revolutionary tradition, established by Kim Il-sung during his anti-Japanese guerrilla struggles, is taught as a major curricular component in all North Korean schools.

The current educational system in North Korea is a result of numerous changes that occurred since 1945. The present eleven-year compulsory and free system of education was put into effect in 1972. It consists of three interlocking levels of schooling. First. there is one-year preschool education, which is provided by the *yuchiban*, or kindergarten class. It is then articulated with a four-year primary education provided by the *inmin hakkyo* (people's school). The four-year course of study is then followed by a six-year course of study provided by the *kodŭng chunghakkyo* (higher middle school).

A variety of post-secondary educational institutions is available in North Korea today. First, there is the *kodŭng chunghakkyo* (higher middle school). *Kodŭng kisul hakkyo*(higher technical school), a two- to three-year course of study that admits graduates from higher middle school. Second, there is the Kim Il-sung University, the only comprehensive university in North Korea. Although they elevated Kim Ch'aek

Engineering University to the status of a comprehensive university recently, it is yet to be determined how comprehensive that institution is in terms of its curricular as well as research developments. The university named after Kim Il-sung offers a five- to six-year courses of study. Other regular institutions of higher learning called *taehak* also offer five- to six-year courses of study. They offer a five-year course of study in social sciences and humanities, while a six-year course of study is offered in the fields of natural science and technology. Third, North Korea established specialized institutions of higher learning at various industries. They are called *kongjang taehak* (industrial college), where a four-year course of study is offered to students working at the industrial complex. Another form of specialized higher education is known as *kongsan taehak*, or communist college. This also offers a four-year course of study, and every provincial center has a Communist college.

All education is free in North Korea. Post-secondary education is, however, not compulsory. Students in colleges and universities have to engage in socially productive work, and they work for their education. Educational administration in North Korea is highly centralized. The Education Committee of the North Korean cabinet oversees all educational institutions. Ultimately, the final authority rests on the Korean Workers' Party (KWP). All teachers are members of the KWP.

6

Current Education in South Korea

The early educational development in South Korea after 1945 was very much influenced by the American Military Government that ruled Korea between 1945 and 1948. The military government tried to transplant the American education system in Korea. As part of their plan they employed many American-educated Koreans to work towards developing an educational system based on democratic principles. During this formative period John Dewey and his ideas of democratic education were adopted as educational principles to forge Korean education. However, perhaps due to lack of understanding of the Deweyian philosophy, in addition to the cultural ethos of the Korean people, democratic education has not been put to practice in earnest. Instead, an "anti-Communist, democratic education" has prevailed in South Korea which has created some serious problems in education. Included among them are the declining quality of education due to expanding educational opportunity, lack of respect for the individual learner due to large class-size, abstract learning instead of learning by doing, indoctrination of students in anti-Communist ideology that has served the political interest of the ruling class, and education for economic development at the expense of moral and ethical development.

In order to amend such educational problems the South Korean government enacted the Charter of National Education in 1968. It declared that the purpose of education was "to help people achieve a firm national identity and develop respect for history and tradition." The

Charter emphasized a balance between tradition and development; it also stressed a balance between individual needs and the national needs. The South Korean government also enacted Education Law in order to define and articulate educational goals. According to the law, a general principle of *hongik ingan* or broad service for benefit of mankind, is to serve as a guiding philosophy for Korean education. Given this philosophy, education is to help all people in "perfecting their individual character, developing the ability for an independent life and acquiring the qualifications of citizens capable of participating in the building of a democratic state, and promoting the prosperity of all humankind."

The school system in South Korea is not too different from that of the United States. It follows a 6-3-3-4 ladder pattern. It consists of primary school, lower secondary school, higher secondary school, and college or university. Although pre-school education is popular and available readily, it is not part of the formal school system. It is not free. Parents have to pay to send their children for pre-school education. As of 1989, there were 8,354 kindergartens with an enrollment of 414,532 children. This number constituted 40 percent of the children four to six years of age.

In general, primary education is free and compulsory. There are, however, private schools accommodating children of rich families who are concerned about adverse educational impact resulting from overcrowding conditions in public primary schools. Primary education offers a six-year course of study. It emphasizes language development, citizenship, development of observation skills, occupation skills, development of quantitative skills, appreciation of music, fine arts, literature, and personal health. As of 1989, there were 6,335 primary schools with an enrollment of 4,868,520 students taught in 117,538 classes by 136,800 teachers.

There are two tiers in secondary education. The first is called *chung hakkyo*, or middle school, and the second, *kodŭng hakkyo*, or high school. Upon successful completion of primary education, students twelve to fourteen years of age move on to middle school. As of 1989, there were 2,474 middle schools with a total enrollment of 2,275,751 students. Middle school education puts emphasis on the development of democratic citizenship, basic skills for a specific occupation, critical thinking, and physical and psychological health. Upon successful completion of middle school education, all students desiring a high school education have to pass the state-administered qualifying examination. The total number of high school students in 1989 was 2,283,806 who were accommodated in 1,683 schools staffed by 92,683 teachers. High school education is basically divided into two categories: academic and vocational. High school education puts emphasis on students' ability to see themselves in relation to their country and society, on improving what they have learned in middle school, and on personal health.

There are basically four different types of higher educational institutions: (1) colleges and universities with four-year undergraduate programs, (2) two-year junior vocational colleges, (3) four-year teachers colleges, and (4) miscellaneous schools with college status. Included among the last type of institutions are schools of theology, military and police academies, and other specialized schools. The student enrollment in these institutions is strictly controlled by the Ministry of Education. No institution may admit students beyond its annually allocated quota. Every year graduates of high schools across the nation wishing to receive higher education have to pass two separate tests. First, they have to pass the state-administered qualifying test in order to apply for admission to a college or university of their choice. Then, the institution that accepted an individual's application administers a test to see if he is qualified for college education. As of 1988, there were 107 colleges and universities with a total enrollment of 1,040,166.

There are three layers of educational administration in South Korea today: district, provincial, and national. The Ministry of Education has authority on all matters relating to educational policies for public education. It controls curriculum development, approves textbooks in the case of primary education or endorses them for secondary education, supervises local administrative personnel, and certifies teachers. There are fifteen Boards of Education in the nine provinces and six cities across the country. Each board has a legislative body chaired by the city major or the provincial governor, and the superintendent of the board is appointed by the President upon recommendation of the board. The district office of education supports the work of the board.

As discussed above, the contemporary education in both South and North Korea has been influenced by a number of historical and cultural forces that were both indigenous and foreign. These forces have worked together to create two separate systems of education. North Korea has vowed to create through education "Communist man" who is imbued with the zeal to work towards the goal of creating a Communist Korea and of liberating South Korea. On the other hand, South Korea has used public education to create "anti-Communist, democratic man" who is eager to work towards building a liberal, democratic, anti-Communist state. These two disparate systems of education with diametrically opposed social and political goals have now become dysfunctional to the Korean people's goals for achieving national re-unification and national reconciliation.

In North Korea today, there is little freedom for the individual. He is totally at the mercy of the state which controls every aspect of his daily life from dawn to dusk. He cannot have a job unless the state approves of it. He is not allowed to live where he wishes without the state's approval. The individual is being sacrificed for the purpose of creating a Communist paradise, where a tile-roofed house, rice, meat, and silk clothes are readily available for all North Korean citizens. Education is used as tool by Kim Il-sung and his followers to indoctrinate people to support Kim's dictatorship. Education in North Korea has become Kim's private property, a means of thought-control to maintain his power.

Education in South Korea has been used as a means of recruiting the elite into government bureaucracy, large corporations, and academic and research institutions. What the formal educational system has done in South Korea over the last four decades has been responsible for creating a meritocracy that rationalizes and legitimizes the inequality between the rich and the poor. Education designed to help create a liberal, democratic state has contributed to developing morally weak individuals uprooted from their cultural tradition and ethical standard of their community.

Suggested Further Reading

de Bary, William and Ja Hyun Kim Haboush (eds.). 1985. *The Rise of Neo-Confucianism in Korea.* New York: Columbia University Press.

Deuchler, Martina. 1980. "Neo-Confucianism: The Impulse for Social Action in Early Korea," *The Journal of Korean Studies* Vol. 2.

Korean Overseas Information Service. 1990. *A Handbook of Korea.* Seoul: Korea Overseas Information Service.

McGinn, Noel F. et al. 1980. *Education and Development in Korea.* Cambridge, Massachusetts: Harvard University Press.

13

Painting
by Junghee Lee

The earliest Korean paintings still extant appear in tombs of the Koguryŏ kingdom (A.D. 4th-7th c.) in the region of what is now southern Manchuria and North Korea. Koguryŏ painting style was highly developed, indicating an elevated and advanced level of culture. The fifty or so extant Koguryŏ murals are painted directly on the stone or plaster wall. Mural painting development may be divided into three periods: early, middle, and late. The murals of the early period (4th to early 5th c.) indicate a trend towards Han Chinese tastes in choice of subject, which included scenes from the everyday life of the deceased, depictions of his family and subjects, auspicious animals, and heavenly bodies such as the sun, moon, and stars. Two inscribed tombs of this period indicate the date and nationality of the tomb occupants as Chinese. One of these, the earliest Koguryŏ tomb excavated, is the well-preserved Tomb No.3 at Anak-kun in Hwanghae Province of North Korea, dated 357, which depicts large idealized portraits of the deceased and his wife in the fluid brush strokes of the Chinese style. (The Lotus flower, a Buddhist motif, appears in this tomb before the official introduction of Buddhism to Koguryŏ in 372.)

Distinctive Koguryŏ characteristics began to appear in the middle period of Koguryŏ wall painting (mid-5th to early 6th century). A simplified flatter style was effectively used to depict fewer topics, commonly hunting scenes and constellations. Concurrently, strong Buddhist elements were introduced from China's Gansu Province through nomadic routes. Portraits of the deceased appear with their wives. A typical example of this period is the tomb at Tian, Manchuria: the Tomb of the Dancing Figures (Muryongch'ong, late 5th c.). This tomb contains two chambers on whose walls and ceilings are depicted numerous scenes of native Koguryŏ customs and culture in action. Scenes portraying sleeve-dancers, jugglers, servants carrying food, wrestlers, and the deceased as a host receiving his guests provide us with a fascinating glimpse of a long-lost way of life. These murals provide scholars with many faithful representations of native costumes, armor, trappings on horses, furniture, and architecture. The section shown here depicts a royal hunting scene (Fig. 1), which provides a sense of the brilliant horsemanship of Koguryŏ warriors. (Note the faithful detailing of the equine saddlery and hunters' accouterments.) The scene depicting the ease with which the horse rider aims his arrow towards his moving prey behind him is not only testimony to his great riding skill but to the skill of the artist in successfully portraying their furious speed. Undulating stripes on highly stylized mountains, loose parallel wisps signifying drifting clouds, and tautly outstretched legs of quadrupeds in flight and pursuit all contribute to a sense of high-speed movement. The warriors' square-jawed physiognomies and double-plumed headgear identify these figures as Korean, for such caps appear on depictions of Korean envoys in murals from such distant locations as Samarkand and as late as a hand scroll from the Sung Dynasty.

By the last and most mature period of Koguryŏ mural development (mid-6th to mid-7th c.), Taoism was a dominant ideological force and dictated that the tomb be a microcosm of the universe. The four directional animals in East Asian art, the blue dragon of the east, white tiger of the west, the black tortoise intertwined with a snake of the north, and two birds of the south are sole occupants on the tombs' proper walls such as at the Great Tomb at Kangsŏ in South Pyŏngan Province. The magnificent vitality and stylistic vigor of these creatures leap from the flatness of the architectural planes. The scenes are charged with mystery in an ethereally-styled atmosphere. The Korean landscape tradition may begin in this period because these animals are sometimes set against sylvan backgrounds.

The Koguryŏ artistic tradition not only influenced paintings in the neighboring kingdoms of Paekche, Old Shilla and Kaya, but the Asuka and Hakuho styles of Japan. The legacy of Koguryŏ art continued into the murals of the Parhae kingdom which was established in Manchuria by Koguryŏ aristocrats fleeing the victorious Shilla and Tang armies.

The unification of the Korean peninsula by the Shilla kingdom in 668 thrust the newly consolidated nation into the international Tang sphere. Buddhism's attendant culture fully blossomed during this period. As with other arts of Unified Shilla, Buddhism was well represented in painting. One of these extant pieces is a fragment of a frontispiece to an illuminated scroll of the Avatasaka Sutra dated 754 to 755. The full-bodied Bodhisattvas painted in gold iron-wire lines on purple-dyed mulberry paper provide a glimpse into this period's sumptuous style. These figures are very similar in form and posture to the large granite Buddhist deities in the contemporaneous Sŏkkuram cave grotto.

In the following Koryŏ Dynasty (918-1392), Buddhism became an even stronger force, patronized by devout royal descendants of the dynasty's Buddhist founder. However, the only extant work from the early Koryŏ period is a partial set of 11th century wood-block prints illustrating an anthology of Buddhist poetry. The pictures display the monumental landscape style of the Five Dynasties and Northern Sung periods.

The Mongol invasions began in 1231, reducing much of the country's cultural heritage, of which many were paintings, to ashes. Once accord was reached with the Mongols which lasted from 1260 to 1356, the influence of Mongolian culture which by then had turned to Lamaist Buddhism set the tone for Koryŏ art. The lavish and highly ornate Mongolian style with its abundant use of gold leaf began to appear. Aristocratic patrons commissioned

Buddhist texts painted in gold or silver on indigo paper.

The extant examples of Koryŏ period paintings all date from the late 13th to the 14th century, that is, after the Mongol invasion. One of the most outstanding of all these Koryŏ paintings is a standing Avalokiteśrara (Kwanŭm) Bodhisattva (ca. 1300). A similar example dated to 1323 and painted by Sŏ Ku-bang currently resides in the Sumitomo collection in Japan. Because many of these works were copied and distributed, several identical types have been found. One large well-preserved example is the Water-and-Moon Avalokiteśvara (Fig. 2) in the Harvard University Art Museums. Here the large bodhisattva in a landscape is seated on the edge of the rock in his abode at Mount Potalaka being visited by Sudhana, the young seeker of enlightenment. Illustrating a portion of the Gandhavyūha chapters in the Avatasaka Sūtra, this piece displays a fully developed landscape style indicated by rocks lit from below through gold brushwork and the meticulous styling of bamboo. Reversed shading modulates the flesh of this Bodhisattva seated in the meditative pose with one leg squarely crossing the other pendant leg. This Bodhisattva's attribute, the sacred willow branch, rests in a celadon kundika vessel. The Bodhisattva is depicted in rich colors, with intricate gold patterns in circular roundels and other geometric forms in thin wire lines, and the diaphanous veil. Gold roundel patterns echo similar patterns found on contemporaneous inlaid celadon ware.

Also commissioned were large elegant visionary paintings of the Amitābha Buddha welcoming the reborn soul in the Western Paradise. These Amitābha paintings employ superb mastery over the gold-painting technique, reflecting the taste of the Koryŏ aristocracy, whose munificence was probably based on their desire to enter the Pure Land. The iconography visible in certain extant paintings provides us with useful information about aspects of Korean Buddhism. The evidence presented in a Ho-am Art Museum scroll depicting the youthful Chijang (Kitigarbha) Bodhisattva, Lord of the Underworld, hints at this Buddhist figure's importance within Korean Buddhism. Yet another category of Buddhist paintings is represented by ink paintings of the five-hundred Arhats, which are idealized, yet detailed portraits of these imaginary subjects, thus paving the way for later portrait painting.

The founder of the Chosŏn Dynasty, King T'aejo (r. 1392 to 1398) established Neo-Confucianism as the official ideology, setting the stage for a dynasty whose morality encouraged a modest and practical lifestyle. Lavish patronage of art was thus shunned, and the status of the professional artist was reduced to that of a mere technician belonging to the intermediate *chung'in* class, between the *yangban* and commoners. The Bureau of Painting, the Tohwasŏ later changed to Tohwawŏn, was established by the government from the onset of the dynasty in a status lower than that of the analogous bureau of the Koryŏ period. The strong adherence to Neo-Confucianism made Koreans readily accept orthodox Chinese painting styles popular in the court of Peking. On the other hand, the Korean artist's skill and willingness to explore allowed them to transcend and at times reinvent the Chinese manner. Chosŏn painting trends may be divided into three periods: early, which went up to the 16th century, middle (16th to 17th c.), and late (18th to 19th c.). The court painter An Kyŏn was the foremost proponent of the early style, characterized by its adaptation of Northern Sung styles following the tradition of Guo Xi's and Chin paintings in the style of Guo Xi. An Kyŏn's *Dream Journey to the Peach Blossom Land* (1447; fig. 3), was commissioned by Prince Anp'yŏng following a dream in which he visited a Taoist paradise. This narrative journey begins with the Prince accompanied by Pak P'aeng-nyŏn, a scholar of Chiphyŏn-jŏn, embarking on a road in the lower foreground surrounded by low hills and small trees. The final destination, the Peach Blossom Land, is depicted in a panoramic view, surrounded by towering peaks, approached by way of huge cliffs and water falls. It is a wide valley filled with peach trees whose peaches when eaten would lead to immortality. Guo Xi's influence is seen in this work's atmospheric perspective and monumental organic mountain forms. However, An Kyŏn's forms are not overpowering or gnarled but more natural. He influenced many later Chosŏn painters, the earliest of whom may be called proponents of the An Kyŏn school. This school invented a style of landscape which combined the lyrical, one-corner style of Southern Sung in the foreground with high mountains in the background that appear in Early *Winter Landscape*, album leaf attributed to An Kyŏn now in the National Museum of Korea (Fig. 3), providing a direct source to 15th century Muromachi period painting in Japan. In the middle period, the Southern Sung Academy's one corner composition and axe-cut strokes were exclusively found on a landscape by the professional painter Yi Sang-jwa in the 16th century.

Also in the early Chosŏn Dynasty was the introduction of Ming Academy and south Chinese Zhe school styles by Kang Hŭi-an, a Confucian literary painter who visited Ming China in 1455. His album leaf entitled *Sage Contemplating by the Stream* (1468) depicts a meditative Confucian scholar in a vigorous spontaneous style amidst damp wet rocks in bold ink wash. Vines hang elegantly from a silhouetted vertical cliff. This painting is notable since its particular style predates any extant Chinese works in the same stylistic genre. The literati painter Yang P'aeng-sŏn whose landscape painting dated to the first half of the 16th century exhibits a new landscape style incorporating Zhe-school influence by the use of wide expanses of water and the introduction of the middle ground.

Portraiture and paintings of animals, birds, and flowers also reached high standards during this period. The so-called four-gentlemen paintings depicting plum blossoms, orchids, bamboos, and chrysanthemums, all symbols of Confucian virtue were important subject matters for literati painters. Two of the best known bamboo painters were the 16th century Yi Chŏng and the mid-15th century painter Yi Su-mun who painted thin bamboo stalks sprouting among rocks in a manner similar to those of Yün literati painters. These bamboo painters strongly influenced Muromachi paintings in Japan.

It was literati painters who painted the famous grape paintings. Hwang Chip-jung (b. 1533) controlled his ink wash with great skill, able to define a diaphanous light illuminating the grapes. During the mid-Chosŏn period, woman artists were also active in ink and color paintings. The most famous of them is Shin Saim-dang, the mother of the Confucian scholar Yi I, whose bright colors and meticulous and intimate rendering of insects, flowers, and vegetables became so famous that all paintings of similar subjects were attributed to her.

Portrait painting was an important genre that reached its full development during the Chosŏn Dynasty. With the supremacy of Neo-Confucianism, portrait painting became a necessary means of remembering and honoring one's leaders and ancestors, being displayed at important Confucian ceremonies, in ancestral shrines, temples, or halls. Various categories of portraits exist, the best represented being those of the *sadaebu*, or scholar-official. With exact likeness of the subject being the goal, the styles combined great attention to detail and use of modeling techniques to depict contours of the face. Conversely, the subject's body was usually flatter, with much less care in presenting volume. These pieces were often life-size, so were quite large. Self-portraits were rare, but one notable example was painted by Yun Tu-sŏ (A.D. 1668 to 1715), who focused exclusively on his visage with a sensitive and meticulous hand. His brooding face, with intense eyes staring from sunken eye-sockets modeled to depict wrinkled flesh, testify to his faithfulness to reality.

The naturalism found in Yun's portrait also appears in the landscape painting of this period which was influenced by the Practical Learning School which emphasized a return to more practical, real matters at hand rather than the philosophizing so popular in earlier generations. Hence the type of landscape known as the True-Scenery Landscape, which espoused the painting of real places in Korea, became the trend for the next sixty years. This scene was pioneered by the literati painter Chŏng Sŏn (1676 to 1759) who was influenced by the Wu school which was later incorporated into the Southern School of Ming China. For the first time, Korean scenes with figures in Korean costumes appeared. It was in this period that the Diamond Mountains (1734; Fig. 4), a representative Chŏng Sŏn landscape, was painted. Chŏng said he merely painted the material force, or *ki*, of the mountain and indeed one can sense the power of these mountains through his calligraphic brush strokes.

In keeping with this trend to depict things Korean, genre painting pioneered by the 18th-century versatile painter Kim Hong-do who included scenes of work and play by members of the working class, became popular. By his masterful use of simple lines and dots, the artist conveyed a wide variety of facial expressions and gestures containing much movement and a sense of humor, the last of which is an important component of native Korean art.

The other well-known 18th-century genre painter was the court painter Shin Yun-bok who painted scenes from the life of the upper class taking part in their worldly pleasures such as their entanglements with the *kisaeng*, or highly skilled courtesan. These paintings are often erotic and suggestive, leaving the observer wondering about their context.

An important undercurrent in Korean painting is *minhwa*, or decorative paintings, often identified as folk paintings. These are the visible product of the native Korean spirit painted in sumptuous opaque colors. Many early extant examples date from as early as the 16th century. Subjects are drawn from Taoist, shamanistic, Buddhist, and Confucian sources ranging from the Sun and Moon over Five Mountains, other Taoist or shamanistic symbols, birds and flowers, humorous tigers and bookshelf paintings, which are paintings of scholarly apparatus.

From the late 19th century, Korean paintings took another turn with the introduction of Western art. As happened throughout the history of Korean painting, foreign styles became transformed through the hands of the Korean painters, ultimately infused with a true Koreanness which can be described as a more vigorous sense of movement, vitality in the spirit of *ki*, and humor and naturalness, all characteristics still alive today in the works of contemporary painters.

List of illustrations

Fig. 1. Hunting scene, from the Tomb of the Dancing Figures; Chi-an, Kirin province, China; Koguryŏ kingdom; late 5th century; after Won-yong Kim, et al., *Korean Art Treasures* (Seoul: Yekyŏng Sanŏp-sa, 1986), pl. 3.

Fig. 2. *Water-and-Moon Kwanŭm Bodhisattva*; hanging scroll; 14th century, Koryŏ period; ink, colors, and gold pigment on silk; Gift of Withrop, Harvard University Museums collection. 1943. 57. 12; h:159.6 cm. w:82.3 cm. Photo: Courtesy of Harvard University Art Museums.

Fig. 3. An Kyŏn, attributed, Early Winter; 15th century, Chosŏn period; ink on silk; National Museum of Korea, Seoul collection; from Yi Tongju (Yongha), *Sansudo*, vol. 1 (Seoul: Chungang Ilbosa, 1983).

Fig. 4. Chŏng Sŏn, *Diamond Mountains*; A.D. 1734, Chosŏn period; Ho-am Art Museum, Yongin, Korea collection; from Yi Tongju (Yongha), Sansuhwa, vol. 2 (Seoul: Chungang Ilbosa, 1983).

Suggested Further Reading

Covell, Alan Carter. 1986. *Folk Art and Magic: Shamanism in Korea.* Elizabeth, New Jersey: Hollym International Corp.

Coepper, R. and R. Whitfield. 1984. *Treasures from Korea: Art through 5,000 Years.* London.

Kim, Chewon and Lena Lee. 1974. *Arts of Korea.* Tokyo: Kodansha International.

Vos, Ken. 1992. *Korean Painting: A Selection of Eighteenth to Early Twentieth Century Painting from the Collection of Cho Won-kyong.* London: Bamboo Publishing, Ltd.

Fig 1. Hunting Scene

Fig 2. Water-and-Moon Kwanŭm Bodhisattva

Fig 3. Early Winter

Fig 4. Diamond Mountains

14

Traditional Music and Dance
by Alan C. Heyman and Andrew C. Nahm

1

Introduction

Korea's music and dance have particular characteristics and stylized forms that are distinctively different from those of other East Asian peoples although there are certain similarities between the Korean forms and those of China and Japan. In this brief essay we will first discuss the origins and developmental aspects of various forms and styles of music and dance of early Korea and examine traditional Korean music and dance of the past and present.

With the demise of the Yi Dynasty in 1910 when Japan annexed Korea, court music and dance as a separate entity ceased to exist. However, traditional court music and dance were preserved by the *A'ak* Department of the Office in Charge of the Affairs of the Yi Royal Clan and other private organizations and individuals. Despite attempts by the Japanese colonial rulers to destroy the ethnic identity and cultural heritage of the Koreans, traditional music and dance of both the upper and the commoner classes survived.

Following the liberation of Korea from Japan in 1945 and its partition into north and south, concerted efforts were made in the south under the sponsorship of the government and the leadership of the National Classical Music Institute of Korea, which replaced the former *A'ak* Department, to revive and promote those aspects of traditional music and dance which were fast disappearing. However, in the communist republic established in the north, much of the traditional music and dance have been replaced by socialist, revolutionary music and dance.

The discussion of the current status of traditional music and dance in Korea is, therefore, limited to that of the Republic of Korea in the south. Despite such limitation, it is our hope that this chapter will help the reader to develop a broad knowledge of the unique musical and dance heritage of the Korean people.

2

Origins and Historical Background of Traditional Korean Music and Dance

During the Neolithic period in Korean history that began around 4000 B.C., the inhabitants of the Korean peninsula and southern Manchuria promoted music and dance. With the dawn of the Bronze Age around 1200 B.C., new tribal units of Tungusic people speaking an Altaic language migrated into the Korean peninsula from central Asia via Manchuria, bringing with them the Sytho-Siberian culture including religion, music, and musical instruments. When the Iron Age began and rice culture developed in the 4th century B.C., shamanistic religion and its music and dance were advanced.

It is difficult to ascertain what type of music was played, what kind of musical instruments were used, and what style of dances were performed, but it is quite safe to assume that both music and dance were of a primitive type associated with religious beliefs and practices, and the musical instruments were mostly percussion instruments. As agricultural life developed, so did music and dance associated with the seasonal religious festivals, creating a new cultural heritage.

The ancient Koreans observed a variety of religious seasonal festivals. For example, the Puyŏ people who lived in north central Manchuria, many of whom migrated into the Korean peninsula, celebrated a shamanistic ceremony called *yŏnggo* ("spirit-invoking drums") with songs and dances of thanksgiving. The people in Koguryŏ, a state which emerged in southern Manchuria in 37 B.C. or earlier and whose territory expanded into northern Korea, practiced a cult of ancestral worship known as *tong-maeng*, honoring the founder-king with song and dance on conjunction with their harvest thanksgiving festival. In a religious festival called *much'ŏn* ("dance to heaven"), the people of the Eastern Yi in northeast-ern Korea worshiped the lord of heaven with song and dance. Those early Koreans who lived in the three Han federations (Chinhan, Mahan, and Pyŏnhan) which emerged in the southern regions of the peninsula in the 4th and 3rd centuries B.C. also believed it important to invoke the blessings of the spirits of heaven and earth. Various Chinese sources such as the History of the Wei, a part of the *History of the Three Kingdoms,* compiled at the end of the 3rd century A.D., stated that singing and dancing were essential for celebrations such as the spring festival to pray for abundance and the autumn harvest festival for thanksgiving. These sources said that when the planting of seeds was completed in the 5th lunar month, people sang, danced, and drank wine all day and night with-out rest. When they danced, a score of people lined up in single file and, following the leader, they raised and lowered their hands, stamping the ground with their feet to the accompaniment of music, invoking the bless-ings of the spirits of heaven and earth. When harvest gathering was com-pleted, a similar festival was held in the 10th lunar month, offering thanks. The farmers' music and dance, known in Korean as *nongak,* may have their origins in such seasonal religious festivals of ancient Korea. Be that as it may, a Chinese source which dealt with the Zhou Dynasty's cer-emonial practices described Korea as being "a land of dance and music that is forever bursting forth anew with an act filled with vigor and vital-ity." In the early developmental stage of music and dance, shaman priests and priestesses seem to have an important role as lyricists, composers, and dancers, since all music and dance were most likely associated with reli-gious practices.

Cultural contacts between the Koreans in the three Han federations and the Chinese, who established three commanderies in north-western Korea following their conquest of that region in 108 B.C., grew rapidly as cultural relations between the Chinese and the nomadic peoples in Manchuria increased. It was recorded that the people in Chinhan and Pyŏnhan played a 25-stringed Chinese zither called *sul.*

The growth of Chinese cultural influence in Korea was rapid follow-ing the introduction of Confucianism, Buddhism, and other cultural pat-terns in the fourth century. While Confucianism fostered studies of Confucian thought, as well as Chinese poetry, music, and dance associated with Confucian rituals, Buddhism nurtured new music (chant) and dance during and after the Three Kingdoms period (57 B.C.-668 A.D.) in

Korea.

The Kingdom of Koguryŏ, being located closer to China, received more cultural influence from the Chinese much earlier than Shilla and Paekche, which emerged in the southern parts of the Korean peninsula where the Chinan and Mahan federations had existed. As a result both new religious and secular music and dance developed in Koguryŏ much sooner than in the other two Korean kingdoms. A tomb which was excavated in 1949 revealed such evidence. This tomb, named the Tongsu Tomb, was built in 357 A.D. near present-day Anak, South Hwanghae Province, North Korea, some forty years after Koguryŏ destroyed the Chinese command of Lolang (Nangnang in Korean). The murals on this tomb show singers and musicians with various musical instruments and in certain costumes at some sort of ceremony. Among these instruments were drums, panpipes, a zither, a lute, a long vertical flute, a horn, and a handbell. A mural on another wall shows a dancer with a large nose wearing a turban, indicating that foreign musicians and dancers from the region beyond China might have already arrived in Korea. The fresco of another Koguryŏ tomb, the Tomb of the Dancers, built in the 5th or 6th century at Tungkuo, Koguryŏ's former capital, shows six dancers, seven singers, and an instrument player in uniforms. Chinese sources, including poems written by Li Bo and Bo Juyi, reveal that musicians and dancers from Koguryŏ performed Korean music and dance at the Tang court. Evidently, such dances as tongdongmu and hosŏnmu were popular dances of Koguryŏ.

As Chinese influence penetrated into the southern kingdoms, music and dance developed in Paekche, including a mask dance known as kamugiak. Many Paekche musicians and dancers were dispatched to Japan in the 6th century and later, promoting new art forms in that country. In Shilla, as Confucian studies grew and studies of Chinese poetry (*hanshi* in Korean) developed, the writing of native songs in Chinese characters began. With the invention of the new writing systems called *idu* and *hyangch'al*, a large number of native songs called *hyangga* (also known as *saenaenore*) such as the "Song of Ch'ŏyong" were written. Those early mask dances that developed in Koguryŏ, Paekche, and Shilla became forerunners of present-day mask dances of both shamanistic and secular nature.

In additions to shaman rituals and seasonal festivals, the people in Korea after Shilla's unification of the Three Kingdoms in 668 A.D. observed the Buddhist Lantern Festival, for the purpose of propagating the Buddha's virtue, as well as a new festival known as *p'algwanhoe*, a mixture of Buddhist and earlier religious elements honoring the spirits of

Heaven, the gods of the mountains and rivers, and the Dragon God, making music and dance of the Koreans more diverse and sophisticated. The Chinese chronicles of the 6th and 7th centuries recorded that invocatory group singing and dancing was characteristic of the sacrificial ceremonies of the Koreans to the gods of heaven and earth.

Meanwhile, new musical instruments were created in Korea. In the 6th century, a Koguryŏ musician, Wang San-ak, created a six-stringed zither called *kŏmungo* (also called *hyŏngŭm*). At about the same time, a musician named U Ruk, in one of the six Kaya states that existed in the south-central region of the peninsula, created a twelve-stringed zither which became known as *kayagŭm* or *kayago*. Meanwhile, in Shilla, a five-stringed lute called *hyang pip'a* was created. It is not clear as to when such wind instruments as large, medium, and small transverse bamboo flutes (known in Korean as *taegŭm, chung'gŭm,* and *sogŭm*) appeared in Korea. But these bamboo flutes and the above-mentioned zithers and lute became the six key musical instruments of Unified Shilla and after. A historical source entitled Memorabilia of the Three Kingdoms, compiled by the Korean monk Ilyŏn in the mid-13th century, included a legend associated with the creation of the sacred bamboo flute, according to which a sea dragon-king told a filial king of Shilla to cut down the bamboo from the hill on the floating island in the East Sea and make a flute with it, saying that "its music will bring peace and happiness to your kingdom." The king had a musician cut down the bamboo and make a flute, and when this was played the "enemies of Shilla retreated, diseases were healed, rains came after drought, the sun shone after rain, the wind became mild and the sea calmed." It was named the "Flute to Calm Ten Thousand Waves," according to the legend.

In Shilla, in addition to shaman priests and priestesses, a group of young men known as *hwarang* ("flowery princes") seem to have played an important role in promoting music and dance. These young men, who were the scions of the nobility, visited sacred places such as mountains, valleys, and rivers throughout the kingdom and prayed for national safety and prosperity while fostering their spirit and physical strength, mutual trust, and composing songs and creating dances.

3

The Classification of Traditional Korean Music

New music developed in Korea in connection with the growing influence of Buddhism and Confucianism during and after the Three Kingdoms period. Such a trend continued through the Koryŏ period (918-1352) and the early period of the Yi Dynasty (1392-1910) promoting what became traditional Korean music that consisted of the court, religious, and folk music. In this section, the first two branches of traditional Korean music will be discussed.

Court Music

The term "court music" (*kungjung ŭmak*) is a modern invention. The traditional classification of this music was kuk'ak, or "national music," which included not only the music associated with various court ceremonies, but also that associated with Confucian shrine ritual and royal ancestral shrine ritual, as well as the secular music of the upper-class Koreans who were known as *yangban* during the Yi period. It is also called *chŏng'ak*, or "authentic music."

The court music consisted of three categories. The Tang music (*tang'ak*), the "elegant" music (*a'ak*), and the indigenous music (*hyang'ak*). This categorization of the court music into these three branches began during the Koryŏ period, but it was during the reigns of kings Sejong

(1418-1450) and Sejo (1455-1468) that such divisions were clearly established.

The term Tang music refers not only to non-ritual music of China of the Tang period which was brought to Unified Shilla in the 7th century and after, but also to other secular music of China of the Song and Yuan periods which came to Korea from the early 12th century onward. It included Song China's long songs of irregular meter called ci (*sa* in Korean), as well as secular music of the Mongols.

Unlike the Tang music in Japan, which retained much of its original characteristics, Tang music in Korea became radically altered and assimilated with local tradition, losing much of its original character and identity. Of some 40 or so pieces of Tang music recorded in the catalog of music of the Koryŏ period, only two were preserved and handed down to the present. They were long ci songs of Song China called "Spring of Luoyang" and another court ceremonial music called *pohŏja*. Ordinarily, the Tang music is played by small ensembles of 13 musical instruments, including *changgo*, a drum shaped like an hourglass, which was brought to Korea in the 12th century from central Asia.

The *a'ak*, or elegant music, is Confucian ritual and ceremonial music, known as *chŏng'ak*, which was introduced to Korea from song in China in 1116, thanks to musical notations and instruments which the Song emperor sent to the Korean court. After its arrival, the *a'ak* became "authentic music" (*chŏng'ak*) for the Confucian shrine and Royal Ancestral shine rituals, as well as for various cŭurt ceremonies. It also became the music of upper-class Koreans.

The *a'ak* was the music of the spring and autumn Confucian shrine rituals called *munmyo cherye* or *sŏkchŏn*, as well as annual ceremonies at the Royal Ancestral Shrine known as *chongmyo cherye*. Two orchestras, one called the Terrace Orchestra (*tŭngga*) and the other called the Ground Orchestra (*hŏn'ga*), played the music. The Terrace Orchestra, positioned on the terrace of the main hall of the shrine, and the much larger Ground Orchestra which sat in the courtyard of the main hall of the shrine played a total of seven long pieces of the "elegant music" (*a'ak*), each taking turns and playing a particular piece of music to the order of the ceremonial act.

Four vocalists were attached to each orchestra and sang ritual songs during the ceremony. Among the major *a'ak* pieces which the orchestras played were "Encounter on the Spiritual Mountain," which had three versions, and "Sharing Happiness with the People," a piece of music whose lyrics were from the epic poem entitled "Songs of Dragons Flying to Heaven," written during the reign of King Sejong.

Up until the reign of King Sejong, mostly the *a'ak* and the *tang'ak* pieces were played at the annual ceremonies at the Royal Ancestral Shrine, but in 1435 two newly composed pieces of Korean music (*hyang'ak*) entitled "Preservation of Great Peace" (*pot'aep'yŏng*) and "Founding of a Great Dynasty" (*chŏngdaeŏp*) became official music for these ceremonies. The first of these praised the civil virtues of the founder of the Yi Dynasty while the second glorified his military skills and achievements.

In the beginning, the term *a'ak* was applied only to Confucian ritual music, but eventually it was used in a broader sense to include the entire musical tradition of the Korean court as well as that of upper-class Koreans. Some *a'ak* pieces were performed by string instruments while other pieces were performed with wind instruments as the core groups. The *a'ak* was normally performed by a large orchestra of 45 instruments. On the other hand, the *chŏng'ak* was played by small ensembles.

The term *hyang'ak* means indigenous music. However, the officials of both the Koryŏ and the Yi periods who established musical divisions failed to include folk music in this category because it was the music of the "low-born" people and not worthy of any consideration by the so-called literary people. The term *hyang'ak* originated during the late Shilla period when native songs of Shilla were called *hyangga*. Such terms were coined to differentiate native songs from Chinese songs of the Tang period. During the Koryŏ period, the *hyang'ak* was named *sok'ak*, which means secular music. The music of both the Shilla and the Koryŏ periods was the court music that was nurtured in Korea, fashioned after Chinese musical theories and patterns. Oddly, however, the music which arrived in Korea from the region beyond China before the 4th century was included in the *hyang'ak* category. At any rate, among some 19 major *hyang'ak* pieces that were handed down are: "Yearning for Mother," "Song of the Western Capital," "Song of Green Mountains," and "Song of Chŏngŏp."

The *hyang'ak* pieces were played by small ensembles of seven instruments such as the zithers, lutes, and flutes, all of which were created in Korea. What differentiates the *hyang'ak* from the Chinese music (both the *a'ak* and the *tang'ak*) was that while most Chinese music is based on the heptatomic scale, most *hyang'ak* music was composed on the pentatonic scale.

Military music was an important part of the court music of traditional Korea. The music which the military bands played was called *ch'wit'a*, which means "blowing and beating," and this type of music fell into two categories. In addition, there was the "marching music" which was played on such occasions as military processions and parades, various activities at the military camps, and the king's visitations to his ancestral shrine or tombs. Two units of military bands accompanied the king's processions, one at the head of the procession and the other at the end.

The military bands used mostly percussion and wind instruments such as drums, trumpets, a conical flute with a brass funnel, cymbals, and a conch-shell trumpet. Members of the military bands were identified by their bright, yellow uniforms with blue belts and yellow hats.

The vocal music that constituted an important part of the court music was called *ka'ak* in Korean. Only songs in this category belonged to what was known as "authentic music." This vocal music (*ka'ak*) included three types of songs: long lyric songs (*kagok*), narrative songs (*kasa*), and short lyric songs (*shijo*). Each of these types of vocal music had its own unique techniques, tonal control, and emotional expression. A solo vocalist was accompanied by a small ensemble, and many ritual and much of the ceremonial music included vocal arts performed by groups of singers.

The vocal tradition that flourished under the sponsorship of the Yi government, which adopted Neo-Confucianism as the state creed of Korea, enjoyed the highest esteem of the upper class of the Yi society. It seems that when the lyric songs emerged in the 15th century they were all in slow tempo. By the early 17th century fast tempo songs were written and gained in popularity so that, by the mid-18th century, slow tempo songs were no longer sung. Most of these songs were written in five-tone mode, but some were four-tone. The entire repertory of some 41 lyric songs (*kagok*), 26 for male and 15 for female voice, were collected in the songs of the *Ten Thousand Years of Joy*. The songs were sung with the accompaniment of a small ensemble which consisted of zither, flute, bamboo oboe, and drum.

The narrative songs (*kasa*) developed in the mid-17th century. In general, these were longer than the lyric songs. Musically, they were also less organized than the lyric genre as they lacked formal structure and a defined singing style, although each narrative song was sung to a particular tune. The twelve existing narrative songs include such titles as "White Gull Song," "Yellow Chicken Song," "Song of the Angler," and "Song of Mt. Suyang." Narrative songs were usually sung without accompaniment, or occasionally with a drum (*changgo*) or bamboo flute (*taegǔm*).

The history of the short lyric song (*shijo*) is brief, beginning in the early 19th century. It is based on a short lyric poem of 42 or 45 words in three lines, the form of which developed in the 13th century and flourished during the Yi period, particularly after the introduction of the newly invented Korean script called *han'gǔl* in the middle of the 15th century.

New melodies were composed for these lyric poems to be sung. Although slow in tempo, the dynamism in vocal expression rendered particular character to these short songs which were usually sung to the accompaniment of bamboo flute (*taegŭm*), drum (*changgo*), a two-stringed fiddle (*haegum*), and a slender oboe (*sep'ilyul*).

The short lyric song developed almost exclusively in the central and southern parts of Korea, and the tunes of the Seoul area were distinctively different from those of the southern provinces.

Religious Music

In addition to ritual music which we have already discussed, there were two types of religious music in traditional Korea, the Buddhist and the Shaman. Later in the 18th century, Christian hymns were introduced, followed by a massive importation of Christian music with the arrival of the Protestant missionaries at the end of the 19th century.

1. Buddhist music

With the arrival of Buddhism in the late 4th century, Indian language chants were introduced. Some of them were long sermons while other were supplications that sought blessings of the Buddha or other Buddhist saints. Still others were chants for reconciliation. Some of the songs were composed in four phrases of seven words each or four phrases of five words each. About seventy such chants are said to have existed, but only ten of them are currently known. Most of these chants were choruses which included solo parts.

The best known Buddhist vocal music was *pŏmp'ae*, a chant without any melodic lines, which was brought to Korea from China in the 8th century. It is often called *Indo sori*, meaning Indian song, and it takes nearly an hour to sing the entire song. It is a song of prayer for the dead so that the departed may gain entry into the Western Paradise. This type of song has two basic styles of singing: the simple chant (*hotsori*) which makes up the majority of the repertory and the more elaborate chant (*chitsori*), which has the most extraordinary melismas and a tone that ranges from a deep basso, basso profundo, all the way up to falsetto. It is not confined to any limitation of time and can be prolonged or abridged in accordance with the requirements of the ceremony.

The *pŏmp'ae* texts are from a Buddhist sutra. Some parts of the *pŏmp'ae* are sung in Sanskrit, the ancient Indian language, and some parts are sung in Chinese. The chant is usually sung with the accompaniment of a large gong, round drum, and a hollowed-out, wooden block with a slit, called *mokt'ak* in Korean.

In addition to the chants, music that was associated with Buddhist dance developed and became a part of the musical heritage of Korea.

2. Shaman Music

Shaman music (*muak* or *musok ǔmak*) is the oldest music in Korea which is associated with shaman rituals (*kut*) of various categories. Many shaman chants that originated during the prehistoric times led to the rise of the three types of shaman chants: those which welcome and bid farewell to the gods when the ritual is performed, long narrative chants which usually describe a certain situation or explain causes for current sickness or ill-fortunes of the host or members of his family, and "pleasure songs" for the purpose of entertaining the gods, much akin to the ordinary folk songs (*t'aryǒng* or *norae karak*).

The shaman ritual, which usually has twelve segments, begins with the songs calling for gods to be present at the ritual. These are followed by songs that praise the virtues and goodness of the gods and entertain them. After that, come the songs which invoke the good wishes of the gods for reconciliation between the gods and the host and his family. At the end, the song of farewell to the gods is sung.

There are many types of shaman rituals (*kut*). Some are elaborate, lasting two or three days, while others are quite simple. The ritual for the village god and that of treading the evil spirits into the ground are rituals in which many people take parts. There is a simple ritual (*p'udakǒri*) to exorcise the devils of disease and another one (*salp'uri*) for the exorcism of evil spirits. Whatever the nature of the ritual, such shaman songs as "Song of Creation," "Song of Princess Pari," and "Song of Warrior Hero" are sung by the presiding shaman priest, who also dances.

Regional variations in shaman chants are unmistakable. The most popular rhythmic pattern in shaman music, naturally enough, is called *kutkǒri changdan*, which simply means "rhythmic pattern of shaman ritual music." The musical instruments most prominently used in shaman rituals were the round drum (*puk*), the hourglass drum (*changgo*), the two-stringed fiddle (*haegǔm*), and the gong (*ching*).

4
Particularities of Traditional Korean Music

There are many particular features of traditional Korean music. Some of these have already been mentioned. In this section, two unique aspects of traditional music are discussed. They are its rhythmic patterns and the musical scale, modes, and the notation system that was used.

Rhythmic Patterns

The Korean word for rhythmic patterns is *changdan*, which means "long and short," and together with the melodic lines known in Korea as karak, they constitute one of the two basic elements of Korean music.

There are two rhythmic patterns of Korean music, the patterns of the authentic music (*chŏng'ak changdan*) and those of the secular music (*minsok'ak changdan*). The rhythmic patterns of the authentic music, which normally have long melodic lines, include some sixteen different patterns. Ten of these are for instrumental and six are for vocal music. During the performance of the music, the rhythmic pattern is maintained by either the round drum (*puk*) or the hourglass drum (*changgo*).

Musical Scales, Modes, and Notation System

The Koreans adopted the Chinese musical scale called *shibiyul* which had 12 pitches (tones), or *yul* in Korean. Counting from the first pitch, the first six odd numbers were called yang *yul* and the even numbers were called yin *yŏ*. The terms yin and yang came from the Chinese cosmic theory related to these dual forces.

5

Folk Music

As already mentioned, the officials of the dynastic period failed to include Korea's truly indigenous music, namely folk music, in any category, including *hyang'ak*. However, they called it secular music (*sok'ak*), the modern terminology for which is *minsok'ak*.

Korea's folk music may be divided into two types: "artistic" folk music and common folk music. To the first type belongs *p'ansori*, *shinawi*, and *sanjo*, and folk music of all types Koreans call *minyo*. Farmers' music belongs to the second type.

P'ansori

Etymologically, *p'ansori* means a "song sung at a place of entertainment." The term *p'ansori* is translated in many ways such as "folk operatic song," "Korean minstrels song," or "a narrative-epic-dramatic vocal art form." It is often mistakenly called "musical drama" (*ch'ang'gŭk*). At any rate, it is an art form of dramatic story-telling by a solo performer in songs (*ch'ang*) and recitation, accompanied by the rhythmic patterns provided by a barrel drum (*puk*) player who, in reality, is more than a mere accompanist. The drum player, usually a male, is a source of inspiration to the singer, a feat accomplished with the use of drum calls. His function may be likened to that of the Spanish flamenco guitarist.

Folk entertainment such as *p'ansori* may have existed for centuries since the days of the three kingdoms, but it is said to have originated in the early Yi period (15th century). Be that as it may, by the mid-18th century it had developed as an art. The songs the *p'ansori* singers sang and the stories they told were orally transmitted from masters to apprentices. Only in the mid-19th century did a patron of the *p'ansori* (Shin Chae-hyo) edit the then existing songs and published attractively written panzer texts with beautifully explained passages thereby elevating this form of art to a higher level. Those songs which Shin wrote were based on well-known folk tales of the time, and the melodic structure of the songs was drawn from satanic ritual music as well as regional folk songs of the southwestern region. Among the songs which Shin wrote were "Songs of Ch'unhyang," "Song of Shim Ch'ong," "Song of the Red Cliff," and "Song of Hungbu."

Shin also wrote short songs which panzer singers sang before their main performance. Among them were "Song of the Peach and Plum Blossoms," "Song of the Angler," "Song of the Crow and Toad," and "Song of a Folk Entertainer." Of these, the last, known in Korea as *kwangdae-ka*, is the most well known. In this the personal sentiments of a folk entertainer were expressed, and the qualities that good folk entertainers must possess were pointed out. Quite understandably, the folk entertainer says that good looks, talent for narration, musical skills, and ability to make dramatic gestures were the ideal qualities.

A total of seven rhythmic patterns were employed in panzer. The most frequently used ones are slow *chinyangjo*, moderate *chungmori*, fast *chungjungmori* and faster *chajinmori*. Tempos employed in panzer singing range from largo to allegro. There is a basic meter and rhythm, but it is primarily used as a point of departure from which the accompanist, the round drum player, must adapt himself to the rhythmic and emotional outflow of the singer.

It is absolutely essential that the voice, rhythm, tone, and techniques of the panzer singer convey the inner meaning of the narrative. In order to be able to do so, a long period of rigorous training and mastery of the various techniques is required of those who aspire to be panzer singers. These artists narrate the tales in a dramatic fashion, invoking emotional responses from the audience, and sing songs in mournful or cheerful voices in accordance with the passages in the tales, making various gestures with their arms, hand, and the fan they hold in the right hand, or a handkerchief in the left in the case of a woman singer. The panzer artists always perform their acts in standing posture, wearing simple costumes.

Shinawi

Shinawi, which is related to satanic music of the southwestern region of Korea, was a heterophonic type of music played by small ensembles, which included the native slender oboe (*sep'ilyul*), the large transverse bamboo flute (*taegŭm*), the two-string fiddle (*haegŭm*), the hourglass drum (*chang'go*), and the gong (*ching*). Later on other stringed instruments such as the six-string and the 12-string zithers (*kŏmungo* and *kayagŭm* respectively) were added.

In a way, *shinawi* is similar to American jazz. It allows maximum freedom to players to improvise lines in accordance with two basic rhythmic patterns of 12/8 time, oddly enough producing a harmonic effect. Some maintain that *shinawi* was the ancient form of Shilla's native music.

Sanjo

Sanjo is a unique type of solo instrumental music that may have been an off-shoot of shinawi. In the beginning, sanjo music was only for the 12-string zither, but later on *sanjo* music was written for other instruments such as the 6-string zither, the large transverse bamboo flute, and the two-string fiddle, thereby enriching Korea's musical heritage.

Contrary to *shinawi*, the *sanjo* music has definite structure and set meter, but it also allows the players to improvise their creative skills. Because of this, the same *sanjo* music will sound different when played by different players.

Sanjo music consists of several movements in different rhythmic patterns. The main ones are the slow movement (*chinyangjo*), the moderate movement (*chungmori*), and the fast movement (*chajinmori*) in a sequential order toward the finale. These three movements are played without a break and at a gradually increasing tempo.

Minyo

Folk songs known in Korean as *minyo* have been part of the oral literature of Korea as much as part of her native musical heritage. These songs are directly related to everyday life, and some of them are as old as history. These songs are known as such-and-such *ka*, *norae*, *yo* or *t'aryŏng.* Some of them are men's songs, some women's songs, and some children's songs. Among the men's songs are the "Rice Planting Song," "Song of the Wood Cutter," "Animal Song," and "Food Song." The Women's songs include such titles as "Sewing Song," "Song of Sea Divers," "Song of Married Women," "Song of the Widow," "Song of Love," and "Grain Grinding Song."

Particular folk songs are associated with certain regions of Korea. Thus, one hears about Kyŏnggi folk songs of the central region, southern folk songs of the southwestern region, western folk songs of the northwestern region, and eastern folk songs of Hamgyŏng, Kangwŏn, and Kyŏngsang Provinces. Such folk songs as *yangsando, toraji t'aryŏng,* and *Pak Yŏn Water Fall* are typical Kyŏnggi songs; *sushimga* and *monggŭmp'o t'aryŏng* are of northwestern Korea; "Song of the Birds," *"yukcha paegi,"* and *kanggang sullae* are of the south and southwest; and *shinkosan t'aryong* is a relatively new folk song of the northeast.

The folk song called *arirang* is by far the most widely known and sung and is common to all regions. The Koreans sing this when they are happy and when they are sad. Nevertheless, there are regional *arirang* songs such as chindo *arirang* and miryang *arirang* of the south, Kangwŏndo *arirang* and Chŏngsŏn *arirang* of the Kangwŏn Province, and long ari of the northwest. Some folk songs are sung in unison while others are sung by two groups in responsive fashion.

Farmers' Music

What the Koreans call farmers' music (*nong'ak*) is not the music of the Korean farmers as such but the music which certain semi-professional musicians in the farmers' bands play for the rural people. The farmers' music played an important role in traditional Korean music in the past and is still performing a significant cultural role today. Various forms of music of the farmers' band may have their origins in the spring and autumn festivals dedicated to the spirits of heaven and earth for their beneficial deeds. Some believe that the tradition of mendicant Buddhist monks who decorated their hats with flowers and played music to solicit donations from the devotees for their temples gave birth to the farmers' band. Following the appearance of the farmers' bands and when the territorial warfare between the three kingdoms became intense, the farmers' bands and their music that had religious ties took on a military aspect as the peasants were recruited into the militia.

Whatever the case may be, in the past the farmers' bands were classified into twelve categories such as the Flower Crown (*hwagwan*) Corps and the Battle Hat (*chŏnrip*) Corps. The members of the former wore hats in the shape of the Buddhist monk's hood decorated with large paper flowers, usually chrysanthemums, and the members of the latter group performed music related to various military activities such as assembling, parading, charging, retreating, and marking the triumphal return of the peasant soldiers.

The traditional farmers' band music consisted of twelve movements or parts, and each movement had three melodic units. Thus, the entire repertory of the farmers' music was often called "twelve movements and thirty-six melodic units." Each melodic unit was played in sequences without any break, completing a movement at the end of the third unit. Then the next movement began without a pause. It has been speculated that these thirty-six melodic units represented the music associated with battle strategies. On the other hand, some believe that farmers' music had the same root as shaman mask plays because many of its melodic lines are identical to those of shaman ritual music and, furthermore, many activities of the farmers' bands are similar or identical to those of the shaman rituals (*kut*).

Due to geographical and climatic factors, farmers' music and dance developed mostly in the southern regions of Korea where the agriculture economy was much more important to livelihood than in the north and where shamanism grew stronger. Northern provinces such as Hamgyŏng and P'yŏn'gan had no farmers' bands.

Today, farmers' bands are normally composed of six members led by flag bearer who carries a long banner suspended from a tall bamboo pole topped with a crown of pheasant feathers. The inscription on the banner reads: "Farmers are the Principals of the World." The band leader (*sangsoe*) wears a tightly fitted hat, often topped with a plume of crane feathers. He carries a small brass gong (*kkwaenggari*) in his left hand and plays it with a small wooden-tipped mallet, and he occasionally dances. Another principal member wears a hat similar to that of the leader, but instead of a plume his hat has a swivel on the top to which a long paper streamer is attached. He carries a small hand drum (*sogo*) which he plays while dancing. Another member wears a large hood-shaped paper hat similar to that of a Buddhist monk, which is covered with large paper chrysanthemums of several colors. He plays an hourglass drum (*changgo*) and also dances. Some members play the double-reed oboe with a brass funnel (*t'aep'yŏngso*), the round drum (*puk*), and a large gong (*ching*). Three other members who frequently take parts in various activities of the farmers' bands are the "gunner," wearing a crown with large Chinese characters saying "Great General," a "gentleman folk entertainer" (*yang-ban kwangdae*), and a singer.

The farmers' band music is high-pitched, loud, noisy, fast tempoed, and highly animated, generating an exuberant and joyful mood that the Koreans call *hŭng*. The farmers' bands play music with such titles as "War Camp Play," "Play at the Well," "Sacred Drum Play," and "Yangban Gunner Play." Many of their melodic units have the same titles as shaman ritual music, indicating the common origins of shamanism and the farmers' music.

Such music is played at various activities, some of which are related to agricultural life such as planting, weeding, and harvesting. Some of the activities are associated with folk beliefs. Thus, from the first day to the 15th day of the first lunar month, the farmers' bands perform the ritual called "Treading the Earth Spirits," playing music and stamping the ground so that evil spirits will stay in the ground all year long. During the rice planting season, they play music in the rice fields. After planting, on the 5th day of the 5th lunar month, they celebrate the spring festival called Tano. In the 7th lunar month, they carry out another religious ritual, praying for a rich harvest, and on the 15th day of the 8th lunar month they participate in the harvest festival of thanksgiving. On the 15th day of the first lunar month and in the 10th lunar month they take part in the rituals dedicated to the village god, paying homage for the safety and well-being of the villagers. In the 12th lunar month they perform, oddly enough, shaman rituals at nearby Buddhist temples.

A Recent Trend in Folk Music

As the government made serious efforts to revive and promote Korea's traditional culture, including music and dance, the new generation of Koreans with creative instincts launched their own movements to produce modern versions of traditional music and dance. In 1978 a group of four such young men introduced what they called "four item play," or *samul nori*. Debuting at the Space Theater in Seoul, this folk percussion quartet played many traditional melodies and new ones of hypnotic rhythms that mesmerized the audience. Since then, the *samul nori* has become extremely popular. The folk quartet consisted of a round drum, a 12-string zither, a large gong, and small gong. The creators of this new genre in Korean folk music said that their aims were to invent sounds of heaven, earth, and man in harmony.

Panzer and the folk songs (*minyo*) are now included in the category of national music (*kuk'ak*) and officially recognized as an essential part of Korea's musical heritage.

6

The Dances of Traditional Korea

The dances of traditional Korea, much like its music, had their origins in various seasonal religious festivals of antiquity. However, as the society changed and secular culture grew, new forms of dance emerged during and after the Three Kingdoms period. The arrival of Chinese dances greatly enhanced the new trends.

As in the case of music, dances of traditional Korea consisted of court dances, religious dances, and a variety of folk dances. While the highly stylized court dances displayed important dimensions of discipline, grandeur, and elegance to create "aestheticism of the inner spirit," folk dances, especially mask dances, showed spontaneity, humor, freedom, and satire.

There are many differences between Korean and Western dances and the ways in which the dancers perform. Some of the conspicuous ones are that, while Western dancers primarily use their legs, Korean dancers use their shoulders, arms and hands more, and while Western dancers dance on their heels as well as their toes, Korean dancers in general use the heels more but with very little leg movement. Another difference is that Korean dancers often sing while they dance.

Court Dances

Court dances, known in Korean as *pŏmmu* or *chŏngjae* consisted of two types: those which were danced to the Tang music and others which were created in Korea and were danced to the tune of the indigenous music. There were a little over 50 court dances. Most court dances were performed by two groups, the main dancers and the supporting dancers. The male parts were played by boys, known as *mudong* in Korean, and the female parts were played be female court dancers, often called *kisaeng*. The *mudong* danced mainly for kings, princes, and their guests, while female dancers performed for queens and princesses as well as in the presence of kings and other male guests at various court ceremonies. The female dancers wore a specially designed small ornamental crown and colorful costumes with long sleeves which covered their hands.

The court dances were sublime, solemn, majestic, ornate, and highly stylized, and they were designed to be an elegant spectacle, sometimes involving as many as 200 or more dancers. To supplement the apparent simplicity of the dances, expensive and ornate costumes and props were used so that the performance would assume a pompous and stately appearance corresponding to the grandeur and glory of the throne. As a rule, in the court dances, as in the court music, meters and rhythms were strictly adhered to. Absent from the dances was the expression of emotion as such, although the court dances are said to have "epitomized the poetry and grace of human emotions."

Many Chinese court dances which the Korean court adopted became known officially as Tang dances regardless of whether or not they were those of Tang or Song China. The Tang dances were different from the indigenous court dances in many ways. One particular difference was the presence of two long poles, about ten feet tall, on the stage when the Tang dances were performed. At the tip of each pole was a red wooden bow plaited with a hundred small sticks. Another difference was that whereas all songs in the Tang dances had Chinese phrases, songs of the indigenous dances were written and sung in Korean.

Several historical sources indicate that many Chinese dances were brought to Korea, but most of them have become extinct. One of the oldest Chinese dances to survive is the "Ball Throwing Dances," which was performed by twelve female dancers. Among other Chinese dances was the "Queen's Unit Dance," which was a spectacular dance performed by a large group of dancers to celebrate the rule of the reigning king. One of the dances created in Korea and performed to the Tang tune was the "Dance of the Golden Measure," which glorified the deeds of the founder of the Yi Dynasty.

Some of the dances which were presumed to have indigenous origins may actually have Chinese roots. Whatever may be the case, the indigenous dances became important repertory of the court dances of Korea during the Yi period. The oldest indigenous dance was the "Dance of Ch'ŏyong," which was created in the late Shilla period. This mask dance of shamanistic nature is related to the legend of the son of the sea dragon who took a human form. The dance is performed to the tune of "Encounter on the Spiritual Mountain" and "Sedgewick." Another Shilla dance which became an important part of the court repertory was the "Dance of the Four Fairies," whose story is related to four "flowery princes" (*hwarang*) of Shilla who promoted music and dance as well as martial spirit. Among the popular indigenous court dances were titles such as the "Boating Dance," the "Nightingale Dance," the "Beautiful Person Picking Peonies," the "Drum Dance," the "Double Drum Dance," the "Sword Dance," the "Crane Dance," and the "Coming of the Phoenix." The "Nightingale Dance" is a solo dance and the slowest of all the court dances, and the "Crane Dance" is a duo dance which mimics the mating ritual of two cranes. The "Sword Dance," one of the most popular of all dances, is said to have originated in Shilla. This dance, which is normally performed by two or four female dancers, became one of the dances which the shamans performed at their particular ritual.

Ritual and Religious Dances

The ritual and religious dances of traditional Korea were those of Confucianism, Buddhism, and Shamanism. The Confucian ritual dances were performed to the accompaniment of "elegant music" (*a'ak*). Ever since its adoption by the Koreans in the early 12th century, the original solemn and stately nature of the Confucian ritual dance has been preserved intact.

The Confucian ritual dances are collectively called ilmu, and they are still performed in the spring and autumn rituals (*sŏkchŏn* or *munmyo cherye*) held at the shrine in Seoul dedicated to Confucius and his main disciples. The identical ritual dances are performed at the annual spring ceremony (*chongmyo cherye*) at the Royal Ancestral Shrine in Seoul.

The ilmu consisted of the "Civil Dance" and the "Military Dance." It is performed by two groups of dancers who form eight lines with eight dancers in each line. Such formation gave the name Eight *Ilmu* (*p'al ilmu*) to this particular form of dance. The dance consists of a series of simple, slow, stylized movements solely for the purpose of ceremony and the offering of sacrifices rather than for the sake of dance as such. The dancers of the "Civil Dance" wear a red robe and a stiff black hat. They carry a type of flute in the right hand and, in the left, a stick with a dragon-shaped head to which pheasant feathers are attached. The dancers of the "Military Dance" wear a red robe and a stiff red hat. They carry a shield with a painted dragon head in the left hand, while the right hand holds a wooden hatchet with a carved dragon head. The two groups of dancers perform to the music played by the two orchestras alternately according to the order of the ceremony. In the annual ritual held at the Royal Ancestral Shrine, the civil and the military dancers perform to the music entitled "Preservation of Great Peace" and "Founding of a Great Dynasty," which were composed during the reign of King Sejong to glorify his ancestor.

The Buddhist dances which were introduced to Korea from India via China in the eighth century were radically Koreanized in the ninth century and after, losing much of their original characteristics. Be that as it may, there remain the four dances that constitute the main repertory of the Buddhist ritual dances. Theses dances have been performed at various Buddhist ceremonies such as the "Spiritual Mountain Ritual" as a supplication to the Buddha for the souls of the departed so that they may gain entry into the Western Paradise.

One of the best known Buddhist dances in Korea is the "Butterfly Dance" (*nabi ch'um*) which is the ultimate in grace, subtlety, and restraint, emulating the ethereal movements of the butterfly. This dance is performed with the accompaniment of a large gong and a conical oboe and the chanting of the Buddhist invocation. Of fourteen variations of this dance, only six are commonly performed at present day rituals. The "Butterfly Dance" is normally performed by two monks wearing long frocks of white or yellow hemp cloth with extremely broad and long sleeves. The hats they wear are the typical monk's pointed hood, but they are made heavier by additional flaps of materials and ornaments. They also wear bright red mantles across their chests and over one shoulder.

The "Drum Dance" (*pŏpko ch'um*) is a Buddhist dance of self-chastisement. It is performed by a monk dancing in front of a large barrel drum about two feet in diameter which gives off a thunderous sound. He makes only simple and slow dance movements as he plays the drum. Along with this dance, the "Cymbal Dance" (*para ch'um*) is regarded as one of the most difficult Buddhist dances. Performed by a solo dancer in colorful costume, it requires the manipulation of two very large and heavy cymbals in two movements: the first, where the cymbals are lifted above the head from waist level, and the second, where they are spun about to face the front and back of the dancer's head in a series of alternating motions.

Another Buddhist dance is known as the "Dance of the Eight-Fold Path" (*t'aju*) which is performed at the end of the "Spiritual Mountain Ritual." In this dance, two dancers make a circle around an eight-sided wooden log painted white and bearing large black letters that symbolize the teachings of the Buddha. As they go around the log, which is placed in the center of the dance area, each stops at intervals and touches the top of the log with a long, thin, wooden mallet. Another Buddhist dance in Korea is the "Dance of the Wooden Fish" (*mogŏ ch'um*), in which a monk makes dancing moves as he plays a fish-shaped wooden drum which is hung in the pavilion at the entrance of the temple.

Both Buddhism and shamanism were mutually influenced by each other. The Buddhists incorporated certain shamanistic beliefs, such as the concepts of the mountain deity of shamanism, and constructed a particular building dedicated to other shaman deities in the compound of the temples, while some 30% of the twelve segments of shaman rituals called kut are Buddhistic. The shaman ritual known as the Seven Star (Big Dipper) kut is a case in point. In this particular ritual, the female shaman, dressed in a monk's robe and wearing the Buddhist rosary, performs the "Dance of the Descending God," employing cymbals as in the Buddhist "Cymbal Dance," and pays homage to the infinite grace of the Buddha.

Only certain segments of shaman rituals have dancing. Most of the shamans who sing, dance, and perform rituals are female shamans called mudang in Korean. In general, shaman dances are highly individualistic since the performers create various moves as the situation calls for while performing the ritual. Among the shaman dances is the shamanist version of the court dance named the "Sword Dance." The dancer carries two unconventional swords whose short blades are connected to the handles by short wires and which produce a rattling noise as the dancer brandishes them. This dance, a colorful and attractive one, is among the most popular in Korea.

One of the most enchanting shaman dances is called *salp'uri*, an improvisational dance which literally means "exorcise the devil" or "soothing the evil spirits." Originating from the shaman rituals of the southwest, it is performed as a postlude to the ritual proper to assure the safe passage of the soul into the Western Paradise after death, thereby comforting the soul of the deceased and soothing the sorrows of the bereaved. Performed to the accompaniment of shaman incantation, the dance expresses such feeling as the loneliness, solitude, emptiness, pointlessness, and futility of life, and the helpless yearning for immortality in the face of eventual death.

In the southern region, the shamans perform the *salp'uri* dance in slow, rippling movements, while in the northern region it is performed to a faster tempo, at times violent in motion, with jumping up and down, and waving of the arms wildly about in what almost appears to be a state of frenzy.

Folk Dances

The folk dance is the oldest of all dances in Korea, which developed in association with religious and farming activities of ancient times. A leading dance critic of Korean dance remarked that the "ideal of the Korean dance is enjoyment of *mŏt* and *hŭng* rather than demonstration of the techniques of dancing for dance's sake." Such an opinion regarding Korean dance may have been expressed in connection with the characterization of the folk dance of the Korean people. The Korean word *mŏt* may be translated as "exotic style" and *hŭng* could mean "exuberantly joyful mood." A writer described *hŭng* as "an irrepressibly joyful mood almost reaching the point of giddiness ... a joy pouring forth from within ... from a deep sense of beauty ... a state of everlasting exhilaration." The folk dances are an expression of these feelings.

Among some unique features of Korean folk dance is the precedence of the dancer's movement over rhythm, and the precedence of rhythm over meter. In the court music and dance, meters and rhythms are, as a rule, strictly adhered to, in contrast to the free, improvisational nature of the native folk medium. With respect to such factors as syncopation, polyrhythms, and counter-rhythms, the folk music and dance are far more developed than those of the court music and dance. The precedence of the dancer's movement over the rhythmic accompaniment reaches its highest peak in the farmer's dance where the performers "walk right through the triple meter as nonchalantly as if they were walking down a country road ... entirely unmindful of the prevailing rhythmic force."

Another important aspect of Korean folk dance is the dispensation of the concept of time, wherein the dancer remains motionless except for the rhythmic motion of the shoulders, which move up and down. In the Korean folk dance, the stillness is directed toward the attainment of the "spiritual executed in quiescence."

Traditional Korean folk dance consisted of two categories. The first was the dance associated with shamanistic mask plays, and the second was secular dance for popular entertainment. Of course, the common folk did dance to a variety of folk tunes as their ancestors had done before. The folk dances discussed here are those which were performed by professional or semi-professional dancers. Some of those dances were solo dances, but most of them were performed by groups of dancers.

1. The Mask Dance.

The mask dances, called *t'alch'um* in Korean, originated with the spring and autumn rituals of the ancient Koreans which were performed to honor the spirits of heaven and earth. However, the ritual they performed of the night of the year to exorcise the evil spirits of the old year and to welcome the new ones may have been the direct ancestor of the later mask dances,

There are two main styles of Korean mask dances: one is the *kodurŏm* dance and the other is the *kkaekki*, each having ten acts of various steps, motions, and rhythms. The first type is performed to the slow tune of Buddhistic chants while the second type is performed to the folk tunes of faster rhythms such as *t'aryŏng* and *kutkŏri*.

Most of these exciting and theatrical mask dances have been associated with shamanistic mask plays. The "Dance of Ch'ŏyong" may have been the first such mask dance created in Korea. One type of the mask plays is known as *sandae togam nori* which developed in Kyŏnggi Province. Other well-known mask plays, which include many exciting mask dances, are those of Pongsan, South Hwanghae Province in North Korea, and the "Lion Dance" of Pukch'ŏng, South Hamgyŏng Province in North Korea. The shaman ritual called *pyŏlshin gut* which is dedicated to the female tutelary goddess of the village of Hahoe, North Kyŏngsang Province, is a unique mask play, while the plays called the "Five Folk Entertainers" (*okwangdae*) of T'ongyŏng, and the "Field Play" (*yayu*) of Tongnae of South Kyŏngsang Province have very popular dances. Although these are religious mask plays, they have certain segments which are secular in character in which the ruling class (*yangban*), including the government officials and corrupt Buddhist monks of the Yi period, are ridiculed and bitterly denounced. Interestingly, as in the "Lion Dance" of Pukch'ŏng, in the mask play of Pongsan and the "Five Folk Entertainers" play, the lion appears and avenges his smaller and weaker animal friends by killing the hunter. In such plays, the audience could easily identify themselves with the defenseless animals in the forest and the hunter as the government official.

The mask dancers wear grotesque painted masks made of gourd or wood and colorful costumes with long sleeves. They are acrobatic and made various physical gestures that are highly comical. The mask plays are often fraught with obscenity and vulgarity.

2. Farmers' Dances

Although the dancing constitutes a minor part in the total performance of the farmers' band which plays farmers' music, it is an important aspect of all activities of the farmers' band that developed long ago in connection with the seasonal economic activities and religious festivals.

The principal dancers are the leader of the band who plays a small hand gong (*kkwaenggari*), the hourglass drum (*changgo*) player, and a small hand drum (*sogo*) player. Only rarely do other members dance. The dance which they perform has no set style, and it lacks artistic form. The movements the dancers make are simple, crude, and unstylistic. Be that as it may, whenever the farmers' band performs, whether in seasonal farming activities such as planting, weeding, and harvesting or in religious rites such as the ritual for the village god or the treading of spirits into the earth, they dance. The dance of the drum player has backward, forward, and pivoting side movements. The small hand drum player makes mostly head and neck movements. Rotating his head right and left, he spins a long paper streamer suspended from the swivel at the top of his hat to wave or make large circles. Occasionally, the dancing boy, dressed in a girl's costume, appears on the shoulders of a man and moves his arms and shoulders, making dancing gestures while the man who carries the boy also dances.

3. Other Dances

Among the many other dances that belong to the culture of the common people are the "Monk Dance," the "Nine Drum Dance," and *Salp'uri*.

Developed in the early 16th century, the "Monk Dance," which is a folk adaptation of the Buddhist "Drum Dance," became one of the most popular secular dances. Performed by a female dancer wearing the robe of a Buddhist monk with long sleeves and red mantle, a white hood, and a Buddhist rosary, this dance tells the story of a Buddhist monk who encounters and succumbs to worldly temptations, represented by a large drum suspended from a wooden frame in the center of the stage.

The "Nine Drum Dance," like the "Five Drum Dance," is a new version of the "Monk Dance" in which the Buddhist aspects are discarded. In this dance a female dancer demonstrates mostly her skills as a dancer as well as a drummer by playing on a large drum and two lines of four smaller drums placed facing each other in front of the large drum. Although it lacks certain artistic grandeur, it is a spectacular dance.

A regional dance named *kanggang sullae* is the only group dance that belongs to the southern coastal region of Korea. This is a circle dance that is said to have its origin in the 16th century when the local inhabitants of Chindo were engaged in fighting against the invading Japanese hordes who rampaged in that region. Today, the women in the coastal regions and elsewhere perform this dance under the full moon of the 15th eve of the 8th lunar month, singing the song *kanggang sullae*.

Recent Trends in Dance

In the Republic of Korea, traditional dances, much like traditional music, were not only preserved but were given new impetus. As a result, many dances of the past were revived. At the same time, young artists in the field of dance made various attempts to create new dances based on traditional principles or to develop new styles for old dances, bringing dynamic activism in dance, and presented them at the new open-air theater similar to that of the traditional days called *madang*. Often such an open-air theater is called *nori madang*, which means "playing stage."

A particular development in the performing arts was the creation of a new genre called "singing drama," or *chang'gŭk*. The *chang'gŭk* had existed in the form of the panzer, but unlike the latter, the new form of "singing drama" is truly a Korean-style opera in which many actors and actresses play the parts. Some sing, some dance, and others play the supporting roles. The dances in the new singing drama are akin to folk and mask dances. Recently, such popular novels as *Tale of Hungbu, Tale of Ch'unhyang,* and *Tale of Pae Pijang"* have been transformed into singing dramas. Meanwhile, a female dancer named Kong Ok-chin created a new genre called "song and dance drama," or *ch'angmugŭk* such as "*Tale of Shim Ch'ŏng,*" the "Dance of a Cripple," "*Salp'uri* Dance," and the "Dance of Profound Regrets of a Crane-Woman." As in the panzer, these dances are performed by a solo dancer.

Suggested Further Reading

Cho, Won-kyung. 1962. *Dances of Korea*. New York: Norman J. Seaman.

Han, Man-yong. 1981. *A Study of Buddhist* Music. Seoul: Seoul National University Press.

_____ . 1990. *Kugak: Studies in Korean Traditional Music*. (Translated and edited by In-ok Paek and Keith Howard) Seoul: Tamgudang.

Heyman, Alan C. 1966. *Dances of the Three-Thousand-League Land*. With an introduction by Faubion Bowers. Seoul. Dong-A Publishing Co.

Howard, Keith. 1989. *Bands, Song and Shamanistic Rituals: Folk Music in Korean Sociey*. Seoul: Royal Asiatic Society, Korea Branch.

Lee, Byong-won. 1980. *Buddhist Music of Korea*. Seoul: Jeongeumsa.

Lee, Hey-kyu. 1977. *An Introduction to Korean Music and Dance*. Seoul: Royal Asiatic Society, Korea Branch.

_____ . 1982. *Korean Musical Instruments*. (Translated by Alan C. Heyman) Seoul: National Classical Music Institute of Korea.

Pratt, Keith. 1987. *Korean Music: Its History and Its Performance*. Seoul: Jeongeumsa.

Si-sa-yong-o-sa Publishing Co. 1894. *Traditional Korean Music*. Seoul.

The Court Music Ensemble

Changgo

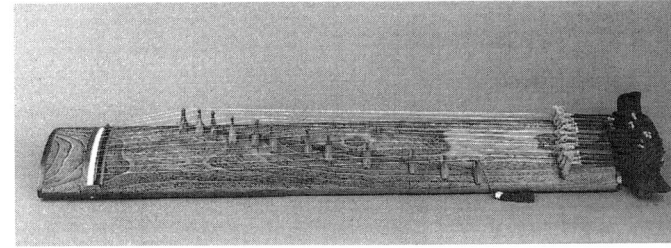

Kayagŭm

A Team of Mask Dancers at Play

15

Stone Pagodas and Buddha Images
by Marylin Martin Rhie

1

Introduction

The stone pagodas and Buddha sculptures of Korea are known for their distinctive and special qualities. Though related to forms developed in China from Indian and Central Asian traditions, they reveal remarkable interpretations and styles which have emerged from Korean aesthetic sensibilities and understanding of the Buddhist religion. Each of these two particular expressions of Korean Buddhist art will be introduced here with respect to iconographic and stylistic factors, using a few of the many splendid examples which still exist in Korea.

2

Stone Pagodas

The pagoda is a form of the Buddhist stupa, which is a memorial shrine or reliquary generally containing the remains (relics or sarira) of a Buddhist. The first Buddhist stupas contained the relics of the Buddha Shakyamuni, who lived in India ca. 563 483 B.C. Although over time the stupa came to be used for the relics of other renowned Buddhists, usually great monks and teachers, it nevertheless kept the symbolism of the shrine connected with the relics of a Buddha and, by extension, acquired the meaning of symbolic representation of the Buddha's body, his enlightenment, and Nirvana. In all these respects the stupa was treated by Buddhists as a sacred object and venerated.

The earliest known stupas in India were solid, hemispherically shaped tumuli structures with a central pole or mast which penetrated the mound and projected above it. The projecting mast held a series of "umbrellas," which, according to texts of the 1st 3rd century A.D., indicated the status of the relics. For example, the stupa of a Buddha's relics would have more umbrellas than the stupa of those of a monk. In later times, the umbrellas came to symbolize the stages to enlightenment according to certain texts. The stupa was worshiped or venerated by circumambulation in a clockwise direction around the structure. Although the origins are obscure, another kind of stupa in the form of a tower (Chinese: t'a; Korean: t'ap; Japanese: to; English: pagoda) developed in Central Asia and China probably by the end of the 2nd century A.D., as it is known in the remains of Chinese art by that time. The tower form is usually square (or octagonal) with an uneven number (usually 3, 5, 7, 9 or more) storeys, each being demarcated by its own "roof." The central axis pole remains an important element and projects above the top storey holding a series of small ringlike forms which probably stand for the original Indian "umbrellas." Sometimes there is a small round hemispherical dome (often referred to as an "overturned rice bowl" shape in East Asian terminology) above the top storey to symbolize the original shape of the Indian stupa. In the tower type of stupa or pagoda the sarira relics are usually buried in the ground below the central axis pole. But in the original Indian stupas the sarira relics were usually placed in the solid dome portion. In the Korean stone pagodas the relics are generally placed in the base or middle sections of the pagoda rather than underground. In most cases sarira relics consist of remains of cremated Buddhist saints and possibly some gems or seeds, all usually placed in a small glass or metal container, which is then placed in a series of other containers. Oftentimes texts, miniature stupas, sculptures, and paintings are included.

There are pagodas made of wood and brick in Korea, but most are made of stone. Stone pagodas became the hallmark of the Korean style pagoda, as distinguished from the primarily wooden pagodas of Japan and the predominantly brick or wooden pagodas of China. Korean stone pagodas are of many different varieties, shapes, sizes, and numbers of storeys, but the symbolism and basic structure remain the same: a base, a storied middle section, and an axial pole which projects beyond the last storey and holds the rings and topmost elements.

One of the oldest known stone pagodas in Korea is the five-storied pagoda at the Chŏngrim temple site in Puyŏ, Ch'ungch'ong Province (Fig. 1). It dates from the Paekche kingdom (18 B.C. 660 A.D.) of the Three Kingdoms period, probably ca. 6th century A.D. Buddhism had been introduced to Paekche in the late 4th century, and the kingdom had developed a strong Buddhist religion which was patronized by the ruling family. By the late 6th century, Paekche was a flourishing Buddhist kingdom and produced a large quantity of Buddhist art.

This pagoda is lofty (H. 27.33 ft.), yet simple in its construction and is made entirely of cut and dressed stone. It has a doublestepped square foundation and a low square base with a rhythmic pattern of alternating projecting and recessed panels. Two large vertical stone slabs form the sides (like doors) of the first story, which also has four square, slightly projecting corner pillars. These walls and pillars support a set of horizontal lintel stones and large, curved cornice-like stones which curve out like a solid bracket to hold up the flaring roof. The roof, composed of six large but rather thin slabs, projects far beyond the walls and has slightly curved up corners. The graceful curve and slender width of the roof slabs impart a delicacy and lightness to the structure.

Above the main first storey rise four more storeys replicating the first, except that each successive storey becomes considerably shorter and decreases in width. The wide extension of the five roofs placed so closely together creates a strong horizontality and a measured upward movement, which is, however, made fairly rapid by the pronounced shrinking in the width of the inner core of each story. The top part with mast and rings is now lost. In the overall simplicity and gently curved linear rhythms, this pagoda emits a calm and graceful dignity.

The Unified Shilla (660-935 A.D.) period produced numerous pagodas and developed a classic style, usually of the three or five-storied pagoda. The style tends to be quite severely austere and abstract with a characteristic roof that has a corbel design structure resembling an inverted step pyramid. The Unified Shilla pagoda generally has a powerful and clear shape without widely flaring roof ash seen in the Chŏngrimsa pagoda of Paekche. The early Unified Shilla pagodas tend to be monumental in style and scale, whereas those of the middle period (8th century) become more elegant, and those of the late period (9th-early 10th century) loose some vigor but have a gentle and sometimes more elaborate design.

The splendid pair of three-storied pagodas at the Kamun temple site near Kyŏngju, capital of the Unified Shilla in Kyŏngsang Province, are majestic examples of the early, forthright, powerfully abstract Unified Shilla pagoda style (Fig. 2). They are part of the famous temple built by King Shinmu (r. 681-692), on behalf of his father, King Munmu (r. 660-681). The site is within view of the Eastern Sea, where King Munmu is believed to have been buried in the huge rock just off shore. It is a common practice during this period for temples to have a pair of pagodas flanking the entrance of a monastery. Though the stone rings have broken and fallen off on both the east and west pagodas, revealing the iron rod symbolizing the axis pole, they nevertheless testify to the broad and massive proportions characteristic of the early Unified Shilla pagodas.

Possibly most famous among the stone pagodas of Korea is the pair at the Pulguk temple in Kyŏngju. They are the three-storied Shakyamuni pagoda and the Prabhutaratna pagoda (*tabo t'ap*). The latter (Fig. 3, H. 34.12 ft.) is a special pagoda of remarkable and unusual design. It represents the stupa which appeared while Shakyamuni Buddha was teaching the *Lotus Sutra text* on the Vulture Peak in India. In chapter 11 of this text, a popular Buddhist scripture in East Asia, the episode is described in detail. Inside the stupa was the Buddha Prabhutaratna, a Buddha of the remote past, who had come to praise the teaching of Shakyamuni in this age just as he had come and promised to come in every age to do the same when a Buddha taught the *Lotus Sutra*.

This complex, splendid pagoda is raised up on a high square base. The first story is approached by a staircase on each of the four sides. These four stairs, each entered through a pair of short, round topped posts, reflect the symbolism of the four cardinal directions, which indicate the universality of the Buddhist teaching and its accessibility to all. A seated lion was placed at the head of each set of stairs, but only one remains today. These may refer to the guardian aspect of the lion, the lions used for king's thrones, or to the early symbolism of the lion as representing the "lion's roar" of the Buddhist teaching.

The first story is composed of four large square corner pillars whose massive curved brackets hold the gently curved roof slab which supports the upper levels. In the center can be seen the huge square central pillar of the axis, so important for the symbolism of the stupa. In fact, the central pillar appears in the levels above as well, even though it is elaborately encased in a series of three superbly fashioned small stories which comprise the whole middle section of the pagoda. The two lower levels act as a base to lift up the lotus which is the base of the topmost level with its octagonal roof. The lower level has a square outer railing and the middle level an octagonal one. The encasing elements are composed of differently shaped posts, those of the lower level being angular and those of the middle level replicating bamboo. The octagonal roof has pointed angles and is held up by bracket-shaped posts. Above the roof the stone mast, much reduced in diameter, holds a series of stone rings, most of which still remain. In its intricacy and complexity, clarity and balance of structural design, this pagoda is unmatched. Moving from square to octagon to circle, this masterfully designed pagoda has monumentality and grandeur, and yet is moderate and approachable in size. It is certainly one of the most unique and interesting pagodas known. In its setting at the Pulguk temple, it contrasts with its pair, the more austere, yet elegant three storied Shakyamuni pagoda. Together both of these remarkable structures contrast with the surrounding wooden galleries and main shrine hall and complement the famous stonework of the entrance stairways and gates, simulating the structures of the Buddhist realms or "Pure Lands."

During the Koryŏ period (918 1392), the last major period of Buddhist art in Korea, the pagodas tend to become exaggerated in height, creating strange effects of proportion which lend an air of awesome wonder to the structure. One of the most beautiful of the Koryŏ pagodas is the octagonal nine-storied pagoda of the early Koryŏ period, around mid-tenth century, at the Wŏlchŏng temple at Odaesan, Kangwŏndo (Fig. 4). From a circular lotus and octagonal base the slender but sturdy pagoda is lifted high, each level echoing the same octagonal structure with little decrease in size. From each angle hangs a bronze bell, which makes delightful sounds in the wind. At the top, rising from a small dome and lotus base, are the rings and finial, all in openwork bronze. The series of rings are termed treasure wheels, and the two balls on the spire above are called the "dragon chariot" (lower) and the "treasure pearl" (upper). Though they are typical of the finial designs on East Asian pagodas, few original ones remain as they do on this pagoda. Other Koryŏ pagodas may be more richly carved with figures, lotus and other decorative designs, but the Wŏlchŏng temple pagoda reveals the elegance of proportion and repetition typical of Koryŏ style pagodas at their best. It seems to simulate the beauties of the visionary mystical pagodas, such as that witnessed by prince Suddana, the seeker of enlightenment in the *Gandhavyuha section of the Avatamsaka Sutra* (*K. Hwaŏm*), one of the most popular and important Buddhist texts in Korean Buddhism.

3

Stone Buddha Images

Images of the Buddha seem to begin to appear in India around the first century B.C. to A.D. period. The schools of Mathura in Central India and Gandhara in present day Pakistan and Afghanistan created portrayals of the Buddha which were most influential on the developments of Buddhist art in Central Asia and China during the early centuries of Buddhist practice in those areas. The Buddha was generally depicted wearing the monk's robe (*sanghati*) which was thrown over both shoulders or covered only the left shoulder. His distinguishing marks (*lakshana*, of which he is said to have 32 major ones) usually included the cranial protuberance (*ushnisha*, which looks like a bun of hair on top of the head), and the spot between the eyes (*urna*, a curled white hair which is said to emit miraculous light at times). The earlobes are usually shown distended, a mark of his youth when he wore the heavy jewels and earrings customary for an Indian prince. He is also said to have golden skin, long limbs, prints of the 1,000 spoked wheel on the palms of his hands and soles of his feet, etc. The Buddha image also has certain hand gestures (*mudra*) and sitting postures (*asana*), which are expressive of teaching, meditation, bestowing, and other attitudes. Specific gestures can sometimes be linked with specific episodes of the Buddha's life or be identified with certain Buddhas, of which there are considered to be countless numbers in the view of Mahayana Buddhism, the developed form of Buddhism which dominates East Asia. Besides Shakyamuni Buddha, the most popular in Korea are Maitreya (the Future Buddha), Amitabha (the Buddha of the Western Pure Land), Bhaishajyaguru (the Medicine or Healing Buddha), and

Vairocana (the Cosmic Buddha).

Stone images of the Buddha appear in the Three Kingdoms period, mostly from the kingdoms of Paekche and Shilla during the 6th first half of the 7th century. Both independent images probably for usage in temple halls or private shrines as well as "in situ" relief cravings on large rocks or cliffs are known from these early periods. The stone is usually the native buffcolored granite which abounds in the land. It is a coarse stone difficult to chisel because it is so hard. However, the Korean artist has a special affinity for this stone and has produced masterworks which are quite unique to Korea and different from the marble, sandstone, and limestone images generally seen in China and the mostly wooden images which appear in Japan. In fact, Korean stone images, both independent and cliff relief images, form a distinctive body of work among Asian Buddhist art and East Asian art in general, just as do the Korean stone pagodas.

The stone triad at Paeri (Fig. 5) on the outskirts of Kyŏngju is a monumental configuration consisting of a standing Buddha (H. 9.02 ft.) attended by two standing Bodhisattvas (beings on the path to enlightenment). Each is made from a single large block of stone, which still seems to assert its massive quality despite being carved into the form of images. In this work, which dates in the later years of the Shilla kingdom just before unification of the peninsula under Unified Shilla, the sculpture maintains a firm, self-contained, somewhat naively disproportionate appearance. The Buddha (Fig. 6) seems chunky and solid with large head and hands. The limbs are short and portrayed as a single mass with the rest of the body. The robe hangs in a few heavy folds and does not always follow naturalistic depiction. Despite these consciously unnatural elements in the image, there is something very compelling and greater than naturalism in the implied power of the mass and in the unadorned, simple, human quality. The emphatically large face with its gentle smile seems to emote a warmth that infuses the whole image, to which the viewer is easily drawn because of its very lack of sophistication. The large right hand is raised in the "have no fear" gesture, and the left hand is shown palm out in a "bestowing" gesture, all signs that also encourage the viewer. As religious sculpture, this naive, earthy, welcoming, yet powerful figure vividly expresses a religious message. Underpinning it all is the primordial power of the stone itself, with its qualities of weight and solid mass.

The masterwork of Korean stone Buddhas from the Unified Shilla period (660-935) is the Buddha of Sŏkkuram (Fig. 7). Sŏkkuram cave temple was begun around the mid-8th century by the donor Kim Dae-sŏng, prime minister of Unified Shilla, and was completed by the government after his death. The founding of Sŏkkuram is recounted in the *Samguk Yusa* (Chronicle of the Three Kingdoms), Korea's oldest major history book.

Sŏkkuram is a structural cave temple made of large cut stones, forming a hall with antechamber and circular rotunda. It was covered with earth like a hill, simulating a natural cave temple. This construction is unique to Buddhist art as far as we know. As one enters this temple all of carved stone, images of guardians in relief line the walls of the antechamber and passage to the rotunda. The large Buddha figure sits alone in the exact center of the domed hall, lifted on a high circular pedestal (total height 10.70 ft.). His presence is impressive, yet he seems near. Surrounding the figure around the walls are relief panels of Bodhisattvas and monks, and above are small niches with celestial beings and Bodhisattvas. The circular lotus halo of the Buddha appears on the wall behind him.

Clearly, the master of the hall is the Buddha image. He sits crosslegged with his right hand resting palm down on his right leg. This is the "earth witness" gesture, a gesture made by Shakyamuni at the moment of his enlightenment, when he pointed to the earth requesting the earth goddess to witness his enlightenment. His other hand lies face up in his lap. The sanghati or monk's robe covers his left shoulder, but is drawn around under his right arm, leaving the right shoulder bare a typical Indian mode. The drapery clings closely to the powerful body, so much so that it seems in places to merge with the body, as in the area of the left chest. In other areas, however, the folds make thick pleats and cluster in patterns which emphasize the natural shape of the form, which is clearly revealed, quite unlike the earlier Buddha at Paeri (Fig. 6).

The body is strong and majestic with broad shoulders, lifted torso and heavy limbs. It appears massive and powerful but at the same time has a fleshy and naturalistic heaviness, unlike the more naive and abstract Buddha at Paeri. The balance of the lordly, majestic and the idealistic with the naturalistic human fleshiness is an outstanding characteristic of this image. It suggests the simultaneity of the transcendent and the natural. This is a basic Buddhist concept, often expressed by the saying Samsara (phenomenal existence) and Nirvana (liberation) are the same. The head of the Sŏkkuram Buddha also suggests this quality: it is perfectly proportioned to suggest the ideal, and also has a naturalistic beauty, softness, and pleasant expression in the features. Though the Buddha is lofty and lordly and thereby assumes power, at the same time he is totally approachable by the radiant, mild, friendly expression and smile of his face. The human and the perfected are harmoniously merged. Here the stone does not govern the representation as it did in the earlier Paeri image, but it lends its mass and power to the figure, which seems borne beyond the limits of flesh or stone in a merging of the human and the ideal that is one of the greatest expressions of the Buddha in all Asian art.

The Korean *"maebul"* or cliff Buddha is an interesting phenomena in Korean Buddhist art. Though carvings on the stone cliffs and boulders which abound in Korea are known during the Three Kingdoms and Unified Shilla periods, they proliferate during the Koryŏ Dynasty (935-1392). Some are spectacularly large, some are high on mountain cliffs, but perhaps none is more handsome than the large standing Buddha carved on a huge boulder on the mountain behind the Haein temple on Mt. Kaya in Kyŏngsang Province (Fig. 8). The image is 24.6 ft. high and is carved in relatively high relief. It has a circular head halo and the shape of the boulder acts as the large encompassing halo. The figure probably dates in the early years of the Koryŏ Dynasty, ca. 930-950, when the Haeina was an influential monastery under the direction of the monk Huiryang, who was patronized by the first Koryŏ king, T' aejo. The precise identity of this Buddha is not known for certain, but it may be a representation of Amitabha Buddha (*K. Amita Pul*) coming into this world. This Buddha was popular in Korea as well as in other East Asian countries, especially for the saving power of his vows and his promise of rebirth in his Western Pure Land for those who had faith in him.

The image is a mixture of Herculean power and gentle beauty, of the mystical and the human, and of the real and the transcendent. Like the Sŏkkuram Buddha in Fig. 7, it relates these apparent opposites as a unified expression, but the emphasis and manner of portrayal are different here. The Shilla lordly majesty and idealism have shifted in this maebul image to a portrayal with more emphasis on the mystical dimension. The emphatic width of the shoulders is beyond the normal, and the thick neck and large square head suggest awesome power. The proportions are not as measured and regular as those of the Sŏkkuram Buddha, and they impart the effect of heightening the "otherworldly power." On the other hand, elegance is suggested in the arms and hands, which, though plump and large, are rather flat and curved in a relaxed and graceful shape, and by the folds of the garments, which describe simple but pleasing arcs suggesting a consciously lyrical beauty rather than simply naturalistic folds. The softness of the carving, especially in the head and its features, which are mild and unpronounced, and in the bunched and heavy folds of the robe over the left arm, imparts a human aura to the statue. Nevertheless, it is balanced by the sense of a mystical apparition which seems to be emerging from the rock like a vision emerges from space, penetrating the veil that separates our mundane world from transcendent vision. Or, to put it another way, the image seems to be displaying the ontological in the noumenal world and to portray that vision as concretely real and solid like the stone.

Koryŏ stone maebul are particularly effective in producing the apparent reality of a mystical vision, since the transcendent can be so readily apprehended or believed when one sees the impressive size of these images. The "unbelievability" of form emerging from rock in the ordinary world of phenomena appears destroyed and one accepts the "reality" of the "unreal." This creates a special form of religious image which can strongly affect the viewer. In the particularly wide range and variety of styles and types of Korea's mae-bul, which explored the possibilities inherent in this type of image more than any other area in East Asia, the Buddhist art of Asia as a whole is greatly enriched. Korean Buddhist art as a whole, not only the pagodas and stone images, offers a vast array of magnificent and beautiful works that are among the great treasures of the world.

Suggested Further Reading

5000 Years of Korean Art. 1979. San Francisco: Asian Art Museum.

Kim, Chewon, and Lena Kim Lee. 1974. *Arts of Korea*. Tokyo: Kodansha International.

Kukpo (National Treasures). 1983. 12 vols. Seoul: Yekang Sanopsa.

McCune, Evelyn. 1962. *The Arts of Korea; an illustrated history*. Rutland and Tokyo: Charles E. Tuttle.

List of Illustrations

Fig. 1   Fivestoried stone pagoda, Chŏngrim temple site, Puyŏ, Ch'ungch'ŏng Province, Three Kingdoms Period, Paekche, ca. 6th century, H. 8.33 m. (photo after Chin Hong-sup, *T'appa*, in *Kukpo* (National Treasures of Korea), vol. 6, Seoul: Yekang Sanopsa, 1983, fig. 4)

Fig. 2   West Threestoried stone pagoda, Kamun temple site, Wŏlsŏng County, Kyŏngsang Province, Unified Shilla, ca. 682 A.D., H. 13.4 m. (photo after *Kukpo*, 1983, vol. 6, fig. 11)

Fig. 3   *Tabo t'ap* Pagoda, Pulguk temple, Kyŏngju, Kyŏngsang Province, Unified Shilla, mid-8th century, H. 10.4 m. (photo after *Kukpo*, 1983, vol. 6, fig.19)

Fig. 4   Octagonal ninestoried stone pagoda, Wŏlchŏngsa temple, Pyŏngch'ang County, Kangwŏn Province, early *Koryŏ*, mid-10th century, H. 15.15m. (photo after *Kukpo*, 1983, vol. 6, fig. 200)

Fig. 5   Stone triad with Buddha and two Bodhisattvas, Paeri, Kyŏngju, Kyŏngsang Province, Three Kingdoms, Shilla, ca. first quarter of the 7th century, H. of Buddha 2.75 m. (photo: M. Rhie, 1968)

Fig. 6   Detail of the Buddha in Fig. 5. (photo: M. Rhie, 1968)

Fig. 7   Seated Buddha, Sŏkkuram cave temple, Mt. Toham, Kyŏngju, Kyŏngsang Province, Unified Shilla, mid-8th century, H. 3.26 m.

(photo: M. Rhie)

Fig. 8　Buddha (*maebul*) on Mt. Kaya, Hapch'ŏn, Kyŏngsang Province, early
Koryŏ, ca. 930−950 AD, H. 7.5 m. (photo after *Hangukŭi* Mi, vol.
10 (Hwang Su Young, *Pulsang* [Buddha Images]), Seoul: 1985,
fig.147)

Fig 1. Five-storeyed Stone Pagoda,
Chŏngrim Temple

Fig 2. Three-storeyed Stone Pagoda,
Kwanŭm Temple

Fig 3. Tabot'ap,
   Pulguk Temple

Fig 4. Octagonal Nine-storeyed Stone Pagoda,
   Wŏlchŏng Temple

Fig 5. Stone Triad with Buddha and Two Bodhisattvas

Fig 6. Seated Buddha, Sŏkkuram Temple

Fig 7. Stone Statue of Buddha on Mt. Kaya

16

Architecture and House Furniture
by Byung-Ok Chun

1

Introduction

Traditional Korean houses have been in existence for several thousand years. Many regional and local adaptations have evolved over this time due to the varying climate within the Korean peninsula, as well as the historical traditions and life styles of the Korean people.

Traditional Korean houses are built mainly of wood with tiled roofs. However, the spatial functions of these Korean houses differ from one region to another. These differences may be attributed to local climatic conditions.

In the following, I will outline some of the characteristics of a typical house floor plan and discuss common national design characteristics and interior decoration of the Chosŏn period.

2

Characteristics of Floor Plans in Traditional Houses

Seoul Type. The main entrance quarters, housewife's quarters, and other components of the house are built along the edges of the compound. The Seoul type includes *anbang* (housewife's room or living room) and *kŏnnŏbang* (room facing *anbang* across a wooden floor), which form a straight line. The kitchen is located perpendicular to the *anbang*.

   Central Korea Type. In the housewife's quarters, the kitchen, *anbang* (living room) and *witpang* (room adjacent to the *anbang*) are built on a straight line. A wooden floor is located perpendicular to the *witpang* and *kŏnnŏbang* at the end.

   Western Korea Type. Generally, two or three rooms are built adjacent to the kitchen side by side in the housewife's quarters. A narrow wooden floor, which is connected to a large wooden floor placed at the end, is in front of the rooms. A complete view of the three sides can be seen from *taech'ŏng* (large wooden floor).

   Southern Korea Type. The kitchen, the wife's room (*anbang*), the wooden floor, and *kŏnnŏbang* are horizontally placed in the housewife's quarters. Also, a corridor runs in front of the rooms. A long wooden floor is built in front of the rooms, which is utilized as a summer living space in this warmer region.

   Northern Korea Type. In this type, exterior wall space is minimized by placing the four *ondol* rooms in the shape of to reduce heat loss in cold weather. (*Ondol* is an arrangement of flues under the floor for heating.) In particular, there exists an *ondol*-heated room, *chŏngji*, beside the earthen-floored kitchen. The two spaces are separated by a change in the ground level rather than a more typical side wall. *Chŏngji(gan)* is a useful space where the family may have meals or do simple household work. This space is unusual in other regions.

The heat from the kitchen warms the attached cow barn and the treadmill during the severely cold winters. The cow barn and the treadmill are hence a part of the main house. The northern type has no wooden floor but instead possesses a narrow verandah which is placed in front of a room.

Earthen Wall

3

Upper-Class Homes

Upper-class homes offer excellent examples of traditional Korean housing. The exteriors of these homes blend well with the surrounding environment and create intimate and elegant atmospheres.

Elevated Base (*kidan*). Upper-class Korean houses are generally built on an elevated base at least 30 cm. to 50 cm. (1 feet to 1.6 feet) in height. The height of the elevated base may differ depending on the size and type of house. The *kidan* is comprised of a brightly colored granite, making the wooden structure on the elevated base appear stable and attractive.

Pillars. Pillars are structurally important. The distance between two pillars, called *kan*, is about eight *cha* (one *cha* is between 30 to 50 cm. depending on the size and region of the house). Pillars also function as a decorative element in relation to important items utilized in daily life (e.g., oil cup of a lamp that might be hung on the pillar).

Roof. The roof of a house is hipped, gabled, or hipped and gabled. The hipped-and-gabled roof is used mainly in large-scale houses.

Ceiling. Two types of ceilings can be found in traditional Korean architecture, one for commoners' residences and the other for aristocrats' residences. In the former case, the ceilings are slanted, revealing rafters because of the low columns. No ceilings are built on the wood-floored hall. The roof structure is thus visible and is plastered or decorated in a traditional *tanchŏng* (red and blue) coloring.

Floor. Floors of Korean houses include *ondol* floors, wood panel floors, recessed verandahs, and mud or earthen floors in areas such as storage rooms, kitchens, and cow barns. In the *ondol* heating system, stone plates are placed over a hypocaust, and a mud floor is spread on the heat-preserving stone plates. Plain paper is glued to the mud floor, and an oiled paper of some thickness is then glued to the plain paper. Narrow or wide wood pieces are used to produce a variety of designs of the wood floor hall. Wide wood pieces are common in the recessed verandah area.

Walls. The composition of walls varies, though there are two basic types. Earthen walls are made with earth and stone. The top of the wall is covered with tiles or rice straw. Stone walls, made of earth, tiles, and stones, are generally built in upper-class houses. Some walls are built of brick masonry and, sometimes, plaster-on-brick masonry. Various designs are created on the walls by utilizing brick arrangements. In regions where stones are easily available, walls may consist of stones without using earth. In this case the top of the wall is not covered with tiles or rice straw.

Doors

There are doors for entrance to a house and doors installed between rooms. Entrance doors to a building usually consist of an outer door and an inner door. This helps keep out the cold draft in winter. Many outer doors are double doors which are papered on both sides. In middle-and upper-class houses, the outer doors are framed and ribbed to express various designs. The doors are designed to facilitate streaming in of sunlight.

House Furniture

Furniture pieces used in a traditional house evolved ornamental characters as well. There was considerable variety in the kinds of furniture pieces of the Chosŏn period. Their ornamental designs were also considerably varied. I would like to discuss here some of the most representative of the Chosŏn Dynasty furniture pieces.

Many of the furniture pieces of the Chosŏn period were lacquered. Articles used by the royal court were mostly crimson lacquered. Furniture for government officials was black-lacquered. Commoners used black-lacquered pieces or pieces decorated in some other manners.

1. Furniture in sarangbang (master's quarters).

Scholarship and academics were emphasized in the Confucian-oriented Chosŏn kingdom. Thus furniture and articles such as a reading table, a book chest, and writing tools (a brush, an ink stone, etc.) occupied an important place in *sarangch'ae*, or the house master's study, and in the drawing room. Some other *sarangch'ae* furniture includes a document chest, an incense table, a sutra table, and a floor lamp. The following describes some of these furniture pieces.

Ch'aeksang (reading desk). One of the furniture pieces in *sarangbang* is *ch'aeksang*, which is low and small and holds one or two open books on it.

Hyangsang (incense table). The shape of *hyangsang* is similar to that of a reading table. It is mainly used for burning incense in *sarangch'ae*.

Kyŏngsang (sutra table). *Kyŏngsang*, like *ch'aeksang*, structurally consists of a top panel, the legs, and sometimes drawers. The top may have everted edges.

2. Furniture in *anbang* (wife's quarters).

The *anbang* is located for easy access to conduct the day-to-day business of the household. Unlike the furniture pieces in *sarangbang* (the husband's quarters), which are characterized by a sense of orderly proportion and simplicity, the furniture pieces for the wife's quarters are elaborately decorated. This ornamentation is somewhat excessive in some instances.

Chang (one-piece chest). The structural and proportional beauty of the large anbang chests is one of the most important aesthetic factors in the traditional Korean home. The type of wood, its graininess, the width of the side concave panel between the legs, use of Chinese character-based designs either in relief or intaglio, inlaid mother-of-pearl, and metal ornaments all contribute to produce a great variety of ornamental combinations on the chest.

The chest is designed to suit the three basic postures taken by Korean women as they put in or take out clothes from the chest; namely, sitting directly on the floor, kneeling, and standing up. The doors and drawers are also positioned for easy access by one of the three postures.

Some designs are intended to enhance simplicity and the class of the chests, some give an overall sense of stability to the chests, and others make the chests look colorful. The chests may be classified according to the use: clothing chest, wardrobe chest, and sleeping mat chest.

The chests can also be classified according to the ornamental designs and the type of wood.

Food-related Furniture. Food-related furniture items include pantry chests, rice chests, cupboards, and portable dining tables (called *soban*). Traditionally, Korean houses had no dining space in the Western sense. Meals were brought on soban to family members scattered in various rooms.

Folding Screen. Folding screens were placed in front of a garret door or a sliding window to protect from the cold weather and to decorate the room as well. Today folding screens are utilized more for artistic appreciation than for blocking drafts. A folding screen may be two-, four-, six-, ten-, or twelve-folded, but is always an even number. Calligraphy, embroidery, or painting is often executed on the screen.

Yŏn'gyŏngdang of Ch'angdŏk Palace

Korean architecture has evolved as an important focal point of understanding Korean aesthetics. Yŏn'gyŏngdang House represents the typical and fundamental beauty of the Korean house. It may be considered the architectural design that most accurately reflects Korean people's character and life style. Yŏn'gyŏngdang House, built in 1829, is representative of the upper civilian class of the Chosŏn period. The prevalent theme of this style is simplicity and serene beauty.

As we enter Chang'nang Gate in the outer servants' quarters, the housemaster's quarters is seen directly and to the east. A pavilion called nongsujŏng is situated on raised ground farther to the east. The housemaster's quarters is built with a large central wooden floor and verandahs running along the front and the back. An open wooden floor is in the east end of the quarters. The large master's room is in the west end.

Unique decorative stones are placed in front of the south wall of the yard. Stone water ponds with floating lotus flower leaves grace the stone ponds adjacent to the southeast wall. Royal azaleas blossom along the wall.

The housewife's quarters are connected to the west wall of the housemaster's quarters. The rooms in this living area are divided by lowrise walls. Sliding doors connect the rooms and allow the lady of the house a view of the chambers and of the yard from her room. The north rooms remain cool in the summer. The wooden floor sections in the housewife's quarters divide living spaces. Pear, persimmon, mulberry, cherry trees, and azaleas in the rear garden complement the house exterior's beauty.

Suggested Further Reading

Chun, Byung-Ok. 1981. *Traditional Artistic Design of Korea.* Seoul:
    Pojinjae.

_____. 1988. *Decorative Designs in the Houses of Chosun Dynasty
    Period.* Seoul: Pojinjae.

McCune, Evelyn. 1987. "The Structure and Ornamentation of Yi
    Dynasty's Architecture," *Koreana.* vol. 1.1.

Yŏnkyŏng'dang in Ch'angdŏk Palace

17

Traditional Ceramic
by Kumja Paik Kim

Although we see ceramic wares exhibited behind display cases in galleries and museums today, until modern times they had always been made for a purpose, utilitarian or ritual. They were used for cooking, serving, or storage, and for this reason their forms met the needs of a community and mirrored the technical ability and aesthetic taste of the potters.

The earliest pottery so far discovered in Korea dates from the 6th millennium B.C. They were made during the Neolithic period by the new stone age people of Korea who chose their dwelling sites near rivers and the sea, engaging in fishing, gathering, hunting, and incipient forms of agriculture. There were regional differences in pottery forms and decorations, depending on the localities of their production. Potters of the east central region of the peninsula made two types of small bowls: some embellished with raised decorations in the applique style, while others with short incised or pricked decoration only around the mouth rim. Potters in the southeastern area also made two types of small bowls. While some had raised decoration in the applique style, others were plain without any surface decoration.

These early neolithic earthen wares came in a variety of reddish or yellowish shades, indicating that they had been fired in an oxidizing atmosphere with an ample supply of air and clear flame. The temperature in which they were fired reached 600 to 1,000 degrees centigrade. These low fired, unglazed pottery are usually called earthen wares because they are not as strong as the pottery of later times, which were fired at a much higher temperature.

The most famous pottery from the Neolithic period are those with the pointed or round bottom decorated with the "comb-pattern," dating between the 4th and 2nd millennium B.C. The so-called comb-pattern decorated neolithic earthen wares do not have a uniform appearance, again showing regional differences. In the southeastern region during the 4th millennium B.C., pottery was made with the round bottom and decorated only around the mouth rim with short parallel diagonal lines, leaving the other areas undecorated. Those made in the western central region had the pointed bottom, and those from the northeastern area came with the flat bottom.

It was not until 3000 B.C. that the classic comb-patterned wares were produced. The famous classic comb-patterned wares had their surfaces completely covered with decoration in a variety of ways using parallel, herringbone, wavy, or semi-circular designs made with incised or impressed lines as well as with dots or comb-tooth lines. It appears that toward the end of the Neolithic period the surface decoration was once again eliminated and the comb-patterned earthen wares were left only with the mouth rim decoration.

During the Bronze Age (ca. 1000 B.C.-300 B.C.) it is believed that Tungusic people from North Asia came into the Korean peninsula, bringing with them bronze making technology and an advanced agrarian culture. The Bronze Age newcomers produced bronze objects such as lute-shaped daggers and mirrors with large geometric designs which, although very distinct, were related to those made in Siberia, Ordos, and North China. They not only built gigantic dolmens all over the Korean peninsula but also initiated new pottery forms, replacing the pointed or round bottomed earthen wares of the preceding Neolithic period. For utilitarian purposes they made flat-based earthen wares which were brownish or reddish in color and without decoration. For ritual or burial purposes they produced burnished earthen wares with thin walls, both in red and black, as well as reddish or brownish earthen wares decorated with elongated marks in black, often called the "eggplant" design.

The third century B.C. was a turbulent era in East Asia due to political upheavals in China. A significant movement of people took place affecting the Korean Peninsula. It was between the third and first centuries B.C. that iron was introduced to Korea, and hence the name of the period, the Iron Age. During the Iron Age (300 B.C.-0), metal technology was further developed, and the bronze mirrors with intricate geometric designs in thin raised lines were produced. The ceramics tradition continued with the production of reddish or brownish earthen wares as well as red and black burnished earthen wares. Some imaginative innovations were made in ceramic forms. Bowls and cups with a long tubular stem were made, forecasting the stemmed stone wares of the Three Kingdoms period (57 B.C.-A.D. 668). Their slender, tall forms, though not practical for everyday use, must have added an air of elegance to a ritual setting. Steamers with perforations on their bottoms and jars with ox horn shaped handles also made their appearance during the Iron Age.

In the beginning of the Three Kingdoms period (57 B.C.-A.D. 668) iron occupied an increasingly prominent place, and iron implements used in farming increased agricultural productivity, bringing relative prosperity to the inhabitants of the walled-town states. In the field of ceramics, many important innovations took place. Ceramic shapes became more varied, from small, flat bottomed bowls to large, globular round-bottomed jars with the mat or cord decoration. Unusual are the ceramic vessels resembling natural forms, such as the hollow bodied, duck-shaped earthenware vessels with the openings on the back and tail, discovered in the southeastern part of Korea. They were fired at temperatures between 800 and 1,000 degrees centigrade, a temperature suitable for making tiles. This is why they are often called the *wajil t'ogi* (tile-quality earthenware). They have been discovered in the lower reaches of the Naktong River in areas that had been part of the Kaya states. Kaya, occupying an area rich in rice and iron, prospered concurrently with the neighboring Shilla kingdom until the middle of the 6th century. Among all the duck-shaped vessels, the one in the Avery Brundage collection of the Asian Art Museum of San Francisco (Plate 1) has the most expressive face with alert eyes. Its grinning face, long bill, and sail-like crest add an air of humor and pomp. It can be dated to the 3rd century because the stand, though it has lost the lowest splayed part, is without apertures, placing it earlier than those with a perforated stand.

The most significant technological advances were made around A.D. 300 with the introduction of the potter's wheel and the climbing or tunnel kilns built on slopes or hills. The gentle slopes enabled the kiln temperatures to rise to between 1,200 and 1,300 degrees centigrade hot, enough for making hard, impermeable pottery called stone wares. In addition to raising the kiln temperature, the potters also learned to manipulate the flow of air in the kiln chamber during firing by closing off the openings, so that at a certain stage in the firing oxygen could be radically reduced. When the pottery was fired in a reducing atmosphere, it took on a dark color from gray to very dark gray or black. It is believed that the introduction of the potter's wheel also brought about the specialists who had to be trained to work with the wheel. These specialists were now men, while during earlier times, especially the Neolithic period, women had been the makers of earthen wares.

The most famous wheel-thrown stone wares are the large round-bottomed globular jars with the mat or cord design paddled on their surface, using a wooden beater covered with rope or hemp. It is possible that the cord or lattice design could also have been carved directly on the wooden beaters. In the past these handsome jars with the mat design were often called Kimhae pottery after the name of the site, Kimhae in the south Kyŏngsang Province, where they were first discovered. It is now known that they were produced in large numbers throughout Korea during the Three Kingdoms period, although they were first made in the areas of the Kaya states which included Kimhae. The potters of the Paekche and Shilla Kingdoms (18 B.C.-A.D. 660, 57 B.C.-A.D. 668) continued to make the round-bottomed globular jars with the mat or cord design long after Kaya's absorption into Shilla in A.D. 562.

Gray stone wares with simple and rugged forms became the hallmarks of the Three Kingdoms period. One type, which is commonly called the long-necked jar, is fashioned with an elongated neck, a wide mouth, and a short foot with openings. Its body is given either a full, round form or an angled silhouette using a line which divides the body and the shoulder. The long-necked jars have been discovered throughout South Korea, once the ancient domains of Shilla, Kaya, and Paekche. The similarities in their forms as well as in their ornamentation testify that there were active cross-regional exchanges between these ancient kingdoms.

Another popular ceramic form was the stemmed cup and bowl. Some of these were discovered in recent excavations with food still in them. It is believed that they had been used not just for burial but for special occasions or rituals. Generally, stemmed bowls and cups from Shilla are decorated with strong geometric designs based on an inverted "V" together with parallel vertical lines, while those from the Kaya area have a saw-tooth decoration. Recent studies show, however, that there were many more cross-regional exchanges than we had previously thought, for vessels which have Kaya characteristics have also been discovered in the Shilla tombs.

One of the outstanding ceramic forms created during the 5th and 6th centuries was the tall pedestal or stand. Although the Shilla and Paekche kingdoms also used this form, the Kaya States again are believed to have been the first to develop this vessel type to accommodate the round-bottomed jars and bowls they preferred. At first these stands came in modest height, but they gradually developed into tall and magnificent forms. From the strength and height of these pedestals it can be surmised that they were used for important outdoor ceremonies and rituals performed to insure the prosperity of the entire state or kingdom and to pray for the continued blessings of the ancestral spirits on the ruling and powerful families.

Many unusual stoneware forms were created during the Three Kingdoms period. Among them are oil lamps made with multiple cups arranged evenly around the rim of a stemmed cup with perforations. The bottoms of the cups are connected to the hollow, tubular rim to allow easy flow of oil, showing the ingenuity of the potters. Although discovered in tombs, they could easily have been lamps used everyday in homes. Less practical is the so-called "chariot cup," which is made of a wheel stand with double cups. Two deep cups on the wheel stand are connected at the base and tied together with a band outside. Although these "chariot cups" might have only served a burial purpose, they seem to have been copied from the existing form for carrying wine and water for important rituals and ceremonies.

Buddhism was introduced to the Koguryŏ kingdom (37 B.C.-A.D.

668) in A.D. 372, to the Paekche kingdom (18 B.C.-A.D. 660) in A.D. 384, and finally the Shilla kingdom (57 B.C.-A.D. 668) officially accepted it in A.D. 527. With the spread of Buddhism, the burial customs of the Korean people changed from inhumation to cremation. By the time Shilla unified the Korean peninsula by defeating both Paekche and Koguryŏ, the practice of cremation had become firmly established.

During the Unified Shilla period (A.D. 668-935), ceramic forms became more stable. Tall pedestals as well as bowls and cups with high stands made during the Three Kingdoms period disappeared, and in their place bowls with a low foot and a matching cover were made. Some of these bowls were cinerary urns to contain ashes of the Buddhist believers. The urns of the late 7th century were sometimes decorated with bands of incised lines or horizontal grooves. They also had twisted dangles as attachments and a modest, low foot with apertures which were vestiges of the pre-Unified Shilla practice.

While stone wares for everyday use were simple and undecorated, the surface of cinerary urns produced during the 8th century were often decorated completely with stamped or impressed designs of rosettes, concentric circles, and other floral patterns. More importantly, many of them were intentionally glazed, unlike the ceramic vessels with the accidental ash-glaze of the Three Kingdoms and early Unified Shilla periods. During the 9th century, ceramic forms became more quiet and subdued. The cinerary urns, for instance, were undecorated, their beauty depending entirely on their forms rather than on the exuberant surface decoration. Stone wares by now had become the backbone of Korean ceramics, ensuring the continued production of strong utilitarian vessels ranging from small cooking bowls to gigantic jars for storage.

During the Koryŏ Dynasty (918-1392), stoneware forms became more refined. This was noticeable not only in the thin walls of the vessels, but also in forms that resembled those in the natural world, such as gourds and melons. The outstanding achievement of the Koryŏ potters, however, was the famous Koryŏ celadons called *ch'ŏngja*. The ceramic technology of the Unified Shilla Dynasty, whose potters produced the ash-glazed stone wares in a reducing atmosphere, led easily to the full development of Koryŏ celadons. Although in the minds of many people celadons and the Koryŏ Dynasty are inseparable, in recent excavations celadon shards dating to the late 9th and early 10th centuries have been discovered in Yong'in, Inch'ŏn, and Sŏsan, placing the beginning of the celadons in the Unified Shilla rather than the Koryŏ Dynasty.

Koryŏ celadons' early connection to Chinese Yue wares appears to be certain, since Yue wares have been recovered in the Anapji Pond excavation in Kyŏngju. There is no doubt that the appealing color of Yue wares inspired the Korean potters in their search for the jade-like glaze. Chinese Ding, Northern Celadon (Yaozhou stoneware), Chingbai, Ru, and Lungquan wares also influenced Koryŏ celadons in their design and form. By the first half of the 11th century, the Koryŏ celadon was fully developed, since the Koryŏ court felt its celadons were fine enough to be used as gifts to the Khitan rulers of the Liao dynasty. The Koryŏ celadon appears to have reached its height during the first half of the 12th century, as attested to by Xu Jing who came to Korea in 1123 with a Chinese mission headed by Lu Yun-di from the court of Emperor Huizong of the Northern Song dynasty.

It is important to remember that the finest jade-colored Koryŏ celadons written about by Xu Jing in his book *Kaoli Tujing* (*Illustrated Accounts of Koryŏ*), which was presented to Emperor Huizong (r. 1101 - 1127) in 1124, are contemporaneous with Chinese imperial Ru wares made at the end of the Northern Song period. Except for a few examples of the famous Ru wares, Koryŏ celadons excel in the beauty of their forms and in the luster and brilliance of their glaze. Without doubt, fine Koryŏ celadons were produced in far greater numbers than the imperial Ru wares. The Celadon Ewer in the Avery Brundage Collection (Plate 2) comes with the cover in the form of a lotus. Originally it must also have had a snugly fitting outside bowl which is now lost. In the simplicity of its form and the beauty of its thin, transparent glaze, the ewer is comparable to those made in the golden age of Koryŏ celadons during the first half of the 12th century.

Koryŏ potters' contribution to the history of world ceramics was not limited to the creation of the most beautiful celadons in the world. They made other significant innovations, the first of which was decorating celadons with inlaid designs in white and black clays. Traditionally, it has been believed that inlaid celadons were first made in the mid-12th century. This was based on the fact that no inlaid celadon was discovered in the tomb of King Injong, who died in 1146, and that the aforementioned Xu Jing had made no mention of inlaid celadons in his book. However, since 1962 celadon shards with inlay decorations datable to the second half of the 10th century have been discovered at kiln sites at Yong'in and Hampy'ŏng. It is now believed that by the mid-12th century the inlay technique was fully mature, as illustrated by the famous celadon bowl dated 1159 in the collection of the National Museum of Korea, Seoul, which is decorated on the outside with an inlay of chrysanthemum sprays and on the inside with a reverse inlay of floral scrolls. Another important invention made by Koryŏ potters is the use of copper oxide under the glaze as part of celadon decoration, adding the bright red color to already existing white and black inlay colors.

While the Koryŏ Dynasty preferred the elegant and refined beauty of celadons, the succeeding dynasty of Chosŏn (1392-1910) promoted the much simpler and austere beauty found in two ceramic forms: *punch'ŏng* and porcelain. *Punch'ŏng* is an abbreviation of *punjang punch'ŏng sagi* meaning "white slip decorated greyish-blue stoneware." Despite its name, the majority of *punch'ŏng* tended to be light yellow or brown because most pieces were fired in an oxidizing or neutral atmosphere. Unlike the porcelain wares which at first were made exclusively for court usage, *punch'ŏng* was made for commoners as well as for court and government offices during the 15th and 16th centuries.

Numerous local kilns produced *punch'ŏng*, using a variety of techniques to decorate them. The earliest decorative technique was the inlaying method, confirming the *punch'ŏng's* connection to the Koryŏ celadon which had been in production probably until the early part of the 15th century. Other techniques used to embellish *punch'ŏng* were stamping, incising, *graffito*, and painting. Regardless of the decorative methods used, white slip always featured prominently in *punch'ŏng* wares.

The most popular *punch'ŏng* wares were those with under glaze iron decorations painted with bold and expressive brushwork, such as the bottle with the painted fish and abstract scroll decoration in the Avery Brundage Collection (Plate 3). They are believed to have been made at kilns in the area of Mt. Kyeryong in the south Ch'ungchŏng Province and are popularly known as *Kyeryongsan punch'ŏng*. The influence of white porcelain became quite noticeable in *punch'ŏng* wares during the 16th century, when the coloring tended to become increasingly white. Many were decorated by brushing white slip over the vessel or simply dipping it in white slip. *Punch'ŏng* wares ceased to be produced after the Japanese invasions of 1592 and 1597. According to some scholars, Toyotomi Hideyoshi (1536-1598) sent two expeditions to Korea partly to raid the Korean kilns and bring back Korean potters. These potters not only supplied tea wares for their captors but also began Japan's porcelain industry during the 17th century. Thus, Japanese ceramics such as karatsu, imari, nabeshima, and kakiemon had Korean connections.

Although completely overshadowed by the more famous celadons, porcelain wares were also produced from the 10th century on. The declining celadon industry toward the end of the Koryŏ Dynasty enabled the porcelain potters to make great strides in their art and develop it further after the fall of Koryŏ and the establishment of the Chosŏn Dynasty. From the beginning of the new dynasty, the Chosŏn rulers and *sadaebu* (scholar-officials), steeped in Neo-Confucianism, preferred the simple, white color of porcelain wares over elegant celadons. To them the color white symbolized the Confucian virtues they strived for, such as purity, honesty, austerity, and modesty. The royal household of King Sejong (r. 1418-1450), for instance, used white porcelain wares exclusively. The most famous official porcelain kilns were located at Kwangju, Kyŏnggi Province, not far from Seoul. Porcelain continued to dominate the ceramics field throughout the Chosŏn Dynasty.

With fully mature porcelain wares of the early 15th century as the backbone, decorated porcelain wares in under glaze cobalt, iron, and copper oxide developed. Attracted by under glaze blue decorations on porcelain wares which came to the Chosŏn court in 1428 as gifts from the Ming dynasty emperor Xuande, the Chosŏn court made an effort to produce *ch'ŏnghwa paekja* (porcelain with under glaze cobalt decoration), commonly known as "blue and white." At the same time they also explored for native cobalt, which was subsequently discovered first in Sunch'ŏn, south Chŏlla Province, in 1463. Blue and white wares were first made with imported cobalt in the middle of the 15th century. Because the native cobalt tended to produce very dark and uneven blue tones, the imported cobalt which produced the clear, light-blue tones was preferred by many people. The finest porcelain decorated in under glaze cobalt with realistic designs was usually painted by court painters sent out to official kilns in Kwangju, Kyŏnggi Province, while porcelain made at local kilns decorated by local artisans often had abstract decorations. The popular motifs used to decorate Chosŏn Dynasty porcelain wares were dragons, phoenixes, plum blossoms, orchids, bamboos, grapes, chrysanthemums, birds, longevity symbols, and landscapes.

The Large Jar (Plate 4) in the Avery Brundage collection decorated with birds in blossoming branches in under glaze blue is a typical 18th century piece in form with the strong, bulging shoulder and the narrow foot. The deftly manipulated empty space balancing its simple and sparse composition and brush strokes executed with speed and spontaneity suggest that it was painted by a court painter who was brought out to official Kwangju kilns to decorate the porcelains which were to be used for the court and official purposes.

Although iron and copper oxide had already been in use during the Koryŏ Dynasty, decorating porcelain wares with iron brown became especially popular during the 17th century. Favorite motifs, such as bamboo, grapes, and tigers, were painted in a bold and expressive manner revealing the vitality of the potters' art. Copper oxide also regained its popularity during the 18th century. While Koryŏ artisans used copper oxide in a limited manner to enliven their inlay decoration, Chosŏn artists of the 18th century used copper oxide as if it were ink, creating wonderful designs. Lotuses, grapes, pines, and cranes were favored motifs painted in an abstract and expressive or in a naturalistic manner conveying a sense of harmony, fun, and whimsy as well as revealing the vitality of brush lines.

During the first half of the 20th century Korean ceramics struggled to survive under the pressures of an efficient, modernized ceramics industry. Special efforts have been made by potters not only to revitalize Korea's long ceramics tradition but also maintain it as an artistic tradition separate from machine-made ceramic wares flooding the markets. Contemporary potters such as Cho Chŏng-hyŏn create quiet stoneware pieces with a modern slant while paying homage to traditional utilitarian stone wares of the past. Another potter, Yun Kŭn-hyŭng, better known by his artist name Hae Gang, has devoted his entire life to recreating Koryŏ celadons, both plain and inlaid, as well as capturing their serene beauty. There are other potters, such as Kim Ik-yong and Yun Kwang-jo, who are creating porcelain and *punch'ŏng* wares. These potters are not only concerned with continuing Korea's ceramics tradition but also with exploring and discovering new ways of expressing their own artistic visions through the medium of clay and fire.

Suggested Further Reading

Kim, Chewon and Lena Kim Lee. 1974. *Arts of Korea.* Tokyo: Kodansha International.

Kim, Won-yong. 1986. *Art and Archaeology of Ancient Korea.* Seoul: Taekwang Publishing Co.

Gompertz, Godrey St. George Montague. 1964. *Korean Celadon and Other Wares of the Koryo Period.* New York: Thomas Yoseloff.

Plates

1. DUCK-SHAPED VESSEL
Earthenware
Three Kingdoms period: Kaya, 3rd-4th century
H: 12 "(30.5 cm); W: 15" (38.1 cm)
Korea B63 P13+
The Avery Brundage Collection

2. EWER
Stoneware with celadon glaze
Koryŏ Dynasty, first half of the 12th century
H: 9 5/8 "(24.4 cm); W: 6 1/2" (16.5 cm)
Korea B60 P123+
The Avery Brundage Collection

3. BOTTLE
Punch'ŏng, Stoneware with glaze over white with iron painted decoration
Chosŏn Dynasty, 16th century
H: 12 "(29.4 cm); Diam: 6 1/2" (16.5 cm)
Korea B65 P 63
The Avery Brundage Collection

4. LARGE JAR
Porcelain with cobalt decoration under the glaze
Chosŏn Dynasty, 18th century
H: 15 "(38.1 cm); Diam: 10" (25.5 cm)
Korea B60 P 1793
The Avery Brundage Collection

Duck-shaped Vessel

Ewer

Bottle

Large Jar

18

Papermaking and Printing
by Mark Peterson

1

Introduction

Korea was the first country in the world to develop metal movable type. The exact date for the invention is unclear; for a time, the easy-to-remember year 1234 was though to be accurate, but more recently the date has been pushed forward and backward. There is one claim that some time in the 12th century metallurgists forged type fonts as well as coins; but another claim, reinforced by UNESCO, claims that a book printed in 1377 was the first printed with metal movable type. Gutenberg published his first work in the 1440s, and his Bible in 1455. Whichever date is more convincing, Korea was well ahead of Gutenberg.

There are some important qualifications to remember about this accomplishment. The Chinese had already printed with movable type made of ceramics and wood, but the Koreans were the first to use metal alloys for the type fonts. The invention did not spawn a renaissance as did Gutenberg's—it was not a use of technology that brought literacy to the common man and thereby lead to universal literacy—but it was nonetheless a giant step forward in the civilization of mankind.

2

Movable Metal Type

That the Koreans were first to develop metal movable type fits into a larger context of inventions unique to Korea. Koreans historically were accomplished metallurgists. The ancient crowns of the Three Kingdoms period were made of gold, the first iron-plated warships were Korean, and the typical bowls and chopsticks in Korea were made of bronze (unlike the ceramic bowls and wooden chopsticks of China or the lacquer-on-wood bowls and chopsticks of Japan.)

The government department that was responsible for making the movable type was the same that made cannons. The secret formula that determined the exact ratios of metals in the alloy used to make cannons was the same as that used for the metal type fonts. Most fonts were forged in government foundries, although the 1377 edition was published with fonts forged at a Buddhist monastery, and private organizations in the 17th century and even private individuals in the 18th century created their own fonts.

The evidence for books printed before 1377 is based on various records in the history, but the oldest book printed with movable type in Korea that still exists today is also the oldest example of printing by movable metal type in the world. It is a Buddhist text that states that it was printed at a temple called Hŭngdŏk in the seventh month of 1377. The copy, kept at the National Library of France, was featured at an international book exhibit in 1972, the year of the book.

It was known that in the area of Chŏngju, there was a temple called Hŭngdŏk-sa, but its precise location was unknown until 1985. A dedicated journalist assisted first by a historian and later by a full team of archaeologists discovered the site, and found incontrovertible evidence that a temple by that name was there. Not only has the temple been reconstructed, but on the site, a museum, The Chŏngju Early Printing Museum, has been built. Therein, various exhibits show how the earliest Korean printing fonts were made, how Korean printing progressed over the centuries, and how Korean printing compares to what was done in other countries.

3

Innovations Under King Sejong

We do not know much about how the fonts developed during the Koryŏ period (918-1392), but by Kind Sejong's reign (1418-1450) in the Chosŏn period (1392-1912), the record is detailed. Since *han'gŭl* was not invented until King Sejong's time, earlier fonts were of Chinese characters. In Sejong's time and after, there were some *han'gŭl* fonts created, but the use of printing fonts was Chinese characters. Even though *han'gŭl* was invented in 1446, most of the educated elite considered it too common, and because they were proud of their use of Chinese characters, *han'gŭl* was not used. Printing in Korea was for government officials and the scholarly elite until there was a revolution that led to wide-spread use of *han'gŭl* and universal literacy at the end of the traditional dynastic period at the turn of the 20th century.

There were two sets of fonts created during the Sejong period, one in 1420 and another in 1434. Both font sets preceded the invention of *han'gŭl*, yet the fonts that were augmented by replacement fonts and also by *han'gŭl* fonts. This pattern was true of subsequent fonts that were forged every twenty to forty years. As augmentation to the Chinese characters, many of the sets included a subset of *han'gŭl* characters, but the *han'gŭl* fonts were seldom used.

Many of the fonts were forged with one set of full-sized characters and one set of half-sized characters. The half-sized were used in the recording of commentaries on the main text, such as the Korean philosophers commentaries on the Confucian classics. From time to time, wooden fonts were carved on short notice to replace missing or broken fonts. Toward the end of the Chosŏn period, iron fonts and then lead fonts were also cast.

4

Wood Block Printing

In some ways, the technology that preceded movable type printing (typography), wooden block printing (xylography), was even more important and continued to be used even after the development of movable type technology. They could carve a text into a wooden block, on the front and the back, smear the block with ink, then apply paper to obtain a printed copy. The wooden blocks were two pages wide. The paper would be folded in half so that the blank side is folded inward and the outside became two pages bearing the text. The folded edge became the edge one felt in turning the pages, the loose edges of the paper were sown together into the binding or spine of the book.

The most famous of the collections of the collections of wooden printing blocks is that at Haein Temple, where can be found the 80,000 wood blocks that contain the text of the Buddhist scripture. It is the most complete text of Buddhist scripture extant today, and is known as the Koreana Tripitaka. The blocks were carved on Kanghwa Island at a temple called Chŏndŭng during the devastating Mongol invasion in the 13th century. Today they are held in Haein Temple near modern-day Taegu where they are preserved in the same buildings that have protected them for centuries.

The great advantage of the wooden blocks is that they can be re-used time and time again. Even today, if a serious student of Buddhism desires a copy of various pages of the Buddhist canon, with permission, a copy can be made by applying ink and paper just as was done centuries ago. It is a kind of original photocopy machine.

Not only were the Buddhist scriptures preserved on wooden blocks, but as Confucianism came to have more influence in the subsequent dynasty (Chosŏn, 1392-1910), other texts were inscribed on wooden blocks. In fact, with the advantage of being readily available for making copies, wooden blocks continued in use long after movable type was invented. Some Confucian-inspired texts were carved as late as the 1940s. The major category of text written by Confucian scholars were called *munjip*, or collected essays. Prominent scholar-officials of the Confucian-dominated Chosŏn period would often write explanations of various theories, and together with possible eulogies, letters, memorials to the throne and sometimes poetry, these would be edited by disciples or descendants of the scholar and printed. These, too, could be copied as needed even years after the initial printing.

5

Papermaking

No less important than printing technology was that of making paper. Korean paper was so highly prized both inside and outside of Korea that the Chinese often required that Korean paper goods be included in the tribute goods. The paper was made from the finest material, the root of the paper mulberry tree — a variety of mulberry unique to Korea.

The history of papermaking is long. The oldest document written on paper found in Korea was discovered in the 1960s when the government was remodeling the Pulguk temple complex in Kyŏngju. They took apart a pagoda in the courtyard and found inside a kind of time capsule that had been put inside the pagoda at its dedication. The date converts to the western calendar date of 751. The document outlines the facts of the dedication of the temple and also of its subordinate shrine known as the Sŏkkuram, the famous granite Buddha in a cave high on the hill above Kyŏngju that overlooks the East Sea.

Korean paper, from earliest times, was made to last one thousand years. Claims like that are often exaggerations, but in this case it is not. There are historical references to the quality of Korean paper that compare it to cloth, and in some ways, although it is not woven, it is as pliable and supple as cloth.

The process by which Korean paper is made is remarkably simple although the process is quite exact. First, one must select the proper type of root; the root of the paper mulberry is the best, but other types are possible. Note that it is the root of the tree, not the bark or pulp or the trunk or stems that are used. The roots are throughly washed and washed again to remove all soil and other matter. They are then soaked in a special solution for a long period of time to soften them and help them to slightly decompose. When the fibers are soaked properly, they float in a milky solution that looks like a kind of paste or soup. You cannot see the individual fibers. Into this solution the craftsmen lower a large wooden frame. It is suspended from the ceiling in such a way that it can either be swung to one side and pulled out of the huge tub, or dipped into the tub to collect the fibers suspended in the solution. Covering the wooden frame is a finely-netted grate. The watery solution drips through the screen leaving the fibers loosely suspended on the grate. If the frame is lowered into the solution in one direction, the fibers all lie on the screen in that orientation. If the grate is then lowered into the solution, with a sweeping motion, at a right-angle to the first motion, then fibers will lie in a criss-cross pattern.

After the proper amount of fiber is collected on the screen, the frame is swung to one side of the tub where, firmly resting on the edge, a large rolling pin (not unlike the ones used in baking in Western kitchens except that it is much longer —maybe five feet) is rolled over the soggy fibers to squeeze out more liquid and to compress the fibers. The large sheets of wet fibers are carefully, by hand, lifted off the frame and laid in stacks to dry. When it is dried, it is paper. It can be cut to any desired size and used for writing, printing or even as wall paper in the home.

Three of the most important uses for Korean paper are found in the finishing of the rooms of a house. In the typical traditional house, the paper is used to cover not only the walls, but the floors, and even the doors and windows. Covering walls with paper is done in the West and does not seem unique, but covering the floors is done in a beautiful and unique Korean way. The floors of the house, as contrasted with the verandas and "living room" (*maru*) which are wooden planks and the kitchen which is clay, are the sources of heat for the house. The rooms are called *ondol* rooms, meaning "hot rocks," describing the under-the-floor heating system used in Korea. Under the paper is clay, and under the clay is a layer of flat rocks that cover flues which wind their way back and forth under the floor and through which hot smoke from a fire passes thus heating the rocks and radiating through the room. Of course, one must remove shoes to enter such rooms, but to strengthen the surface of the paper a kind of shellac is applied that also gives a shiny golden hue to the resulting floor covering.

The windows and doors are also covered with paper. The paper is not treated in any way (in the West, paper was saturated with oil to make it almost transparent), but it is glued to a lattice work or thin strips of wood arranged in uniquely and beautifully Korean designs. Covered with the white paper, both windows and doors easily slide to the sides to provide openings for passage or ventilation. Often the doorways are insulated with a double set of doors, one set that swings outward on hinges and one set that slides. The doors and windows provide adequate privacy though they were part of a traditional prank, it is said, on wedding nights. A family member or villager would repeatedly moisten a finger and hold it against the paper until the paper gave way and provided a peep hole and an opportunity to harass the newlyweds.

6

Bookmaking

Returning to the subject of the use of paper in printing, not only was Korean paper used to print the text, but a thicker paper, wax-coated and imprinted with a subtle design, was used as the protective cover on the front and back of the book. The spine of the book was bound in a thick thread. This type of traditionally bound book, in modern times to distinguish it from Western style hard-bound or paperback book, is called *hansŏ*, literally, a Chinese-style book.

In papermaking and in printing technology, Korea was like no other country. Although the technology did not lead to universal literacy, as did Gutenberg's invention, still it lead to a scholarly tradition appropriate for traditional times. With the dawning of the modern age, however, with the widespread use of *han'gŭl*, Korea quickly became universally literate. Today, with a literacy rate close to 100%, Korea has one of the best-educated people in the world. It is often noted that the education miracle proceeded the economic miracle that has made Korea an important player in the community of nations today. In large measure, the roots of that miracle can be found in traditional Korea as is evidenced by its ancient development of paper and printing.

Suggested Further Reading

Im, Young-joo. "A Kaleidoscope of Papercraft," *Koreana.* Vol. 7/No. 1.

Lee, Chong-sang. "Hanji: Sturdier Thank Silk or Leather," *Koreana.* Vol. 7/No. 1.

Ven, Young Dam. 1993. "Hanji," *Koreana.* Vol. 7/No. 1.

19

Oral Literature
by In-hak Choi

1

Introduction

Oral literature means literature that has been transmitted by word of mouth, thus distinguished from literature transmitted through written records. The Koreans created a rich oral tradition throughout their long history, and as the literature of the masses, it took deep roots, becoming an important part of the cultural heritage of the Korean people as well as part of their belief system.

Although certain segments of oral literature had been written down in the 12th and the 13th centuries, it was after the 15th century that much of Korea's oral literature was transformed into written literature, creating a new cultural heritage. Nonetheless, most literature of oral tradition remained as a genre as it was in the past.

The scope of oral literature in Korea may be divided into three categories: (1) narratives, (2) songs, and (3) sayings. They may then be subdivided as follows:

(1) Narratives: myths, legends, and folk tales

(2) Songs: folksongs, shaman songs, and *p'ansori*

(3) Sayings: proverbs, riddles, taboos, and auspicious words

2
Narratives

The term "old tales" (*yet iyagi*) means tales that have been transmitted down by word of mouth from a long time ago. Professor Kim Tong-uk has held that as *niyagi* (story) is an archaic form of *iyagi* (story), the original form of the word for "story" (*iyagi*) should be be traced from *nireuda* (to tell), the original verb form of *niyagi*. He has also suggested that both *niyagi* and *nireuda* contain the meaning of "to pronounce" or "to report" to a king or god. Therefore, he concludes that *iyagi* means "to pronounce" or "to report" to a king or god. Recently, scholars have tended to widely use the Chinese word *sŏlhwa* in place of the Korean word *iyagi*.

The classification of folk narratives into three categories of myths, legends, and folktales was introduced from the West in the early 20th century. This trisection method was not used in Korea's first folktale collection, *Chosun Mindam-jip*, complied by Son Jin-t'ae (1930). The first publication that adopted the trisection method was *Folk Tales from Korea* by Zŏng In-sŏp (1952). Since then the Western method has been the standard, and all the folk narrative materials in Korea have been classified as myths, legends, and folktales. However, at times we have difficulties in classifying some of the tales on the basis of the trisection method.

Myths

Korean myths can be divided into written myths and oral myths. Written myths mainly consist of the national foundation myth and the founder myth, while oral myths include the creation myth, the culture developing myth, etc. The written myths describe actual individuals who can be found in historical records, while the oral myths describe folktales containing motifs which are mythical in content. Representative myths from both the written and oral categories are briefly summarized below:

1. Written Myths

Tan'gun myth (the foundation myth of ancient Korea). Hwanung, the son of the Heavenly King, descended to earth and established a sacred city. At that time, a bear and a tiger, who wished to be human beings, received from the Heavenly Prince taboos to keep in a cave. The tiger failed the task, but the bear was able to transform into a woman and married Hwanung. She gave birth to a prince, who was named Tan'gun. He established the kingdom of Chosŏn and reigned for 1,500 years. He became a mountain god upon his death.

Chumong myth (the foundation myth of Koguryŏ). Kŭmwa succeeded to the throne of Eastern Puyŏ. He took Yuwa, the daughter of Habaek, as his queen. One day, sunlight beamed in and fell upon her. As a result she became pregnant and gave birth to a large egg. The king cast it out to be destroyed, but animals helped to save it. Before long it hatched, and a boy appeared. His name was given as Chumong. His mother's other sons were jealous of Chumong and tried to kill him, but he escaped from danger and fled to Cholbonju, where he founded a new kingdom called Koguryŏ.

Kim Suro myth (Kŭm'gwan Kaya foundation myth). When the chiefs of nine tribes gathered at the top of Mt. Kuji, a voice was heard from Heaven, saying that a new kingdom would be founded. As they rejoiced with dancing and singing, a box wrapped in red cloth came down from Heaven. In it was a boy, who eventually took the throne and founded the kingdom called Tae Karak (Tae Kaya).

2. Oral Myths

The Creation of Heaven and Earth. In the beginning, the heaven was stuck to the earth. Mirŭk, the Buddha of the Future, separated the two by erecting an iron pillar on each of the four corners of the world. At that time, since there were two suns and two moons, it was too hot during the day and too cold at night. Mirŭk thus made small and large stars with one of the two suns, and made the Seven Stars of the North and the Seven Stars of the South with one of the two moons.

The Sun and the Moon. The god of Heaven made the sun and his sister the moon. The moon said that she was too shy to be gazed upon by people and asked her brother to change his role with hers. The brother refused this request, and the two began to fight. During the scuffle, the brother poked his sister's eye with his long tobacco pipe. Ashamed by injuring her, the brother conceded to become the moon.

The Fire Dog (The origin of eclipses of the sun and the moon). There once was a land of darkness in Heaven. Its inhabitants wished to have some light. The king of the land ordered the fiercest of his fire dogs to bring the sun and the moon to him. The chosen fire dog raced off and tried to seize the sun in its mouth, but it was too hot. He then went to the moon, but he found it too cold to bite. The king never gave up his dream for light, and to this day he often sends out his fire dogs. It is said that eclipses of the sun and the moon are caused when the fire dog bites the sun or the moon and then spits it out again. This is the explanation of what we call eclipses.

The Origin of Mountains and Rivers. A princess of the Heavenly Kingdom once dropped her favorite ring on the earth while she was playing. The king sent one of his generals to the earth to search for the ring. The general began to dig into the ground with his bare hands. The holes which he dug eventually became the oceans, the piles of dirt which he created around the holes became the mountains, and the places where he ran his fingers through the ground became the rivers.

The Flood and the Multiplication of the Human Race. The human race was drowned by a great flood except for a brother and a sister who drifted to the top of a mountain. As the brother and the sister had no one to marry, they decided to ask god's will. They split a hand mill into two parts, and each of them climbed onto a different peak of the mountain, carrying a mill part. Then they rolled them down opposite sides of the mountain. As the halves of the mill rolled down, their course caused them to merge, so they were once again a whole mill. The brother and the sister concluded that god approved their marriage. Thus they became husband and wife, and repopulated the world.

In the national foundation myths, we find heroes' birth motifs centering on the descending to earth of a heavenly being and on hatching from eggs. We can also notice more extraordinary birth motifs such as intercourse between humans and animals or between gods and humans, etc.

It is interesting to note that during the Yi Dynasty, the upper classes who advocated rationalism and utilitarianism under the strong influence of Confucianism tried to eliminate stories whose contents they found to be nonscientific; they accepted only those which emphasized the divinity of the dynasty. As a result, myths explaining the origin of the universe or the founding of human race were not recorded in written literature; but they continued to be transmitted orally.

Legends and Folk tales

The word 'legend' is more familiar to the general reader than are the terms 'myth' and 'folktale.' While folktale is the term used in the academic world, *yennal iyagi* (old tales) is used among the masses. Generally, folktales open with the phrase, "once upon a time" or "long long ago."

In the days when oral literature was not yet a discipline of scholarship, myths and folktales were included in the category of legend. Around 1900, the formal study of folktales began in Korea with the publication of folktale collections. In 1979, Choi In-hak attempted to make a motif index of legends, classifying 637 Korean legends. They were as follows:

1. Origin and explanatory legends (92 tales)
2. Historical and local legends (239 tales)
3. Mythical and religious legends (291 tales)
4. Folktale-legends (15 tales)

One thing we should keep in mind is that in early times a legend was considered history. Therefore, specific dates and places were clearly described in legends. Folktales were transmitted orally in the form of legends, and many of them were linked with actual historical characters. Of the legends collected in Korea, the highest percentage (14%) are legends explaining the names of certain places. Second (10%) are legends relating to geomancy.

The traditional name of a place in Korea was often established by the term symbolizing the origin of the place or by reference to a historical event of the place. It thus becomes more plausible why legends describing the names of places are the most numerous of all the legends. Another noticeable feature of the Korean legend is geomancy, which even today exerts an influence on the popular mind. Besides these, there are many other common motifs such as the significance of dreams, *tokkaebi*

(Korean goblin), filial piety, a woman of chastity, the Japanese invasion of Korea in 1592, and so on.

Dreams are often interpreted by Koreans as indications of reality and predications of the future. It is believed that the births of heroes or great men are often predicted by dreams. It is, therefore, not uncommon to observe people altering their daily behavior based on their interpretations of their dreams.

The typical Korean *tokkaebi* or goblins frequently appear in folktales. They usually take pleasure in making people happy but at times bring troubles to people. Traditional Korean folk belief places the original *tokkaebi* on a fairly dignified level of the spiritual hierarchy. However, *tokkaebi* has lost its divinity status with modern social changes. Today it remains only as a goblin or a ghost.

3

Songs

In the category of songs, there are songs of labor, songs of ritual dance, and songs of recreation, all making up a major part of the ballads. The shaman song, sung by the shaman while performing her shaman rites, contains mythical elements. Hence, some scholars in the past used the term "divine song" for the shaman song. Many shaman songs have elements of divine pedigree and describe the roles of divine beings, the world after death, and so on.

P'ansori is a lengthy narrative music played by two performers, one singer and one drum accompanist. It was a literature of the populace. The *p'ansori* players were vagabond entertainers. *P'an* means a place where one can perform music or a play, and *sori* means "sound" or "song." *P'ansori's* audience included not only common people but aristocrats as well.

P'ansori has two types of musical forms: one is the main *p'ansori* song called *ch'ang* and the other is the rhythmically articulated spoken portion called *aniri*. The *ch'ang* is the main part, while the *aniri* is a sort of passage connecting scenes, recounting simple conversations, or creating interludes. The text of *p'ansori* includes dramatic structures, realistic expressions, and humorous, satirical themes. Satire at the expense of the *yangban* (the upper-class people) is a mode found in every genre of orally transmitted literature.

There were no special rules governing the performance site of *p'ansori*, and the same procedure was generally followed whether the performance was before a large public gathering or a small select audience. The singer would sit on a mat, facing the audience, with a fan in one hand; the drummer would sit facing the singer. *P'ansori* is enjoying a renaissance in modern Korean society.

4

Sayings

1. Proverb
A proverb is a terse statement that was drawn from the experiences of daily life of the common people and has been handed down orally through generations. Proverbs contain the wisdom, wit, humor, and irony of the people and express many of their norms. We assume that proverbs had been used from much earlier than the days of the Three Kingdoms to which we trace their origin through historical events and literature. The following is a proverb showing that a woman was held in contempt in the traditional Korean society:

>   *Amt'ak-i ulmyŏn chipan-i manghanda.*
>   (When a hen crows, the house is doomed.)

Another proverb suggests that we cannot be too cautious in our life's dealings:

>   *Tol tarido tuduryŏpogo kŏnnŏ kanda.*
>   (Tap even a stone bridge before crossing.)

2. Riddles
A riddle is an expression of metaphoric language in which an object is guessed by means of questions and answers. It serves to develop mental sequences of wit, tricks, knowledge, and humor. More than 5,000 riddles

have been collected in Korea. One riddle is:

If we put 6 dogs, 3 cats, and 2 rats into one confined area, how many animals are there?

The answer is, of course, 9 because the cats will devour the rats.

3. Taboos

There are many taboo words, signs, and actions in Korean society. In Korea, when there is a childbirth in a household, a rope called *kŭmjul* made out of straw with pieces of charcoal and branches of pine trees is hung across the gate of the household in order to mark the restricted area that protects the household from the entrance of any uncleanness. The *kŭmjul* is also often tied around jars of soy sauce. The following are taboo words giving a lesson which discourages people from using evil words:

kannan agirŭl mugŏptago hamyŏn sari ppachinda.
(If one says a baby is heavy, the baby will lose its weight.)

Mari sshiga toenda.
(Words become seeds.)

4. Auspicious Words

Unlike taboo words, auspicious words serve to predict favorable things. There are many auspicious words relating to humans, animals and plants, water, fire, sky and heaven, dreams, ancestor rituals, objects, and so forth. Some of the auspicious words are as follows:

If a thread is given to a child on the first anniversary of his birth, he will live long.

If a magpie sings in the morning, one will have a welcome guest or good news.

Suggested Further Reading

Cho, Dong-Il. 1982. "Oral Literature and the Growth of Popular Consciousness," *Folk Culture in Korea*. Seoul: Si-sa-yong-o-sa Publishers, Inc.

Choi, In-hak. 1979. *Type Index of Korean Folktales*. Seoul: Myongji University Press.

Zŏng In-sŏp. 1952. *Folk Tales from Korea*. London: Routledge & Kegan Paul Ltd.

20

Modern Poetry and Literature
by David R. McCann

1

Introduction

An introduction such as this can hope only to suggest the historical breadth of Korean literature, and indicate but a few of the most prominent sights along that landscape: the major writers and their works, the typical themes, the characteristic genres. This introduction is divided into two parts: Korean literature from the late Koryŏ period, of 13th and 14th centuries, up to the end of the 19th century, from what might be called premodern or traditional Korean literature; and from the year 1908, the date of publication of the first so-called modern poem in Korea, to the decades of the 1960s and 1970s, for modern — but not contemporary — literature.

Korean literature is characterized by several very general features. First, there is a discernible split between the formal genres and themes and the informal. Some works seem primarily to have been intended to record an event, describe some situation, explore some issue, while others seem to have come into being solely to express some sudden, powerful emotional impulse. Second, there is an authoritarian strain to Korean literature, just as can be noted in its society and, particularly, in the culture of its modern governments, both north and south. A strong, didactic current runs through Korean literature from the essays of the 12th century scholar Yi Kyu-bo to the stanzas of Korea's first modern poem, *From the Sea to Children*. This authoritarian strand is opposed by a humorous, satirical side to Korean literature which can be found in a wide range of genres, from the pun-filled poems of the 19th century poet Kim Sakkat, through the *p'ansori* narratives, puppet plays, *shijo* songs by anonymous composers, and fiction of various kinds. Finally, it should be noted that the great dynastic histories, other compilations of history and legend, essays and miscellanies, and a great array of poetry written upon formal, calendrical occasions, all share one peculiar feature in Korean literary history: they were written in the Chinese language, using Chinese characters. For the entire chronological span of the pre-modern period — that is, at least until the beginning of the 20th century — works written in Chinese occupied and defined the center of Korean literary culture, while works written in the Korean language were defined as peripheral, informal, occasional. The modern age has had to reverse this relationship, bringing Korean language works to the center of Koreas literary history, while treating the works that were written in Chinese, known as *hanmun*, or Chinese (*han*) literature (*mun*), as a vast and weighty but somehow not-quite-Korean appendix to the story of Korea's own literature. (In the broader perspective of Asian literary culture, hanmun was written anywhere that the Chinese writing system enjoyed favor, from Japan to Korea, Vietnam, and other regions of Southeast Asia. Because Classical Chinese was not the contemporary spoken language in any of the periods when it was used even in China itself, it could be argued that *hanmun* within China was no more native there than it was in Korea.)

The foreshortened perspective of historical hindsight determines the structure of the sections that follow. The first part of this introduction, on traditional Korean literature, surveys by centuries representative works, authors, genres, or other noteworthy features of Korean literature from late Koryŏ to the 19th century. The second part, on the 20th century, moves by decades, from just before the end of Korean independence at the beginning of the Japanese colonial occupation in 1910, to the near present.

2

History and Memorabilia of the Three Kingdoms

The Koryŏ Dynasty (10th to 14th centuries) brought the first peninsula-wide (or peninsula-long) unified rule to Korea. The Shilla kingdom had managed, through a 7th century alliance with Tang China, to subdue the kingdom of Paekche in the southwestern quadrant of the Korean peninsula, and to extend its territories to a line north of the presentday capital of South Korea, rather near the infamous 38th Parallel; but Shilla was unable to subdue all of Koguryŏ, the kingdom to the north. When Shilla control began to fragment in the 8th and 9th centuries, Koguryo revivified. The founder of the Koryŏ Dynasty took the name, dropped the *gu*, and established the kingdom which the west first encountered by that name, Latinized as *Corea*, or *Korea*.

There are only fragmentary written records from prior to the 12th century, so the history of Korean literature is in that literal respect, at least, constrained to begin with the Koryŏ period. The beginnings, though, are indeed monumental. The multivolume, official history of Koryŏ and its origins, known as the *History of the Three Kingdoms,* or *Samguk Sagi,* was assembled by a scholar, Kim Pu-sik, upon royal commissioning of the project, and completed in 1145. An even more monumental creation, two sets of the Buddhist scriptures — the first was destroyed by Mongol invaders were carved on 80,000 wooden blocks. These stupendous projects were undertaken as official state actions in confronting the threat and then the actual devastation of a series of Mongol invasions which wracked the country in the 12th and 13th centuries. The History, compiled under the orders of the monarch, was designed to enact through its compilation and publication the legitimacy of the kingdom as a national entity allied with China. As an enactment of supreme faith and dedication to the protection of the Buddha, the wood block carvings of the scriptures, known as the *Tripitaka Koreana*, were meant to preserve the kingdom from future attacks. While neither of these creations seems very much like what is normally meant by the term literature, one might make the case that as written works both written in Chinese characters they are texts, at the very least, and illustrate the connection in Korea between the written word and some formal intent, some predetermined purpose, to be accomplished through its deployment.

The next major compilation of Korean history, the *Memorabilia of the Three Kingdoms*, or *Samguk Yusa*, from its title to its contents is a very different kind of work than its predecessor, Kim Pu-sik's History. Where the History was assembled on royal commission, the Memorabilia was the informal product of the eminent Koryŏ monk Ilyŏn's idle hours in semi-retirement. Where the History sought to establish a formal and authoritative record of the kingdom, Ilyŏn was moved to preserve the unofficial, informal, legendary materials from Koreas past, to supplement Kim Pu-sik's work. Ilyŏn assembled his Memorabilia near the end of the 13th century, at a time of considerable discouragement in Korea at the devastation caused by the disastrous Mongol raids and invasions. One has the sense in reading Ilyŏn's work that he is looking back through the wreckage of Koryŏ Korea to the previous golden age of Shilla, when the Buddhist temples and statues were built which the Mongols destroyed, and when government ruled according to religious and philosophical precepts which no longer possessed the same authority. In short, Ilyŏn was trying to preserve, in his work, the Memorabilia of Korea's less troubled historical past, while at the same time endeavoring to record those parts of Korean history which Kim Pu-sik had omitted from his.

The *Memorabilia* is a difficult text to know how to read, in part because it is written in Chinese and therefore *a priori* represents a translation of the Korean materials, and in part because the compilation was assembled several centuries after the events it describes, from a variety of materials that had in the interval been lost or destroyed. Because it is such a conglomerate mixture of legends, history, songs, and other materials, it is difficult to sort out the narrative and descriptive strands. One of the best examples of these complications is a chapter called Chŏyong and the Sea Viewing Temple. Part of the brief narrative describes the reign of King Hŏn'gang. The alert reader will notice that in the first part of the story, the king takes appropriate actions when meeting a dragon, and the kingdom is reported to be in excellent moral, economic, cultural condition. By the end of the short tale, things are not going well; in fact, the kingdom is about to collapse, and the narrator suggests that the collapse of Shilla was due to the courts failure to attend to the proper ceremonies.

The story also includes an interpolated narrative about someone named Ch'ŏyong, about whom there are many questions that scholars and other readers have raised. Who was Ch'ŏyong, and where did he really come from? Why did he not act more heroically? Or did true heroism lie in his restraint? One explanation for what seems to be the anomaly of the story Why record the legend of someone so weak-minded as Ch'oyong seems to be? is that the story really is about a shaman who cures the beautiful woman in the story from a disease caused by a demon.

Although the story was written in Chinese, there is a song at the center of it which Ch'ŏyong sings to provoke the demon to speak, and that song is recorded in the Korean language. Ilyŏn used Chinese characters according to the *hyangch'al* system, developed in Korea at the time to represent the sounds, the meanings of Korean words, and their grammatical inflections. It is as if a tape recording had been discovered, not in perfect condition but audible, nonetheless, of a Korean song (*hyang'ga*) performed in Shilla times, one thousand years ago.

3

Young Man Ch'ŏyong and Sea View Temple

In the time of Hŏn'gang, the 49th King, from the capital all the way to the sea, the walls of the houses touched, and there was not a single thatched roof. Piping and songs were constant along the roadways, and the wind and rains were in harmony with the four seasons.

The king had gone out to Kaeunp'o, in the southwestern part of Haksŏng, now called Ulju, and had turned his carriage to return. As he ordered a rest beside the shore, clouds and fog suddenly obscured and darkened the way. They lost the road. The king asked his retinue, and the soothsayer said that it was the changing of the dragon of the Eastern Sea, and that it would clear away if an appropriate thing were done.

The king thereupon issued a royal command, that a Buddhist temple be built for the dragon near the border. As soon as the command went forth, the clouds broke up and the fog scattered. Therefore the place is called Kaeunp'o, Port of Opening Clouds.

The dragon of the Eastern Sea was pleased, and appeared by the royal carriage with his seven sons. Praising the kings virtues, they offered dances and music.

One of the sons accompanied the royal carriage back to the capital, to assist with the administration. His name was Ch'ŏyong.

The king gave him a beautiful woman as his wife, and bestowed upon him the office of *kŭpkan*, so as to retain his loyal intentions.

The wife was so beautiful, the plague demon adored her. Changing into human form, it came at night to the house and secretly joined her where she was sleeping.

Ch'ŏyong came back to the house from outside, and saw two people asleep. He thereupon sang a song, made a dance, and withdrew. The song went as follows:

> *In the bright moon of the capital*
> *I enjoyed the night until late.*
> *When I came back and looked in my bed*
> *there were four legs in it.*
> *Two are mine,*
> *but the other two—Whose are they?*
> *Once upon a time what was mine;*
> *What shall be done, now these are taken?*

At that time, the spirit appeared in its own form, kneeling before him, it said: I desired your wife, and now I have despoiled her. But because you did not show anger, I am moved and dazzled. I swear that from now on, if I so much as see a likeness of your self, I shall not enter the gate.

Owing to this, the people of this country make gate plates with Ch'ŏyong's likeness. In this way, misfortune is kept at a distance and happiness drawn near.

After the king returned, he chose a place on the eastern side of Yŏngch'u (Spirit Eagle) Mountain where he had a temple constructed. The temple was called Sea View Temple, and also, Bridal Room Temple. It was established for the dragon.

The king went out again, to P'osŏkchŏng. The spirit of South Mountain appeared and danced before the ruler. The attendants did not see it; only the king was able to see it, as a person who had appeared, dancing before him. The king himself performed the dance in order to demonstrate its form.

The spirit's name was Sangsim, Fortunate manifestation. Form that day until now, the people of this country have passed on this dance, calling it Omu Sangsim, the Reign Dance for Sangsim. It is also called the Reign Dance for Sansin, the Mountain Spirit.

Furthermore, following the spirit's appearance in a dance and the examination of the basic forms of its manifestation, he ordered that it be carved in stone and thereby taught to succeeding generations. It was therefore proclaimed as Form Examination. It was also known as the Frosty Beard Dance. In this way its form makes praises.

At the time the king went to Diamond Pass, Kumganyon, the spirit of the northern hills appeared and danced. It was called Oktogom, Jade Blade Clasp. Again, as the same ceremony was being held at a palace banquet, the earth spirit came forth and danced. It was called Kupkan of the Earth Elder.

According to the Grammaticalia, at another time the mountain spirit presented a dance and sang a song which went: *chi ri da do p'a do p'a.* This meant: *Those who rule the country with wisdom understand and flee in great numbers.* This was a revelation that the capital and districts were going to ruin. The earth spirit and the mountain spirit knew that the kingdom would be ruined, and for that reason, made the dance to serve as a warning. The people of the country did not realize this, but took the warning as a happy omen, and let their pleasures and enjoyment go from plentiful to extreme. For this reason, the kingdom ended in ruin.

(Trans. by D. R. McCann)

The Alphabet and After: 14th and 15th Century Literature

The 14th and 15th century are characterized by a much greater variety of literary materials. There are Koryŏ songs that describe life in dissolute times, such as the Song of the Turkish Bakery, which follows a rather promiscuous person on her round of meetings with various lovers. The Song of the Green Hills, with its refrain of *Let us live, Let us live, I say; Up in the green hills, let us live,* will strike one as either a cheery excursions ditty, or a depressing ode on hard times, when life in the city was insupportable and people retreated into the hills to survive.

From the 14th and 15th century materials, two literary events, of vastly different magnitude, stand out in major historical perspective. The first is a song poem in the brief, three-line *shijo* form, said to have been composed by the preeminent Koryŏ statesman and scholar Chŏng Mongju. Late in the 14th century as the Yi family and their followers were maneuvering for their takeover of the Korean state, they found their plans frustrated by Chŏng Mŏng-ju's refusal to alter his allegiance to the Koryŏ state and side with the upstart Yi faction. Legend has it that one of the sons of Yi Sŏnggye, the·general who became the first ruler of the Chosŏn Dynasty, accosted Chŏng at a gathering one evening with a brief, metaphorical *shijo* suggesting that Chŏng try to adopt a more flexible way of responding to the changes then taking place in the state. Chŏng replied with his own, bravely direct rejoinder, a *shijo* that has become one of the most famous in the history of Korean literature, perhaps more for the nature of the event which it captures than its actual literary merit. Chŏng made clear that his loyalty to Koryŏ would never change. Soon after, he was assassinated. The two *shijos* are as follows.

> *What does it matter*
> *if you do this or that ?*
> *Who cares if the arrowroots*
> *go entangled on Mansu Hill ?*
> *We could be like those vines,*
> *enjoying ourselves for a hundred years.*

Shijo song by Yi Pang-wŏn (13671422), fifth son of Yi Sŏng-gye, founder of the Chosŏn kingdom.

Eschewing metaphor, Chŏng Mong-ju replied with the following:

> *Though I should die and die again.,*
> *though I die a hundred times,*
> *Though my bones turn to dust*
> *and whether my soul exists or not,*
> *What can change this single-minded faith*
> *that glows toward my lord?*

(Translation by Jaihiun Joyce Kim)

At the midpoint of the 15th century, the invention and promulgation of the Korean phonetic alphabet, now known as *hangŭl*, marks the second reference point, and the true beginning for a history of Korean-language Korean literature. The alphabet was the inspiration and most likely also the personal creation of Sejong, the third ruler of Chosŏn Korea. The alphabets promulgation in 1446 was an event which caused two immense waves in the expanse of Korean literature: first, a multiplication of new writing in the new alphabet, by all kinds of people on all kinds of subjects, from naturalist treatises to farmer's calendars to songs, long and short; second, a vigorous reaction among the Confucian upper class, who read it as a serious threat to their entrenched positions in society and government, founded as they were upon the long and intensive course of study leading to the civil service examinations, which in turn were based upon knowledge of Chinese Confucian classics. King Sejong marked the promulgation of the new alphabet by commissioning a dynastic foundation song, the Songs of Flying Dragons, *yongbiŏch'ŏn'ga*. The song commemorated the accomplishments of the founder of the dynasty, the many signs by which it became known that he was chosen to establish a new kingdom, and the skillful rule of the first few monarchs. It closes with a long series of admonitions to the future kings as to the dangerous seductions of power. Each time the song was performed, and Sejong was said to have liked it a great deal, it would have sounded the praises of the dynastic founders, and harder on the ears of the officials in attendance at the royal concert, of the new alphabet as well. Structurally and thematically, then, it is quite strongly reminiscent of Ch'ŏyong's song performed as it was before a potentially hostile audience, and embedded in the Chinese-based textual setting of the government. Each verse in the main body of the song begins with the naming of some important event or portent in Chinese history, and then balances it in the second half by referring to a similarly portentous moment in the young dynasty's history. The opening two verses include one of the most well known of all phrases in Korea in the line about the deep-rooted tree as a symbol of the Korean people and their culture.

I

The six dragons of Haedong (Korea) fly;
Their works all have the favor of Heaven:
Their auspices are the same as the worthies of old.

II

A tree with deep roots,
Because the wind sways it not,
Blossoms abundantly
And bears fruit.
The water from a deep spring,
Because a drought dries it not,
Becomes a stream
And flows to the sea...

(Translation by James Hoyt)

Although the Confucian scholar-official class managed to limit the use of the new alphabet, which did not really come into general use until the last decade of the 19th century, outside of that narrow upper band at the top of the society, among women, monks, clerks, and other middle-level government officials, as well as men writing informal or genre pieces, the alphabet and literary expression in Korean became a powerful force in Korean cultural history. Works written in *han'gŭl* were compiled and published in large numbers. The greater majority of these materials comprise philosophical works on government and its activities, or practical philosophy directed toward the improvement of living conditions for the people of the Korean kingdom, and better understanding of, and therefore adherence to, the proper moral, Confucian code of conduct. Literary works in Chinese, as Kim Si-sŭp's (1435-1493) peculiar prose tales, *New Tales from Gold Turtle Mountain*—the name of the hill where he wrote the pieces—also circulated relatively widely, even in Japan.

4

Sixteenth Century Korean Verse Literature

Viewed by most any measure, Korea's 16th century was a perilous one. Four major purges of the scholar-official class, in which hundreds were executed or exiled, tore apart the group from which the state drew its leadership. The economy was strained, then devastated at the end of the century, precisely two centuries after the founding of Chosŏn, when Japanese troops mounted a huge invasion of Korea in their campaign to attack China. Factional rivalries, added to the general malaise, ensured that the initial efforts to halt the invasions would prove futile. The Japanese troops rampaged more or less at will up and down the peninsula until the court reinstated a previously banished admiral, Yi Sun-sin, who went south to take up his command. The admiral recorded his experiences in a diary which makes fascinating reading because of the circumstances in which it was written: near anarchy among the coastal towns, as the local administrators and military officers—as well as great numbers of the local population—had taken flight; the difficult effort to assemble and train the troops and sailors to mount the defense; and then the campaign itself against the Japanese invaders when the Korean navy used its turtle boats, armored vessels, to devastate the Japanese fleet. All of the glorious promise ended for the admiral on the final day of the coastal engagement that broke the Japanese fleet but cost admiral Yi his life when he was struck by a stray bullet. The admiral left the following *shijo* song, said to have been composed on the night before the final engagement with Japan.

On Hansan Isle, high upon the battlements
I sit alone this moonlit night.
Deep in anticipation,
with my great sword by my side,
Suddenly I am pierced to the core
by the single note from a flute, somewhere out there.

(Trans. D. R. McCann)

Where an admiral might be expected to keep an interesting diary in such circumstances, Korea's difficulties both foreign and domestic might suggest a rather more cramped and limited literary life. But the 16th century witnessed an astonishing number of significant literary works, especially in poetry. And where the 16th century can be cited for its remarkable output in poetry, the 17th century, replete with Manchu invasions and continuing problems in the administration of government, is known for a series of pioneering prose works. One lesson from the Korean 16th and 17th centuries may be simply that there is no direct correlation between works of literature and their historical times, or that all such connections are indirect and mediated by the act of writing. It may be no accident, after all, that many of these works are escapist, in one sense of the term or another; that is, they were written during and about periods of enforced exile by officials who had been removed from office in the factional disputes of the day, or they are projected fantasies describing times and places which the author may never have seen, but where themes of peaceful seclusion and such rustic pursuits as fishing reveal all too clearly a desire for less troubling times.

5

Sixteenth Century Korean Verse: A Sampler

Two Korean verse forms came into their own in the course of the 16th century. The *shijo* is a short, three-line verse form, originally sung to a musical setting, and the *kasa*, a long verse form having the same line structure as the *shijo*—four rhythmic groups, rather like dactylic feet in English meter—with an unlimited number of lines. In actual practice, the *kasa* ranges in length from forty or so lines, to texts of several thousand. The brief sampler that follows presents the works of the 16th century's poets, Pak Il-lo (1561-1643), Yun Sŏn-do (1587-1671), and Chŏng Ch'ŏl (1536-1593), all men who occupied various government offices during their lives, but never quite the office they had hoped for, nor for the length of time they had wished; and Hwang Chini, a *kisaeng*, or woman entertainer trained in the literate ways of the world of the bureaucratic officials. The excerpts are chosen to suggest something of the range of subject mater which these representative authors addressed in their works.

The 16th century may well seem remote, distant, classical; and the fact that such a number of its poets are known in the Korean literary canon for having established a standard against which other works and writers are measured compounds the classical interest. But while the four writers gathered here have indeed come to be seen as defining the classi-cal, at the same time they demonstrate in their works just how misleading the label can be, for they were also experimental in practice, and modern, colloquial, and at times quite informal in outlook.

Pak Il-lo wrote *kasa* and *shijo*. His *shijo* are rather pedestrian, often no more than didacticism, reiterations of Confucian moral sentiments, as in:

> *My father begot me;*
> *My mother reared me:*
> *How hard it is to repay their kindness,*
> *Boundless as heaven.*
> *Great Shuns lifelong devotion*
> *Was not enough, it seems.*

(Trans. by Peter H. Lee)

Pak's *kasa* are another matter entirely. They seem to have arisen more directly from Pak's actual experience, and they take their form and diction in a remarkably colloquial use of the Korean language, some four centuries before poets and novelists in Korea are usually reported to have evinced interest in the colloquial. The following passage from Pak's *Song of a Humble Life is* an example of unforced colloquiality carrying the story.

> *... On a moonless night I push my steps*
> *to the house where I had a king of promise*
> *for the loan of an ox.*
> *I stand alone*
> *outside the tightshut gate,*
> *cough loudly,*
> *and after a while hear*
> *"Well, who is out there?"*
>
> *"Shameless I."*
> *"What brings you out*
> *at this hour of the night?"*
>
> *"I am in need like this*
> *every year, I know,*
> *but there is no ox at my poor house,*
> *only many debts, so I have come."*
>
> *"I know I said I would loan it*
> *for nothing, or for a little,*
> *but last night the fellow from across the way*

cooked up a redthroated pheasant
all dripping with juices,
and had me drinking fresh spring wine
till I was tipsy.
Thinking I simply had to repay
such generosity
I made him a promise
for the loan of my ox tomorrow.
I would be ashamed to break a promise.
what can I say?"

"Well if that is so
there is nothing to be done."

Wish shabby hat drooping, in worndown sandals,
dispiritedly I trace my way home.
At my crestfallen appearance
the dog starts barking.

(Trans. by D. R. McCann)

Yun Sŏn-do is generally acknowledged to be the master of the *shijo* form. Among his many innovations, he followed a deliberately relaxed pattern of syllable count in the lines of his *shijo*, and added onomatopoetic phrases or refrains as he wished. One of his best known compositions is the *Fisherman's Calendar*. Two verses from the *Spring* section are:

An east wind springs up;
waves get up a lovely swell.
Hoist the sail, hoist the sail!
I leave East Lake behind,
move on through to West Lake.
Chigukch'ong, chigukch'ong, osawa!
The mountain in front passes by,
giving way to the mountain behind.

Is that the cuckoo singing?
Is that the willow grove greening?
Row the boat, row the boat!
A few fisher houses
glimmer in and out of the haze.

Chigukch'ong chigukch'ong, osawa !
Shoals of fish flash
in a clear deep pool.

(Trans. by Kevin O' Rourke)

Like Pak Il-lo, Chŏng Ch'ŏl composed both *shijo* and *kasa*. His "Drinking Song" is widely admired as an example of what is known as the *sasŏl shijo*, an expanded form of the *shijo* which became more widely practiced and popular during the 18th century.

Drink a cup, then drink another cup;
Plucking flowers to keep the count, drink, and endlessly drink.
After this body dies, covered with a straw mat
and roped to a pack frame,
or borne on a bier as thousands weep
it will pass among reeds and ruches, or willows and oaks;
and when the sun shines yellow, the moon white,
rain drizzles down, or chill winds whirl the heavy snows,
who will there be to say Drink a cup ?
And when some monkey is sadly whistling on your grave,
what good will regrets be then ?

(Trans. by D. R. McCann)

Chong Ch'ŏl's *kasa* poems are said to epitomize the genre. He wrote travel poems and lyric laments that worked the theme of an exile's life: the travel poems described his journeys to places of exile, when he had lost his office position, as happened after during the factional struggles of the time; the laments, in the *persona* of a rejected woman lover, remonstrate with the ruler for the sentence of exile.

from The Wanderings

Giant boulders in front form
the Fiery Dragon Pool.
A thousandyearold dragon,
coiling round and round,
floats day and night
and reaches the open sea.
when will you gain winds and clouds,

and send sweet rain for three days
to yelling leaves
on a shadowy cliff?
Seeing Maha Chasm, Maitreya on a cliff,
and Goose Gate Hill,
I cross a rotting log bridge
to Buddhas Head Terrace,
a cliff hanging in air
over a thousand fathoms deep.
The Milky Way
unrolls its filaments
showing the warp and woof
of its hemp cloth.
Twelve cascades on natures map;
but I can see a few more!
Had Li Po been here
and compared two views,
he would not have bragged
of the waterfall at Mount Lu.

(Trans. by Peter H. Lee)

Hwang Chin-i is known for her *shijo* One, a clever series of puns upon the official title of a scholar official—a homophone with *Jade Green Stream* and her own sobriquet, *Bright Moon*, is among the best known in the language. Another matches the formal use of enjambment, a second line that runs on into the third, to suggest the impetuosity of impulse that led her to send away her lover. The third offers a metaphysical conceit in a most memorable fashion.

Jade Green Stream, dont boast so loud
of your passing through these blue hills.
Through your way runs swiftly down to the sea
there in no such easy return.
While Bright Moon fills these empty hills
why not pause, then go on, if you will.

Alas, what have I done?
Knew I not how I would yearn?
Had I but bid him stay, how
could he have gone? But stubborn

I sent him away,
and now such longing learn!
I will break the back
of this long, midwinter night,
folding it double,
cold beneath my spring quilt,
that I may draw out
the night, should my love return.

(Trans. by D. R. McCann)

6

Seventeenth and Eighteenth Century Prose

As early as the 16th century, the poetry, especially, of Korea exhibited several of the characteristics that are commonly associated with the idea of "the modern" as compared to "traditional" or classical. These characteristics might include the use of the colloquial language as Pak Il-lo employed it, or the experimentation with formal rules displayed in Yun Sŏn-do's and Hwang Chin-i's *shijo*. Yet these same characteristics—an enthusiastic appreciation, let us say, for the informal, the playful, the mildly subversive—are a feature of Korean culture more broadly viewed as well, and elsewhere in its history. Even the earliest Chinese chronicles refer to Koreas people as loving dance and song.

Rather than seeing early signs of "modern" tendencies, then, we can see Korean literature as having been engaged, in its own terms, with issues and objectives, and employing linguistic and formal, literary resources, that suggest the outlines of a far more complex literary tradition than might normally be thought of as "classical Korean literature." This is a useful premise for several reasons. As non-Korean readers of Korean literature—in English translation—we are more likely to apprehend its qualities if we do think of it as innovative, accomplished, and in some ways engaged with its own political and cultural spheres rather than viewing it as a simple, conservative, somewhat disconnected set of formal exercises waiting for the breathe of modern western literary influence to touch its frozen soil.

Late 19th century editorialists such as Sŏ Chae-p'il were fond of using the image of the Korean people awakening from a centuries-old slumber to move into the modern world. Sŏ's imagery reflected, in turn, the western assumptions and prejudices about countries and cultures like Korea: that they were somehow stagnant backwaters needing the dynamic influence, the dynamite of western ideas and technology in the log jam of traditional culture, to get things moving. Such also was the substance of Japans rationalizations of its expansionist, imperialist policies in Korea and the rest of Asia.

Such notions have been pervasive in literary history. Especially in histories of 20th century literature, one finds repeated references to Korea's "borrowing" of forms, trends, schools, or other literary coinage from Europe and the United States in the effort to create a modern Korean literature. This analysis is based on an insidiously teleological argument, in that it assumes that history does have some ultimate goal or purpose, and in this case, that the goal of history is modernization. Because it seeks to read the history of a country like Korea as proceeding from nonmodernized, traditional forms and behaviors to modernized versions of the same, such an analysis must perforce ignore those aspects of Korean literature which the modernizing project wants to claim as the product of its own work—those aspects of "pre-modern" literature that seem somehow modern.

Korean writers of many different forms and types, from story writers to natural philosophers, were engaged in their own series of critiques of contemporary Korean society and culture during the period from the 17th century on. The movement, outlook, and philosophy is called *shirak*, or practical learning, and among other things included the direct observation of conditions as they were in an attempt to understand, and then suggest methods for more equitable or scientific management of them. The literary ramifications of this movement, and more generally of a practical and skeptical view of the given social and political order in Korea, can be found in several representative though quite disparate literary works. *The Tale of Hong Kiltong* by Hŏ Kyun (1569-1618) is a wildly fantastical story about the struggles of the illegitimate son of a government official to win acceptance by his father and by society. Young Kiltong leaves his home when his father, despite his feelings for his son, rebukes him for complaining about his disqualified status as the son of a woman servant in the household. Kiltong roams the countryside, perfecting his Taoist military arts, and gathering about him a band of merry outlaws rather like Robin Hoods. (The actual model for the adventure, mentioned in the story as Kiltong is bidding farewell to his mother, is a Chinese story.) At the end of the story, Kiltong becomes a king himself, and embarks on an appropriately just reign. The very heights of the story's fancy seem to be an even stronger criticism of present conditions in Korea in which the ambitions and loyalties of those who were born outside the narrowing band of upper level aristocracy were frustrated by laws and practices designed to prevent them from gaining office. Ironically, although the mythically accomplished hero of Hŏ Kyun's story enjoys an eventual mastery over the social forces that had initially blocked him, the author was himself implicated in a plot by a group of upper class, illegitimate sons, and was executed.

The Nine-Cloud Dream, by Kim Man-jung (1637-1692), may have been written first in either Chinese or Korean, and translated into the other; it is not clear which was the case. In any event, the story, said to have been composed to console the authors mother during a period when Kim Man-jung was in exile, follows the spiritual journey of the principal character, a Buddhist monk named Hsing Chen, whose wishes to experience life more fully are granted. The story is an extended parable on the transitory nature of life's pleasures and accomplishments, and Hsing Chen, though he experiences worldly success in government office, and harmonious love with eight lovely women, eventually comes to yearn for the spiritual truths he had been seeking as a young monk. This wish, too, is granted, and he awakens to discover that his life of worldly accomplishment had been, both literally and figuratively, nothing but a dream. The story seems like a spiritual counterpart to the worldly social critique implicit in Hŏ Kyun's *Tale of Hong Kiltong*, only the fantasy world that Hsing Chen enters in his dream is a thoroughly Chinese one. Chinese place names, Chinese names and titles for the characters in the story, including the protagonists, demonstrate the author's familiarity with similar Chinese works, and also the rather interesting use of Chinese images to suggest a realm of fantasy, imagination, and otherness.

Princess Hyegyŏng's (1735-1815) *Record in Sorrow*, or *Hanjungnok*, is a remarkable, true account of the events leading up to the unprecedented execution of a royal crown prince. The princess was married at the age of nine to Crown Prince Sado, son of King Yŏng-jo (1724-1776) who, in attempting to lead Korean politics and government out of a period of debilitating factional rivalries, dedicated himself to becoming an exemplary, Confucian ruler. The king's sternness, and the extremely high standards by which he judged his son's actions, may well have contributed to the latter's problems, but the crown prince began to show signs of mental illness and eventual breakdown. The crown princes behavior eventually became so bizarre that in 1762 his father, the king, declared that he was a threat to the stability of the kingdom, and had him buried in a large, wooden rice container, where he died. The official records were purged of references to the incident, but unofficial stories circulated in abundance, including rumors that the crown prince's wife, Lady Hong, was somehow implicated in a plot to undo the crown prince. Partly to save her own reputation, therefore, and partly to clarify the circumstances of the case to her grandson, who became King Sunjo (1800-1834), Lady Hong wrote her memoir over the last sixteen years of her life. The record is written in Korean, with a very steady, clear focus on events that could have come from the imagination of an Edgar Allen Poe. For example:

> The Prince could not help killing people when he was suffering from an attack of his illness. Hyŏnju's mother, Ping-ae, used to take care of the princes robes, and one day in the first month, 1761, just as the prince was about to change his robes in order to travel incognito, he suffered a sudden attack of his illness and beat Pingae so severely that he injured her critically. He went out and Pingae died at the palace not long after. It was a tragedy not only for Ping-ae herself, but also for her children, who were so wretchedly bereaved!
>
> Since the king might visit at any time, we could not keep the body in the palace for even a little while, and indeed we felt pressed to keep it overnight. We sent it out in the morning and arranged for the funeral to be held at the *Yongdongun* Palace, providing plenty of money for the funeral expenses.
>
> ... Suddenly, in the fifth month, he started excavating and in the cavity built a house with three rooms, putting in sliding doors between each room, so that it looked just like the inside of a grave. The door was situated in the ceiling, giving just enough space for the people to creep in between the top panel and the door, and the top panel was then covered with grass so there was no sign of the house built underneath. The prince was very pleased with his work, and shut himself up in the house, which was lighted by a hanging jade lamp. All this was done simply to provide somewhere to hide his weapons and even horses, in case the king came to visit and investigate what the prince was doing.

(Trans. by YangHi ChoeWall)

7

Modern Korean Literature

The history of modern Korean literature has been powerfully influenced by two related constellations of events. The first was the Japanese occupation of Korea in 1910, a colonial regime lasting until Korea's liberation in 1945 at the end of World War Ⅱ. Immediately following liberation, however, Korea was partitioned between the United States and the Soviet Union, an action originally intended to establish temporary zones for the two sides to accept the regional surrender of Japanese forces. The temporary turned long term, however, as Cold War rivalries prolonged the confrontation of the Western powers. In 1950, a civil war broke out between the political Left and Right, aligned geopolitically with the northern and southern regimes, and eventually drawing the two major powers as well as a host of other participants notably including the Peoples Republic of China—into its wake.

Lasting from the end of the war in 1953 until the present, the prolonged division became one of the major concerns of an influential group of writers in the 1980s. Coupled with the repeated invocation of the North Korean threat, the division provided the handiest rationale during the Park Chung-hee regime (1961-1979) for severe repression of political dissent and of literature that in any way articulated it. Only in the relatively recent past, the first few years of the decade of the 90s, has reunification lost its taboo status as a subject, and therefore come to be seen less as the (hidden) object of writing than an accepted premise.

The Japanese occupation of Korea has exerted its influence on the post-1950 writing scene in a number of ways, both direct and indirect, and it may be useful to note a few of these in order to establish for the reader who may be less familiar with the history, or who may think that Koreas cultural and political history as a modern nation really started only after the end of the Korean war, that the themes, subjectivities, objects, and loci of tension in Korean literature have in fact been relatively consistent through the 20th century; or at least until the past few years.

What are these influences, conditions, contexts, loci ? First and most obviously, the Japanese repressed and then imposed an outright ban on literary or other expression in the Korean language. Nationalists who removed themselves from Korea, or who stayed and wrote in Korea until it was no longer possible and then still kept on, are heroes in the cultural histories of the period. Many accommodated, some completely, others to a lesser degree. The former—writers like the pioneers Yi Kwang-su and Ch'oe Nam-sŏn—had been vilified during the post-liberation period, but recently have been offered some degree of literary and ideological rehabilitation. The latter, writers who cooperated with the Japanese in less obvious ways, continue to occupy a supremely tendentious zone in Koreas history. A scandal broke out in 1986, for example, with the publication of the first two volumes of *Selected Pro-Japanese Literary Works*, among which are essays, poems, and other materials by a number of prominent writers in the South Korean literary world.

As an instance of foreign economic and political power exercised in Korea, the Japanese occupation evokes bitter memories, but also raises questions about the so-called Western democratic powers for their evident neglect, even collusion, at Korea's status as an occupied territory. The United States did not discourage Japan's moves leading toward the 1910 occupation, and failed to respond in any significant way in 1919 to the March First Korean Independence Movement, even though the events of 1919 clearly were intended as a respond to President Woodrow Wilson's Fourteen Points. The United States did respond to South Korea's perilous situation in 1950, and for decades after the Korean War, the sense of appreciation for the American intervention was palpable nearly everywhere in the south. More recently, though, it has been noticed in the south that the United States was the initial instigator of the 1945 division; that the U. S. commitment of troops in 1950 was at least as much motivated by anxiety about the supposed Red menace as by concern for the people of (South) Korea; and that lingering American implication in the Cold War was a factor in the continuing division. Again in 1980, when the citizens of Kwangju, a city in the southwestern part of Korea, were brutally assaulted by Korean government troops, the United States not only failed to intervene, but seemed to have given at least tacit approval to the detailing of the troops to Kwangju.

Such political issues have formed a significant strand in Korean literature throughout this century, one that shapes a reading of even the most "aesthetic" or purely literary works, and gives a pejorative sense to the term *sunsup'a*, the pure literary school as contrasted with the *ch'amyŏp'a*, or commitment group. It spills over into the assumption that when one speaks of Korean literature, one normally means—without meaning to—either literature written in Korea prior to the 1945 division, or literary works written in South Korea in the years since. North Korean literature is almost universally excluded. And until just a few years ago, South Korea had banned the publication not only of works by North Korean writers that is, citizens of the Democratic Peoples Republic of Korea—but even those who wrote and published prior to 1945 but then, for whatever reason, whether freely or not, "went north."

Modern Korean Literature to 1945

Out of the great variety of works, of schools and movements, of changes in any given writer's orientation toward the world, language, or literary form that make modern Korean literature such a rich potpourri, it is possible to condense the history to a short, decade by decade synopsis. From the first decade of the century, Ch'oe Nam-sŏn's (1879-1961) poem *From the Sea to Children, Hae egesŏ sonyŏn ege*, stands out in the histories as the first modern poem. Ch'oe published the poem in the first issue of the journal he had just started publishing, *Youth*, or *Sonyŏn*. The poem articulated, with rather heavy didactic force, the authors hope to inspire the younger generations of Korea to take up the challenges of the modern age. The first and last stanzas will give a sense of the poems structure and tone, in several respects reminiscent of the Songs of Flying Dragon.

I

Ch'ŏlsŏk, ch'ŏlsŏk, ch'ŏk, sswa-a.
Rolling, smash, demolish.
Mountains high as Taesan, rocks huge as houses,
What are they to me, what are they?
Know you my strength? Or do you not? Roaring out,
Rolling, smash, demolish.
Ch'ŏlsŏk, ch'ŏlsŏk, ch'ŏk, t'yururung, kwak.

Ch'ŏlsŏk, ch'ŏlsŏk, ch'ŏk, sswa-a.

> *There on earth, the people;*
> *I despise them all. The only ones I love,*
> *Full of courage, the purehearted children.*
> *Come then, sweetly to my arms and be embraced.*
> *Come and let me kiss you.*
> *Ch'ŏlsŏk, ch'ŏlsŏk, ch'ŏk, t'yururung, kwak.*

(Trans. by D. R. McCann)

Following the Japanese annexation of Korea in 1910, the literary as well as the political and social modernization movement were engulfed by the Japanese efforts to assimilate, or erase, Korean culture. Still, writers such as the pioneering novelist Yi Kwng-su, whose 1917 new novel *The Heartless, Mujŏng*, articulated a vision of modern enlightenment thought leading to the rebirth of Korean national energies, continued to grapple with the doubled challenges of creating a modern, Korean literature even as Japan's policies seemed to block the very idea of a Korean nation and culture.

In 1919, in direct response to Woodrow Wilson's Fourteen Points, including especially the principle of national self determination, Ch'oe Nam-sŏn, on consultation with Yi Kwang-su and other leaders, drafted a Declaration of Korean Independence, which was read at Pagoda Park in Seoul on March First. The movement spread rapidly throughout the country, despite the concerted and violent efforts of the Japanese government-general to suppress it. But the international community failed to respond, in part because of the difficult negotiations then underway at Versailles to settle the end of World War I, and in part because of American interests in having Japan as a balance to Russian ambitions in Asia. The Japanese government did alter its policies for a time, however, easing an array of the publishing restrictions, among others. As a result, the decade of the 1920s became a true Renaissance of Korean literature. Fiction writers such as Kim Tongin (1900-1951) and Hyŏn Chin-gŏn (1900-1943) developed the short story, while poets such as Kim So-wŏl (1902-1934) and Han Yong-un (1879-1944) exploited both Korean and other resources in creating a Korean literature. Theirs was a truly cosmopolitan, international world of literature. Korean writers exchanged ideas, and occupied positions in their social and political perspectives, that were closely allied with Japanese as well as Chinese and European counterparts. So-wŏl's famous poem *"Azaleas,"* for example, published in his only collection of poems in 1925, expresses a wistful melancholy to those who read it as a love poem. It echoes a poem by William Butler Yeats,

"He Wishes for the Cloths of Heaven," for those who have read the Irish poets work. Like Yeats, So-wŏl deploys in his poem a traditional diction and rhythm that evoke the Korean cultural past, like the Irish Romantic past of Yeats's early work. That cultural evocation can be interpreted as both a literary gesture, and a political statement in being Korean, or Irish, rather than (colonial) Japanese or British.

Azaleas

When you go away,
weary of me,
without a word, gently I shall let you go.

I shall gather
the beautiful azaleas of Yŏngbyŏn and Yaksan
and scatter them on your path.

Step by step
on the flowers placed before you
tread softly, just lightly, and go.

When you go away,
weary of me,
though I die I shall not shed a tear.

(Trans. by D. R. McCann)

Despite the increasingly severe restrictions placed upon Korea during the decades of the 1930s and 1940s, Korean writers continued to pursue their craft. The poet, short story writer, essayist, Bohemian, Dadaist, architect, teahouse owner Yi Sang(1910-1937), in being the most unusual of Koreas writers then and, in the estimation of many readers, since, can be viewed as the most representative. His novella *Wings, Nalgae,* published less than one year before his death, combines the literary device of the naive narrator—a man who refuses to realize that his wife is a prostitute—with a remarkably avant garde literary style, filled with numerous references to the cultural products of the west, and constantly doubling and redoubling back upon itself in an infinitely regressive process of introspection. The narrator, as the story progresses, comes to resemble Ch'ŏyong, or a modern, urban version of him, more and more, even to the moment when he stumbles into his wife's room as she entertaining a client:

> No sooner had I got home than I discovered my wife had a
> guest. I was cold and wet and, in the confusion, forgot to
> knock. I witnessed a scene that my wife would have liked me
> not to. With drenched feet I strode across her room and
> reached mine. Casting off my dripping garments, I covered
> myself with a quilt. I kept on shivering; the cold became
> intense. I felt as if the floor under me were sinking. I lost con-
> sciousness.

(Trans. P. H. Lee)

The narrator becomes sick, and in a reversal of Ch'ŏyongs story, his
wife nurses him with sleeping pills, rather than cold medicine.
Commentators on the story, of whom there are many, have suggested a
correspondence between the narrators psychic paralysis and the colonized
mentality of those who were living in Korea at the time.

9

Post-Division, Post-War Korean Literature

For an interval during and immediately after the Korean War, a number of writers grappled either wishfully or realistically with the challenge to national identity, and the vast devastation, caused by a war that quite literally decimated the population of 30 million Korean people. Several prominent writers who "went north" were dropped from the literary realm, officially ignored, or worse. The case of Lee In-soo is a representative, if horrific, example. Educated in Korea, Japan, and England, a truly masterful translator of modern Korean poetry, Lee was "recaptured" by South Korean troops after the ceasefire in 1953, but through a hasty trial on charges of treason, and despite extensive and vigorous protests from the international community, summarily executed by the South Korean government.

The 1950s also saw a return to the modernist experiments of the 1930s most notably started by Yi Sang. The poet Kim Su-yŏug (1921-1968) was one of the most influential of the neo-modernists, a group known as the "Latter Half." Other writers pursued a more lyrical, traditional poetic practice notably the poet Sŏ Chŏng-ju, whose passionate, intense poems continue to inspire and exasperate other writers. Sŏ's *Beside a Chrysanthemum, Kukhwa yŏpe'sŏ*, has been learned by several generations of school children in Korea.

Beside a Chrysanthemum

To bring one chrysanthemum
to flower, the cuckoo has cried
since spring.

To bring one chrysanthemum to bloom,
thunder has rolled
through the black clouds.

Flower, like my sister returning
from distant, youthful byways
of throattight longing
to stand by this mirror:

for your yellow petals to open,
last night such a frost fell,
and I did not sleep.

(Trans. by D. R. McCann)

Among a number of novelists and short story writers from the post-liberation period, perhaps the most remarkable is Hwang Sun-wŏn (b. 1915). Hwang has been criticized for writing one after another perfectly realized short stories, thereby avoiding the more harsh and unsettling realities of a divided, and repressive Korea, the Korea appealing in the works of writers like Yi Ho-ch'ŏl, Sŏnu Hwi, and others. Hwang is a master, nevertheless, of perspective refracted through the narrative, of a final shift in a story's resolution which the reader is left to assemble. His *Crane, Hak,* for example, seems to be about the reconciliation still possible between north and south despite the division and bloodshed of the Korean War; yet the deeper perceptual plot of the story unfolds as the reader realizes that the narrator's perspective, the perspective of the South Korean, has made an entirely innocent, north Korean farmer into a communist guerrilla. The reader's deconstruction of the initial reading of the story's characters is itself, potentially, a political act.

The 1960s and 70s were defined by the increasingly heavy-handed measures of the repressive Park Chung-hee regime, and the concomitantly serious focus in Korean literary works upon social and political issues. Kim Su-yŏng came to be even more widely recognized as one of Korea's leading modern poets, and his death in 1968, run down by a bus in the before-curfew rush, was a tragic and ironic urban waste. He was at the time one of Korea's most accomplished and paradoxically most promising writers

Among those who count themselves as descendants of Kim Su-yŏng's are the political satirist Kim Chi-ha, and the rural-urban genre scene poet Shin Kyŏng-nim. Shin and other writers and critics were associated at the time with the influential journal *Creation and Criticism*. The 1970s and 80s, with rapid industrial and economic growth locked in the close embrace of a series of repressive political regimes, seemed to call forth a large number of outright protest poets, such as the former Buddhist monk Ko Ŭn, Kim Chi-ha, and such metaphorical dissenters as Hwang Tong-gyu and Chŏng Hyŏn-jŏng.

The National Literature Movement was organized in the 1980s to refocus effort and attention on the issue that many writers and others believed was the single, defining aspect of Koreas national political life — the continuing division of the country. Many of the writers and critics associated with the movement had come together before in the offices and pages of *Creation and Criticism*. There have been such bizarre moments in the group's history as the expulsion of Kim Chi-ha for his urging students not to kill themselves in their anti-government protests, and the even more bizarre twist when the poet protested in turn that he had not known he was a member of the organization in the first place. Nevertheless, the organization has had a profound influence in Korea's literary history, as it marked a point when writers took action as a polity rather than as isolated individuals or groups of individuals.

As it drew away from the Kwangju Uprising of 1980, the decade marked a period when writers took unambiguous stands on politics and human rights issues, many against the then current government of Chun Doo-hwan, and a few in support. The latter, or those who simply refused to speak out, were subjected to severe criticism and threats.

Many new voices and subjects began to appear, in the latter years of the 1980s, in writing about the world of the laboring class, then works by the laboring class; in works by and about women; and in works from and about Kwangju. With the substantial changes in the domestic political climate in South Korea giving freer reign to the forces of a voracious reading market, poetry, stories, essays, confessional literature, and novels have flooded from the publishing houses. It can be argued that the variety in all its myriad facets had been a constant presence, though confined by the tectonics of the Japanese occupation and the political division. The tremendous release that has happened in South Korea, and may also, at some time, in the north, is perfectly captured in one of Ko Ŭn's most gloriously political poems, *Great Springtime.*

Great Springtime

Warm east winds blow,
the earth is melting.
It's a sight to open
the eyes of the blind.
Kinds are clustering
close like chicks,
underground insects
are wriggling restless too.
Just look! The fish rising
from deeper water
are using their backs
to break the ice!
How on earth
can heaven keep silent?
The wild goose fathers
are leading their broods
away towards the Sungari River.
Now in this land
wonders are happening.
One great springtime is coming!

(Trans. by Young-Moo Kim and Brother Anthony of Taize)

Suggested Further Reading

Kim, Jaihiun Joyce. 1982. *Master Shijo Poems from Korea, Classical and Modern.* Seoul: Si-sayoungo-sa.

Lee, Peter H. 1974. *Flowers of Fire: Twentieth-Century Korean Poetry.* Honolulu: University Press of Hawaii.

_____. 1980. *The Silence of Love. Twentieth-Century Korean Stories.* Honolulu: University Press of Hawaii.

_____. 1981. *Anthology of Korean Literature: From Early Times to the Nineteenth Century.* Honolulu: University Press of Hawaii.

_____. 1991. *Pine River and Lone Peak: An Anthology of Three Chosŏn Poets.* Honolulu: University Press of Hawaii.

McCann, David R. 1988. *Form and Freedom in Korean Poetry.* Leiden: E. J. Brill.

O'Rourke, Kevin. 1989. *Tilting the Jar, Spilling the Moon: Poems form Koryŏ, Chosŏn, and Contemporary Korea.* Seoul: Universal Publications Agency.

Rutt, Richard. 1971. *The Bamboo Grove. An Introduction to Shijo.* Berkeley: University of California Press.

APPENDIX
Holidays and Festivals

Korea officially follows the Gregorian calendar, the calendar used in Western countries. The government of the Yi Dynasty (1392-1910) adopted the Gregorian calendar as the official calendar in 1896 in an attempt to modernize and reform Korea. Since then it remained the official calendar of Korea.

Many Korean holidays originated centuries ago when the ancient the ancient lunar calendar was prevalent. Most holidays have been assigned fixed dates but some still "float" to correspond with phases of the moon (as does Easter in Christian countries). The traditional holidays are still celebrated in the old ways, particularly in the countryside. The following are the national holidays and festivals with brief descriptions.

> New Year's Day (January 1 by the Gregorian calendar)
> Lunar New Year's Day (1st day of the 1st lunar month)
> Indepenence Movement Day (March 1)
> Arbor Day (April 5)
> Buddha's Birthday (8th day of the 4th lunar month)
> Children's Day (June 6)
> Constitution Day (July 17)
> Liberation Day (August 15)
> Ch'usŏk (15th day of the 8th lunar month)
> National Foundation Day (October 3)
> Christmas (December 25)

Lunar New Year's Day

In Korea, the Lunar New Year's Day is considered the most important traditional holiday starts early with a solemn ceremony in memory of deceasedancestors. Relatives gather at the house of the head of their clan to pay respect to their ancestors. The relatives pray before the Household altar where ancestral tablets and food offerings are placed. Every one in the family, adults and children, dresses up in their best clothes, often newly made for the occasion. This rite is called *ch'arye* or *chesa*.

The New Year's morning *ch'arye* which consists of offering wine and delicacies, is followed by the New Year traditional homeage called *sebae*, a formal bow to the floor before living elders of the clan, to wish them much happiness and good health throughout the coming year. After performing *sebae*, children are given a sum of pocket money by their elders. The younger generation call on their elders or acquaintances for *sebae*.

The food for the rite normally comprises of rice cakes, meat, fish, vegetables, and fruit. The use of fish is usually limite to the dried and steamed pollock and cod-fish, and the color of the fruit should not exceed three, namely the colors of apple, pear, and perimmon.

The menu for the morning must include rice cake soup, *ttŏkkuk*, which is made of thin oval slices of white rice cake in a seasoned broth. By tradition, one is not a year older until one has eaten the soup. Without *ttŏkkuk*, a New Year's celebration is unthinkable.

Among the popular games long associated with New Year are yut, kite-flying, *nŏlttwigi*(board-jumping) or Korean seesaw, and the Korean shuttlecock game of *chegi*.

Yut is enjoyed by people of all age groups. The game makes a jolly family pastime. In *yut*, four wooden oblong sticks(each with a flat side and a round side) are tossed. The players are divided into two or more teams. Each player throws the *yut*(the four wooden oblong sticks) into the air to see how they fall, either flat or round side up. This, in turn, determines the number of moves to be made on the game board and the player's score.

In the old days, girls were not permitted to wander outside of the courtyard. It is said that this restriction along with natural curiosity led the girls to adopt the board-jumping game to gain fleeting glimpses to the passing outside world over the courtyard wall. Kite-flying was and is still popular among boys during the New Year holidays.

During the Japanese colonial rule, Koreans were put under an official ban denying them their traditional major seasonal celebrations. In spite of all the prohibitive measures imposed by the colonial government, the majority of Koreans somehow maintained their traditional customs, as an expression of their national pride.

In 1985, the Korean govenment proclaimed the designation of the lunar New Year as a public holiday, because the general preference for the old customs were so much a part of Korean culture.

Ch'usŏk

Ch'usŏk is one of the two major national holidays. It is officially celebrated on the 15th of the 8th lunar month, which falls in September of October by the Gregorian calendar. This is the day of the full moon. *Ch'usŏk* is the traditional harvest festival, which may be referred to as Koran Thanksgiving Day.

People visit family tombs and make food offerings. *Ch'usŏk* is celebrated in much feasting. *Songp'yŏn*, rice cakes made of glutinous rice and filled with sweets or bean paste, is a must at this time. On this day, traditional dress is usually worn, especially by the women.

In the country the young people go out to the hills to view the full moon, each trying to catch the first glimpse as the round moon rises above the autumnal hills.

Independnce Movement Day (March 1)

Koreans observe the anniversary of the independence movement against hte Japanese colonial rule. On March 1, 1919 the Proclamation of Independence was signed by thirty-three Korean patriots. Annually, the proclamation is read at Pagoda Park in Seoul.

Buddha's Birthday (8th of the 4th lunar month)

On this day, Buddha's birth is commemorated. In 1975 this day was designated as a national holiday by the government. This is one of the most colorful of festival days. Elaborate and solemn rituals are held at many Buddhist temples while lanterns are displayed in the temple courtyard.

Constitution Day (July 17)

This day is celebrated as a legal national holiday to commemorate the proclamation of the Constitution of the Republic of Korea on July 17, 1948.

Liberation Day (August 15)

On this national holiday, Koreans commemorate the liberation from the Japanese rule in 1945.

National Foundation Day (October 3)

On this day, Koreans commemorate the founding of the first Korean kingdom called Chosŏn by the legendary founder *Tan'gun* in 2333 B.C. *Tan'gun*, the mythical king of the Korean people, is said to have established his kingdom with its capital at P'yŏngyang.

Some of the other traditional festivals are:

Tano Day (5th day of the 5th lunar month)

Tano is one of the three great holidays of the lunar year. On this day, people dress up in their best and feast as they do on New Year's Day or *Ch'usŏk*. Special events include wrestling matches for men and swinging competitions for women. As a prize, the wrestling champion receives a bull and the swinging champion gets a gold ring.

Hanshik (105th day from the lunar New Year's Day)

Hanshik falls about the fifth of April by the solar calendar. On this day, rites for ancestors are observed early in the morning, when the whole family visits the tombs of their ancestors to pay respects to them, to tidy up and repair the grave site, and plant on or two trees if necessary.

INDEX

Index

A

a'ak 64, 325
Allen, Horace N. 183, 215
Allied for Korean Independence 85
Allied Occupation 86
Altaic language family 101
Analects of Confucius 293
anbang 265, 378
An Kyŏn 316
Anp'yŏng, Prince 316
An Yu 295
Appenzeller, H. G. 299
April Student Revolution 235
Arirang 342

B

Book of Rites 294
Buddhist music 166, 335

C

Cairo Declaration 87
Central People's Committee 94
changgo 127, 332
Chang Myŏn 235

Chinbŏn 44
Chindan Academic Society 84
Chinhan 45, 328
Chinhŭng, King 293
Chin State 44
Chinul 169
Cho (dowager), Queen 73
Chogye order 56, 165
Cho Man-shik 89
Chŏndŭng temple 406
chong'ak 332
Chŏng Ch'ŏl 442
chŏngjae 347
chŏngji (gan) 378
Chŏngjo, King 181
Chŏng Mong-ju 436
Chongmyo 348
Chŏngrim temple 361
Chŏng Sŏn 318
Chŏng Yak-yong 66
chosang tanji 122
Chōsen 79
Chosŏn 59, 137, 221
Choson Ilbo 83
Chumong 46
Chumong myth 417
Chun, King 44
Chun Doo-hwan 239

chung'gum 330
Conduct of the Three Roads 64
Constitution Day 469
court Music 331

Ch'

ch'ang 339, 421
Ch'angdŏk Palace 383
ch'ang'gŭk 339
ch'iwit'a 333
Ch'oe Che-u 69
Ch'oe Chung 56
Ch'oe Nam-sŏn 453
ch'ŏllima movement 94
Ch'ŏndogyo 162, 228
ch'ŏnghwa paekja 394
ch'ŏngja 392
Ch'ŏngsan-ri method 95
Ch'ŏnjugyo 226
ch'ŏntae 56
ch'ungunggi 225
Ch'ung'yŏl, King 295
ch'usŏk 468

D

Declaration of Independence 82
demilitarized zone (DMZ) 19
Democratic People's Republic of Korea (DPRK) 90, 18
dialects 104
Diamond Mountains 21, 318
Dong-a Ilbo 83
Dongguk University 163

E

Eastern Learning 69
Eastern Puyŏ 417
Eastern Ye 51
Economic Planning Board (EPB) 237
Ehwa Haktang 299
Ehwa Womans University 183
Emille's Bell 50

F

Five Rites of State 64
Four Colors 65

H

Haedong T'ongbo 56
Hae Gang 395
haegŭm 335
Haein temple 57
han'gŭl 63, 102, 404
Han'gŭl Day 103
han 197
Han China 44
Han River 48
Hanshik 470
hansŏ 411
Hansŏng 17
Hansŏng Sunbo 75
Hanyang 79
Han Yong-un 163, 456
Ho-Am Art Museum 316
Hodge, John R., Gen. 230
Hŏ Kyun 449
Hongik in'gan 289
Hong Kiltong 449

Hong Kyŏng-nae 225
honorifics 105
Hwang Chin-i 442
Hwang Chip-jung 317
Hwang Sun-wŏn 460
Hwang Tong-kyu 461
Hwang'yong temple 49
Hwanung 417
Hwaŏm 49
hwarang 48, 330
hwarang-do 48
hyang'ak 331
hyangch'al 329
hyangga 52, 329
hyanggyo 61, 294
hyang pip'a 330
Hyŏn Chin-gŏn 456

i 295
idu 49, 329
ilmu 348
Ilyŏn 160
Injong, King 294

Japanese annexation 228
Juche 94, 290, 303

Kabo Reform 76, 228
Kaegyŏng 52
Kaehwadang 74
Kaesŏng 52

kagok 64, 334
Kanggang sullae 342
Kang Hui-an 317
Kanghwa Island 73
karak 336
kasa 334, 442
Kaya 51, 390
kayago 330
kayagŭm 330
Keijo 79
ki 295
Kija Chosŏn 44
Kim Chi-ha 461
Kim Dae-jung 240
Kim Dae-sŏng 266
Kim Hong-do 318
Kim Il-sung 89, 302
Kim Jong-il 95
Kim Man-jung 68, 450
Kim Ok-kyun 74
Kim Pu-sik 160
Kim Si-sŭp 439
Kim So-wŏl 456
Kim Suro myth 417
Kim Su-yŏng 459
Kim Tong-in 456
Kim Young-sam 240
kisaeng 277, 442
Koguryŏ Kingdom 46, 313
Kojong, King 73
kolmaegi 125
kŏmungo 330
Kong Chiu 141
Kong Fuzi 141
konnŏbang 378
Korean Armistice 93
Korean Central Inteligence Agency

(KCIA) 237
Korean Communist Party 83
Korean Linguistics Society 84
Korean Patriotic Youths Society 85
Korean Restoration Army 85
Korean War 91
Korean Worker's Party 89, 304
Korean writing 102
Koryŏ celadon 57, 392
Koryŏ Dynasty 169
Ko Ŭn 163, 461
kukchagam 294
kukchahak 294
kuk'hak 293
kŭmjul 424
Kungnaesŏng 47
kut 205, 336
Kwangju massacre 239
Kwangju Uprising 461
Kyŏngbok Palace 72
kyŏngdang 292
Kyŏngju 362

Later Koguryŏ 52
Later Paekche 52
Later Three Kingdoms 52
Lee In-soo 459
Liberation Day 469
Long Wall 54

MacArthur, Douglas, Gen. 92
maebul 368
Mahan 45, 328

makkŏlli 25
March First Movement 82
maru 122, 409
May Military Movement 95
Memorabilia of the Three Kingdosa
    44, 432
Min, Queen 76
minhwa 318
minjung Buddhism 164
minsŏk'ak 337
minyo 339, 341
Mirŭk temple 49
mokt'ak 336
Moon Sun-myung 198
mudang 206
mudong 347
munjip 143
Munmu, King 362
munmyo 296
Myŏngkyŏngdang 296

Naktong River 48
Namhan sansŏng 161
National Classical Music Institute
    of Korea 325
National Confucius Academy 148
National Foundation Day 469
National Liberation Movement 82
National Museum of Korea 317
Neo-Confucianism 61, 139
norae 336, 341
North Korea 17, 91
North Korean People's Assembly
    90
North Korean Workers' Party 89

Okchŏ 46
Old Chosŏn 43
ondol 378
Onjo 46
onomatopoetic words 108

Paechae Haktang 299
Paekche Kingdom 361
Paektu Mt. 20
Pagoda of Many Treasures 50
Pagoda Park 456
Pak Che-ga 66
Pak Chi-wŏn 66
Pak Hon-yŏng 92
Pak Hyŏkkŏse 46
Pak Il-lo 442
Pak Paeng-nyŏn 316
Pak Yŏng-hyo 74
Parhae 52
Pari, Princess 130
Park Chung-hee 236, 452
People's Army 90
People's Republic of Korea 87
pŏmmu 347
Pŏmŏ temple 49
Pomp'ae 335
Pomun order 174
Pongdŏk temple 50
pori kogae 25
Practical Learning Movement 66
Provisional Government of Korea 83
puk 336
Pulguk temple 362, 408

punchŏng 63, 393
Puyŏ State 44, 327
pyŏlshin mask dance 68
Pyŏnhan 45, 328

p'algwanhoe 49, 329
P'anmunjŏm 93
p'ansori 339, 415, 430
p'udakkori 336

Republic of Korea (ROK) 89
Rhee Syngman, Dr. 83, 232
Righteous Uprising of Students 234
Roh Tae-woo 239

sadaebu 58, 317
saenaenore 329
sahak 294
salp'uri 336
samgang oryun 142, 296
Samguk sagi 160
Samguk yusa 160, 366
samul nori 344
samunhak 294
Sangp'yŏng Tongbo
sanjo 341
sarangbang 265, 382
sarangch'ae 382
Saro State 46
Scranton, M. F. 299
Second March First Movement 84

Sejong, King 59, 102, 404
Seoul 59
sep'ilyul 335
shijo 57, 334, 430
Shilhak 66, 449
Shilla Dynasty 169
shinawi 341
Shin Kyŏng-nim 461
Shinmu, King 362
Shin Saim-dang 317
Shin Ton 58
Shin Yun-bok 318
Sino-Korean words 110
soban 383
So Chae-p'il 185, 448
So Chŏng-ju 459
sŏdang 61, 294
Sŏgang University 192
sok'ak 333
sŏkchŏnje 148, 348
Sŏkkuram 50, 163, 366
So Ku-bang 315
sŏlhwa 416
Sŏn 49
Sŏngdo 52
Sŏnggyungwan 61
sŏnhwang 125
South Korea 91
South Korean Interim Government
  (SKIG) 88
South Korean Interim Legistative
  Assembly (SKILA) 88
South Korean Workers' Party 91
sŏwŏn 148, 296
speech levels 106
Student Uprising 95
Sunjo, King 451

Sunjong, Emperor 78
Supreme Council for National
  Reconstruction 236
Supreme People's Assembly 90

T

taech'ong 378
Taedong River 48
taegŭm 330
taehak 304
Tae Karak 417
Tae Kaya 417
Taewŏngun 72
Tang'ak 331
Tan'gun 289
Tan'gun myth 417
Tano Day 470
Taoism 210
Tasan 66
Three Kingdoms 389
Tohwasŏ 316
Tohwawŏn 316
tokkebi 420
Tonghak 228
Tongsŏ Haktang 294
Tongye 45
Tripitaka Koreana 57, 432
Tumen River 17

T'

T'aego order 169
t'aehak 292
T'aejo, King 53, 368
T'aejong, King 209
t'aryŏng 342

U

U. N. Temporary Commission on Korea 88
U. S. Army Military Government 230
U. S.-U. S. S R. Joint Commission 87
Underwood, Horace, G. 215
Unified Shilla 314, 362
U Ruk 330

V

vowel harmony 106

W

wajil t'ogi 389
Wanggŏmsŏng 44
Wang Kŏn 52
Wang San-ak 330
Wiman Chosŏn 44
witpang 378
Wŏlchŏng temple 363
Wŏngang 293
Wŏnhyo 169

Y

Yalu River 47
yangban 55, 60, 241
Yang P'aeng-son 317
ye 296
Ye State 44
Yi Cha-gyŏm 57
Yi Dynasty 59
Yi Hwang 63

Yi I 63
Yi Kwang-su 453
Yi Sang 457
Yi Sŏng-gye 221
Yi Su-mun 317
Yi Sŭng-hun 181
Yi Sun-sin, Admiral 440
Yi T'oegye 63
Yi Yul-gok 63
Yŏngjo, King 450
Yŏngyŏngdang 383
Yŏn Kaesomun 51
Yonsei University 191, 299
Yŏsu-Sunch'ŏn Rebellion 91
Yŏŭido Full Gospel Church 195
Yŏ Un-hyŏng 85
Yun Ch'i-ho 185
Yun Po-sun 238
Yun Sŏn-do 442
Yun Tu-sŏ 318
Yushin 192

Z

Zŏng In-sŏp 416